Live&Work in

Australia

Jodie McMullen Seal

original edition by
Deborah Penrith

Dear Zuzana
To help you with your plans! ☺

Jeremy

crimson

The author and publishers have every reason to believe in the accuracy of the information given in this book and the authenticity and correct practices of all organisations, companies, agencies etc. mentioned: however, situations may change and telephone numbers, regulations, exchange rates etc. can alter, and readers are strongly advised to check facts and credentials for themselves. Readers are invited to write to Crimson Publishing, Westminster House, Kew Road, Richmond, Surrey, TW9 2ND, with any comments, corrections and first hand experiences. Those whose contributions are used will be sent a free copy of the Live and Work Abroad title of their choice.

Publishing, a division of Crimson Business Ltd
www.crimsonpublishing.com

4501 Forbes Blvd., Suite 200, Lanham MD 20706

Westminster House, Kew Road, Richmond, Surrey TW9 2ND

Distributed in North America by National Book Network
www.nbnbooks.com

Distributed in the UK by Portfolio Books
www.portfoliobooks.com

A catalogue record for this book is available from the British library.

ISBN 978 1 85458 418 2
Printed and bound by Colorprint Offset Ltd, Hong Kong

Acknowledgements

The author would like to thank the following people and organisations, in no particular order, for their invaluable help in compiling this book:

For the brilliant photography: David Aidekman, Grant McMullen, Linda Sumner; Robert McMullen, Shane McMullen, Yvonne Bischofberger, Zennie McLoughlin, Fintan McLoughlin and the Mcdougalls. To the good looking Aussies who feature in the pictures; Tara, Beryl Baker(Nan),Mary Sinead, Rosco, Shaneo the Amazeo, Scott Sumner, Jaqs , Mick and Fast Eddie McDougall, Lisa Hagenmeir, Wa ,Puppy Yuill and Tippa.

To Matthew Hurst, Sandy Thomas and Timothy Edwards for allowing us to use the Railcorp maps of Sydney and Melbourne; All maps were reproduced with permission from Railcorp

For advice on anything petrol/economy related: Robert McMullen; On pensions, Geraint Davies from Montfort International plc; On visas; Geoff Taylor and Ian Wallace at The Emigration Group; On anything real estate related, Paul Liddy.

For trawling the supermarket aisles, Mausie McMullen and for advice on film and entertainment, Jake Seal.

And also a big thank you to all our case study participants, Simon, Rebecca, Scott, Mike, Matthew, Anna, Natasha, Joanna and Jane – May you all live many happy years in the sun drenched country!

Expats Scott Sumner and Joanna Davies have the last word:

'Absolutely do it. Don't wait, just do it. Just be sure what you want out of the experience and if it is a holiday, then be prepared to see and do everything and pay the money it takes to do it. If you are hoping to travel and go home with money in your pocket, you will not have made the most of your trip. If you are coming to live, my advice would be to be gentle with yourself and allow at least twice the time you would expect to get really settled. If you are non-English speaking, you will be able to get by, but you will have to work especially hard to rise to the level of standing that you might enjoy in your home country. Whatever you do, don't limit yourself to backpacker hostels as you will see the country, but not get to know the people. Stay in one place long enough to work – that is how you will get to know the true Australian' **Scott Sumner**

'Be prepared to embrace your new life, try not to look down on new things, people or experiences simply because they are different. Try not to be too suspicious of friendly people. Don't worry about making mistakes, most people make mistakes when they move to a new country, whether it's choosing the wrong place to live or buying the wrong fridge! Most things like this don't matter. Give yourself time, and credit yourself for the huge change you have made, don't expect to feel settled in straight-away but take each day as it comes. Acknowledge the hard work you have done in making the move and don't try to achieve too much too soon. It is harder to settle in and learn about the new culture than you think. Even now, three years later, there are still new words and phrases which remind me I am originally from a different place! Working and socialising with Australians helps you absorb the new culture easily. Above all, have fun and make the most of what Australia can offer!' **Joanna Davies**

OVERVIEW**OF**AUSTRALIA

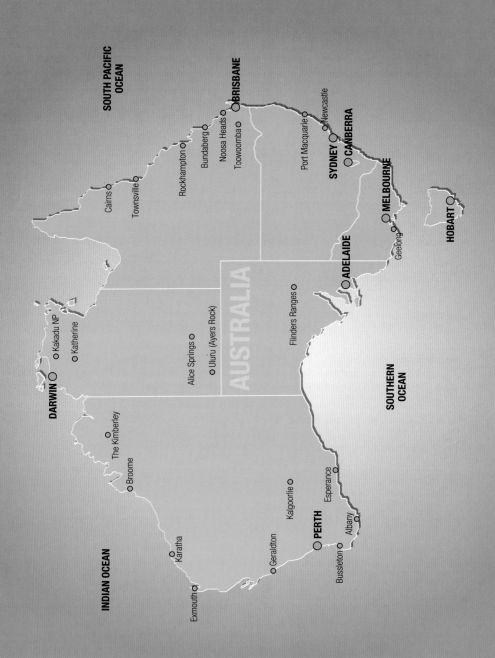

STATES OF AUSTRALIA

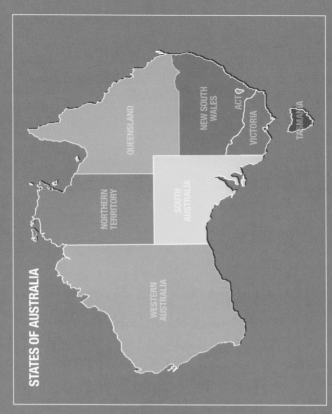

- QUEENSLAND
- NEW SOUTH WALES
- ACT
- VICTORIA
- TASMANIA
- NORTHERN TERRITORY
- SOUTH AUSTRALIA
- WESTERN AUSTRALIA

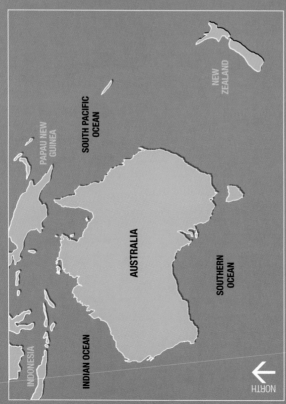

- INDONESIA
- PAPAU NEW GUINEA
- SOUTH PACIFIC OCEAN
- NEW ZEALAND
- AUSTRALIA
- INDIAN OCEAN
- SOUTHERN OCEAN
- NORTH

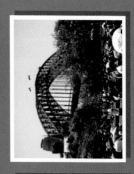

Contents

Contents

About Australia 433

Appendices 481

Telephone numbers

Please note that the telephone numbers in this book are written as needed to call that number from inside the country you will probably be calling from. For example, a British removals company to Australia will be given as a UK number; an Australian removals company from the UK will have its international prefix.

To call another country from Australia dial 00 before the number for the country concerned, then the subscriber's area code minus the first zero, then the subscriber's number.

To call Australia from another country dial 00 61 followed by the number minus the first zero.

Exchange rates

Throughout the book, Australian dollars have been used. The table below gives an indication of the exchange rates for other countries:

Australian dollar A$	British pound £	US dollar $	Euro €	NZ dollar NZ$
A$1	£0.49	$0.95	€0.61	NZ$1.25
A$10	£4.85	$9.54	€6.13	NZ$12.60
A$20	£9.70	$19.08	€12.27	NZ$25.20
A$50	£24.25	$47.70	€30.67	NZ$63
A$100	£48.50	$93.38	€61.35	NZ$125.95
A$1,000	£485	$935.80	€613.50	NZ$1,260

(at time of press)

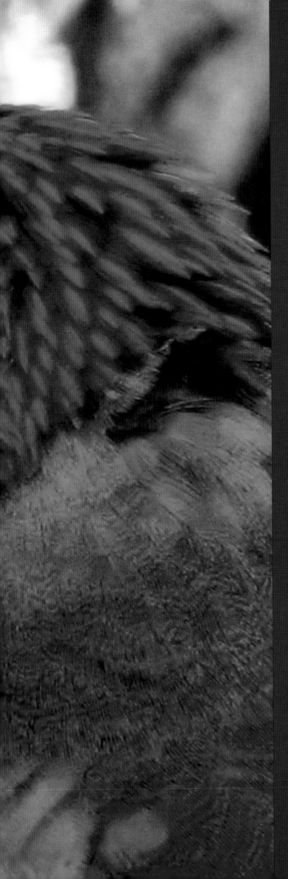

Why Live & Work in Australia?

▮ ABOUT AUSTRALIA

Capital:	Canberra
Geographic coordinates:	27 00 S, 133 00 E
Lowest point:	Lake Eyre, 15m
Highest point:	Mount Kosciuszko, 2,229m
Currency:	Australian dollar (A$)
Population:	21 million
Gross domestic product:	A$674.6bn (2006 estimate)

Australians all let us rejoice, for we are young and free. We've golden soil and wealth for toil, our home is girt by sea Our land abounds with nature's gifts of beauty rich and rare In history's page, let every stage advance Australia fair'. This first verse of Australia's national anthem sums up why 25% of the 200,000 Britons who left their home soil for a new life in 2007 chose the land 'down under'.

Once the home of the world's largest and most remote penal colony, Australia is now seen as the perfect destination for Britons, Europeans, Americans, Canadians and South Africans wanting to escape the confines of the low grey sky a fast-paced lifestyle and instead live the sun-drenched good life. Current figures show that Australia receives one international migrant every three minutes (Australian Bureau of Statistics, March 2008).

Australia comprises six states and two territories, with the ACT (Australian Capital Territory) being the capital. Each state is renowned for the uniqueness of the terrain and of the folk that live there. The most popular cities to settle in are Sydney, Melbourne, Perth and Brisbane.

Australia boasts clean air, safe streets, sunshine, clean natural beaches, untouched coral reefs, vast desert with rich red soil, lush rainforests, national parks, stunning harbours, and people who stop and say hello, or at the very least smile.

> 'I like it (Australia) a lot, I think it's a terrific country; they really know how to live. The natural history of the place is endlessly fascinating.'
> **Bill Bryson, Down Under**

A myriad of creatures are found only in Australia – strange breeds such as the duck-billed platypus (a cross between a reptile and a mammal), wallabies, echidnas, lorikeets, tree kangaroos, wombats, koalas, bats (that fly overhead every evening), tree frogs, kookaburras, ostriches, dingoes, Moreton Bay bugs, Tasmanian devils, blue bottles, barramundi and huge jellyfish. We won't even get started on the little critters, such as redback spiders, funnel web spiders and Christmas beetles.

The best bits about living in Australia include the laid-back nature of life and the 'you beaut', get-up-and-give-it-a-go attitude, all contained in the largest island in the world, where the underdog prospers and you are never far from your 'mates'.

Live the *dream*

with the help of

THE EMIGRATION GROUP

Visa and Migration Experts since 1992

If you are seriously thinking about emigrating to Australia or have already decided to emigrate, you are probably wondering just how to go about it. Where do you start? What help will you need and from whom? Are you eligible for a Visa? Will you find a job and how will you face the challenge of starting a new life overseas? Well, help is at hand.

The Emigration Group was established in 1992 to provide expert guidance to people wishing to emigrate and to ensure they achieved a happy and prosperous new life overseas. Our successful track record over the years has seen us help more than 10,000 people make a fresh start and enjoy a terrific lifestyle 'Down Under'.

We offer not only a wealth of experience, but full assistance with each aspect of migration: **Visa Preparation and Management; Employment Search; Homes and Resettlement**. How we can help you with each of these vital elements of emigration is covered in the next few pages. As you will see, our complete service provides the essential one point of contact for all your migration needs. Enlisting our expertise to help you 'Live the Dream' assures you of unrivalled personal service in the months ahead as we guide you and your family through one of the most important moves of your lives.

Over the following pages, in letters sent to us, clients Danny and Cheryl Gardiner recall their famliy's experience of their new life in Australia.

The Gardiner's (right) with Cheryl's brother and family (left).

Cheryl and Danny (above).

Ethan with his grandmother.

Email letter received on 10th December, 2007

Hi Andrew

We were just going through some old emails and clearing out some of the no longer needed stuff and came across this one from you.* This was sent to us after our first meeting with you at your office in London and reading it has reminded me that we never did write and thank you all for helping us to achieve our dream of living in OZ.

So first I would like to say a huge thankyou to all of the staff at The Emigration Group, as I'm sure you can imagine picking the right company to manage our application was the first of many important decisions to make once we had set our hearts on living in Australia. After trying one of the other companies and feeling like we were getting nowhere, we made the trip to London for an interview with you, by the end of which we had decided to put our trust in you.

Well, as you can see. that was in October 2005 and I am pleased to tell you that we landed in Sydney on February 5th 2007, so just a little more that one year from start to finish (in fact I think we were told our application had been passed around November 2006).

We now live in South Australia, about a twenty minute drive from the city of Adelaide. We have bought a beautiful house overlooking the sea next to a 15 km board walk that goes along the cliff edge, which Cheryl walks our new dog along almost every day. Our son Ethan has not needed steroids for his asthma since we arrived, and has now joined the local surf lifesaving club which is only a ten minute drive away or thirty minute walk. He is growing like a mushroom and eating us out of house and home, so I think its safe to say that Australia agrees with him (in fact it agrees with us all!).

We all love it here and wouldn't swap it for anything. We feel that the help and support that we had from your company was invaluable and would be more than happy to recommend you to anyone, including our closest friends. By the way we have just had our first visitor from the UK and she loved it so much that she has gone home to tell her husband and children that they should all move out ASAP so I hope that this will be another success story for The Emigration Group.

We cannot say THANKYOU enough but please know that we are so grateful to you all.

Many Thanks,
Danny, Cheryl, Ethan & Snoopdog

* this email (abridged), sent by our consultant, Andrew James to the Gardiner's on 7th October, 2005 appears below.

Dear Danny and Cheryl
Thank you for taking the time to visit our offices today to discuss your plans for a new life in Australia. I hope you found our meeting useful in considering further your options but should you have any further questions over the weekend please do not hesitate to telephone me. I am acutely aware that you are likely to be feeling saturated with information from all the various meetings you have had and so I thought it would be useful to send you this e-mail to attempt to distill the key issues and options.

It is clear that beyond the simple desire to live a different kind of life in a new country the critical concern you have is the need to move Ethan to a country where the climate will be much more appropriate for someone with asthma. I recognise fully the depth of your concern and your need to ensure that you will, not may, will be able to make this move to Australia. One way or another we will, if you choose to use our service to manage your application, ensure that whatever it takes if it can be done it will be done.

One way or another there is a way for you all to be in Australia. My feeling is that you are worrying unnecessarily and creating anxieties for yourselves that do not need to exist and are allowing the situation to become overcomplicated by trying to answer in your minds in advance all the various questions, issues and possible permutations. This does not have to be complicated.

If you choose to use our service you will be paying us to do the worrying and to deliver the goods. In which case let us do just that – just give us the information that we request, to the best of your ability and as promptly as you are able and leave the rest to us. It matters to me that we get you into Australia, and one way or another, should you choose to use our service, if it is do-able, we will do it, and **it is do-able**.

Having approached the family for permission to use their testimonial letter, on 23rd May, 2008 Cheryl Gardiner wrote further to The Emigration Group's Managing Director, Geoff Taylor.

Hi Geoff…

Thank you so much for your email…yes you can welcomely use our letter. I have included a few photos which you are welcome to use also, some of which include my brother who has also recently visited. He was amazed at how warm the sea was, how you could sit on the beach and be warm (until so late) and watch the sun set and then see a star filled sky (and I mean **'see it'** as in the UK vision is not so great), whilst toasting to another wonderful day as we all sat and enjoyed a cool bottle of Australian wine…my brother said it was one of the most magical times he had ever spent…his words. We are really living a privileged life…after a year of getting here. Would we want to go back…Never!!!!!!!!

Thank you again…we have recommended The Emigration Group to a number of friends, who also wish to live the dream. Again, would we choose anywhere else to live? No! Would we have chosen anyone else to get us here? No…The Emigration Group really held our hands every step of the way.

Regards
Cheryl Gardiner

Top: Ethan and his cousin at sunset.
Top right: The Gardiner family with Snoopdog.
Middle: Danny and Ethan (right) with Cheryl's brother and nephew (left) enjoy the sunset on the local beach.
Bottom right: Cheryl and son, Ethan show off their new car.

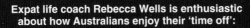

Expat life coach Rebecca Wells is enthusiastic about how Australians enjoy their 'time off':

'People here have a greater sense of work/life balance. It's common for people to go to the beach after work for a surf (people actually do that) and the 'family unit' is clearly very important here, which is refreshing.'

▌ PROS OF LIVING IN AUSTRALIA

Good lifestyle

Beautiful weather, golden beaches, national parks, untouched coral reefs. Believe the hype. It really is 'beautiful one day, perfect the next!'

Fitness and outdoor activities are a must for those living down under. Australians spend a large part of their day outdoors, so days feel endless (in a good way). Every year outdoor festivals take advantage of the balmy evenings, including the outdoor cinema in the Sydney Botanical gardens,

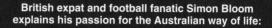

> **British expat and football fanatic Simon Bloom explains his passion for the Australian way of life:**
>
> *'People here don't generally work the length of hours they do in the UK, so there's plenty of time to do things in the evenings and weekends. Obviously it's a very outdoorsy culture – beach, sport, walking etc. I get fairly involved in football over here so spend most of my time with guys from that.'*

with the screen popping up in the harbour, and the annual Big Day Out, the sunny equivalent to Glastonbury.

Outdoor leisure activities are plentiful with the emphasis on extreme sports such as bungee jumping, whitewater rapids, surfing and caving. There are also plenty of activities for the non-thrill seekers out there – national parks and beaches (with gorgeous coastal walks) are ten to the penny.

Climate

Australia's climate and way of life have always been a motivating factor in the decision of many international migrants to leave their home shores. The

warm, sunny weather in most coastal regions allows people to enjoy an outdoor lifestyle with an emphasis on leisure. Even hardship seems better when the sun shines. There are acknowledged health and psychological benefits to living in a favourable climate. Vitamin D, known as the 'sunshine vitamin' (because the skin makes it from ultraviolet rays, and you cannot extract it from food and fortified milk alone), is believed to be beneficial in preventing some cancers. So a little bit of sunshine a day not only improves one's outlook on life, but may even sustain it.

People

Aussies are friendly, laid-back people who are willing to give anything a go. They are fiercely patriotic, which makes the entire country feel connected as a wider community.

Uniqueness is also a very Australian characteristic. In fact Australians are a juxtaposition of seemingly opposite traits. On one side, they are built tough enough to sustain the harsh Aussie terrain, wildlife and climate; yet on the other, they are (rightly) famous for their laid-back, no fuss attitude. This is a country where a visit to the outback toilet ('dunny') in the middle of the night could evoke a life-threatening bite from a spider, snake, or even plant. Yet, Australians have an inbuilt thick skin, which could be a result of their humble beginnings as convict stock, 'spaghetti Western' type outlaws, indigenous Aboriginals or general outcasts of European society.

> 'Aussies are vehemently patriotic which is really energising'
> **Rebecca Wells**

Multicultural population

Australia is a huge melting pot of cultures, religions, customs and people. There are large Asian, European (most of Melbourne's immigrants are Greek) and Lebanese communities.

Economy

Most Australians live in large, modern cities that compete successfully in the global economy. Australian scientific and technical research lead the world in many areas, and technology, engineering, commerce and banking are now as important to the economy as its agricultural and mining industries. Salaries are nowhere near as high as in the UK, when converted dollar-to-pound, but with a much lower cost of living, an average wage goes much further.

Lower cost of living

Wages may be relatively smaller than what you're used to back home, but housing, education, healthcare and groceries are all better priced here.

New Government

After 11 years of a liberal parliament, new Prime Minister Kevin Rudd has taken Australia to a Labor government. The defeat was disastrous for John Howard – his Liberal Government lost office to Labor and he lost his own seat of Benalong. Even in opposition he could not be leader, since losing your own seat in an election effectively means you are out of politics altogether. A Prime Minister losing his own seat is almost unheard of and gives some indication how unhappy the electorate was with John Howard.

Since becoming Prime Minister, Kevin Rudd has made good on promises to apologise to the Aboriginal community's 'Stolen generation'. The apology comes more than 10 years after a Government investigation, which discovered that at least 100,000 children were forcibly removed from their parents from 1869, which continued right up until 1969. They were placed in orphanages, or fostered out, in an attempt to socialise them with European culture. It is reported that many were abused.

Let's not forget that life began in this country well before Captain Cook landed in 1770. The first Australians to toil the land were the indigenous ones, the Aborigines. It is estimated they have inhabited the land now known as Australia for some 50,000 years, and many tribes still speak a variety of 200 different forms of their language. Their population was approximately between 318,000 and 750,000 before the British invaded and changed their world forever. Three years after the arrival of Europeans, two-thirds of the aboriginal population had been wiped out by European diseases and a deliberate policy of annihilation. Today, about 1% of Australians have aboriginal blood, and of these, 10,000 are pure-blooded aboriginals.

FACT

■ Aborigines means 'first or earliest known, indigenous'.

High level of home ownership

Most Australians own their homes (which are large by European standards). Home ownership is a notion drilled into them since childhood – the pursuit of the Great Australian dream. Aussies are particularly houseproud and love nothing more than asking you round to see their new water feature or gazebo.

Although real estate is considerably cheaper than in the UK, prices have risen in the past three years, making it harder for first-time buyers to get on the property ladder. However, if you arrive with savings in pounds, you will get a place three times as large as your current abode. Sydney and Melbourne are the most expensive cities in which to purchase property, and although these cities have a higher population density than others in Australia, residents retain the expectation of a large, detached house with a garden, pool and garage. Relatively few people live in flats (or 'units' as they are known).

Matthew Morrison observes the differences in renting:

'Rent is cheaper here and you can live in your first choice location. Flats tend to be unfurnished, so you need to either buy/rent furniture, flat-share or pay a premium for furnished. People tend to continue flat sharing well into their 40s and 50s here!'

Good-quality food

Fruit and vegetables are abundant, fresh, and almost invariably locally grown. There is a huge variety, including many tropical and exotic fruits in the north of Australia that are rarely seen on European shelves, such as the pawpaw.

Australian produce was once very reasonably priced, but with inflation creeping up, things such as fruit and vegetables, have started to bear the brunt. Also, natural disasters like the 2006 cyclone, which wiped out most banana plantations in Queensland, have meant that the price of bananas has increased threefold. However, meat is still reasonably affordable and of excellent quality, and there is no risk of bovine spongiform encephalopathy (BSE) infection in Australian beef. Some people say you haven't experienced seafood until you have tasted what Australia has on offer. Local delicacies such as Moreton Bay bugs make this a haven for crustacean lovers.

Inexpensive domestic travel

Although getting a flight out of Australia is incredibly expensive, getting a flight internally is extremely reasonable! Airlines such as Virgin Blue and Jetstar will get you from Sydney to the Gold Coast for as little as A$70 return (if you book online in advance).

First-class educational standards and facilities

The Australian school system aims to develop the individual talents of students, in a safe, caring and culturally rich environment. Its schools are world leaders in applying technology such as computers, multimedia

materials and internet access to everyday learning situations. Schools are both state and privately funded and offer large roaming playgrounds and sporting fields, which often take up acres of land. Australia's highly interactive teaching style also encourages student participation, which in turn develops confidence and high personal skills.

Excellent medical facilities

The World Health Organization said this about Australia's healthcare system:

Australia is known for its medical advancement, clean hospitals and state of its public health system. They have the Medicare system, which provides free treatment to patients in public hospitals and free or partially subsidised treatment by practitioners such as dentists, doctors, optometrists and specialists. Medicare is available to all Australian/New Zealand citizens, those who hold a permanent residence visa, and people from countries that have an agreement with Australia such as the UK. It is funded by contributions made through taxes and levies. There are also over 50 private health insurance funds available in Australia.

Gay and lesbian scene

Sydney is renowned as the second gay and lesbian capital of the world, with only San Francisco beating it to the title.

■ CONS OF LIVING IN AUSTRALIA
Geographical isolation from Europe

New arrivals are sometimes painfully aware of their geographical isolation on this remote island. Homesickness and the prohibitive cost of international air travel to Europe and North America occasionally promote a sense of exile. It is a country so remote that when you arrive you must declare any fruit and vegetables you may be hoarding, before being sprayed with a type of disinfectant, ensuring you are not inadvertently introducing any exotic wildlife to this gigantic island.

Many are overwhelmed and it is common for immigrants to return permanently to their home country within a couple of years. However it is still a good idea to see as much as you can of the southern hemisphere before coming home. Fly to Bali, New Zealand or one of the many South-East Asia destinations located close by. With a country so large and full of diversity, travel within Australia walls is a must. You will spend a lot of time on road trips, as it can often take days to reach other cities. To give you an idea, Sydney to Brisbane takes approximately 10 hours to drive, yet is only a one hour flight. Perth to Sydney can take four or five days, and a treacherous four-wheel drive through the unforgiving outback.

Strict immigration laws

The days of the 'ten pound pom' (POM meaning Prisoner of Mother England) are long gone. Australia no longer needs to offer inducements to build up its population and skill base, and immigration quotas are now strictly regulated. The application procedure is lengthy, complex and expensive, with an emphasis on the net gain to Australian society. Nurses, police and other key workers are still desperately needed, but mostly in remote outposts. While the country actively pursues a programme of humanitarian immigration, most applicants will need to be able to either demonstrate financial security and significant professional experience, or Australian ancestry.

> *i* Read: *Ten Pound Poms: Australia's Invisible Migrants,* by A James Hammerton and Alistair Thomson

Creatures that bite

One big turn-off for the thousands of potential new residents is creepy crawlies. Australia is notorious for its unpleasant insects, harmful plants, life-threatening snakes and its many species of shark. With the warm weather come flies – swarms of them – and if you live near fresh water, probably mosquitoes too. Aussies refer to the swatting away of flies from one's face as the 'Aussie salute'. You will even see newsreaders waving at you in this fashion when out on location. It is wise to assume that **any** spider you encounter is venomous until you learn to recognise those that pose an actual danger. Redback, funnel web, and trapdoor spiders are all potentially fatal to adults as well as children, and Australians learn from an early age where these are likely to lurk. As scary as this may seem, you may go through your entire life living down under, and never see a redback.

You will soon get into the swing of thumping your outdoor shoes against a brick wall, before leaving the house, to rid them of any accidental tourists. Even local bushland parks may harbour snakes such as dugites, whose bite will be lethal unless treated immediately. Many Australians know how to apply a tourniquet and suck out venom from a snake bite (Relax! most

> **Simon Bloom encountered his fair share of outdoor life when he first arrived:**
>
> 'The scenery and wildlife here is pretty amazing. When I was younger I remember wondering how Australians survived – so there are many dangerous animals that could kill you just by looking at you. Since I've been here I've only seen one redback spider, no Sydney funnel webs, plenty of Huntsmen spiders and one snake – although it was a red-bellied black snake and I did grab its tail (Google it, and you'll realise how cool I am!!)'

never need to use this knowledge), but it may be reassuring to take a first aid course when you arrive, especially if you have a young family.

Sharks live in some of Australia's coastal waters and many beaches have an aerial shark patrol, as well as lifesavers on duty. Again, relax! Shark attacks are extremely rare and their possibility does not discourage Australians from beach life. However, it is important to be alert, and born-and-bred Australians do not swim at dawn or dusk, which is known to be the sharks' feeding time. Also, ensure you have a lifesaver looking out for you at all times if you aren't a strong swimmer, as 'rips' or strong currents have caused more than one death on the picturesque beaches of Australia.

Sun warning

This can be classified as both a pro and a con as Aussies have a love–hate relationship with their sun-drenched climate. Australians have the highest rate of skin cancer in the world. Some argue that this is as a result of a significant hole in the ozone layer above Australia. Children on beaches in Australia wear total body, zip-up swimsuits to protect them against the sun. They also have a huge ad campaign telling all to 'Slip, Slop, Slap' – slip on a shirt, slop on sunscreen and slap on a hat.

Modern Australians have learnt to deal with sun exposure and make the most of the beneficial year round sunshine – which provides vitamin D, makes people happier and more laid-back and promotes an agreeable outdoor culture.

Cost of imported goods

Although the cost of living is, in general, low, imported goods carry a substantial luxury tax, which may place familiar or favourite brands and items outside financial reach. Local alternatives are always available, but there are those migrants for whom no amount of sun, sea and sand can compensate for an over-priced packet of Jaffa cakes.

Economy

Australia's inflation rate has been pushed higher by record petrol prices, increases in rent and house prices. To offset the impact of high inflation in 2008, the new Prime Minister has announced significant cutbacks in spending for the year.

Driving

Most Australians own their own vehicle, as long driving distances are a part of everyday life (unless you live in the centre of town). There is also a great deal of policing on the roads, so cars rarely speed, and drink-drivers are almost a thing of the past.

Droughts

There are often water restrictions in place, for many Australian cities such as Brisbane, Sydney, Melbourne and Perth. This can mean your water usage is monitored, and fines if you don't conform, so, you are often only permitted one shower a day and definitely no washing your car. However, the end of 2007 and start of 2008 saw an uncustomary rainy season, which has filled some of the reserves.

Pros and cons of moving to Australia

Pros
- Warm, sunny climate
- Friendly, welcoming people
- Multicultural diversity
- High standard of living, including better pay
- Better work conditions
- Lower cost of real estate
- First class educational standards and facilities
- Excellent medical facilities
- Good economy
- Lower cost of living and high quality produce

Cons
- Geographical isolation
- Strict immigration laws
- Annoying and dangerous insects and animals
- Expensive international travel
- High cost of imported goods
- Skin cancer
- Droughts

■ PERSONAL STORIES

Rebecca Wells

Rebecca Wells made a brave and inspired life decision some 12 months ago when she opted to change careers entirely, and move to the other side of the world! No stranger to travelling, she was born in England but raised in the busy metropolis that is Hong Kong. It was this upbringing that helped Rebecca decide to give up her unsatisfying job in London, with the long-term view of studying to become a life coach. She now spends her days helping expats settle more quickly and achieve their personal and professional goals. She currently lives in Bondi with her British partner, Ross.

What was your life like before you moved to Australia? What did you do for work?

Hectic. There was a great deal to balance. I have a lot of friends in London, had a great social life and was out most nights and busy most weekends. I also run my own business, which is busy; I'm a coach specialising in working with expatriates. I was living in London – the working hours are particularly long and I didn't much enjoy the invariably grey weather.

What were your first impressions of Australia?

I visited Cairns in 1996 and then backpacked around the west and east coasts nearly four years ago. I now live in Sydney.

My first impressions of the west coast – well I just loved it. It's home to the most glorious national parks and host to some beautiful, booming red gorges. The beaches around that coast are idyllic – gorgeous fine sand near Turquoise Bay and some spectacular snorkelling spots! I was disappointed with Perth though – being a city girl at heart I found it highly underwhelming.

And then the east coast – I just fell in love with Sydney. It has everything: a buzzing city, stunning mountains, gorgeous countryside, weird indigenous animals (which I love, being a big animal buff) and beautiful, rolling, sandy beaches. There are also some fantastic spots along the coast but many are inundated with backpackers in the summer and are not so ideal.

The local people are extremely friendly, welcoming and have a really good sense of fun. They tend to keep things more in perspective than I am used to with those back in UK.

The weather is also an obvious bonus – the sunshine and resultant endorphins are both welcome!

Why did you relocate?

My partner and I loved it so much in Australia that we were keen to move here as soon as the timing was right.

It's also true that Ross and I wanted some adventure and to experience a new environment – and also throw ourselves a little out of our comfort zones!

Neither of us wanted to settle in the UK long-term and Sydney was a city we both instinctively loved – and it will be a great place to raise a family when that opportunity arises.

What is your visa status? Is it easy to change the status once you are in the country?

We have a four-year visa. We have no need to change the status of our visa; my partner is sponsored and I am self-employed so our visa is the perfect solution for both of our career needs.

What is Australian bureaucracy like? How does it compare with British?

It takes forever to get anything done in the UK. In Sydney we continue to be very impressed with the service: we've had furniture delivered on time and extremely quickly; companies you deal with are extremely helpful and knowledgeable. Upon arrival we set up bank accounts in 30 minutes.

In the UK it seems there are complicated processes for almost everything you do and for no apparent reason; here, it's extremely straightforward all round.

Has it taken long to acclimatise?

Not really. Ross and I both love warm climates. Growing up in Hong Kong definitely helped me as I am used to the heat and humidity. We are also lucky to have some friends here already from London and Asia, and we've met new friends through them too. Moving to a new city was quite a natural thing to do for us: we love travelling and grab every new opportunity.

What is the social life like?

It's great! Sydney has a rich and varied social scene. There's a great deal of cultural things to do – theatre, gigs, museums. We've already been to Sydney Opera House to see a show like Cirque de Soleil!

There are also loads of social clubs, gyms, Pilates classes where you can meet people and 10 restaurants or bars per square metre in Bondi!

The weather has a massive impact on what you can feasibly do – there are a lot of outdoor-based activities here and people enjoy socialising more as a result.

How does the standard of living compare with England?

We used to live in central London, in a relatively small one-bedroom flat. Now we're living a stone's throw away from Bondi Beach in a much more spacious unit (they don't call them flats here) and we have brilliant orange and green parakeets careering past our patio window!

Public transport here is much cheaper than London, relatively straightforward and easy to use.

Shopping is excellent here – Bondi Junction has one of the best shopping centres I've ever been in (and I've been to a few!).

The fresh produce is extremely varied and very cheap and there are many local bakers and butchers, often offering local meats like kangaroo and crocodile! Must try cooking one of those steaks soon!

What do you like most about Australia?

The people are just fantastic. They invariably say 'G'day – how y'going?' and expect a response; they're genuinely interested in how you are. It's quite alien coming from London where most people seem to think they're too busy to be interested in your welfare!

The climate's fantastic. The fact that it doesn't rain that much means your options are far wider: you can invite people to a BBQ and not end up cooking on your grill; you can go to a wedding and wear your favourite silk shoes; you don't need to carry a heavy umbrella around everywhere you go! There are seasons of a kind, though, so you still get a sense of those natural cycles.

People here have a greater sense of work–life balance. It's common for people to go to the beach after work for a surf (people actually do that) and the 'family unit' is clearly very important here which is refreshing. Aussies are vehemently patriotic which is really energising.

What do you like least?

There is quite an obvious divide among Australian people: some are really well travelled and some have never left their home town. Although that's the case in every country worldwide, I have encountered a surprising amount of ignorance here about the world around us.

On a similar vein, it drives me potty that the newspapers here are so Australian-centric and only have one or two pages of world news coverage in them (usually right at the back). I find it baffling that there are wars going on around the world and these stories don't make front-page news.

There isn't a great deal of reference to the indigenous people here – especially when you're in the cities. I think a lot of travellers who come to Australia sense that too. Having traveled all over New Zealand where the Maori people and their heritage are truly celebrated, I find it upsetting that a similar pride isn't replicated here.

Do you think you will stay in Australia?

Absolutely. It's very exciting living in a new environment, meeting new people from different backgrounds and increasing my awareness of different attitudes and approaches to life.

Sydney has everything I have ever wanted in a place to settle. It is vibrant, cultured, multicultural, warm, extremely friendly and relatively close to Asia, a part of the world that I love to visit regularly.

Do you have any regrets about leaving England?

Not one. It's a beautifully historic place and I think the British countryside is one of the most stunning places to be in the warm hazy sunshine – but unfortunately that's only three days of the year these days! I do miss the buzz of London and my family and friends but you're only ever a day away from any of them. And there's always Skype!

What advice would you give someone thinking of coming to live and work in Australia?

Being an expatriate coach, to help someone decide whether they should move abroad, I would ask them one question:

'What will living abroad be *worth* to you?'

If their response showed that emigrating would make them happier, lead a more fulfilled life or empower them to be the kind of person they've always wanted to be, then the answer is obvious!

Rebecca's advice to expatriates:

Many expatriates I have met or worked with tend to agree on these pieces of advice:

■ Do extensive research into the country before you apply for any visas

■ Make sure you're aware of what the exchange rates are

■ Be sure you can afford to live on the kind of salary you will receive abroad

■ Join social groups, sporting teams or gyms to make friends and build networks

■ Be brave – just get out there; you won't meet anyone new at home!

■ Keep in touch with your family and friends back home

 To contact Rebecca for life coaching: see www.clearhorizoncoaching.com

Joanna Davies

British expat Joanna Davies and her Aussie husband were drawn to the warmer climate and cheaper cost of living in Australia. So they packed their bags and settled in the cultural capital of Australia, Melbourne.

What was your life like before you moved to Australia?

Leisure time was spent with family and friends, although many friends were in London (50 miles away). Family were fairly far away (250 miles) which meant only seeing family around four or five times a year. Social events mainly revolved around pubs and dinner parties, eating and drinking lots of comforting, warm food!

Exercise routines were difficult to maintain as cold, dark winters meant it was hard to get motivated. We had a high level of car use due to inclement weather or poor public transport links.

How is it that you came to move to Australia?

My husband grew up in Australia and wanted to return for a better quality of lifestyle and outdoor leisure pursuits. We were attracted by the cheaper cost of living and the warmer climate.

What were your first impressions on arriving in Australia?

We found Australia to be brighter, more vivid, warmer and friendlier than the UK. We were excited but easily tired by absorbing so much information. We did a lot of research and reading about setting up a new life, which I think helped.

How did you settle in?

We feel very settled. We have avoided going back to the UK since we left three years ago as we felt this would unsettle us in the critical period when we were trying to settle into our new life. We have missed family and people rather than things and places. We don't miss the highly competitive atmosphere we felt while in the UK. We find Australians more friendly and helpful than people in the UK. We were initially quite mistrustful of people's intentions when they spoke to us or tried to offer help – thinking they were out to con us – but we soon got used to the more friendly nature of people and have let our defences down. We are pleasantly surprised that generally teenagers and children are not as abusive or disrespectful to adults and mostly we feel safer in Australia than the UK. We have probably become much more laid-back ourselves.

We have tried to avoid having only expat friends, although have unavoidably made a couple of English friends as there are so many of them here, and you do share cultural backgrounds that make it easy to relate to each other and share support. We no longer think of the UK as 'home' and have tried to embrace our new life in Australia as completely as possible. I think this has meant less homesickness for us.

What is the social life like? How is it different to back home?

Social life revolves around barbeques and other gatherings, usually having a sporting theme as an excuse, like the Australian Football League (AFL) Grand Final or the Melbourne Cup. We find Australians always bring food to a gathering and are happy to share. We find neighbours friendly and they will always pop over for a coffee or a chat. Social events revolve around food and drink, but meals seem lighter with more importance placed on the company and location than the food provided. Eating out seems more affordable (plenty of reasonably priced Asian restaurants) and social events can be organised spontaneously because the weather does not affect things too much.

How did you go about looking for work? Did your qualifications and/or experiences translate easily to Australia?

I found it easy to get work as a graphic designer, as my skills are relatively hands-on and practical. I started with a temp agency and while I wasn't working in the same industry as in the UK, and was doing a slightly different job, I obtained valuable corporate experience and learnt a lot in the year I was in the 'temporary' job.

My husband has found it much harder to find work, despite being an Australian citizen! Australia is a highly regulated country and recruitment firms look for qualifications and exact industry matches, especially in careers such as IT. Qualifications need to be up-to-date and you may need to take a different role or lower position to get a foot in the door. We found that recruiters is very specific about the person they want to fill the role, and even if a candidate is flexible and resourceful, they will not necessarily be considered if they don't have the exact experience required.

What comments do you have about the Australian working environment? In what ways do you find it similar, different?

I think in some ways British people are more resourceful and driven than Australians. Some Australians seem quite happy with the status quo and like to be led rather than to take initiative in things. Perhaps this is why recruiters are cautious about hiring anyone without a proven track record. A lot of UK expats I have encountered have done well in Australian companies, reaching higher levels of management because of their can-do attitude and ability to problem-solve. The most important thing to remember is that salaries do not translate between the UK and Australia, and you need to adjust your expectations to local market rates, and try to avoid comparing things to your previous earning status in the UK! You also will need to rebuild your entire industry knowledge and contacts (unless you are very lucky), because when you arrive in Australia, you find yourself in the very strange position of having a certain number of years experience in a career, but having the same level of industry knowledge or contacts as a new starter – quite frustrating!

What is your visa status? Is it easy to change the status once you are in the country? Did you encounter any difficulties? Do you have any advice for people who are trying to do the same thing?

I am currently on a permanent visa as I came in on the temporary spouse visa and after 2 years was granted permanent residency. I would like to obtain citizenship but will have to wait a little longer for this. Having temporary or permanent residence instead of citizenship has not really affected my daily life in Australia, except I cannot vote, yet still have to pay taxes to the Government! As a new immigrant I found it much easier to obtain tax file numbers and a Medicare card than my husband who was a returning Australian citizen!

What is Australian bureaucracy like? How does it compare with English?

Australia can be a very bureaucratic country, and often it is impossible to obtain one piece of paper without having another piece of paper and sometimes the only way to get something is to find an official who is willing to 'bend the rules'. Most things will require original documents or 'certified copies' or statutory declarations; these are easy but it can still take a lot of organising to get all documentation sorted out. I would advise you to keep as many records as possible and obtain as many official documents before you leave the UK, as this will help you when you get to Australia!

What do you like about the Melbourne area?

I like the cooler, drier climate. It is less humid than other areas of Australia and has a more European/Mediterranean climate. It does not have the long weeks of endless rain, or grey damp depressing skies like the UK. Generally the weather enables you to be outside most of the time and is more conducive to outdoor pursuits than the UK.

Melbourne is a fairly quiet and clean city with relatively good transport links. It sprawls a long way, but you can live near the beach or in the hills and still be able to commute to the city by public transport for work. There are lots of cycle paths and parks. Trees line most streets so most suburbs are quite pleasant places to live.

How does the standard of living compare with England?

There are lots of cheap and free events and you don't need to earn a lot of money to have a good lifestyle. Housing is getting more expensive but currently my husband

and I are managing to survive on one salary, rather than both of us having to work full-time.

What do you like most about Australia?

Positive attitudes of most people and laid-back atmosphere.

What do you like least?

Frustrating bureaucracy and red tape.

Do you have any regrets about leaving the UK?

Leaving family and friends.

What advice would you give someone thinking of coming to live and work in Australia?

Be prepared to embrace your new life, try not to look down on new things, people or experiences simply because they are different. Try not to be too suspicious of friendly people. Don't worry about making mistakes, most people make mistakes when they move to a new country, whether it's choosing the wrong place to live or buying the wrong fridge! Most things like this don't matter. Give yourself time, and credit yourself for the huge change you have made, don't expect to feel settled in straight-away but take each day as it comes.

Acknowledge the hard work you have done in making the move and don't try to achieve too much too soon. It is harder to settle in and learn about the new culture than you think. Even now, three years later, there are still new words and phrases that remind me I am originally from a different place! Working and socialising with Australians helps you absorb the new culture easily. Above all, have fun and make the most of what Australia can offer!

Scott Sumner

Toronto born expat Scott Sumner decided to pack in his Canadian life as a lawyer and time counter, to follow his heart and follow his new Aussie bride, Linda, down under. He had backpacked his way around Australia, years before and knew that trading long office hours for the promise of sea, sun and sand was a winning formula. Now, happily settled in Sydney, he tells us of the trials and tribulations of making new friends, dealing with lying realtors, approaching 30-year-old Aussie women and buying the perfect couch!

What was your life like before you moved to Australia? Where did you work?

Life was good but the new career I had embarked on as a lawyer was not turning out to be quite as exciting as it appeared on the various TV shows I had based my entry into the profession upon. I was working at a very large law firm as a litigator in downtown Toronto. I was working 12–14-hour days, which were measured in docketable six-minute increments, and not seeing too much daylight. On the more positive side, I was close to family and friends and had a cool downtown apartment with city and water views at the bargain price of Car $137,500 (A$140,000); which would get me a nice parking space in Sydney. Weekends were dedicated to making the two-hour drive to my family cottage at Long Point, a 42km peninsula that extends into Lake Erie, one of the Great Lakes. Life seemed to be in transition well before I moved as I was evolving from being a student, to full-time work with grown-up responsibilities.

Why did you move?

In short, I chased an 'Australian Skirt' back to Australia. This may have been as much a way to escape a career that I hated but struggled to find a way out of. Having previously backpacked through Australia, the promise of sea, sand and sun was simply too much to dismiss when compared to the drudgery of my long working hours, and cold winters. At the time, I anticipated only coming to Australia for one year, but after I upgraded my love interest to Linda (now my wife) and found a job that provided me with a car and the autonomy to drive around the Eastern Suburbs of Sydney, which usually never saw me more out of sight from the ocean, one year stretched on.

What were your first impressions of Australia?

Australia lived up to its reputation of being vastly different to any place I had been previously, while still having so much in common with Canada that I felt quite at home with the people, their sense of humour, and their culture. In short, Australia seemed like Canada with more sun, far fewer clothes on the women (which is not too much of a challenge when you compare the topless beaches to the north of Canada where exposed skin can freeze in a matter of minutes), and a *laissez faire* attitude towards everything including political correctness. Quickly learning that Australian women saw their the men of the country as louts without manners, and commenting that I was amazing since 'I returned their calls', I figured that I was on to a good thing in Australia. The other wildlife, ranging from sharks, whales, kangaroos and koalas inspired me given that my first degree was in environmental biology. Australia struck me as a naïve place where anyone with a dream could have a chance to achieve it.

What is your visa status? Is it easy to change the status once you are in the country?

I am now an Australian citizen. It took five years to get this sorted out given the approach that I took. I was fortunate that my provisional residency was granted in five days of applying and provided that I ticked all the boxes along the way, there was not too much trouble in progressing to full citizenship; I just had to let the clock run.

What is Australian bureaucracy like? How does it compare with Canadian?

Bureaucracy the world over is out of control, and Australia is no exception. This being said, Australia, being a slightly younger country, has not had quite as much time as Canada to implement as many layers of red tape. Give it time! During my time in Australia, I have already noticed an increase in bureaucracy without any corresponding increase in efficiencies or fairness. Wasn't it Shakespeare who coined the phrase *'The first thing we do is kill all the lawyers'*? This was likely in response to having to deal with a bureaucrat who had a lawyer on staff drafting policy! When it comes to immigration, I have to be a little condemning of Canada as my wife and I struggled to get her residency there for over a year, as opposed to my five days when I came to Australia.

Has it taken long to acclimatise?

It took me the better part of a year to really feel at home. Arriving at the age of 30, I discovered that most people – while friendly enough – weren't actively looking for new friends as they were struggling to find the time to maintain their childhood friendships. I think that this would be the case in any country and is a reflection of the challenge of growing up and having different commitments. The catalyst for me in adjusting was making that one first friend who I really connected with, and who then allowed me to share his massive network of friends. This friend, let's call him Dave, is a 'true blue Aussie' who would drop anything when a mate needs a hand.

In return, he simply asks that when you join him for 'just a short drink', that you don't turn into a 'soft cock' and go home before the sun comes up the following day.

What is the social life like?

There is plenty going on. If you are in a big city like Sydney or Melbourne, you have a wide range of places to go and spend your hard earned money. The people in the cities tend to be a hard crowd to break into. The lament of most 30-year-old women is that they can't ever meet anyone when they go out, but then again, they almost refuse to speak to anyone who finally gets up the courage to walk up to them – they like the guys who show them no interest which makes them grown-up versions of 15-year-old girls. Most guys quite like that! The guys are far more approachable and are happy to be your best friend if you have something in common – like drinking beer or enjoying sports. The small towns are pretty cool, and every one of them has its 'local', regardless of the size of the town – for example, the town of Young is essentially comprised of the pub and a church, which is directly across the road. I am not sure whether the drinking leads to regret and atonement or whether it is the other way around, but it seems to be a formula that works! Once you have found a few friends, you can be as busy as you like. The hard part in the first few years is forcing yourself to accept all social invitations for fear that you won't get any more, regardless of whether you really want to do what is on offer.

How does the standard of living compare with Canada?

That is hard to answer, but overall, it is pretty similar. In Canada you can certainly get a much nicer house than you can in Australia and people really put a huge effort into making sure that their homes are well presented at all times. At first glance, most things appear more expensive in Australia, but this is because Australia builds all taxes and tips into the price that goes on the tag, whereas in Canada you have 15% added in taxes, and tips for service, after you arrive at the cash register. After all is said and done, most items are about the same. The one huge exception outside of property are couches, chesterfields, loungers – call them what you like. In Australia, they are so dear that you need a second job if you don't want to sit on a piece of garbage. Consequently, most people happily sit on their age-old piece of garbage, not realising that there are plush, comfortable ways to relax in front of the television. Clearly this is a pet peeve of mine – which I am reminded of every night as I sit on my piece of garbage dreaming of the day when I can get a nice couch. If you want to enjoy yourself without spending money, this is easier to do in Australia than in Canada. Australia has beaches and oceans, which are fabulous playgrounds, and they are all free to enjoy. Just don't think that the parking adjacent to them will come for free.

What do you like most about Australia?

The weather – hands down!

What do you like least?

The price of property and ridiculous games that get played by lying real estate agents which make it virtually impossible to buy a house, even if you have the money and are willing to pay a fair price.

Do you think you will stay in Australia?

My wife and I have a five-year plan – and God laughs at plans that people make! We figure that we will always have a foot in both Canada and Australia and thus will likely live parts of our lives in both countries. If we have kids, we think it will be important for them to live in both countries and know both sides of their heritage. This plan promises to be expensive and exhausting so don't think that we are completely deluded about reality!

Do you have any regrets about leaving Canada?

I have sadness over leaving a country I love, and being so far from my family and friends. I knew that this would be the case before I left, and I have been right. If I were to regret it, I would be on a plane tomorrow. Life is too short to have regrets. I have been blessed to have the opportunity to live in two amazing countries and now to be a citizen of both of them. As with most expats, I am sure that I will never stop missing my home country, but I am thrilled that my new country has become home too.

What advice would you give someone thinking of coming to live and work in Australia?

Absolutely do it. Don't wait, just do it. Just be sure what you want out of the experience and if it is a holiday, then be prepared to see and do everything and pay the money it takes to do it. If you are hoping to travel and go home with money in your pocket, you will not have made the most of your trip. If you are coming to live, my advice would be to be gentle with yourself and allow at least twice the time you would expect to get really settled. If you are non-English speaking, you will be able to get by, but you will have to work especially hard to rise to the level of standing that you might enjoy in your home country. Whatever you do, don't limit yourself to backpacker hostels as you will see the country, but not get to know the people. Stay in one place long enough to work – that is how you will get to know the true Australian.

Matthew Morrison

Londoner Matt Morrison thought he had gone back in time when first arriving in Sydney. Now, fully acclimatised to the locals' quirky fashion sense and melting heat of the city, he tells us his favourite parts of being an Australian resident.

What was your life like before you moved to Australia?

It was good, as I lived and worked in London, with lots of friends, although work life was a bit hectic at times, and commuting is always a pain in London.

What were your first impressions of Australia?

On the train into Sydney, it felt as though I had gone back a little in time with fashion and people. But overall, good. They are such laid-back, friendly people!

What is Australian bureaucracy like? How does it compare with British?

Not too bad. In London you basically have to go to the embassy for anything, as the phone line is on a charge and offers general information only! The people in the embassy were helpful though.

It's all fairly straightforward in Australia in comparison, as there are less people, so they are better catered for.

Has it taken long to acclimatise?

Not really. People tend to take a bit more time with you, similar to living outside of London, and I have found them to be very friendly and helpful.

Getting used to the heat on some days is a challenge – no long walks at lunchtime unless you can take a shower afterwards!

Banking systems and health systems are slightly different. You need to find out what you need, rather than expecting anyone to tell you or having the knowledge you do at home.

What is the social life like?

Brilliant! There are loads of great bars with fantastic views, whether over the harbour or by the sea. I've built up a knowledge of some great restaurants and favourite haunts!

As far as the social life goes, many people are already in relationships, so it can be hard to break into groups at times, or to socialise with locals/work colleagues at weekends.

How does the standard of living compare with England?

Rent is cheaper here and you can live in your first choice location. Flats tend to be unfurnished, so you need to either buy/rent furniture, flatshare or pay a premium for furnished. People tend to continue flatsharing well into their 40s and 50s here!

That said, I was surprised to find food more expensive, in general, which I believe is due to lack of choice of supermarkets (one in each suburb as a rule, rarely with competitors). You often find that alcohol is the same price in bars and shops! They also don't sell alcohol in supermarkets here, just at bottle shops (or bottle-ohs as they call them) Salaries tend to be lower here, however, they seem to go a bit further.

What do you like most about Australia?

The beach at the weekends, it's very relaxing. Also, the positive nature of most of the people. In Sydney, I find it very clean and chilled out, you never feel threatened or stressed walking around, at any time of night. People are also very respectful and family oriented, especially at places where people meet, like the beach.

What do you like least?

In Sydney, the transport system relies heavily on buses only. Cost of food, as mentioned. The reliance on having a car, and a car mentality (dangerous being a pedestrian at times!). Really poor quality of television, and lack of cultural shows, with a heavy reliance on American imports. Also lack of world news, they only seem to report on local events, as if the rest of the world doesn't exist! Flights anywhere out of Australia, cost the same in pounds – no exchange rate benefit!

Do you think you will stay in Australia?

Absolutely!

Do you have any regrets about leaving England?

You miss your friends and family and being part of Europe, and what is going on in the world. I also hate that it's so expensive if I want to visit different countries and cultures.

What advice would you give someone thinking of coming to live and work in Australia?

Go for it! Ensure you are committed to living far away from friends/family as you will probably only average one trip a year, as it costs a lot and requires time. That said, it's a great outdoor lifestyle and a great place to be, whether you're young or old.

Before You Go

■ VISAS, WORK PERMITS AND CITIZENSHIP

Immigration has currently become a contentious policy area in Australia with many people reacting to economic stringencies by calling for an end to Australia's migration programmes. The rationale for this position (that 'foreigners take our jobs') has been proved to be completely erroneous. This has not prevented anti-migration activists, generally operating from a distinctly racist platform, from continuing to dominate the debate on the issue in the media. In response, the Government has stressed its commitment to Australia as a *'deeply tolerant, fair-minded and generous society'.*

The new Labor Government recognises that migrants have made, and continue to make, an enormous contribution to Australian society, bringing new skills, ideas and technologies to the nation's economy and skill base. In the context of the globalisation of Australia's economy, migrants' awareness of the nuances of international cultures provides an important asset for its international and domestic competitiveness.

Migration to Australia is dependent on your ability to meet the migration criteria of the day and Australia's interest and needs. The migration programme is carefully managed, with annual quotas imposed on each

The Australian Flag

area of temporary and permanent residency category after extensive assessment of the current economic circumstances. Migrants are chosen from three broad categories:

- Family Stream
- Skilled Stream
- Humanitarian

Family Stream

The Family Stream of Australia's migration programme enables the reunion in Australia of close family members such as spouses, fiancé(e)s, interdependent partners, dependent children and adopted children. It also includes other family members such as parents, orphan relatives, carers, aged dependent relatives, and remaining relatives. In 2006–2007 there were 46,000 family stream places. This shows a marked increase from 2004–2005 when there were as little as 41,740 successful family applicants.

Skilled Stream

The Skilled Stream of Australia's migration programme is designed to target migrants who have skills or outstanding abilities that will contribute to the Australian economy. The migration to Australia of people with qualifications and relevant work experience helps to balance specific skill shortages in Australia, and enhances the size and skill level of the Australian labour force.

There are four main categories in the Skilled Stream:

- General skilled migration
- Employer nomination
- Business skills migration
- Distinguished talent (which has the least number of places)

The Skilled Stream planning level

The Skilled Stream planning level for 2007–08 is 108,500, with a continued emphasis on:

- employer-sponsored migration
- state/territory government sponsored applications
- applicants who nominate an occupation which is on the Migration Occupations in Demand List (MODL)

General skilled migration

This shows slight growth from 2006–07 when there were 97,500 successful Skilled Stream applicants and a massive leap from 2004–05 when there were only 77,889.

The Government's intention is that migration should become more focused on the intake of skilled migrants, although it retains a commitment to bona fide immediate family migrants.

Which countries are accepted?

Although racist polemics in the popular press would suggest otherwise, Australia operates an entirely non-discriminatory immigration programme. It is selective on the basis of skills, age and language ability, but is open to anyone in any part of the world, regardless of their country of birth, ethnic origin, race, sex or religion.

Immigration statistics

Figures from the Australian Bureau of Statistics show that from June 2001 to June 2002, the number of settlers arriving in Australia, by country of birth were: UK 9.8% China 7.5%, South Africa 6.4% and North America 1.9%.

However, in the 2007–08 period, the figure increased to reflect over 17.7% were from the United Kingdom (totalling 23,300) and 14.4% coming from its close neighbour New Zealand (19,000).

Other large migrating countries during this period were:
- China (excludes SARs and Taiwan Province) (10,600) 8.0%
- India (11,300) 8.6%
- Sudan (3,800) 2.9%
- South Africa (4,000) 3.0%
- Philippines (4,900) 3.7%
- Singapore 2,700 2.0%

Applying to live in Australia can be a time-consuming and expensive exercise, and a number of migration consultancies offer services to help prospective applicants with the procedures. The Australian consular service advises prospective visa applicants that, although such consultancies cannot 'get round the system' and guarantee success, a reputable firm will definitely ease the pressure and provide valuable advice to those unfamiliar with the migration application process. Migrants, either permanent or temporary, must undergo comprehensive health examinations and provide evidence of good character.

Humanitarian programme

A total of 13,000 places have been maintained for the 2006–07 Humanitarian Programme which is comprised of two main components – refugee and humanitarian.

Over the 2007–08 period, a total of 6,000 places have been allocated to the Refugee category, which is for people who are subject to persecution in their home country and who are in need of resettlement.

A further 7,000 places have been allocated to the Special Humanitarian Programme (SHP) category, for people outside their home country who are subject to substantial discrimination amounting to gross violation of human rights in their home country, and to meet Onshore Protection needs. Onshore Protection visas are granted to those assessed as refugees in Australia.

 Department of Immigration and Citizenship: www.immi.gov.au
www.emigrationgroup.co.uk

Emigration Group

The Emigration Group was established with the sole aim of helping people achieve a new life overseas. Together with their New Zealand sister company Taylor & Associates, who specialise in migrant employment search, they provide an effective and total emigration service.

 Emigration Group: (from UK 0845 230 4374) www.emigrationgroup.co.uk

The Emigration Group is experienced in preparing many types of visa applications. The rules and regulations for each are complex and often change. They recommend a full personal eligibility assessment of your residence prospects by their experienced personnel, two of whom each have over five years experience in the Australian Department of Immigration.

All migration agents and consultants charge for their services.

 Tip: Australian Outlook is published monthly by Consyl Publishing Ltd: 01424 223111; www.consylpublishing.co.uk. Aimed specifically at migrants, this publication is a useful way of keeping up with Australian migration policy and entry regulations. In the UK six issues cost £12 and 12 issues £18 in Europe six issues cost £15 and 12 issues £24 elsewhere six issues cost £18 and 12 cost £32.90.

Entry for Australian, NZ citizens or permanent residents

New Zealand passport holders have a co-agreement with Australian immigration. In general, if you wish to visit Australia as a tourist you will need a Visitor's visa; if you are planning to go on a working holiday or to retire, you will need a Temporary Residence Visa in the appropriate category; and if you are hoping to settle permanently in Australia, you will need to be accepted as an immigrant and be granted permanent residence. When booking a flight to Australia, your travel agent will often add your tourist visa to your ticket.

Australia is known for its strict immigration rules

Under various arrangements since the 1920s, there has been a free flow of people between Australia and New Zealand.

The 1973 Trans-Tasman Travel Arrangement has allowed Australian and New Zealand citizens to enter each other's country to visit, live and work, without the need to apply for authority to enter the other country. (Source: www.immi.gov.au)

Visitor's visa

You may be wondering how your friends and family will gain entry for visits once you have settled, or perhaps you want to go and have a look around before you make your final important decisions. In these cases you will need a Visitor's visa.

The department of Immigration and citizenship states that in 2006–07, there were 3,627,803 Visitor visa grants offshore, a record number of grants, increasing by 1.8% over the 2005–06 figure of 3,563,372. The highest number of offshore Visitor visas was granted to people from the United Kingdom. The rate of grant for Visitor visas continued to improve during 2006–07.

 To visit Australia as a tourist, you will require a Visitor's visa obtainable from the Australian High Commission and most travel agents. This form can also now be downloaded as a pdf file from the Internet at

FACT

■ The 1973 Trans-Tasman Travel Arrangement has allowed Australian and New Zealand citizens to enter each other's country to visit, live and work, without the need to apply for authority to enter the other country. (Source: www.immi.gov.au)

www.immi.gov.au/allforms/index.htm. Visitors' visas are classed as either 'short-stay' (three months) or 'long-stay' (up to one year), are multiple entry visas and are valid for 12 months from the date of issue. The application fee for the short and long-stay Visitor's visas is a non-refundable A$75 if lodged outside Australia. Travellers visiting Australia to conduct business of a short-term nature which is deemed not to disadvantage local residents should also apply for a Visitor's visa. Retired parents of Australian residents are entitled to a Visitor's visa valid for a period of 12 months. To be eligible for this extended visa, you need to provide proof of funds sufficient to support yourself during the entire period of the visit. If you intend staying with family or friends for any or all of this time, the level of funds required will be assessed at a lower level than that for a tourist.

The three-month Visitor visa can be applied for by post, with a processing time of approximately three weeks. Enclose a large, stamped, self-addressed envelope for the return of your documents. Applications can be made in person at the Australian High Commission in London, the Australian Embassy in Washington and from Australian Government offices elsewhere. The Australian High Commission in London can be very busy, especially from September to February, and you should expect a long wait; Mondays to Wednesdays are generally the busiest days.

It is possible to extend a three-month Visitor's visa to one of six months duration while in Australia; however, if you wish to stay longer in Australia, it is vital that you extend the visa before it expires. The Department of Immigration and Multicultural and Indigenous Affairs will immediately deport any applicant who holds an expired visa. You must leave the country on a valid visa and renew it overseas before returning, although some travellers following this procedure have been refused re-entry into Australia, despite leaving Australia on a valid visa and renewing their visas in New Zealand or Singapore.

Electronic Travel Authority

The Visitor's visa has now been pretty much superseded by Australia's state-of-the-art Electronic Travel Authority (ETA) system. This is available to passport holders from 34 countries and locations, including British and US citizens and most citizens of EU countries. The ETA system was introduced in 1996 and is an 'invisible', electronically-stored authority for short-term (three-month) travel to Australia which can be issued (at the time of making travel bookings) in less than 10 seconds at the time of making travel bookings. It is claimed that the ETA is the most advanced and streamlined travel authorisation system in the world, permitting visitors to be processed in seconds on arrival at their destination. At this end, the advantages include an end to form-filling, queues and embassy visits: the whole process is completed on the spot. The ETA system can be accessed by 300,000 travel agents worldwide, and by more than 75 airlines.

Worldwide internet access to the ETA system now enables tourists and business travellers intending to visit Australia for three months or less to apply online at at a cost of A$20 (payable by credit card only).

 Electronic Travel Authority applications: www.eta.immi.gov.au

More than 17 million travellers have chosen to visit Australia on ETAs, which now account for around 85% of all tourist and short-term business visas issued worldwide. There are three different types of ETA and travellers should make sure that they obtain the one appropriate to their needs: tourists and those visiting family or friends for a period of three months or less need a Short Validity Tourist ETA, while business visitors need a Long Validity Business ETA, or a Short Validity Business ETA. It has currently been reported that some British travel agents are charging their clients to issue an ETA. The amount of work involved in supplying this visa can in no way justify this charge, and travellers should be alert to this potential rip-off.

 More details: www.immi.gov.au/visitors/tourist www.emigrationgroup.co.uk

■ TEMPORARY RESIDENCE

Visitors intending to enter Australia temporarily for the purpose of work or otherwise need to obtain a temporary residence visa. These can last from six months to four years depending on the type of visa. In some cases you can roll over from a temporary residence visa to a permanent visa, such as the spouse temporary to permanent visa. The temporary visa is a policy requirement in some areas.

Skilled, long-term temporary residents make a major contribution to Australia. By filling specific skill gaps in Australian businesses, they help

> **Expat Joanna Davies explains her current visa situation:**
> 'I am currently on a permanent visa as I came in on the temporary spouse visa and after two years was granted permanent residency. I would like to obtain citizenship but will have to wait a little longer for this. Having temporary or permanent residence instead of citizenship has not really affected my daily life in Australia, except I cannot vote; yet still have to pay taxes to the Government!

Australia to remain a strong competitor in the international market. Skilled long-term temporary residents also bring with them new ideas, international contacts, access to cutting edge technologies and business practices. Many are also helping businesses to train their Australian staff. It is anticipated that demand for the programme will continue to grow while Australia's economy remains strong and Australia's population continues to age. (Source: www.immi.gov.au)

There are currently 21 different temporary residence sub-classes, which are issued according to the type of activity the applicant will undertake in Australia. The temporary residence programme is designed to allow people from overseas to come to Australia for specific purposes, which are expected to provide some benefit to Australia. This includes the Retirement visa (see page 366). The programme consists of three streams: economic, social and cultural, and international relations.

The costs of gaining a temporary visa are high:

- Skilled – Sponsored (Migrant) visa (subclass 176) –
  1st instalment: A$2,060, 2nd instalment: A$2,860
- Skilled – Regional Sponsored (Provisional) visa (subclass 475) –
  1st instalment: A$2060, 2nd instalment: A$2,860
- Skilled – Recognised Graduate (Temporary) visa (subclass 476) –
  One payment: A$190

Economic visas

Visa	Allows:
Business entry	employers to recruit skilled personnel from overseas for a stay of up to four years
Educational	entry of staff to fill academic, teaching and research positions in Australian educational institutions, which cannot be filled from within the Australian labour market *A letter of appointment is required*
Temporary medical practitioner	entry of suitably qualified medical practitioners, sponsored by Government, community bodies, or prospective employers, which satisfy labour market requirements *There is a strong focus on providing service to rural and remote communities*

Social and cultural visas

Visa	Allows:
Entertainment	entry of actors, entertainers, models and their associated personnel for specific engagements or events in Australia *Visa assessment will take into account the need to protect the employment of Australians in the industry*

(Continued)

Media and film staff	entry of foreign correspondents to represent overseas news media organisations in Australia, and television or film crew members or photographers, including actors and support staff, involved in the production of films, documentaries or advertising commercials in Australia which are not being produced for the Australian market
Sport	entry of amateur and professional sportspeople, including officials and their support staff, to engage in competition with Australian residents and to improve general sporting standards through high calibre competition and training
Religious worker	entry of religious workers, including ministers, priests and spiritual leaders to serve the spiritual needs of people of their faith in Australia
Family relationship	secondary school-age children to have an extended holiday with relatives or close family friends who are Australian citizens or residents
Retirement	people over 55 an extended temporary stay in Australia *Individuals can work for up to 20 hours per week*
Public lecturer	entry of specialists and recognised experts to deliver public lectures in Australia
Visiting academic	entry of people as visiting academics at Australian educational and research institutions, with the intention that their presence will contribute to the sharing of research knowledge *A letter of invitation is required and you may not receive a salary from the host institution*

International relations visas

Visa	Allows:
Working holiday	young people to holiday in Australia, while working to supplement their funds *Aims to promote international understanding. Many conditions apply (see Working holiday, page 48)*
Foreign government agency staff	foreign government officials to conduct business or teaching duties on behalf of their government, where that government has no diplomatic or official status in Australia
Exchange	visitors to come to Australia to broaden their work experience and skills under reciprocal arrangements by which Australian residents are granted similar opportunities abroad. Includes people seeking entry under certain bilateral exchange agreements *A letter of invitation is required from the organisation offering the position*
Special program	people visiting under approved programmes to broaden their experience and skills – generally used for youth exchanges and programmes such as the Churchill Fellowship *A letter of support is required from the organisation*

Diplomatic	temporary entry of people wanting to travel to Australia in a diplomatic or official capacity
	Those who are eligible should apply for this visa regardless of their intended period of stay
Domestic worker (diplomatic/ consular)	entry of private domestic staff for work in the households of diplomatic and consular staff posted to Australia where Australian Department of Foreign Affairs and Trade (DFAT) supports the entry
Domestic worker (overseas executive)	entry of domestic staff of certain holders of visas in class 457 long-stay temporary business entry
	Only granted where it can be shown that the entry of such staff is necessary for the proper discharge of representational duties
Occupational trainees	entry of persons for occupational training appropriate to their background and/or employment history, for the acquisition or upgrading of skills useful to their home country
	A nomination must be provided unless the training is to be given by the Commonwealth of Australia
Supported dependent	temporary stay of dependents of either an Australian citizen or a holder of a permanent residence visa who is usually resident outside Australia and intends to remain temporarily in Australia
	A letter of support is required from the Australian citizen/ permanent residence visa holder
Expatriate	temporary stay of certain spouses or dependents of persons employed by international companies in remote locations near Australia, such as South-East Asia, the South Pacific or Papua New Guinea
Professional development	temporary entry of groups of professionals, managers and government officials from overseas who are seeking to enhance their professional/managerial skills by taking part in tailored training programmes designed by an Australian sponsoring organisation

Student visas

Visa	For overseas students:
Independent ELICOS	undertaking an ELICOS (English Language Intensive Course for Overseas Students) as a stand-alone course, and not as a prerequisite to commencing another course (for example, a degree course)
Schools	undertaking a course of study at a primary school or a secondary school
	This subclass is also for overseas school students participating in a formal registered secondary exchange programme
	The period of exchange may vary from one month to one year
Vocational education and training (VET)	studying certificate I, II, III and IV, Diploma, Advanced diploma and Advanced certificate

(Continued)

Higher education	studying for a Bachelor degree, Associate degree, Graduate certificate, or Graduate diploma
Postgraduate research	taking a Masters degree by coursework or by research, or a Doctoral degree
Non-award founda-tion studies/ other	taking foundation, bridging or other courses that do not lead to the award of a degree, diploma or other formal award
AusAID or Defence	undertaking full-time study sponsored by *AusAID* or *Defence* for the whole or part of an education or training course offered by an Australian education provider

Health and character check

People who wish to enter Australia on the temporary residence visas listed above must meet the normal health and character requirements for entry. Some applicants may be asked to have a medical examination before a visa will be granted. In most cases, if you have your application for temporary residence approved, you will then be granted a multiple entry visa for the period of the approved stay.

If you need a further re-entry visa, you will need to apply to an office of the Department of Immigration and Multicultural and Indigenous Affairs (DIMIA). Fees for temporary residence visas are currently £190.

Temporary residence visa processing times are currently around three to six weeks.

Students

Since 1985, numbers of transnational students seeking to study in Australia have skyrocketed. In 2006–07, visas granted to overseas students totalled 450,664, an 18.8% increase on the previous year. Of these 4,631 were granted to students from the UK, a 10.6% increase from 2006. Chinese students, however, came in their droves and represented a massive 106,221 student visas in 2007.

 Statistics on student enrolment: http://aei.dest.gov.au/AEI/MIP/Statistics/StudentEnrolmentAndVisaStatistics/2007

How to apply for permission to work on a student visa

 Working while studying: www.immi.gov.au/students/students/working_while_studying

Applying online is the quickest way for students and their family members to lodge permission to work applications. Applications received by post may take up to seven days to process and applications lodged in person may take up to 28 days.

◼ **Applying online**

1. Ask your education provider to notify the department electronically to confirm that you have started your course.

   Allow at least one hour for the transfer of this information into the department's system before going to Step 2.

2. Check the charges for lodging an application for permission to work.

   See: Charges (Fees) – Student visa charges at www.immi.gov.au/students

3. Complete the online application and follow the prompts to pay for the application.

   See: Online applications – Students at www.immi.gov.au/students

4. Register for Visa Entitlement Verification Online (VEVO) whilst you are applying for your visa online. You can use VEVO to check the progress of your application and your visa details.

   Note: You no longer require a visa label to be put in your travel document.

 Visa Entitlement Verification Online (VEVO) for eVisa holders: www.immi.gov.au/students

Note AusAID and Defence (subclass 576) visa applicants must bring a letter from your Australian education provider, to any departmental office, stating that you have started your course before commencing your online application.

■ Applying by post or in person

1. To apply, you must have one of the following:
   - ■ a letter from your education provider stating that you have started your course
   - ■ the front of Form 157P Application for a student visa with permission to work signed and stamped by your education provider.
2. Check the charges for lodging an application for permission to work. You can pay the application charge by electronic funds transfer, credit card, money order, or bank cheque made payable to the department.
3. Complete Form 157P, found at www.immi.gov.au/students
4. Post or deliver your application to your nearest departmental office.

 Application forms, addresses and fees : www.immi.gov.au/students/students/working_while_studying/how-to-apply.htm

Students may work full-time during holiday periods. Note that student visas are subject to cancellation if a student works in excess of his or her entitlements. Currently student visas take four weeks to process and cost A$430.

 2009 fee charges: www.immi.gov.au/allforms/990i/students-visa-charges.htm

The Government now offers eVisa, a convenient electronic visa application as an alternative. You can lodge an application 24 hours a day and no more than four months before your course commences. As from November 2004, a new facility allows accompanying family members to be included in a student eVisa application lodged outside Australia. The student visa application charge includes an International Education Contribution of A$115. This contributes to Australian Government initiatives to support international education through the Department of Education, Science and Training.

Working holiday

The Working Holiday programme aims to promote international understanding by giving young people the opportunity to experience the culture of another country. It allows working holidaymakers to enjoy an extended holiday by supplementing their travel funds through incidental employment, thus

experiencing closer contact with local communities. Australia has reciprocal working holiday arrangements with Belgium, Canada, Cyprus, Denmark, Estonia, France, Germany, Hong Kong, Finland, Ireland, Italy, Japan, Republic of Korea, Malta, the Netherlands, Norway, Sweden, Taiwan, United Kingdom and, since 2007, the United States. Although there are specific arrangements with these countries, the Australian working holiday scheme is applied globally, and applicants from other countries are considered where there might be a benefit both to the applicant and to Australia.

When you apply for a Working Holiday visa, you must demonstrate that your main purpose in visiting Australia is to holiday, and that any work you expect to undertake will be solely to assist in supporting you while on vacation. You must have a good chance of finding temporary work, and may study or train for up to three months. You must also have a return ticket or sufficient funds for a return airfare, in addition to being able to demonstrate A$5,000 in funds for your travels (or a parental guarantee for the same amount). A Working Holiday visa usually allows for multiple entry, which means that you may leave and re-enter the country as many times as you like (in the time restriction of your visa). When the visa is granted, ensure that it has been stamped 'multiple entry'. The only way you can renew your working visa for an additional 12-month period, is if 3 months' worth of work has been undertaken in a primary industry.

You cannot get an extension on a Working Holiday visa under any other circumstances (though you can apply to change your visa status if you meet requirements), and must leave the country on or before the expiry date of your visa.

The Working Holiday visa is available to applicants between the ages of 18 and 30. Applicants may be either single or married, but must not have any dependent children. You must not have previously entered Australia on a Working Holiday visa and you will also need to meet health and character requirements and be outside Australia at the time of the visa being granted. The visa is valid for 12 months from the day of issue, and allows a stay of 12 months from date of entry into Australia.

A limit (reviewed annually) may be imposed on the number of Australian Working Holiday visas granted. A number of factors influence the volume of applications for Working Holiday visas, such as the strength of various economies around the world, and the popularity of some kinds of tourism. Some prospective working holidaymakers have suffered under the new 'capping' rules, and have had their application for a visa refused after paying for their travel. Travel agents who specialise in Australian travel suggest that one way of avoiding this is to plan to commence the working holiday shortly after the beginning of July, which is the beginning of the annual visa allocation period. Applications made at this time have a good chance of succeeding. According to the Department of Immigration and Citizenship, the number of people in Australia on Working Holiday visas has grown from 85,200 in 2001–02 to 126,600 in 2006–07, with the largest number of successful applicants coming from the UK.

Once in Australia, surveys show that most working holidaymakers find temporary or casual employment in farming, clerical and hospitality industries. Fruit picking, bartending, secretarial and clerical work obtained through temp agencies, and labouring are all popular options for travellers, and this work tends to be widely available on a seasonal basis (see page 257, Working in Australia). Most travellers, on average, undertake three or four different jobs over the period of their visit, holding each for six to eight weeks at a time. The Working Holiday Maker scheme permits you to work for a maximum of three months for any one employer. If you are found to be working beyond the approved time limit you may have your visa cancelled. At present Working Holiday visas cost A\$190 and processing takes about four to five weeks. Form 990i available from DIMIA contains additional information on the scheme. It is also now possible to apply directly through DIMIA's website for an electronic visa. Processing priority will be given to applications lodged in this way, while those lodged at an Australian mission abroad may take considerably longer.

i **Working Holiday Maker visa applications:** www.immi.gov.au
Advice: www.emigrationgroup.co.uk

■ PERMANENT RESIDENCE (MIGRATION)

Migration numbers to Australia continue to prosper and a study conducted in June 2005, revealed that over 23.6% of Aussies were born in the UK. The level of migration places for 2006–07 totalled 144,000.

Generally, a successful applicant for migration to Australia must meet the personal and occupational requirements of the category for which he or she is applying, be able to settle in Australia without undue cost or difficulty to the Australian community, and be of good health and character. In addition, successful applicants will need enough money to travel to and settle in Australia. In 2003–04, 114,362 migrants were selected in the Migration Programme. In 2005–06, 143,000 had their applications accepted.

Family Stream migration

Approximately 32% of the migrants entering Australia each year do so under the Family Stream of the Migration Programme. The Family Stream had grown steadily from 31,310 visas in 1997–98 to 46,000 visas in 2006–07 *(Source: Australian Immigration)*. However, over the same period, the Family Stream's overall share of the Migration Programme fell from 47% to 35%. Family Stream migrants are selected on the basis of their family relationship with their sponsor in Australia, and there is no test for skills or language ability as there is for Skilled Stream migrants; they are still required, however, to meet the requirements of health and character which are applied to all migrants. Family Stream applicants can be sponsored for migration (permanent residence) under four main categories: Partner, Child, Parent and Other Family. The level for Family Stream places in 2006–07 stood at 46,000 visas.

Partner/spouse

Issued to a husband, wife or *de facto* partner of the Australian sponsor. Since May 1997, it has been required that a *de facto* or interdependent partner of an Australian citizen or permanent resident must be able to demonstrate one year of cohabitation with the sponsor. The cohabitation requirement also applies to gay and lesbian partners of Australian sponsors, who should apply for an Interdependency visa, but who otherwise are assessed in the same way as those applying for a Spouse visa. In compelling cases, such as where a child of the relationship exists, the cohabitation requirement may be waived.

Prospective marriage

Fiancé(e)s overseas must apply for a Prospective Marriage visa, which is valid for nine months from the date of issue. They must travel to Australia, marry their sponsor, and apply to remain permanently during that period.

It is a requirement that the parties to a prospective marriage have met and be known to each other in person. If all requirements are met, applicants will be granted a temporary visa, followed by a permanent visa if the relationship is still continuing at the end of two years.

Interdependent partner

Interdependency visas are for people who have an interdependent relationship with an Australian citizen or permanent resident that demonstrates a genuine, continuing and mutual commitment to a shared life together. The application process is the same as for the spouse visa, although the number of visas given out is considerably lower; for example between 2006–07 there were only 570 visas for Interdependents.

Child

During the 2006–07 period, a total of 2,547 visas were granted for children. There are three separate categories for child visas:

- **Dependent Child.** Parents are able to sponsor for migration their natural or adopted child, or a stepchild of an Australian spouse. The granting of a dependent child visa must not prejudice the rights and interests of any person who has custody or guardianship or access to the child.
- **Adopted Child.** A child adopted overseas who is under 18 years of age.
- **Orphan Relative.** This visa permits the migration of orphans (as defined in the Migration Regulations), who are under 18 years old, unmarried and a relative of the sponsor.

Parent

- **Parent.** Applicants must be the parent of a person who is a settled Australian citizen or an Australian permanent resident.

  You can only be granted a Parent visa when applying in Australia if you are old enough to be granted an Australian age pension. This does not mean that you will receive the age pension, as you must have been an Australian permanent resident for 10 years to access the age pension.

  The Age Pension is paid to Australian residents who, on the day the claim is lodged, are over 65 years (for men) or aged between 60.5 and 65 (for women whose date of birth is between 1 July 1935 and 1 January 1949).

- **Contributory parent.** Applicants must be a parent of a child who is a settled Australian citizen or an Australian permanent resident. There are more visa places available in this category, but the visa application charge is substantially higher. The parent must be an aged parent (pensioner) who holds a Contributory Parent (Temporary) visa (subclass 173) and wants to apply for the permanent Contributory Parent (Migrant) visa (subclass 143). You can apply for this visa any time before your Contributory Parent (Temporary) visa expires. Your spouse

FACT

 You can only be granted a Parent visa when applying in Australia if you are aged. An aged parent is one who is old enough to be granted an Australian age pension. This does not mean that you will receive the age pension, as you must have been an Australian permanent resident for 10 years to access the age pension.

and other family members may be included in your application if they meet certain requirements. This visa allows you, your accompanying spouse and dependent family members to live as permanent residents in Australia.

You can also:

- work and study in Australia
- receive subsidised healthcare through Medicare and the Pharmaceutical Benefits Scheme (PBS)
- access certain social security payments (subject to waiting periods)
- be eligible to apply for Australian citizenship (subject to the residency eligibility criteria)
- sponsor people for permanent residence (subject to waiting periods). Over the 2006–07 period, 3,500 contributory parent visas were issued.

 Parent visa: www.immi.gov.au/migrants/family/parent

Other family visas

- **Carer.** To apply for a Carer visa you must be willing and able to give substantial, continuing assistance to an Australian relative (or a member of their family) that has a medical condition that is causing physical, intellectual or sensory impairment of their ability to attend to the practical aspects of daily life. The need for assistance must be likely to continue for at least two years. You must be sponsored or nominated by the relative requiring care in Australia, who must be an Australian citizen, Australian permanent resident or eligible New Zealand citizen.
- **Aged dependent relative.** To apply for an aged dependent relative visa you must:
  - be old enough to be granted an Australian age pension (for males 65, for females the qualifying age is gradually being increased from 60 to 65)
  - be single, having never married, been divorced or formally separated from your spouse or widowed
  - have been dependent, and remain dependent, on your Australian relative for a reasonable period (normally three years).
- **Remaining relative.** This visa allows for entry of the last remaining brother, sister or non-dependent child outside Australia. You or your spouse must not have a parent, sibling or non-dependent child or step-relative (in the same degree of relationship) living outside Australia, and again your sponsor must have lived in Australia for at least two years before the sponsorship is lodged.

The Australian Government has established processing priorities for applicants under the Family Stream scheme. Priority is given to dependent

> 'In 2007–08 there will again be 4,500 visa places available – 1,000 in the parent category and 3,500 in the contributory parent category'
>
> **(DIMC)**

children (including adopted and interdependent families). Lower priority is given to all other Family Stream categories.

Some Family Stream applicants are subjected to a mandatory Assurance of Support (AoS). This is a legal commitment to repay the Commonwealth of Australia any recoverable social security benefits paid by Centrelink to those covered by the assurance. Other applicants may be subject to a discretionary AoS if they are at risk of becoming a burden on the Australian social welfare system. An AoS is also a commitment to provide financial support to applicants so that they will not have to rely on any government forms of support. There are also limitations on the number of sponsorships any sponsor can make and the timeframe in which they may be made. A number of visa classes, such as Prospective Marriage and Interdependency, can be subject to 'capping.' This means that once the number of visas for a visa class in a particular programme has been reached, no further visas can be granted in that class for that year.

Skilled stream migration

The Skilled Stream of Australia's migration programme is especially designed to target migrants who:

- have skills or outstanding abilities that will contribute to the Australian economy
- have a high level of English
- are under 45 years of age

Numbers of skilled migrants continue to increase annually, and in 2006–07 there were some 97,500 visas offered, which compares to 77,889 places in 2004–05. Skilled Stream visas make up 67.7% of total migrant visas.

Current Government policy is committed to increasing migration in the Skilled Stream, and seeks to address specific skill shortages in the Australian labour market, as well as to enhance the size and skill level of the Australian labour force. There are five main categories of skilled migration.

- **Independent.** Independent migrants are people selected on the basis of their education, skills and work experience, who are likely to contribute to the Australian economy. They are not sponsored by an employer or relative in Australia. This group is the largest sector of the skilled migration programme. In November 1997, a component of the Independent migrant category was announced, known as the State/Territory Nominated Independent Scheme (STNI). This scheme enables State and Territory Governments to sponsor skilled migrants and their families on the condition that the selected migrants live and work in nominated regional areas. Regions and skills are identified through a skill-matching scheme, providing a resource for potential employers who are considering nominating overseas workers to fill their requirements. In 2006–07 there were 46,200 Independent visas granted, this compares with 38,120 in 2003–04. Applicants must meet the pass mark (see below), which changes from time to time.

■ **Pass Mark:** This is the total number of points you must score to pass the Points Test. You must reach the pass mark applicable to your application at the time it is assessed (note: not at the time the application is lodged). If you pass, your application will be processed further.

■ **Pool Mark:** If you do not achieve the pass mark, the pool mark is the total number of points you must score if your application is to be held in reserve for up to two years after it is assessed, in case a new, lower pass mark is set. If your application scores sufficient points to meet the new pass mark, your application will be withdrawn from the pool and processed further. (Source: www.visabureau.com)

With effect from July 2004 there is also the Skilled Independent Regional (Provisional) Visa for individuals who cannot meet the Skilled Independent Pass Mark and are not eligible for the STNI scheme. The visa is a temporary one providing three years' residence in a regional area of Australia, and the visa holder and family can apply for permanent residence on completion of two years' residence including at least one year's employment.

Employer nomination

Employers may nominate personnel from overseas for migration through the Employer Nomination Scheme (ENS), the Regional Sponsorship Scheme (RSMS), and a Labour Agreement. These options are available only when the position cannot be filled from the Australian labour market. Employers may also sponsor skilled workers under a Labour Agreement, which was negotiated to allow the recruitment of an agreed number of personnel subject to various conditions. Labour Agreements provide for the permanent entry of workers with skills in demand in certain industries. In 2006–07, 15,000 employer-nominated visas were given out.

■ **Distinguished Talent.** This small category (only 200 successful visas granted in 2006–07) permits distinguished individuals with special or unique talents to enter Australia, and is generally reserved for outstanding sportspeople, musicians, artists and designers who are internationally recognised in their field. It is open to very few applicants.

■ **General Skilled Migration.** The General Skilled Migration (GSM) Program is the only path for skilled workers to emigrate to Australia. Migrants in this category are selected on the basis of skills, age, English language ability, and family relationship. Chances of success in this category are improved if the candidate is sponsored by a relative already living in Australia. In 2006–07, 17,700 skilled migrants were granted this visa. A points test provides the criterion for selection under this programme (see explanation below) Applicants must meet the pass mark which changes from time to time. There are six categories of visa:

- *Skilled – Independent:* This visa subclass is the most popular skilled migration category for immigration to Australia and is geared to skilled workers who can make an immediate contribution to the Australian economy.
- *Skilled – Sponsored:* An Australian skilled immigration category for skilled applicants who have close family members living in Australia or who are sponsored by an Australian State or Territory.
- *Skilled – Regional Sponsored:* This visa is for skilled migrants who either have sponsorship from a participating state government or have sponsorship from a relative who lives in a designated area of Australia who is willing to sponsor them.

Designated areas

To qualify for the Skilled Regional Sponsored Visa under the relative sponsorship nomination, your sponsor must have lived in Australia for at least one year and still be a resident of one of the Designated Areas outlined below.

State or territory	Designated area
Victoria	Anywhere
South Australia	Anywhere
Northern Territory	Anywhere
Tasmania	Anywhere
Australian Capital Territory	Anywhere
Queensland	Postcode areas: 4019–4028, 4037–4050, 4079–4100, 4114, 4118, 4124–4150, 4158–4168, 4180–4899 (anywhere except Brisbane metropolitan area)
Western Australia	Postcode areas: 6042–6044, 6051, 6126, 6200–6799(anywhere except Perth metropolitan area)
New South Wales	Postcode areas: 2311–2312, 2328–2333, 2336–2490, 2535–2551, 2575–2739, 2787-2898 (anywhere except Sydney, Newcastle and Wollongong)

- *Skilled Regional:* An Australian skilled migration category for skilled migrants who have been living in Australia on a Skilled Regional Sponsored visa and are seeking a permanent visa pathway.
- *Regional Sponsored Migration Scheme (RSMS):* The Australian Government's RSMS is limited to certain areas of Australia. It allows employers to sponsor skilled migrants for job vacancies. The RSMS visa provides permanent residency.
- *Skills Matching visa:* The Australian skilled migration visa for those who may or may not meet the Points Test and are seeking to be nominated by an Australian State/Territory or employer.

- *Labour Agreements:* Labour Agreements enable Australian employers to recruit a specified number of workers from overseas in response to identified skills shortages in the Australian labour market. Employees may come to Australia on either a temporary or permanent basis.
- *Graduate – Skilled:* An Australian skilled immigration category for foreign students who have family in Australia and have recently completed a program of study in Australia.

> *i* Online assessment and points test: www.visabureau.com/australia/emigrate-to-australia.aspx

Business Skills migration

The Business Skills programme is designed to encourage successful entrepreneurs and other business people to settle in Australia and develop new businesses of benefit to the Australian economy. The current government has a strong commitment to increasing the entry of high quality business migrants, with numbers of visas granted almost doubling every year since 1994. In 2006–07, 5,400 Business skill visas were successful. Australia is actively encouraging Business Skills entrants to set up businesses in regional, rural, or low growth areas. Applicants may seek sponsorship from a state or territory government. For more information on government sponsorship go to: www.visabureau.com

The Business Skills programme is divided into four categories:
- Business owner
- Senior executive
- Investor
- Business talent

You may be eligible for a Business Skills visa if you have a reasonable ownership share in a business in your own country, have significant business and personal assets, and have achieved significant annual turnover; if you are a senior executive employed in top tier management of a major business; or if you make a significant investment in a government-approved investment for four years. The expectation is that a business migrant will establish a new business or become an owner or part owner of an existing business in Australia, and participate in the management of that business. The progress of business migrants is monitored after arrival in Australia, and where no significant steps are taken towards these goals in three years, the visa may be revoked. In 2006–07, the top 10 source countries of citizenship for Business Skills visas were China, UK, Malaysia, South Africa, Singapore, Taiwan, Zimbabwe, South Korea, Hong Kong and Indonesia.

Business Owner visa

To be eligible for the permanent Australian Business Owner (Residence) Visa, you will need to fulfil the following requirements:

- You are the holder of Business Owner (Provisional), a State/Territory Sponsored Business Owner (Provisional), a Senior Executive (Provisional), a State/Territory Sponsored Senior Executive, State/Territory Sponsored Business Owner (Residence) Visa, an Investor (Provisional) or a State/Territory Sponsored Investor (Provisional) Visa
- Throughout the 12 months immediately before the application is made, your (or you and your spouse's) main business employed at least two full-time employees who are Australian citizens, Australian permanent residents or New Zealand passport holders and who are not members of your family unit
- Throughout the 12 months immediately before the application is made, the net value of your (or you and your spouse's) personal and business assets in Australia has been at least A$250,000
- Throughout the 12 months immediately before the application is made, the net value of your (or you and your spouse's) assets in the main business in Australia is at least A$100,000
- In the 12 months immediately before the application is made, your main business had a turnover of at least A$300,000
- You have had, and continue to have, an ownership interest and direct and continuous management, in one or more actively operating main businesses in Australia for at least two years immediately before application is made
- For each business, an Australian Business Number (ABN) has been obtained and all Business Activity Statements (BAS) required by the ATO for that period have been submitted to the ATO, and are included in the application
- Neither you or your spouse have a history of involvement in a business or investment activities of a nature not generally acceptable in Australia
- You have been in Australia as the holder of one of the qualifying visas for a total of at least one year in the two years immediately before the application is made

Business Talent visa

To be eligible for the permanent Business Talent (Migrant) Visa to Australia, you will need to fulfil the following requirements:

- You have been sponsored by a state/territory government
- You have had an overall successful business career
- For at least two of the last four fiscal years immediately before the application is made, you had an ownership interest in a main business,

or main businesses with an annual turnover of at least A$3m (each year)

- For at least two of the last four fiscal years immediately before the application is made, you (or you and your spouse together) have net assets in a qualifying business (in which you held an ownership interest) of at least A$400,000
- Your business and personal assets (including those of your spouse) have a net value of at least A$1.5m which are available for the conduct or establishment of a business in Australia and are lawfully acquired and available for transfer to Australia in two years of the grant of your visa
- You are aged less than 55 at time of application, or you are proposing to establish or participate in a business that your sponsoring State/Territory has determined is of exceptional economic benefit to the State/Territory
- Neither you or your spouse has a history of involvement in business or investment activities of a nature not generally acceptable in Australia
- You have a genuine and realistic commitment to establish or participate actively in a qualifying business in Australia and to maintain and hold a substantial ownership level

State/Territory Sponsored Investor visa

To be eligible for the State/Territory Sponsored Investor (Residence) Visa, you will need to fulfil the following requirements:

- You must be sponsored by an appropriate regional authority of a State/Territory government
- You are the holder of a State/Territory Sponsored Investor (Provisional) Visa
- You have been a resident, as the holder of a State/Territory Sponsored Investor (Residence) Visa, in the State/Territory in which the sponsoring appropriate regional authority is located for a total of at least two years in the four years immediately before application is made
- Neither you nor your spouse have a history of involvement in business activities that are of a nature that is not generally acceptable in Australia
- You have a genuine and realistic commitment to continue to maintain a business or investment activity in Australia
- At the time of your decision, the Designated Investment made by and held in the names of you (or you and your spouse together) has been held continuously for at least four years

i Designated Investment: www.visabureau.com/australia/designated-investment.aspx

Australian Permanent Business Investor (Residence) Visa

To be eligible for the Australian Permanent Business Investor (Residence) Visa, you will need to fulfil the following requirements:

- You are the holder of an Investor (Provisional) Visa
- You have been in Australia as the holder of an Investor (Provisional) Visa for a total of at least two years in the four years immediately before the application is made
- Neither you nor your spouse have a history of involvement in business activities that are of a nature that is not generally acceptable in Australia
- You have a genuine and realistic commitment to continue to maintain a business or investment activity in Australia
- At time of decision, the Designated Investment made by and held in the names of you (or you and your spouse together) has been held continuously for at least four years

i Designated Investment: www.visabureau.com/australia/
designated-investment.aspx

State/Territory Sponsored Business Owner (Residence) Visa

To be eligible for the State/Territory Sponsored Business Owner (Residence) Visa, you will need to fulfil the following requirements:

- You have been sponsored by an appropriate regional authority of a State/Territory government
- You hold a Business Owner (Provisional), a State/Territory Sponsored Business Owner (Provisional), a Senior Executive (Provisional), a State/Territory Sponsored Senior Executive, State/Territory Sponsored Business Owner (Residence) Visa, an Investor (Provisional) or a State/Territory Sponsored Investor (Provisional) Visa or a Business (Long Stay) Independent Executive Visa
- You meet certain criteria set by the appropriate regional authority regarding employment of Australian citizens and hold appropriate investments in business of at least A$75,000 or personal assets of at least A$250,000
- You have had, and continue to have, an ownership interest and direct and continuous management in one or more actively operating main businesses in Australia for at least two years immediately before the application is made

Common questions about the Business and sponsored visitor visa

Q: What is the difference between a 'Business Visitor' and a 'Sponsored Business Visitor'?
A: Very little. The only difference is that a Sponsored Business Visitor has an approved sponsor in Australia and is prepared to vouch for the applicant's purpose of visit and period of stay and lodge an application in Australia, on behalf of the applicant.

Q: Who is eligible to become a sponsor?
A: Australian State/Territory and Commonwealth Government agencies, as well as organisations specified by the Minister of Immigration, are able to provide formal sponsorship for individuals and business delegations intending short-term business visits.

Q: Can Business Visitors lodge an application on their own behalf?
A: No. The application for a Sponsored Business Visitor must be lodged in Australia, by the sponsor. This provides sponsors with the opportunity to become more closely involved with the visa application process and to liaise with their local Business Centre in Australia.

Q: Can a sponsor offer sponsorship to more than one applicant?
A: Yes. A sponsor can sponsor more than one applicant at a time. If a sponsor wishes to sponsor more than one applicant, each applicant will need to complete a separate visa application form. The sponsor only needs to complete one sponsorship form and lodge this together with all the visa application forms.

Q: Can a sponsor offer sponsorship to an applicant who is already in Australia?
A: No. The applicant must be outside Australia at the time the application is lodged. However, the sponsor must lodge the application form and the sponsorship form in Australia.

Q: How long will the application take to process?
A: To ensure that applicants meet the relevant criteria for a specific visa, the time it takes to assess each application may vary. However, it is expected that a new application for an Australian Government Sponsored Business Visitor Visa would take approximately five working days to process.

(Source: www.visabureau.com)

- For each of these businesses an Australian Business Number has been obtained and all Business Activity Statements required by the Australian Taxation Office for that period have been submitted to the Australian Taxation Office and are included in the application
- In the 12 months immediately before the application is made, your main business, or main businesses together, had a turnover of at least A$200,000
- Neither you nor your spouse have a history of involvement in business activities that are of a nature that is not generally acceptable in Australia
- You have resided in Australia as the holder of one of the qualifying visas for a total of at least one year in the two years immediately before the application is made

(Source: www.visabureau.com)

The points test

The Department of Immigration and Multicultural and Indigenous Affairs operates a 'points system' for international immigration applications under the Skilled Migration programme. Applicants must meet certain criteria, based on their skills, experience, age, language ability, occupation in demand, Australian qualifications, regional (low population growth areas) Australia (see delegated area explanation in our visa section above), and spouse skills and relationship. Regional Australia Points are awarded for each criterion, and applicants must gain sufficient points to reach the Pass Mark. The Pass Mark currently stands at 120 points, but changes from time to time.

Applicants who score close to the Pass Mark are held in a reserve pool for up to two years following assessment. However, if you do hit the pool mark your chances of making it to Australia as a migrant are considered to be slim. There are a number of consultancies, advertised in *Australian Outlook*, which help you prepare for the points test by advising applicants on how to maximise the number of points they can accrue. Consultants are useful if you are unsure about the points test or your eligibility and need to have it explained in detail by professionals.

 Government's Immigration website: www.immi.gov.au
Australian Outlook: www.consylpublishing.co.uk/australianoutlook.htm
Expert advice: www.emigrationgroup.co.uk

Generally, the baseline requirements for success in the Points Test are that you must:

- be under 45 years old at the time your application is lodged
- reach either the pool or Pass Mark in force at the time of assessment of your application (which may not necessarily be the same as the marks at the time your application was lodged)
- be proficient in English

Points for skill are awarded on the basis of your usual occupation, which is determined by the migration officer. Normally, you will have worked in this occupation continuously for at least 12 of the last 24 months. If you have held more than one job that fits this description, you will be assessed against both of your usual occupations, and will be allocated the one that provides you with the best score. The Australian authorities will also assess your qualifications and experience, and the resulting 'skill level' of your occupation will affect how many points you can score.

The occupation that you nominate as fitting your skills and qualifications must be on the 'Skilled Occupations List' (see page 486) at the time of assessment.

 Skilled occupations: www.immi.gov.au/skills/index.htm

You receive points allocated for your nominated occupation; skill is considered to be the primary attribute in the points test, so is scored higher than other attributes such as age and English language ability.

The points for occupations are allocated as follows:

- 40 points – generalist occupations that require diploma or advanced diploma-level qualifications.
- 50 points – generalist occupations that require degree-level qualifications but which do not necessarily require occupation specific training.
- 60 points – occupations that require degree or trade certificate level qualifications, where entry to the occupation requires training in a body of knowledge specific to the occupation and which are generally regulated or self-regulated.

Points are awarded for the amount of time you have worked in your nominated occupation and also if that occupation is in demand in Australia. You can earn further points if you have gained an Australian qualification from an Australian educational institution, studied for at least one academic year in Australia, or have Australian work experience (you must have legally worked in Australia in any occupation on the Skilled Occupations List for at least six months in the four years before you apply). You can achieve this by entering the country on one of the many temporary visas outlined above.

You may also be eligible to claim points for having lived and studied for a minimum of two years in regional Australia or low population growth

 The Skilled – Recognised Graduate (Temporary) visa (subclass 476): 'This visa allows current graduates of selected overseas universities to gain up to 18 months of skilled work experience in occupations in demand in Australia. As a holder of this visa, you may apply for permanent residence at any time if you are able to meet the pass mark on the General Skilled Migration points test.' (Source: www.immi.gov.au)

metropolitan areas. You may earn extra points depending on the skills of your spouse; if you have capital investment in Australia or fluency in one of Australia's Community Languages (other than English). For Skilled – Australian Sponsored applicants you may receive points if you have or your spouse has a relative who is an Australian citizen or permanent resident who is willing to sponsor you.

Current pass and pool marks for the points-tested visas in the General Skilled Migration category (March 2008)			
Category of Skilled Migration visa	**Subclass**	**Pass mark**	**Pool mark**
Independent (Migrant)	175	120	100
Sponsored (Migrant) visa	176	100	80
Regional Sponsored (Provisional) visa	475	100	100
Independent (Residence) visa	885	120	120
Sponsored (Residence) visa	886	100	100
Regional Sponsored (Provisional) visa	487	100	100

(Source: www.immi.gov.au)

Migration application packages and charges, January 2008	
Application for Long-Stay Visitor's visa (up to one year)	A$75
Application for Temporary Residence visa (most categories)	A$170
Application for Student visa	A$430
Application for Working Holiday visa	A$190
Application for Temporary Business Short-Stay	A$85
Application for Temporary Business Long-Stay	A$190
Application for Partner Migration	A$1,390
Application for Prospective Marriage visa	A$1,390
Employer Sponsored Migration (1st instalment) (if you are outside Australia when the visa is granted)	A$1,390
Employer Sponsored Migration (1st instalment) (if you are in Australia when the visa is granted)	A$2,060
Application for General Skilled Migration (1st instalment)	A$2,060
Application for Business Skills Migration (1st instalment)	A$2,735
Application for Sponsored Business Visa	A$85

For costs 2009 and beyond: www.immi.gov.au/allforms/990i/visa-charges.htm

A second instalment of charges for permanent residency is payable only after the application has been accepted. Religious workers are fee-exempt in the Employer Nominated category. These costs are quoted in Australian dollars and will vary according to the exchange rate. The Australian High Commission will be able to advise of the current cost in local currency. Applicants for permanent residency should also allow for the cost of a medical examination by an approved practitioner, which will include screening for tuberculosis (chest X-ray), human immunodeficiency virus (HIV) and hepatitis.

Visa processing times vary according to the type of visa, and according to current demand. As a general guide, a spouse visa will take around six months, while Family and Skilled Stream migration visas can take up to 20 months. DIMIA has decided that priority is to be given to applications sponsored by Australian citizens; those sponsored by non-citizens will now go to the back of the queue, and it is expected that waiting time on such applications will become even longer. Visitor's visas can be issued the same day, or instantly if applying for an ETA (Electonic Travel Authority).

Five-year Resident Return visa

The purpose of this visa (subclass 155) is to allow current or former Australian permanent residents, or former Australian citizens to re-enter Australia after travelling overseas. This visa will allow you to maintain your status as an Australian permanent resident on your return to Australia.

i Application for a Five-year Resident Return visa: www.immi.gov.au/migrants/residents/155/index.htm

> **TIP**
>
> ■ Important: You are advised to apply for this visa before you leave Australia.

■ BECOMING AN AUSTRALIAN CITIZEN

As you will soon find out, Australians are fiercely patriotic and being an Australian citizen is something Australians are immensely proud of. Many migrants, once they have completed all the requirements of permanent residency and feel settled in their new home, decide they too want to show a commitment to Australia by becoming a citizen. Approximately 62% of migrants take up citizenship in five years of arrival and 76.7% do so after 15 years of residence. In current years the Australian Government has strongly encouraged immigrants to take up citizenship, and now offers various incentives for them to do so. There are, of course, various rights that come with Australian citizenship: you will have the rights to:

■ vote
■ apply for any public office

- apply for an Australian passport and to leave and re-enter the country without a Resident Return visa
- seek assistance from Australian diplomatic representatives while abroad
- enlist in the Australian armed forces
- apply for Government jobs
- register your child as an Australian Citizen by descent

Many public sector jobs, especially in areas of national security, are now open only to Australian citizens. The booklet *What it Means to be an Australian Citizen* is available from the Department of Immigration and Multicultural and Indigenous Affairs.

 Australian Citizenship: www.citizenship.gov.au

People who became permanent residents on or after 1 July 2007 must have been lawfully resident in Australia for four years immediately before applying including: 12 months as a permanent resident and no absences of more than 12 months, including no more than three months before applying.

If you became a permanent resident before 1 July 2007 and make your application before 30 June 2010, you must have been physically present in Australia as a permanent resident for a total of two years in the five years before applying, including one year in the two years before applying.

As of 1 October 2007, people who satisfy the general eligibility criteria are also required to pass a test before applying for citizenship.

So the new rules stipulate: you must be 18 years and over, be a permanent resident, satisfy the residency requirements, be likely to reside, or to continue to reside, in Australia or to maintain a close and continuing association with Australia, be of sound and good character and have passed the test (unless you are exempt).

 Application for citizenship: www.citizenship.gov.au/applying/application-process/general/eligibility.htm

The application fee for conferral of Australian Citizenship – general eligibility is A$240. This figure has almost doubled in the past three years. A concession fee is available to applicants who have a permanent financial disadvantage and are recipients of pensions from Centrelink or the Department of Veterans' Affairs. The fee payable is A$40. You are not required to pay a fee at the time you sit the test. A fee is required to be paid when your Australian citizenship application is lodged. You will need to make an appointment to sit the test, phone 131 880 (in Australia).

An increasing number of Australians are migrants, children of migrants, or were born overseas. This means that many Australians are dual nationals, or could be regarded as dual nationals by another country.

 within How many people passed and sat the citizenship test? Go to www.citizenship.gov.au/resources/facts-and-stats/citz-stats.htm

Useful resources

UK Passport Service (UKPS): London Passport Office, Globe House, 89 Eccleston Square, London SW1V 1PN; 0870 521 0410 (UKPS Adviceline); www.ukpa.gov.uk. There are also offices in Belfast, Glasgow, Liverpool, Newport, Durham and Peterborough.

Australian High Commission, London: Australia House, The Strand, London WC2B 4LA; 020 7379 4334; Recorded Information Line (24 hours) 09001 600 333; www.australia.org.uk. Open: Mon–Fri 9am–5pm (office hours); 9am–11am Mon–Fri (Migration/Visas); telephone service hours 2pm–4pm Mon–Fri.

Australian Consulate, Manchester: First Floor, Century House, 11 St Peter's Square, Manchester M2 3DN; 0161 237 9440; www.australia.org.uk. Passport interviews only. Open: Mon–Fri 1pm-3pm.

Australian Embassy, Dublin: 7th Floor, Fitzwilton House, Wilton Terrace, Dublin 2, Ireland; 01 664 5800; www.australianembassy.ie. Open: Mon–Fri

8.30am–4.30pm. There is no visa office at the Embassy. Visa services for those living in Ireland can be obtained from the Australian High Commission in London only.

Australian Embassy Washington DC: 1601 Massachusetts Avenue, NW, Washington DC 2006; 202 797 3000; www.austemb.org.

Department of Immigration and Multicultural and Indigenous Affairs (DIMIA): DIMIA North Building, Chan Street, Belcommen Street, ACT; 02 6264 1111; www.immi.gov.au. For all immigration and visa information.

Language

You may assume all Australians speak the same language, albeit with an unusual inflection. In theory, this is correct. However, there is another language in Australia that still survives in the indigenous Aboriginal community. This language once had between 350 and 750 distinct groupings and a similar number of inner languages and dialects. However, with the immigration of British and European people over 200 years ago, there are now only 200 remaining indigenous Australian languages which continue to be spoken, and all but 20 of these are thought to be in danger of becoming extinct. These languages are unique to the indigenous population, and are not related to any spoken anywhere outside of Australia

There are two strains of this dialect – *Pama-Nyungan* languages and the *non-Pama Nyungan*. The difference is partially to do with geography. In the north of Australia, stretching from the Western Kimberley to the Gulf of Carpentaria, are a number of groups of languages which have not been shown to be related to the *Pama-Nyungan* family or to each other: these are known as the *non-Pama-Nyungan* languages.

As for the remainder of the Australian population, they speak with a very upbeat and nasal voice. They inflect their sentences up at the end, so at first you may think they are posing a question to you.

For example, if you bump into someone on the street, and you say 'Oh, excuse me', they might respond 'You're right'. They sound as if they are saying 'Are you all right?' But they mean,' Oh that's OK', or more commonly, 'No worries'.

Most words are spelt in the British format, but occasionally Americanisms creep in to the spelling. Australians spell colour with a 'u' and likewise with 'labour', except when it is dealing with the current Government, which is spelt 'Labor'. Items have different names as well – a pepper is known as a 'capsicum', an aubergine is an eggplant and flip-flops are known as 'thongs'.

Also, abbreviating names is a fast track indicator you have made an Aussie mate. You may think you have got away with no shortening of your name, only to find they have added an 'O' to it (i.e. Dave becomes Dave-o). This is a very Australian trait. For example, if you are going to purchase some beer from the bottle shop, you would be going to the 'Bottle-oh', if you were ill you may go to hospital in an 'ambo' or you might wave to the 'garbo' (dustman) in the morning before buying milk from the 'milko'.

Often Aussies will add 'ie' or 'y', so they get mail from the 'postie', feel 'toastie' (too warm) drink a 'bevvie' with their morning 'bickie'. Other slang isn't so clear-cut, and it has simply evolved over the years, much like cockney rhyming slang has in the UK.

Aussie colloquialisms

amber fluid	beer
ankle biter/tin lid	small child
arvo	afternoon
Aussie wave	swatting away flies with the hand
back of Bourke	a faraway place
banana bender	Queenslander
bastard	(term of endearment)
battler	someone who works hard to earn a living
beaut, beauty	really good
billy	teapot, container for boiling water
bizzo	business ('mind your own bizzo')
bloke	man, guy
bloody	very 'bloody hard yakka'
bloody oath!	that's certainly true
blowie	blow fly
bludger	lazy person, layabout, somebody who always relies on other people to do things or lend him things
blue	fight ('he was having a blue with his wife')
bluey	blue cattle dog (named after its subtle markings) which is an excellent working dog; everyone's favourite all-Aussie dog
bluey	bluebottle jellyfish
bog standard	basic, unadorned, without accessories (a bog standard car, telephone, etc)
bogan	person who takes little pride in his appearance, spends his days slacking and drinking beer
bogged	stuck in mud, deep sand (a vehicle)
bonzer	great, ripper
boogie board	a hybrid, half-sized surf board

(Continued)

booze bus	police vehicle used for catching drunk drivers
brass razoo, he hasn't got a	he's very poor
brick shit house, built like a	big strong bloke
brickie	bricklayer
BrisVegas	Brisbane, state capital of Queensland
Brizzie	Brisbane, state capital of Queensland
buck's night	stag party, male gathering the night before the wedding
Buckley's, Buckley's chance	no chance ('New Zealand stands buckley's of beating Australia at football')
budgie smugglers	men's tight swimming trunks – such as mini Speedos
bull bar	stout bar fixed to the front of a vehicle to protect it against hitting kangaroos (also 'roo bar')
Bundy	short for Bundaberg, Queensland, and the brand of rum that's made there
bunyip	mythical outback creature
bush	the hinterland, the outback, anywhere that isn't in town
bushranger	highwayman, outlaw
cark it	to die, cease functioning
chewie	chewing gum
chook	a chicken
Chrissie	christmas
chuck a sickie	take the day off sick from work when you're perfectly healthy
chunder	vomit
Clayton's	fake, substitute
coathanger	Sydney Harbour Bridge
cobber	friend
cockie	cockatoo
cockie	cockroach
coldie	a beer
conch (adj. conchy)	a conscientious person, somebody who would rather work or study than go out and enjoy him/herself
cooee:	a greeting, or meaning a long way away

corker	something excellent (a good stroke in cricket might be described as a 'corker of a shot')
corroboree	an Aboriginal dance festival
cozzie	swimming costume
cranky	in a bad mood, angry
crook	sick, or badly made
cut snake, mad as a	very angry
dag	a funny person, nerd, goof
daks	trousers
dead dingo's donger, as dry as a	dry
deadset	true, the truth
dero	tramp, hobo, homeless person (from 'derelict')
digger	a soldier
dill	an idiot
dinkum, fair dinkum	true, real, genuine ('I'm a dinkum Aussie'; 'is he fair dinkum?')
dinky-di	the real thing, genuine
dob (somebody) in	inform on somebody (hence 'dobber', a tell-tale)
docket	a bill, receipt
dole bludger	somebody on social assistance when unjustified
drongo	a dope, stupid person
durry	tobacco, cigarette
esky	large insulated food/drink container for picnics, barbecues etc.
fossick	to prospect, eg for gold
fair go	a chance ('give a bloke a fair go')
fair suck of the sav!	exclamation of wonder, awe, as in fair suck of the sausage
galah	fool, silly person, named after the bird of the same name because of its antics and the noise it makes
good onya	good for you, well done,
grog	liquor, beer ('bring your own grog, you bludger')
grundies	undies, underwear (from Reg Grundy, a television person)

(Continued)

Harold Holt, to do the	to bolt (also 'to do the harold', after this PM drowned at sea)
hoon	hooligan
hooroo	goodbye
lollies	sweets, candy
larrikin	a bloke who is always enjoying himself, harmless prankster
lob, lob in	drop in to see someone ('the rellies have lobbed')
Manchester	bedding, linen, e.g. sheets and pillowcases
mongrel	terrible person
mozzie	mosquito
never never	the outback, centre of Australia
nipper	junior lifesaver
no drama	not a big deal
no worries!	also not a big deal, can be used to forgive someone as well
no-hoper	a loser
nuddy, in the	naked
ocker	vest and flip-flop wearing, uncouth type
oldies	your parents
op shop	charity store/ opportunity shop
pash	same as French kiss or the UK 'snog'
piece of piss	not a problem – easy task
pig's arse!	said in disagreement
pike	dip out of an occasion – leave early
rack off	go away!
ratbag	mild insult
raw prawn, to come the	to speak bulls**t, said in disbelief
ridgy-didge	the real deal
rip snorter!	brilliant!
ripper	said in excitement (such as 'you little ripper!')
rock up	to arrive at someone's house
snag	a sausage
sook	someone who is soft and cry's a lot – 'sooky baby!'

stickybeak	nosy person
stoked	extremely happy/ pleased
strides	trousers
stubby holder	polystyrene insulated holder for a 'stubby' (375 ml beer)
stuffed	to feel tired ('get stuffed' means to tell someone to leave you alone)
sunbake	sunbathe
swag	rolled up bedding
swagman	tramp, hobo
tall poppies	successful people who need to be cut down to size
throw-down	small bottle of beer which you can throw down quickly
tinny	can of beer or small aluminium boat, or to be lucky
togs	swimming costume
trackie daks/dacks	tracksuit pants
true blue	patriotic
tucker	food
turps	turpentine, alcoholic drink
unit	flat, apartment
ute	utility vehicle, pickup truck
vee dub	Volkswagen
veg out	relax in front of the TV (like a vegetable)
vejjo	vegetarian
walkabout	a walk in the outback by Aborigines that lasts for an indefinite amount of time
walkabout, it's gone	it's lost, can't be found
whinge	complain
wog	flu or trivial illness (such as 'I have a wog in my belly')
Woop Woop	invented name for any small unimportant town ('he lives in Woop Woop')
XXXX	Aussie beer company, known as four x
yakka	work (noun) (as in hard yakka (working hard))
yewy	U-turn in traffic
yobbo	someone seen as uncouth

Find more colloquialisms on: www.koalanet.com.au/australian-slang.html

As Brisbane only has one rather small casino, the Vegas tag was made in jest, as Brisbane was like a big country town before the developers and interstate residents moved in. The term was originally made up by Sydney and Melbourne journalists, as a comedic attempt to parody the current Brisbane tourist campaign to attract business and tourists to its city – they made out that Brisbane was the Mecca of entertainment, when in reality it was seen as a backwater and rather dull. These days it is said in good humour, as Brisbane offers a much more sophisticated nightlife and tourist scene. Some say the hot and dry weather of Brisbane, likens it to Las Vegas.

FACT

■ As Brisbane only has one rather small casino, the Vegas tag was made in jest, as Brisbane was like a big country town before the developers and interstate residents moved in.

Banks and finance

Banking in Australia is fairly straightforward and the tellers (cashiers) are generally courteous and helpful. All banks are open the same hours nationwide: 9:30am–4:00pm Monday to Thursday, and from 9:30pm to 5:00pm on Fridays. Building societies and some banks may open on Saturday mornings from 9:00am–12noon, but regional and remote branches may have more restricted opening hours. Australian banking has all the usual electronic facilities that a customer will expect, plus a few extras. Cashpoint

cards can be used in all supermarkets, and Electronic Funds Transfer at Point of Sale (EFTPOS) facilities are available in most stores, petrol stations, grocery stores and boutiques, with the larger outlets also allowing cash withdrawals. The major difference you will encounter is that you only need your signature for the transaction – the chip and pin revolution in stores has not fully reached Australia yet. You will still need your PIN number when withdrawing cash from cashpoints. You will be asked whether your card is a checking, credit or savings account whenever you make a purchase. Most debit cards are either cheque or savings and credit cards are known as credit transactions, but it may be worth finding out from your local branch before travelling.

Australians are big on the idea of a cashless society. The four largest national banks (known as 'the big four') are Westpac, the National Australia Bank, the Commonwealth Bank of Australia, and the ANZ (which also has branches in New Zealand). Many building societies, including the St George, have gone through the same demutualisation process as those in the UK and now operate as banks.

Bank accounts

If you are going to Australia for more than six months, or to work, it is worth opening a bank account either before you leave your home country, or immediately on arrival in Australia. It is much easier to open an account with an Australian bank when you are actually in Australia, but accounts can also be arranged through bank offices in the UK. The Commonwealth, ANZ and Westpac all have branches in London which offer services particularly geared to new arrivals and migrants. Their advisers are extremely helpful and will guide you in choosing the best accounts to meet your requirements, as well as providing general advice about services. The Commonwealth Bank, for example, will establish a bank account for you with a convenient branch in Australia and transfer your funds before your departure. This means that when you arrive in Australia you have immediate and full access to their range of banking facilities (including cashpoints throughout the country). Australians also use the internet banking options now widely available. The Commonwealth Bank can only establish an account for you before your arrival if you intend to work in Australia, if you are migrating, or if you are a resident returning home after an extended period abroad. To qualify for their services in the UK branch you will need to be able to show them evidence that you have been given the relevant visa. Contact the Commonwealth Bank of Australia's Migrant Banking Services for further details or to speak with one of their consultants, 9am–5pm Monday to Friday.

 Commonwealth Bank Of Australia: Senator House, 85 Queen Victoria St, London, EC4V 4HA www.commbank.com.au

The 100 points system

Banking is relatively open and available in Australia and there are very few people who will be excluded from having an account, even with a bad credit record. References or proof of income are not required, however, proper identification is crucial and all banks must, by law, operate the '100 points system' of identification. Under this system you must conclusively demonstrate your identity and place of residence by providing various forms of identification, which are scored by the level of their official authority. A passport, for example, will provide you with 70 points, which you might back up with a Visa or MasterCard (25 points), a birth certificate (70 points), or a driver's licence (50 points). When you go to the bank to open an account, be sure to take a selection of appropriate documents with you, as you will be sent away empty-handed if you cannot comply with this government requirement. However, if you apply for a bank account in six weeks of arrival in Australia you will only need to show your passport as proof of identification.

International and internal money transfers

If you wish to send an international money transfer to Australia, it will cost you a flat fee regardless of the amount of money sent and the transfer may only be sent through a bank, using the 'Swift' service. The Commonwealth Bank offers customers a superior foreign exchange service and highly competitive exchange rates.

 Commonwealth Bank: 020 7710 3999, www.migrantbanking.co.uk

You can also send money through American Express and Western Union offices, but these services, although quick, are expensive. In Australia, international money transfers are made either by bank draft, or electronically. Within the country, travellers without a cheque (current) account may send money in the country by bank cheque (costing approximately A$8, although the charge varies from bank to bank), or by Australia Post Money Orders, which can be bought to a maximum value of A$1,000 for a cost of around A$4 and are easy to buy – they can be cashed at more than 3,800 postal outlets nationwide. They can either be deposited directly into a bank account, or cashed on the spot, just like an ordinary cheque.

 Internet money transfer: www.transferz.com
Western Union: www.westernunion.com

Australia Post Money Orders are the ideal way to make a variety of payments. Express Money Orders can be bought to a maximum value of A$10,000 and cost around A$20 – they are then sent within the hour.

Money Orders are generally the cheapest way to send money and can be cashed at any of Australia Post's 3,900 post offices throughout the country.

Making use of a specialist currency broker can help you to obtain the best rate of exchange.

> *i* Specialist currency brokers:
> (UK) www.hifx.co.uk
> (USA) www.hifx.com
> (Australia) www.hifx.com.au

Other banking services

- **Credit cards.** All Australian banks offer a credit card facility, and all the usual international credit cards, including MasterCard, Visa, Diners Club and American Express, are available via your local bank branch. If you intend to stay in Australia for less than 12 months, you may prefer to apply for a credit card in your home country before you leave and then establish a standing order to pay off your monthly credit card bill. It is a good idea to deposit any savings in a high interest account while you are away, allowing the interest from this account to cover the approximate charge of 2% on cash advances made against your credit card in Australia.

- **Direct debits.** Australian banks offer direct debit facilities, known as standing orders, for the payment of regular bills, and most now also offer telephone and internet banking facilities, which enable you to authorise and conduct transactions by telephone and online from your home or office. If you don't want to organise a direct debit, you can also use B-Pay which is a simple number found on the back of bills for you to call and pay over the phone. Just have your account details and debit/credit cards handy.

- **Cheque accounts.** The chequebook facility only applies to specific accounts, and it is important to check whether the account you are considering offers this service. There is no cheque card system in Australia, so there is also no limit as to the amount of the cheque you are able to write. However, to write a cheque, you will need to have your driver's licence with you or another acceptable form of identification showing your full name and address, and this information will be noted on the reverse of the cheque. Having said this, most retailers are phasing out the acceptance of cheques, so it may be worth having a card or cash with you for back up. With smaller shops, ask first if they are prepared to accept a cheque.

  Almost every shop now prefers the cashless transaction, and even the smallest corner shop will accept your credit or debit card. Very few Australian bank accounts offer free cheques and as a result, Australians use cheques sparingly, preferring to use cash or credit cards. Cheques take three working days to clear, but foreign cheques may take up to four weeks and you are likely to be charged a commission on the exchange of cheques made out in a foreign currency.

■ **Investment advice.** Many expatriates tend to seek advice on money related matters such as employee benefits, retirement income funding, personal investments and savings.

Worldwide financial services

Brewin Dolphin Securities; 020 7247 4400; email info@brewin.co.uk; www.brewindolphin.co.uk

Aon Consulting, 020 7767 2000; www.aon.com/uk/en/

Money

Australia has had a decimal currency for more than 40 years, abandoning the archaic imperial pounds, shillings and pence system in 1965. The basic unit of currency is the Australian dollar (A$), which is worth 100 cents. In 1993, 'coppers' – one and two cent pieces – were withdrawn from circulation, having become virtually worthless and more of a nuisance than an item of value. Their withdrawal has complicated Australian shopping, which will confuse the new arrival. Although coppers are no longer available to be given as small change, goods for sale are still marked up in terms of single cents (for example, A$2.98). Your shopping will be rung up in these hypothetical numbers and the final total will be rounded off – always, by law, in favour of the customer. Thus, if your supermarket till total comes to A$47.68, it will be rounded down to A$47.65 or, if it was A$47.99,you would pay A$48.00. Items paid for by cheque or cash card, however, will cost the precise amount as stated, and not rounded off. This system sounds complicated but has been quickly accepted by Australians, and few people are nostalgic for the 'bad old days' of a wallet full of dirty, little coins. Australian coinage consists of the silver-coloured, cupronickel 5, 10, 20 and 50-cent pieces, and of gold-coloured A$1 and A$2 coins (with the A$1 coin dwarfing the smaller A$2 one), which replaced notes of the same value in 1994. The 5-cent coin is very similar in size to an old sixpence, the 20-cent coin is easily confused with a UK 10 pence (although it is much bulkier), and the 50-cent coin has the same hexagonal shape as its UK equivalent. The A$1 coin is about the same size as the 20-cent piece, and has irregular milling which allows it to be easily distinguished by blind people. The A$2 coin is smaller and thicker, and is much like a UK £1 in dimension. Australian notes are in denominations of A$5, A$10, A$20, A$50 and A$100. In current years the Australian currency has been gradually redesigned to make it both counterfeit-proof and longer lasting. New A$5, A$10, A$20, A$50 and A$100 notes have now been released, and are made of a kind of plastic, which mimics paper but cannot be torn and is cleverly water resistant. It is considered virtually indestructible. So for those of you who are prone to washing your jeans with money still in the pockets, you can breathe a sigh of relief. The plastic notes bear a forgery-proof transparent seal in the corner (you can see right through the note), and a hologram in the centre of the seal. All notes and coins bear the head of Queen Elizabeth II on the reverse side. Old paper notes have been quickly withdrawn from circulation and destroyed.

The Australian mint also coins gold bullion and coin, known as Australian Nuggets. Each coin has a set purchase price (from A$15–A$100), but the actual value is determined by the daily-fluctuating price of gold, and the demand for the coins. The Australian Nugget can be bought Australia-wide at banks as individual coins or as full sets. They are popular as souvenirs for wealthier visitors.

Visitors are permitted to import and export an unlimited amount of foreign currency into Australia, but if you intend to import or export more than A$10,000 you need to contact customs or the Australian Transaction Reports and Analysis Centre (PO Box 5516, West Chatswood, NSW 1515; 02 9950 0055; www.austrac.gov.au), Australia's anti-money laundering regulator and specialist financial intelligence unit. Should you be lucky enough to clean up at that illegal Australian coin game, 'Two-up', you might have to leave your winnings behind or, if you've been really lucky, invest it in Australian business or property. Banks are also legally obliged to report deposits of more than A$10,000 in cash made into Australian bank accounts, primarily to safeguard against money laundering activities.

Australian banks in UK and USA

Australian and New Zealand Bank (ANZ):] Minerva House, Montague Close, London SE1 9DH; 020 7378 2121; www.anz.com

National Australia Bank Ltd: 88 Wood Street, London EC2V 7QQ;020 7710 2100; www.national.com.au

Reserve Bank of Australia: Basildon House, 7 Moorgate, London EC2R 6AQ; 020 7600 2244; www.rba.gov.au; and 46th Floor, 1 Liberty Plaza, New York, NY 10006–1404; 212 566 8466

Commonwealth Bank of Australia, Financial and Migrant Information Service: Senator House, 85 Queen Victoria Street, London EC4V 4HA; 020 7710 3999; www.migrantbanking.co.uk

Westpac Banking Corporation: 2nd Floor, 63 St Mary's Axe, London EC3A 8LE, 020 7621 7000; www.westpac.com.au

The cost of living

Australia can boast having some of the least expensive cities in the world. The per capita gross domestic product (GDP) – when it comes to the purchasing power of the country – is higher than compared with the United Kingdom. In fact it was ranked in sixth place in the 2005 *Economist*

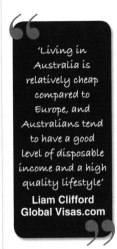

'Living in Australia is relatively cheap compared to Europe, and Australians tend to have a good level of disposable income and a high quality lifestyle'

**Liam Clifford
Global Visas.com**

worldwide quality of life index, and third place for the second consecutive year in the 2007 United Nations Human Development Index.

In the meantime, economists are foreseeing an upcoming crisis due to the poor performance of GDP. It has increased by more than 7%, which is the fourth biggest deficit in terms of current accounts.

However, due to other areas which Australia has been excelling in very much in current years, foreign debt is still significantly low and the economic state is generally as stable as it can get.

Some of the notable cities which boast quality living and low expenses are Adelaide, Brisbane and Melbourne. All of Australia's major cities made it in to the top 30 best places for expatriates list, 2006. *(Source: United Nations Human Development Index in 2006, as quoted on www. expatforum.com)*

The World Competitiveness Yearbook, published by the Institute of Marketing Development (IMD) analyses and ranks the ability of nations to create and maintain an environment that sustains the competitiveness of enterprises. Considered the worldwide reference point to world competitiveness, it has been published without interruption since 1989 and ranks 55 national economies using 323 criteria. In 2004, the *Yearbook* remarked that Australia is the third best worldwide country when it comes to low cost of living. The 2007 results have been pushed back to sixth place, but this still reflects an astonishing score of 82,387 out of a points criteria of 100,000. This compares with the United Kingdom sliding into 20th place with a score of 75,447, and Canada coming in at seventhth place with 83,824.

 World Competitiveness Yearbook: www.imd.ch/wcy

Daily costs in Australia

- **Monthly rent:** varies from state to state, with Sydney and Melbourne having the highest rents. On average you are looking to pay anywhere between A$300–A$700 per week for a two-bedroom apartment.
- **Water and electricity rates:** depend on your usage and what area you live in.
- **Council rates:** include water to a point. Excess use (during drought) is charged above that and usually passed on to tenants. Rates range from A$250 a quarter in unpopular areas to about A$850 a quarter in the more sought-after suburbs.
- **Dinner for two:** varies from state to state, but in general a dinner for two without wine will cost about A$60.
- **Lunch for two:** depends on where you eat. All the generic fast food joints are in Australia – Kentucky Fried Chicken, McDonalds, Subway, PizzaHut, Burger King (also known as Hungry Jacks). If you are eating

Café culture

out at a restaurant it will cost about A$20–A$30 for a lunch for two excluding drinks.

- **Cinema ticket:** Hoytts is the major cinema chain throughout Australia and an adult ticket is currently A$16.
- **Music CDs and film DVDs:** quite expensive to buy in Australia as most are imported. An average CD will cost about A$32 and DVD A$40. Your UK DVDs will play in Australian machines, but NTSC format from North America will not.
- **Single journey on train:** varies from state to state, but on average A$7, more for longer journeys. In Sydney you can go from Holsworthy station (out in the Western suburbs) to the domestic airport for A$11, a 40-minute journey.
- **Visit to doctor:** you must pay at least A$30 (but you can be charged up to A$60) each visit, and if you are eligible for Medicare benefits, this will be partially refunded to you afterwards.
- **Coffee:** has its own language down under. An Americano is known as a long black and an espresso is a short black. A long black will cost you between A$3.00–A$3.80.

- **Glass of beer:** beer is always cold, and a schooner (pint) will set you back from A$5.00–A$7.00 (see measures table on page 188).
- **Haircut:** There are several budget hairdressers throughout Australia, one being Base Cuts. A cut from one of these cheap snippers will cost you about A$12 for men and A$20 for women. However, most hairdressers will cost nearer A$60 for a women's cut and A$30 for a men's.

 Quick currency converter: www.xe.com

Food and drink

An average family of four would expect to spend around A$1,180 every month for food and drinks. Usual meats in Australia are lamb, pork or beef, which are reared and processed locally. Fish is generally reasonably priced, but cities further from the sea and ocean will charge more.

Fruits and vegetables are grown throughout the country (but can be known to fluctuate in price) and are always fresh and abundant. Meat and fish are also plentiful and reasonably priced and locally sourced, thus maintaining freshness. Australian wine is quite affordable and tap water is fresh, clean and drinkable. It is also free of coarse ingredients like limescale and you will automatically notice a difference in your hair after you have washed it. Also, take a close look at Australians' teeth; they are usually whiter and cleaner than their British ancestors, due to the fluoride in the water.

A well-known supermarket

Lamb chops flaming on the BBQ

The things that tend to cost more are imported products, such as cheese, biscuits, beer and imported wine. The Government impose a GST (Government state tax)on all imported products, which bumps up the costs of the more exotic brands to high levels. Australia is widely popular for exporting milk, beef for world-famous steaks and some exotic products such as kangaroo meat and King Island cheeses.

Food and drink costs

To give you an overall idea of a general shopping list, here's a breakdown of costs from Coles (a leading grocery chain) on the Gold Coast in Queensland (February 2008)

Item	Quantity	Price
Broccoli	1kg	A$5.98
Cauliflower	each	A$4.98
Avocado	each	A$1.58
Bread rolls	6-pack	A$1.99
Milk	2 litres	A$2.59
Bacon	250g	A$3.29

(Continued)

Kanga bangas (kangaroo sausages)	1kg	A$3.04
Potatoes (baby)	2kg	A$4.98
Diced beef	1kg	A$16.99
Mixed juice	3 litres	A$4.89
Tea bags	100	A$3.65
Ham (sliced)	100g	A$2.59
Pizza	500g family size	A$3.08
Toilet cleaner	500ml	A$3.15
Iceberg lettuce	each	A$2.22
Bananas	1kg	A$2.48
Butter	500g	A$1.98
Choc ices	10	A$4.69
Nutrigrain cereal	805g	A$7.99
Palmolive washing up liquid	375ml	A$2.49
Ice cream	2 litres	A$4.98
Sausage (Lamb and leek)	500g	A$4.99
Lamb leg roast	1kg	A$10.49
Toilet tissue	9 rolls	A$4.99
Brussels sprouts	1kg	A$12.98
Cordial	2 litres	A$4.27
Strawberry jam	500g	A$2.29
Cadbury chocolate	250g	A$3.49
Chicken	whole	A$9.89
Greencare laundry washing liquid	2 litres	A$4.10
Hellmann's mayonnaise	400g	A$5.34
Sanitarium weet-bix	1kg	A$5.48
Condensed milk	395g	A$1.45
Sugar	1kg	A$1.16

Petrol

Petrol prices differ in each state of Australia because there are two taxes applied. Federal Tax applies to all states and State Tax differs in each state. Prices also differ significantly between capital cities and country areas.

There are two reasons for this. First, there is a freight component to deliver the product, which is higher the further inland you go. The more important factor is the competition arena. In the city you have many service stations (servos) competing for the motorist's business, with price boards continually showing the price of the day. This fierce competition keeps prices in check. In the country regions you may only have a couple of service stations dotted around the town and thus much less competition. There is very little brand loyalty in the petrol industry, and it is very much price driven. A huge impact on loyalty these days are the shopper dockets (receipts) offered by the two big oil companies (Shell and Caltex). If you shop at Woolworths supermarket and present your docket to a participating Caltex service station you will receive a 4 cent per litre discount off your petrol price, the same deal applies with Coles and Shell. This scheme has now created customer loyalty depending on where the motorists shops for groceries. Independent service stations find it very hard to compete with this scheme and are coming up with their own loyalty programs.

Queensland prices are a little lower than other states because the State Tax is smaller than the others. In June 2008 the price for petrol was around A$1.50 and diesel A$1.69. There are pricing cycles in Australia, with the lowest prices on a Monday and Tuesday. The long-term view about pricing is that it will rise to about A$1.80 per litre if trends in crude oil pricing continue to rise. Over the last couple of years the cost of crude has risen from about A$60 a barrel to A$100 a barrel in early 2008. Prices are governed by world output by the major suppliers in the Middle East, and supply and demand with countries like China (which is experiencing huge growth and consuming a lot of the world's output) affecting the supply and demand on a barrel of oil.

Clothing and accessories

Locally made Australian clothes and items are cheaper than their imported counterparts. The major items Australia has been known for in the fashion stakes are the sheepskin 'Ugg' boot, the 'Akubra' hat and rising Melbourne fashion house 'Sass and Bide'.

Australia's fashion scene is usually one season behind the UK and France. Australian designers are becoming more popular in a global sense, with such stars as Collette Dinnigan, Wayne Cooper, Akira Isogawa, Lisa Ho, Martin Grant, Carla Zampatti, Easton Pearson, Michelle Jank and Nicola Finetti in high demand.

The underwear company Bonds is world-known for its fashionable yet comfortable undergarments and can be found in all top department stores. The average cost of ladies' underwear is A$6 and men's boxer shorts A$12.

Australia doesn't lag behind when it comes to modern fashion. Although the locals typically prefer a more casual appearance, several designers can be found in most of the major cities.

Victoria is still considered as the most fashionable place in Australia, with Melbourne boasting some of the best shopping experiences in Australia. The clothes and accessories designed by local designers are expensive since most are created for exportation purposes. The products are still made available to locals if they want them and can be purchased after fashion festivals and publicised catwalk shows.

Most Australians dress for the climate and are known to dress stylishly, yet casually. Jeans will cost from A$50–A$200 depending on the brand, and dresses, shirts and trousers all vary accordingly. You will find plenty of budget clothing stores in shopping malls and inexpensive fashion in clothing chains such as Kmart, Target and Woolworths. Higher end department stores include Myers and David Jones where fashion will be up to date and on the more expensive side. As with other countries, Australia has its fair share of fashion outlets in the suburbs, which provide fashion at a discount.

There are also flea markets and various charity shops (sometimes called 'op-shops') which can provide a cheaper alternative for kitting yourself out.

◼ GETTING THERE

These days, if you want to get to Australia, you have to fly (or take a very long and expensive cruise). Qantas is Australia's number one carrier, and is legendary for its flawless safety record, although its reputation for quality and service allows it to charge premium fares. More than 30 international airlines fly direct to Australia, usually to Perth or Sydney from destinations all over the world. These include Korean Air, Thai Airways, British Airways, Virgin and Emirates). The flight time from Europe to Australia, depending on your route, point of departure, and destination, is likely to be between 19 and 27 hours from the UK. From the west coast of the USA the flight to Australia takes approximately 14 hours.

Fares

Fares to Australia vary dramatically according to the time of year, and are also hugely influenced by special events, such as Christmas and New Year's Eve. Prices skyrocket in early December, for example, but drop dramatically

on 6 January, so delaying your departure by a few days may save you the cost of a couple of internal flights once you arrive in Australia. The cheapest time to fly to Australia is during their winter (approximately March–June). July to November is known as the 'shoulder', or mid season and is reasonably priced. The season to avoid is peak season, from December to early February which is best avoided from a financial point of view, unless you can only travel at that time. Seats fill up very fast, and flights during the Australian Christmas and peak season may be fully booked as early as June.

Many airlines offer the possibility of a stopover in their home country, which allows a welcome break for you to stretch your legs, get some foreign fresh air, and taste some local delights, as well as providing an inexpensive mini break in an unknown country. If you fly with Malaysian Airlines, for example, you may be offered a stopover in Kuala Lumpur as well as a free internal flight, so that if you choose, you can fly to the resorts of Penang or Langkawi for a few days. Alternatively if you fly Korean Air, you may opt to stay over for the night in Seoul and have the airline pick up the cost of the hotel and transfers. Return fares are usually valid for 12 months, and travel agents are required to request proof of residency if you wish to purchase a one-way ticket. An open-jaw return ticket will allow you to enter Australia via one port and leave from another, but this type of ticket is likely to be more expensive.

Tour companies often offer charter flights when they have spare seats on their scheduled package tours. This is usually the most cost effective way to travel to Oz. They are often old planes without much pizzazz, but they are ideal for travellers on a budget.

> *i* Cheap deals:
> www.expedia.com
> www.lastminute.com (be aware they don't always allow you to cancel/amend tickets)
> www.skyscanner.net
> Last-minute and budget flight deals from locations worldwide:
> www.cheapflights.com
> www.deckchair.com
> www.expedia.com

Currently, you can expect to pay around £600+ for a London to Sydney return flight; from US$1,000 for a return flight from Los Angeles and from US$1,100 if you are starting your journey in New York. The disadvantage of charter flights is that they generally operate on a short-term return basis, so that you are likely to have to return two weeks after arrival. Flights book up very early, and stopovers are not permitted. Many airlines also offer savings on Australian internal flights once you have booked with them.

Remember, it is an arduous journey, so it may be worthwhile paying a little bit extra to go the faster route (with fewer stopovers) or with the more well known carrier (so you have better leg room and facilities).

Jetlag

One of the most unavoidable side effects of travelling to the other side of the world is jetlag. You often lose an entire day in transit (depending on your exit port). The first leg of your trip (if departing from the UK) will take you approximately 10 hours, and then a further 12 hours to reach Australia. With the time difference you literally cease to exist for a number of hours.

With this comes the draining vortex of sleep deprivation and a body clock that has been thrown completely off kilter. The best solutions include trying to stay awake on the flight (avoiding the temptation of free alcohol, instead hydrating with plenty of water) until it's Australian night time. Or, when you arrive, try and get some sunshine on your face and the backs of your legs (it works!) and try to stay awake, eating meals at the right time until it is Australian nightfall. It will most likely affect you more in one direction than the return, and will take up to three days to get your body clock back into order.

Travel insurance

Working travellers and those on speculative job finding trips to Australia are strongly advised to take out comprehensive travel insurance. Insurers offering reasonable and flexible premiums include:

Atlas Insurance: 020 7609 5000; www.atlasdirect.net

Columbus Direct Travel Insurance: 020 7422 5505; www.columbusdirect.net

The Travel Insurance Agency: email info@travelinsurers.com; www.travelinsurers.com.

Worldwide Travel Insurance Services Ltd:
01892 833338; sales@worldwideinsure.com; www.worldwideinsure.com

Discount fare specialists for Australia and New Zealand

STA Travel: 0870 160 6070; www.statravel.co.uk. Specialises in student and youth travel with more than 450 branches worldwide. Offers budget to luxury accommodation, adventure tours, round the world flights, package holidays, city breaks, and insurance.

Austravel: 0870 166 2140; email knightsbridge@austravel.com; www.austravel.net. Offices in London, Manchester, Leeds, Edinburgh, Bristol, Bournemouth and Birmingham, and produces a fares guide which gives price comparisons between all the major airlines.

Bridge the World: 0870 814 4400; email info@bridgetheworld.com; www.bridgetheworld.com

Cresta World Travel: 0870 013 0303; www.crestaworldtravel.co.uk

Platinum Travel Centre: 40 Earls Court Road, Kensington, London W8 6EJ; 020 7937 5122.

Travelbag plc: 0870 814 4440; www.travelbag.co.uk. Offices in London, and other parts of the UK including Nottingham, Cheshire and Solihull.

Australian Youth Hostels Association: 02 9565 1699; email yha@yha.org.au; www.yha.com.au. Offers complete travel packages including accommodation and 12 months coach travel. Offices in Sydney, Darwin, Brisbane, Adelaide, Hobart, Melbourne, and Northbridge.

Domestic travel

Although Australia is a vast country, transport networks are extremely reliable and it is relatively easy to explore it by air, rail and coach. There are around 913,000km (567,310 miles) of roads and 5,877 miles (9,458km) of rail networks cross the continent, and several reputable airlines offer a choice to travellers. Qantas was one of the world's first commercial airlines and has an unrivalled safety record. If you fly to Australia with Qantas, you can choose between four fare types – Super Saver, Flexi Saver, Fully

Flexible or Business Class – to explore Australia. A single economy class ticket from Sydney to Melbourne will cost approximately $160. As with all airlines, offers are constantly changing, but look out for regular specials available for overseas visitors. Make sure you constantly check the internet and your local travel agency for specials.

 Qantas: www.qantas.com.au

Virgin Blue and Jetstar, Australia's two only low-fare carriers, combined, currently serve 26 destinations throughout the country. Scheduled domestic flights carry more than 25 million passengers a year. It is worth checking out these two airlines as soon as you have made your travel arrangements as the earlier you book, the better. You may even get a single flight from the Gold Coast to Sydney, for as little as A$50.

 Virgin Blue: www.virginblue.com.au
Jetstar: www.jetstar.com.au

Trains operate in all states except Tasmania, and there are interstate lines travelling deep into the outback and along the lush coastline of the eastern seaboard. Rail Australia provides a nationwide service linking the major tourist orientated passenger rail operators Queensland Rail, Countrylink, and the Great Southern Railway. In addition, Australia has about 70 ports of commercial significance, used mainly for trade, although cruise ships are enjoying a prolonged popularity and regularly call at the ports of Sydney and Fremantle.

◼ REMOVAL AND RELOCATION

Removal companies

Unless you are starting your trip to Australia as a backpacker, you are likely to have excess baggage or belongings that you will need to send separately. Most people do this ahead of departure so it is at least en route when you arrive. You can send your belongings via ship or air. Sending items by air is a faster option but can be expensive. You need to work out what you want to send and how you want to send it before contacting removal companies. It is advisable to contact two or three reputable companies to get a quote. Be sure to ask how long it will take, including customs, processing on arrival in Australia and whether your items will be insured.

Relocation

Although there are many relocation service companies offering assistance with intra-European and transatlantic moves, the Antipodean sector of

the market is poorly served. Relocators can assist corporate and domestic migrants with establishing the basis for life in a new home abroad, including finding accommodation, schools and employment. However, many of those that operate between Europe and Australia concentrate almost entirely on the corporate market. The cost of using such services can be prohibitive for the individual, and in many cases removal companies may be more helpful for people undertaking a domestic move. Many of the larger removal companies offer more than a shipping service, and may be able to advise and assist in many other aspects of your relocation. There are a number of relocation companies in Australia, and these will usually be better able to act on your behalf in organising the essentials for your arrival.

You must also be aware of hidden charges with shipping your goods to Australia. This may include a customs/tax charge, or door-to-door delivery costs (freight companies usually charge by weight), and holding costs (if by some extraordinary incident, your goods arrive before you). Also, check with the customs department before sending any wood or plant products as they can quite often be incinerated at the other end, if customs deem them unsuitable for Australian soil.

And lastly, if the company offers an insurance policy at a reasonable cost, it is wise to take one out as items often go missing in transit.

Relocation services

Expat International Pty Ltd: 03 9670 7555; info@expat.com.au; www.expat.com.au. Expatriate human resources consultancy to corporations worldwide, visa documentation, international and interstate relocations, and cultural awareness programmes. They are affiliated with the Migration Institute of Australia and the Employee Relocation Council (USA) and have offices worldwide: check the White Pages telephone directory of your capital city.

Four Winds International Movers: 07 3890 6800; sales@fourwindsmovers.com; www.fourwindsmovers.com

Nuss Removals: 02 9425 4600 (Sydney) 03 9569 6277 (Melbourne); email sydney@nuss.com.au; www.nuss.com.au. Nuss belongs to FIDA, the *Federation Internationale des Demenageurs Internationaux*, the British Association of Removers, the Household Goods and Forwarders Association of America, Omni, and is an accredited IATA (International Air Transport Association) agent.

Weichert Relocation Resources International: 020 7802 2500; www.wrri.com. One of the largest relocation firms in the world.

Freedom Shipping: 0800 019 6969; www.freedomshipping.com. Part of the Freedom Group and has, over the last 15 years, provided quality services to over 100,000 customers. Bonded by The Bank of Scotland, all of their shipments are secure, arrive in the fastest time, and have prices starting from only £69 for the first box to Australia, New Zealand or South Africa.

Excess International Movers: 0800 783 1085; www.removals-shipping.co.uk

Britannia Movers: 0845 600 6661; www.britannia-movers.co.uk

Setting Up Home

■ HOW THE AUSTRALIANS LIVE

As a nation, Australians choose to buy their home, rather than renting. It is ingrained into them from a very young age that one day they will own 'the Great Australian dream'.

The Great Australian dream is a dream shared by many Australians. They believe that owning one's own slice of Australian real estate is truly reaching the pinnacle of success. It is an expression of security and prosperity. Although this standard of living is enjoyed by many in the existing Australian population, rising house prices (in the city centres) compared to average wages are making it more of a nightmare than a dream for many.

In general, those who are newly moving to Oz will undoubtedly think about renting initially, until they sort out a mortgage, or at the very least research which area they would like to settle in. This chapter focuses on renting and liveable areas. If you want to jump on to the Australian property ladder, go straight to page 153.

Without a doubt, the most sought after areas to live in are Sydney and Melbourne, which reflect the strong employment opportunities in

Many houses in Australia have their own swimming pool, particularly in the hotter northern states

both cities. The rental costs here support this fact. The inner city suburbs of St Kilda in Melbourne, and the beach suburbs of Bondi in Sydney are where the new residents flock (and are generally priced accordingly). Most rentals in the inner city and beach suburbs are two to three-bedroom units, some have back gardens or balconies but you are mainly paying for the location, not the size of the apartment. If you live on the outskirts of the city, the prices come down considerably and you will definitely get more space for your money.

If you have been lucky enough to visit Australia before your big move, you may be familiar with the different suburbs and what they offer. Make sure you take time before your move to consider what is important to you when looking for a new house to live in. Does it need to be close to good schools, or your new office in the Central Business District (CBD)? Or is living close to the beach your reason for upping sticks and moving to the other side of the world? Perhaps it's a view you are after, or a short commute? Last but not least, think about the number of bedrooms needed (and if it is a house or a unit you require) and your total budget including utility bills.

A good place to start looking for different rental properties before you leave are Australian based estate agents. If you know vaguely where you want to settle, then look up an estate agent in that area, for example, The online Professionals are a leading Australian company. www.professionals.com.au

Real estate search engines:
www.domain.com.au
www.realestate.com.au
www.myhome.com.au

◼ THE RESIDENTIAL NEIGHBOURHOODS OF SYDNEY AND MELBOURNE

There is a good reason why the Australian Capital Territory (ACT) is Australia's capital city. It's not because it's the largest or most popular, in fact it's completely the opposite. The reason that this parkland city governs the rest of Australia, is that it lies bang in the middle of the two most popular and sought after cities to live in – Melbourne and Sydney. State governments from New South Wales (NSW) and Victoria fought hard to have their city named the capital, and as the Federal Government couldn't decide which was more suited, they decided to play fair and give it to neither. The war between the two cities continues to simmer, even today. You are either a Sydneysider or a Melbournian. One has the most diverse collection of culture, shopping, restaurants and style and the other is renowned for its picture perfect harbour, beaches and laid-back lifestyle. They both offer equally strong employment growth, and a great quality of lifestyle to their residents. Property is slightly more expensive in Sydney, but is by no means affordable in the heart of Melbourne. The following is a brief guide to the most sought after suburbs for real estate in both cities. Now all you need do is decide whether you are a Sydneysider or a Melbournian!

■ SYDNEY

With a population of over 4,284,379 people, Sydney is the most densely populated city of Australia. Sydneysiders have lived in this picturesque city from the outset of European settlement, as it was the first city to be populated by the English on 26 January 1788 (which is now Australia Day).

Sydney has over 300 suburbs in an area of 12,144.6km² (4,689.1 sq miles) and is:
- 881km (547 miles) north-east of Melbourne
- 938km (583 miles) south of Brisbane
- 3,970km (2,467 miles) east of Perth
- 1,406km (874 miles) east of Adelaide
- 4,003km (2,487 miles) south-east of Darwin

Australia Day, 2008 on Sydney habour

Sydney suburbs are divided North–East–South–West. Most of the population opt to live either in the trendy eastern or the more affordable, sprawling western suburbs. You are either a city dweller or a 'Westie'. The eastern Suburbs are the more expensive, picturesque and popular, while the western suburbs are further from the CBD but offer larger land opportunities at a fraction of the price. Sydney has approximately 38 local government areas, each consisting of several suburbs. There are many small neighbourhoods to choose from; it depends if you want to live close to the beach, the harbour, the CBD, ferries to commute, markets, restaurants, or whether you seek a larger more inexpensive property in the outer western suburbs.

There are so many areas to choose from in Sydney, it is difficult to pinpoint the best. Below is a summary of the most sought after suburbs and the pros and cons of living there.

Find Sydney property:
www.realestate.com.au
www.domain.com.au

The Sydney metro area can be defined as the Hawkesbury/Nepean River in the north/north-west, and then the outer boundaries of the City of Penrith, Camden Council, the City of Campbelltown and Sutherland Shire and Kurrajong Heights.

SUBURBS**OF**SYDNEY

NORTH →

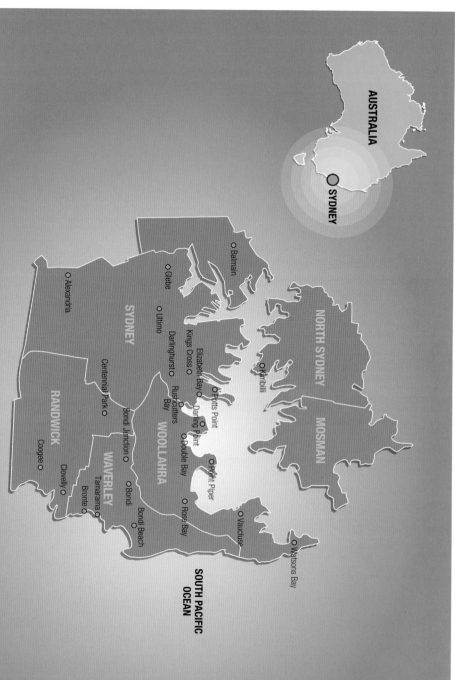

AUSTRALIA

○ SYDNEY

○ Balmain

○ Glebe

○ Alexandria

SYDNEY

○ Ultimo

Darlinghurst ○

Kings Cross ○

Elizabeth Bay

○ Potts Point

Rushcutters Bay ○

○ Daring Point

○ Kirribilli

NORTH SYDNEY

MOSMAN

Centennial Park ○

Bondi Junction ○

RANDWICK

○ Coogee

○ Clovelly

Tamarama ○

WAVERLEY

○ Bronte

○ Bondi

WOOLLAHRA

○ Double Bay

○ Point Piper

○ Rose Bay

○ Vaucluse

○ Watsons Bay

○ Bondi Beach

SOUTH PACIFIC
OCEAN

Bondi Beach

Sydney

Balmain

Sydney Opera House

The most sought–after and expensive areas to live in Sydney are found in the east by the bay: Bellevue Hill, Darling Point, Diamond Bay, Double Bay, Dover Heights, Edgecliff, Rushcutters Bay, Parsley Bay, Point Piper, Rose Bay, Vaucluse, Watsons Bay and Woolhara.

In Sydney's eastern suburbs you will find a mix of low–rise new builds (made of brick, brick veneer or sandstone) and two–three bedroom apartments in Victorian–designed houses with impressive high ceilings and large rooms (3-4 bedrooms with a garage). You rarely find places with back gardens in the eastern suburbs, unless of course you are Russell Crowe who bought Lachlan Murdoch's house 'Berthong' in Elizabeth Bay back in 2003. It features a sprawling back garden with a swimming pool and to-die-for views of the harbour.

Loft conversions and studio flats are also popular in the CBD and eastern suburbs but virtually non-existent in the western Suburbs (except near universities). Many hotels were built for the 2000 Olympics, and have since been regenerated and turned into unusual apartment complexes (often with amazing views). In the western suburbs you are likely to find brick or weatherboard houses with large back yards, often with swimming pools, garages (sometimes with double parking spaces), driveways, front gardens and 4–5 bedrooms.

Eastern suburbs and north shore

One of the most popular areas to live in Sydney is the eastern foreshore and north harbour facing properties of the Eastern Suburbs; these include the areas hugging Sydney Harbour from Watsons Bay to Darling Point. Many Sydneysiders aspire to live in these suburbs, with a mix of successful executives, celebrities (such as Nicole Kidman and Russell Crowe) and retirees who have set up base here. These suburbs have excellent access to the city, a cosmopolitan population, some of the country's best private schools, netted (i.e. sharkproof) harbour beaches, nearby ocean beaches, a plethora of large shopping precincts and even bush walks on the harbour foreshore. If you are financially sound, then the Eastern Suburbs of Sydney will reveal your dream property.

As the real estate is expensive, there is a greater denomination of older residents than in most other areas of Sydney. However, when you are looking on the rental market, you will often find reasonably priced two-bedroom units and options in shared accommodation.

 Shared accommodation: www.gumtree.com.au

The bonus of living in the Eastern Suburbs is its location and style. From almost every vantage point you will see the harbour or park. You can easily stroll into Kings Cross and all of the transport links to the CBD from the Eastern suburbs. If you moved to Rushcutters Bay for example, you could have a twilight drink or sail at the Rushcutters Yacht Club, or the more casual café in the middle of Rushcutters park. The houses are covered in gorgeous greenery and are for the most part Victorian in design.

Bayside living

Double Bay

Also known as 'Double Pay' this area is the Rodeo Drive or Bondi Street of shopping districts and you will find all the most glamorous boutiques, restaurants, bars and salons here. The neighbouring suburbs of Darling Point and Rushcutters Bay sit snugly on the harbour with views to kill for. There are great transport links to the CBD (it is only 4km away), including trains from Edge Cliff railway station, ferries and regular buses. It is also not too far from Bondi Beach, and so has the best of both worlds – a bustling and stylish city feel, with a location close to the beach. You will however, pay dearly for this privilege and an apartment for two will set you back anywhere from A$650 to A$4,000 per week.

Rose Bay

Has much more of a village feel to it than its neighbour Double Bay. It has a charming shopping street, which is full of local cafés, bakeries and shops. Buses run regularly from here (it is 7km from the CBD), as do ferries. Rose Bay has its own scenic park on the harbour which offers views of both the Sydney Opera House and the Sydney Harbour Bridge. It is known as one of Sydney's most desirable and affluent suburbs. A two-bedroom apartment will cost between A$350–A$1000.

Potts Point/Elizabeth Bay

Found at the bottom of Kings Cross and trendy Darlinghurst, this area is an oasis after walking through the neon lights and grime of the red light district. With an inner city living feel (fantastic cafés, expensive boutique hotels and deli's), doubled with harbour views and a close vicinity to Rushcutters Bay, this is a much sought after area. Mainly units and flats are on offer as houses are rare in this suburb. A two-bedroom apartment will cost between A$350–A$650 per week. Many of the old hotels have been renovated and turned into apartments, so boast amazing views.

If you want to live in the Eastern Suburbs, but cannot afford the price tag of Darling Point, Rose Bay or Potts Point, you can opt for inner city Paddington.

Bordering on Oxford Street from Hyde Park eastbound towards Paddington you'll find this precinct very different from the rest of Sydney and probably the rest of the world. The upper half has a bustling high street, which has affordable clothing boutiques, trendy bars, restaurants,

> **Rebecca Wells loved her first experiences of the East Coast of Australia:**
>
> 'I just fell in love with Sydney. It has everything: a buzzing city, stunning mountains, gorgeous countryside, weird indigenous animals (which I love, being a big animal buff) and beautiful rolling sandy beaches. There are also some fantastic spots along the coast'

supermarkets and an excellent Saturday market in the school ground. The lower half, towards the city, is at the heart of the Sydney gay and lesbian scene and is laden with X-rated shops and colourful bars. On every turn you will find fetish shops, gay nightclubs, gay–friendly cafés and pubs, which are mainly populated with the locals. This is the Mecca of the Sydney Gay and Lesbian Mardi Gras, which is held in February of every year.

Paddington is perfectly located for commuting into the city for work, or for nights out, as well as being equidistant to the glory of both Bondi Beach and Rushcutters Bay. It is made up of some of Australia's earliest dwellings and terraced houses. You will pay between A$400–A$900 per week for a two–three bedroom terraced house.

Woollahra

Famous for its quiet, tree-lined residential streets (with a stylish feel of London's Mayfair about it), trendy bars and restaurants and a village-style shopping centre in Edgecliff station, which is like a mini food hall, with, butcher counter, bread, fresh pasta and a Harris Farm Market store. It is located extremely close to the CBD, (only 4.8km away) with brilliant train and bus links. It also has the advantage of being close to Centennial Park (Sydney's largest park), Bondi and Double Bay/Rushcutters Bay. Expect to pay between A$350–A$800 for a two-bedroom apartment. Typical houses here are mostly one to two-storey terrace houses made of brick or weatherboard.

Rooftops of historic houses in Glebe

Inner city

Alexandria

An inner-city suburb of Sydney, 4km south of the Sydney central business district, Alexandria is extremely handy for commuting into the CBD, as it is close to bus routes to the Sydney CBD and situated between two railway lines on the City Rail network. It is served by Green Square railway station, located on the north-eastern fringe, Erskineville railway station and St Peters railway station. Although not the prettiest of suburbs, residents mainly choose to reside here for its proximity to the city. Two-bedroom apartments start from A$300 per week.

Glebe

This inner-city suburb is a convenient 15-minute bus journey or 30 minute walk (3km south-west) to the CBD.

Broadway is a locality around the road of the same name, which is located on the border of Glebe, Chippendale and Ultimo. There is a huge student/creative vibe to the area as one of the leading colleges in Australia is located in Ultimo.

The Sydney Fish Markets, which sell fish straight from the boats, is a 15 minute walk away and in the grounds of Glebe Primary School on Saturdays, you will find the Glebe alternative lifestyle markets. Expect to pay between A$350–A$550 for a spacious two-bedroom unit.

Balmain

Visiting Balmain is like stepping back in time, as many of the original shopfronts and buildings remain as they were back in the 1880s. Balmain is 5km west of the Sydney CBD, in the Municipality of Leichhardt and its neighbouring suburbs are Rozelle, Birchgrove, Iron Cove and Mort Bay. It is seen as a very creative and studenty suburb, with many of the residents enjoying the local art and culture scene. Café shops and popular bars (such as the Exchange Hotel) line the streets and the houses on the leafy streets are often the original Victorian terraces. It once had a reputation as the tough side of town, which bred hard working-class men; it is now an extremely trendy suburb which has residents such as Rose Byrne and Bryan Brown.

It has decent (but not terrific) transport links into the CBD, which include the Balmain ferry from Balmain Thames Street Wharf, and local buses. Traffic can, however, be demanding on weekdays, so this is seen as a slight problem living here. Expect to pay anywhere from A$350 to A$700 for a two-bedroom apartment.

Leichardt

The historic centre of the early 20th century Italian community, this hantag can still be seen in both the local residents and wide array of delicious Italian restaurants, bakeries and delis. There is still a huge sense of community here and it is located very close to Glebe, and so has the same transport networks and close proximity to the CBD. Expect to pay between A$350–A$500 for a two-bedroom apartment here.

If this all too inner city for you, then there are hundreds of suburbs to choose from in the sprawling western of Sydney. From Strathfield to Penrith area are Campbelltown, Bankstown to Concorde, you will gain a house for the same price as a two-bedroom unit, but lose the views, and easy commute to work. An average price of a three-bedroom house to rent in Penrith is A$300 and it will take you approximately 45 minutes (by train) to get to the CBD. However, not all expats will be working in the city, so living in one of the outer suburbs might just do the trick for you.

Beachside

If you are moving to Australia for its iconic beaches, these are the most popular beach suburbs to live.

Bondi

You must start your quest for property with Australia's most photographed and iconic beach – Bondi. The beach is spectacularly large and Campbell parades' neighbouring cafés, restaurants and boutiques make this a very popular local and tourist hangout. Favourite views include the one from the terrace at the Iceberg club, an awe-inspiring art deco building that has the view of the Iceberg's public swimming pool; which for a small admission fee will have you swimming beach side, with the waves constantly crashing into the pool while you do your laps. Other landmarks include Bondi Pavilion, Bondi Hotel, and the amazingly scenic walkway south of Bondi to Tamarama beach.

Bondi Icebergs Club: 1 Notts Avenue, Bondi Beach ; 02 9130 4804 ; www.icebergs.com.au. Pool open Monday to Friday 6am–6.30pm, Saturday and Sunday 6.30 am–6.30 pm, A$4.50

Drawbacks of living in Bondi include the sheer mass of backpackers settling here (Christmas Day on Bondi Beach resembles Oxford Street in London on Christmas Eve) and tourists on weekends. However, while some properties are extremely expensive, it is worth shopping around as there are still some reasonably priced units, if you are willing to live a few streets away from the promenade. There are great transport links from here, including the bus, which will take you to neighbouring Bondi Junction and links to the major train networks. Two-bedroom apartment between A$400–A$1,000 per week here.

Bronte

A pretty green beachside suburb that sits on Nelsons Bay and is surrounded by the lush Bronte Park. It offers awe-inspiring scenic cliff top walks to Coogee and north towards Tamarama and Bondi and is 2.5km from Bondi Beach. It is easy to reach by public transport or car but expect parking space to be extremely limited on weekends) and is 8km east of the Sydney CBD. You will pay between A$400–A$2,000 per week for a two–three-bedroom apartment.

Clovelly

Another popular beachside suburb, clovelly is situated 8km south-east of Sydney. It has an unusually shaped and unique little beach which is popular for snorkellers and bathers. By the late 1980s it was known as 'the safest beach in Sydney'. Its access to several private schools and decent transport links to the City, (Randwick and Bondi Junction railways) has ensured that it remains a desirable residential location, with property prices increasingly moving upwards at increasing rates, in line with other Sydney beachside suburbs. You will pay from A$400–A$2000 per week for a three-bedroom apartment in this suburb.

Camp Cove–Watsons Bay

This is one of Sydney's best-kept secrets. Watsons Bay has several small beaches tucked inside its coves which are protected from high winds and tourists. Camp Cove is steadily becoming one of Sydney's most expensive suburbs as it is a small suburb with limited beachside properties. Local attractions include Doyle's restaurant and the Gap lookout. Expect to pay from A$500 to A$1,500 per week for a two–three-bedroom apartment.

Coogee

Pronounced Could-gee. This is a beachside suburb, 8km south-east of Sydney which shares similarities with the famous Bondi, but has a smaller and more local feel to it. There is an abundance of cafés, pubs and restaurants in the adjacent area. It has public transport links (via Randwick and Bondi Junction) and a mostly young crowd. Expect to pay between A$350 and A$900 for a two-bedroom apartment.

Southern beaches

Cronulla

The Cronulla peninsula is one of Sydney's younger and most prospering suburbs. It features several excellent beaches and neighbouring shops and

FACT

■ 'Bondi' or 'Boondi' is an Aboriginal word meaning water breaking over rocks or noise of water breaking over rocks. The Australian Museum records that Bondi means place where a fight of nullas (Aboriginal clubs) took place. (Source: Book of Sydney Suburbs, Frances Pollon (Angus & Robertson) 1990 cafés. It is 26km south of the Sydney CBD, in the local government area of Sutherland Shire, and is often busy with people visiting from the western suburbs (as it has easy parking and is close to the train network). For those wanting to dwell by the beach, without paying Eastern city prices, this may be the solution. It will take considerably longer to commute to the CBD (approx 48 minutes to Central station), but it has very good transport links. Surf beaches are at the northern part of the peninsula including North Cronulla, Elouera and Wanda beaches. You can rent a sunny two-bedroom apartment here from A$250–A$600 per week.

The 2005 Cronulla riots were a series of racially motivated mob confrontations which originated in and around Cronulla. On Sunday, 11 December 2005, approximately 5,000 people gathered to protest against currently reported incidents of assaults and intimidatory behaviour by groups of non-locals, most of whom were identified in earlier media reports as Middle Eastern youths from the suburbs of Western Sydney. The crowd assembled following a series of earlier confrontations, and an assault on three off-duty lifesavers which took place the previous weekend. The crowd initially assembled without incident, but violence broke out after a large segment of the mostly white Australian crowd chased a man of Middle Eastern appearance into a hotel and other youths of Middle Eastern appearance were assaulted on a train. Thankfully, there have been no repeated confrontations.

Maroubra

Considered to be one of Sydney's best surfing beaches, Maroubra is 10km (6 miles) south-east of the Sydney CBD. It falls under the Eastern Suburbs area code and a two-bedroom apartment will cost between A$350–A$800 per week.

Northern beaches

Manly

Manly falls under the 'Northern beaches' umbrella and is often the first port of call for expats wanting to live in one of Sydney's most attractive and diverse places. Its attraction lies in the fact that it has one of Sydney's best beaches and the commute to work can involve crossing the sparkling harbour, using the Sydney ferry or the faster Jet Cat, via the Harbour Bridge and Opera House. Although this is appealing, one must note that the ferry has limited operating times, and driving or taking the bus (there are no rail connections) can often mean a laborious journey in traffic on Military Road. Manly is located 17km north-east of the Sydney CBD.

Manly was once part of a former holiday and resort centre and to this day retains this fresh, holiday atmosphere. Expect to pay from A$450–

A$700 per week for a two-bedroom unit. You must also factor in the transport costs to get to work from Manly.

 Ferry information www.sydneyferries.info

Mosman

This is one of the most picturesque suburbs of Sydney. It is 8km (5 miles) north-east of Sydney and is part of the lower North Shore district. It is made up of the smaller suburbs of Balmoral, Beauty Point, Clifton Gardens, Georges Heights, the delightfully named Spit Junction and the Spit.

From these suburbs you can stroll through the Sydney Harbour National Park and you can see Watsons Bay on the opposite shore. Taronga Zoo is quite close by and living here means a picturesque Jet Cat or Sydney Ferry commute across the harbour to work (the nearest train stations are Milson's Point or North Sydney) . The beaches are largely empty during the week (and Balmoral is known as one of Australia's nicest beaches) and quite calm on weekends as well, and the overall area has a 'villagey' feel to it. Federation era houses sit comfortably alongside modern townhouse developments. Mosman has all the attractions of the Eastern suburbs but with better prices and more variety with choices of accommodation. It costs between A$350–A$700 for a two-bedroom apartment.

Balmain waterfront

Kirribilli

A 3km car drive or train trip over the majestic Harbour Bridge will take you to the North Shore suburb of Kirribilli. The suburb contains Kirribilli House (the official Sydney residence of the Prime Minister), so it must be a nice area! It has all transport links in order, including a six-minute ferry journey to Circular Quay (two services per hour) which caters to its many residents and will cost about A$25 for a taxi into the city. It has a really nice community feel to it, to-die-for New Year's Eve firework views and plenty of decent restaurants. The closest train station is Milson's Point and regular buses depart from the main streets. A two-bedroom apartment will cost between A$400 and A$3,000 per week.

Western Sydney

Strathfield

Residents derive from many different nationalities, of which the three largest non-Australian-born groups are South Korean, Chinese, and Sri Lankan. It has a population of almost 31,000 people and is a 20-minute drive to the CBD (depending on traffic) via car and a similar time via bus and train. There is a large shopping mall, yet no real sense of community here. Expect to pay between A$380–A$550 for a large two–three-bedroom property.

Neighbouring suburbs to look out for are; Homebush, Homebush West, Flemington, Greenacre, Enfield, Strathfield South, Chullora and Belfield.

Burwood

Another popular choice for Sydneysiders wanting to escape the madness of the CBD and rent a larger property, Burwood is 12km (8 miles) west of the Sydney CBD. You can get a train from the station, which will take 20 minutes to the city, and you are also only 6km away from the 2000 Olympic Park at Homebush. Expect to pay A$300–A$360 for a two-bedroom property.

Parramatta

A western suburb of Sydney, 23km west of the Sydney CBD, on a good morning it will take you, about 45 minutes to drive into town (Parramatta

The evaluation of Sydney

Here's an extract from an Australian Broadcasting Corporation (ABC) programme, *Inside Business*. Andrew Geoghegan is the reporter, Bernard Salt is a corporate adviser on demographic trends and Allan Moss is Chief Executive of Macquarie Bank.

Allan Moss: *You know, we felt we had to change because really this is where the action is.*

Andrew Geoghegan: *30,000 new residents a year, Australia's fastest growing economy, and home to 150 of the country's top 500 companies, western Sydney is undergoing a structural shift, according to corporate adviser on demographic trends Bernard Salt.*

Bernard Salt: *My expectation is that over the next 10 years with the completion of the Sydney Western Orbital, there will be a paradigm shift in the location of key businesses in Sydney.'* (*Source: Transcript of Transurban moves to secure M2 8 May 2005. Reporter:* Andrew Geoghegan www.abc.net.au/insidebusiness)

A bird's eye view of Parramatta golf course

Road is one of the most congested in Sydney). Average property value in Parramatta is A$421,150, and for that you are likely to get a three or four-bedroom house with a garage and generous back garden.

Parramatta has many high-density commercial and residential developments and is home to the eighth largest shopping centre in Australia, Westfield's. Parramatta railway station is a major transport interchange on the City Rail network. It is served by the Blue Mountains line, Cumberland line and the Western line. The Parramatta ferry wharf is at the Charles Street Weir, on the eastern boundary of the Central Business District. The wharf is the westernmost destination of the Sydney Ferries River Cat ferry service which runs on Parramatta River. Prices range from A$200–A$350 per week for a two-bedroom apartment here.

Penrith

A suburb in western Sydney, with a growing population (currently at 178,233), it is the 10th largest city in Australia by population. It is located 50km west of the Sydney CBD. Penrith lies east of the Nepean River, at the

Birrarung Marr, parkland along the river in Central Melbourne

foot of the Blue Mountains, part of the Great Dividing Range. As it is located so far from the city centre, house prices start from as little as A$213,000 (two-bedroom apartment). Rentals cost as little as A$200–A$300 for a three-bedroom property. Penrith Railway Station is a major railway station on the Western Line of the CityRail network. It has frequent services to and from the City and is also a major stop on the intercity network.

 Rental costs update: www.homehound.com.au/rent/apartments/penrith

MELBOURNE

Melbourne is known as the style, food and culture capital of Australia. This is a result of its hugely cosmopolitan mix of 3.4 million residents. There are over 200 different nationalities represented in the mix, with Greek being the largest (it has the world's third largest Greek community). It is notable for its contemporary and Victorian architecture, parks, gardens and impressive tram network. It was also the host city for the 2006 Commonwealth games and the 1956 Summer Olympics, and sport maintains an important cultural significance to the city. Melbourne is such a liveable city that it earned second place in the 2005 Economist Intelligence unit's (EIU) Liveability Ranking.

ABC.net.au reported on July 28, 2007 that:

'Melbourne's median house price has reached a record high. Figures released by the Real Estate Institute of Victoria reveal the median price jumped more than 10% in the June quarter to a new high of A$420,000.

Elwood, Surrey Hills, Middle Park and Balwyn have joined the list of suburbs where the median price has pushed past A$1m.

The figures also showed there are now no metropolitan suburbs where the median price is below A$200,000.

Institute chief executive Enzo Raimondo says Melbourne is the third most expensive capital city for real estate behind Sydney and Perth.

'Most suburbs now, the inner and middle suburbs you wouldn't get much for a million dollars,' he said.

'If you go a bit further out at Donvale, Parkdale, Blackburn, they're about half a million.

'So you have to be going out about 30km to get something in the A$300,000–A$400,000 bracket.'

SUBURBS**OF**MELBOURNE

NORTH →

AUSTRALIA

MELBOURNE

SOUTHERN
OCEAN

MARIBYRNONG

Footscray

MOONEE
VALLEY

MORELAND

DAREBIN

25km to Craigieburn
from centre

PORT PHILLIP

St Kilda

Elwood

STONNINGTON

Toorak

Fitzroy

Richmond

Brunswick

YARRA

5km to Ivanhoe

30km to Warrandyte and
Park Orchards from centre

GLEN
EIRA

BOROONDARA

Camberwell

Surrey Hills

12
13
14
15
1
11
2
3
4
8
5
10
6
7
9

North Melbourne

Carlton

Southbank

Fitzroy

The city of Melbourne is made up of the Central Business District (CBD) and numerous inner-city suburbs. As with Sydney, it also has a massive East and West divide. It is seen as more desirable to live in the East where many of the residents are middle class and well off. However, the West offers more land and bigger houses for a fraction of the cost and was traditionally where the working class resided. Obviously the closer you are to the city (with its private schools, cafés, restaurants) the more expensive the real estate becomes. This rings true for trendy suburbs such as Camberwell, Surrey Hills and Ivanhoe. Besides the sought-after bayside suburbs, these may be the more desirable for people moving with families. Current developments popping up in the outer suburbs of Cragieburn and Pakenham have proven affordable and popular for young families, happy residing a little bit further away from the CDB. The choice is yours in Melbourne – sprawling suburbs with great family orientated services, trendy inner-city suburbs with bars and cafés, beachside living, or semi-rural retreats.

Central Business District apartment

It is obvious, therefore, that the housing market is continuing to increase and choosing the right area is crucial to striking a balance between cost and location. Below is a list of the more popular suburbs to move to in Melbourne. For more details on Melbourne as a city go to our *About the Country* section.

Central Business District and inner city suburbs

The Central Business District (CBD)

Melbourne's business and financial centre the CBD is home to over 62% of Melbourne's overseas residents. The 1990s saw an abundance of office space, which has now been regenerated and turned into trendy inner city dwellings, such as one and two bedroom apartments and studio flats. There are currently about 10,000 residents, who are mostly young professionals working in the CBD or students attracted by the 24–hour lifestyle of their surrounds (there are many bars, clubs, restaurants and nightclubs in this area).

Docklands

This area has been described as a 'city in a city', and the regeneration project looks set to take a decade to fully complete (although parts have

View from Southbank, Melbourne

already been finished and have turned into residential areas). There will eventually be over 8,000 apartments, with up to 20,000 residents and a daily stream of tourists and visitors (up to 20 million each year). For now, however, it has a small but growing population of mainly middle-aged people who have downsized and professionals seeking to live close to the CBD. At night it can seem quite deserted, but this will surely change as more and more people move into the area. It can be found on land adjacent to Southern Cross railway station, the central city and industrial areas. Tramlines, river boats and road extensions are all being extended to service this new metropolis. Currently a two-bedroom rental costs between A$500–A$750 per week.

 Up to date real estate prices: www.domain.com.au

Southbank

Southbank a large overseas population residing in its midst, in fact over 44% were born outside Australia. It is located a mere 2km from the city centre and is bordered to the North by the Yarra River. It is best known for its flashy, buzzing riverside promenade stretching along the south side of the Yarra River, from the Southgate shopping and dining complex to the high rolling Crown Casino.

This area has changed in leaps and bounds throughout the years, as it was once part of South Melbourne and known as an industrial area. Its

transformation began in the 1990s as part of an urban renewal program. Now it is the jewel in the crown of Melbourne's elite – you will find high-rise buildings, upmarket hotels, trendy restaurants, designer shops and cafés and is known as a local hotspot for taking in the splendid views while dining or strolling along the promenade.

The population has increased drastically since 2005, and the residential buildings are all apartments; houses are unknown in this development. You will expect to pay between A$600–A$1,000 per week for the privilege of living in this sought-after area.

Brunswick St, Fitzroy

Local attractions include: the Melbourne Arts Centre, Concert Hall, National Gallery of Victoria, the Malthouse Theatre and the Australian Centre for Contemporary Art and Victorian College of the Arts. It also includes the Melbourne Exhibition Centre (known locally as Jeff's Shed after a former premier) and the Polly Woodside Maritime Museum.

A number of tramlines run through Southbank, making it easily accessible to the CBD.

Carlton

This area is only 2km from Melbourne's CBD, and is also known as little Italy, as it's the traditional home of Melbourne's Italian community. Locals and tourists alike visit this lively area to experience its authentic coffees and the atmospheric Italian restaurants of Lygon Street. In more current times, migrants from South-East Asia, Africa and the Middle East have been drawn to its many attractions and now make up a large percentage of its residents.

Local attractions include the iconic Optus Oval (found in Princes Park and popular with joggers) worshipped by the Carlton

Football Club's league of loyal followers, the historic Melbourne General Cemetery, the majestic Carlton Gardens, the Royal Women's Hospital, the contemporary Melbourne Museum, the domed 19th century Royal Exhibition Building, the University of Melbourne and the Royal Melbourne Institute of Technology (RMIT). Students make up a significant part of Carlton's lively population (it is known as one of Melbourne's largest residential areas) and its affordable terrace and public housing apartments (which makes up 23% of total housing) reflect this.

 Shared accommodation: www.gumtree.com.au

Expect to pay between A$350–A$550 for a two-bedroom unit. Shared accommodation prospers in this area.

In *Settling In* we mention the Melbourne government's initiative to promote street parties – this all began with the Carlton police community consultative committee which was the first area to trial it.

Fitzroy, including Brunswick Street

This trendy inner suburb (3km from the CBD), which annually hosts the Melbourne Fringe festival (Sept–Oct) is at the heart of Melbourne's bohemian culture. It is Melbourne's oldest suburb, and includes the bustling Brunswick Street (at the core of Melbourne's eating, drinking, shopping and entertainment district), with its lively bars, trendy cafés and atmospheric

restaurants, which spill out on to the pavement. The cafés seem to serve breakfast all day and stay open till the wee, small hours. The shops on Brunswick also have an artistic element and house a collection of up and coming designers, retro stores, bookshops (both second hand and new) and modern art galleries.

The architecture of Fitzroy is as diverse as its residents and features some of the finest examples of Victorian era architecture in Melbourne. The entire suburb is a heritage precinct with many individual buildings covered by heritage controls. Average house prices in the area are A$600,000 and two–three-bed rentals range from A$350–A$500 per week. Other typical buildings in Fitzroy include: workers' cottages, terraces, corner shops and pubs, warehouses and factories (many now converted into trendy loft apartments). The 1970s also have a lot to answer for in this suburb as there are many examples of infill developments, such as 'six-pack' style flats and units, along with the large-scale results of 'slum clearance' programs in the 1960s, which resulted in the high-rise, mass populated buildings still evident today. This suburb is definitely for the young, or the young at heart who enjoy city living and fun, local attractions.

Parham and Albert Park are mainly frequented by young professionals lured by the large parks (Albert and Fawkner) and numerous cafés. Parham is also known for its excellent nightlife and shopping, while Albert Park hosts the annual Melbourne Grand Prix and sits in an enviable position next to the CBD and the beach. Expect to pay from A$200,000 for a one-bedroom apartment. Houses range from cute Victorian terrace houses to modern apartment developments. The average sale price for a two-bedroom Victorian timber cottage, on a tree-lined street close to the water is around A$700,000. Rentals are approximately A$400–A$550 for a two-bedroom property close to the beach in Albert Park.

Parkville

Once the home of the 2006 Melbourne Commonwealth Games village and also the base for most of the international athletes and officials, for the duration of the games. It is located 4km from the CBD. Since the games have ended, the village has been regenerated and made into semi-affordable housing for low-income earners and young professionals. It is estimated that 90 of the 155 houses in the Commonwealth Games village have been refurbished and sold on. This development will continue till the year 2011 and on completion, there will be more than 1,000 new private and 200 social houses on this site.

Parkville boasts impressive Victorian era heritage houses, tree-lined streets and an energetic atmosphere, due to the main campus of the University of Melbourne and residential housing for students nearby. Other local attractions include the Melbourne Zoo and the Royal Park, which is the city of Melbourne's largest area of open space.

This area is relatively more affordable than others, due to the student and low-income earners residing here. Expect to pay between A$350–A$500 per week for a two–three-bedroom apartment.

East Melbourne

An affluent suburb, East Melbourne is separated from the central city by a number of historic green gardens, such as Fitzroy, Treasury and Parliament. It is also home to some of Melbourne's most iconic landmarks (including the Melbourne Cricket Ground and Parliament House) and 19th century homes. There were 4,500 people living in this suburb in 2006.

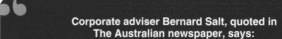

**Corporate adviser Bernard Salt, quoted in
The Australian newspaper, says:**

'Melbourne's celebrity suburb is undeniably Toorak. But
whereas the peninsula positioning of the Points Darling and
Piper protects residents from the prying eyes of the proletariat,
the same effect is achieved in Melbourne by jamming the
city's richest suburb hard up against the Yarra River. Like
a medieval moat, the Yarra River separates leafy Toorakian
order from the scrambled chaos of Richmond.'

Although there are a number of hospitals and businesses in East Melbourne, it is predominantly a residential area. Housing mainly comprises of flats and units in converted houses. Expect to pay A$320–A$650 per week for a two-bedroom apartment.

Southern suburbs

Toorak

You know you have made it when you are searching for real estate in this inner Melbourne suburb. Think Chelsea, Kensington or Mayfair in London or Double Bay in Sydney (without the harbour views). Prices start at the A$1.5–A$2m dollar mark and increase at a rapid rate. Houses are picturesque and feature two–three-storey mansions (often hidden behind huge fences or opulent trees) with sweeping driveways and manicured lawns. There is also a villagey feel to Toorak as it features clusters of expensive shops and cafés on the Toorak road. The suburb is 6km south-east of the CBD, on a rise at a bend in the Yarra River. Expect to pay between A$400–A$1500 per week for a two–three -bedroom property.

South Yarra

Situated close to the wealthy Toorak, you will find South Yarra, which is popular with young professionals. Also an incredibly expensive address, property prices begin at A$800,000. South Yarra has several local attractions, with the jewel in its crown being Chapel Street. This street is shopping heaven; people from all over Australia take day trips (as you would to New York) to shop up a storm. The South Yarra section of the famous street is the most fashionable and upmarket end. Houses are large and well kept in this area and it also contains some notable clusters of terrace houses. These can largely be found on Park Street, which has rows of preserved and highly sought after terraces built in the Victorian era.

Some of these terrace houses are up to four storeys tall (check out Domain Road, Toorak Road West, and Caroline Street). Heritage registered houses include Como House (1847) one of Melbourne's earliest mansions, which is now open to the public and managed by the National Trust. South Yarra also has an area which dates back to the art deco style of housing. This tiny village of 1920s and 30s style buildings can be found overlooking the river in Lawson Grove. Expect to pay A$380–A$500 per week for a two-bedroom apartment.

St Kilda and Elwood

A popular beachside suburb located on Port Phillip Bay, about 7km south-east of the CBD, where young professionals, arty folk and a large proportion of young UK immigrants reside. It is the area you will find the highest density of restaurants, bars and clubs and boasts the largest population of any suburb in the City of Port Phillip.

In the Edwardian and Victorian eras, this seaside suburb was frequented by Australia's élite, and during this period many palatial mansions were erected. In later years, it fell into disrepair and became notorious as Melbourne's red-light district, with many of the large mansions converted into low-cost rooming houses. This is now becoming a thing of the past, as the area has enjoyed a regeneration and is once again a tourist and local favourite. Local attractions include: Luna Park (for amusements and rides),

the Esplanade Hotel (for a real Melbourne pub experience), Acland Street (famous for its European cake shops and cafés) and Fitzroy Street (for its lively bars and cafés). It is home to many theatres the popular St Kilda Beach and many of the city of Melbourne's big events (including the annual Gay Pride march in February). It is also home to the Edwardian built St Kilda pier, which was devastated by fire some years ago and subsequently reconstructed. The St Kilda harbour houses a little penguin colony beneath it.

St Kilda, had, until recently, the highest population density for a metropolitan area outside of Sydney. This density was shown in the number of low and high-rise strata title units, apartments and flats. In current years a high-rise apartment trend in suburbs like Southbank, Docklands and the Melbourne CBD and St Kilda Road all rival the suburb's population density.

For those looking for less of a party atmosphere, neighbouring Elwood offers larger houses and a more family-feel, while enjoying equally close proximity to the beach.

Expect to pay between A$350–A$700 per week for a two-bedroom apartment.

Western suburbs

Footscray

This area which is named after Foots Cray in south-east England, is an inner western suburb of Melbourne, and was once seen as an undesirable address, due to the presence of heavy industry. Migrants have notoriously flocked here since the 1950s when the Greek, Italian and Croatian communities settled here, lured by both the local employment opportunities and the affordability of housing. In current years, Vietnamese and North African migrants followed suit and a massive regeneration project has seen affordable period housing bought by young locals, seeking to live close to the CBD.

Local attractions include a large Chinatown market, known as 'Little Saigon', which caters to both the growing Asian community and customers from all over the city, tempted by the exotic cuisine and noisy atmosphere. Another popular fresh produce and seafood market is the Footscray Market, which is popular with locals and restaurants picking up the catch of the day. The average price for a three-bedroom house is A$390,000.

Kensington and Flemington

These two neighbouring suburbs have a quirky, village type atmosphere. They are well known for their residential character, cool village shops and unusual housing. Local attractions include the infamous Flemington Racecourse (home to the annual Melbourne Cup) and the Melbourne Showground.

Typical houses to be found in these popular neighbourhoods range from public housing apartments to new townhouses, small period dwellings and the Kensington Banks housing development on a former

Footscray family homes.

army depot site and abattoir. Expect to pay A$350–A$500 per week for a two-bedroom house.

Northern suburbs

North Melbourne

This suburb is home to the one of the city's most dynamic and coolest café and restaurant streets – Errol Street. With a population of 8,500, local attractions include the Metropolitan meat market and the North Melbourne Town hall. The area has an agreeable mix of both new and old residents and commercial and industrial properties mixed with retail and community facilities. Expect to pay between A$350–A$500 per week for a two-bedroom apartment.

Brunswick

Brunwick has a population of 21,000, of which 23% were born overseas. It can be found 4km north of Melbourne's CBD and is well connected with transport. Traditionally it has been home to many diverse migrant groups but is increasingly seen as a desirable suburb by young couples and families priced out of neighbouring Fitzroy, and attracted by the larger houses and gardens. Sydney Road is the main street that intersects this suburb and contains a lively and interesting mix of ethnic Middle Eastern and Mediterranean shops, (such as the bustling Italian supermarket Mediterranean Wholesalers), as well as an increasing array of trendy gourmet restaurants.

Brunswick is located on relatively flat terrain, which makes it perfect for cyclists and walkers. It also has transport links to the CBD via the bus and tram networks.

The population is also largely filled by tertiary students, who are drawn to the area for its proximity to the University of Melbourne, the RMIT University and its affordable apartments. Expect to pay A$320–A$360 per week for a two-bedroom unit.

Ivanhoe

This historical and affluent suburb, which steals its name from a bestselling Sir Walter Scott novel, can be found 12km to the north-east of Melbourne's CBD. The area is renowned for its architecture, found on some of Melbourne's oldest historical homes; many were built in the late 19th and early 20th centuries (this may not seem old to UK residents, but Australians only

Traditional brick houses seen accross Melbourne

began building their houses in the 1800s). As a result, many properties in the area are sold for over A$1m. The area hosts two of the few private schools in the northern suburbs: Ivanhoe Grammar School and Ivanhoe Girls' Grammar School.

Other local attractions include the art deco inspired Heidelberg Town Hall, which is found on top of a hill on Heidelberg road. This road also features supermarkets, trendy cafés, banks and other local amenities. There is also a local golf course to be found on the edge of the Yarra river.

Over 100,000 people annually visit The Boulevard in Ivanhoe, where residents put on a Christmas light spectacular like no other. Houses, cars, trees and basically anything that stands still for long enough will be covered by twinkling Christmas lights that would make Santa Claus proud and the electricity board happy.

FACT

■ Hollywood actress Cate Blanchett grew up in Ivanhoe.

Eastern suburbs

Camberwell

This is a popular suburb, located 13km from the CBD of Melbourne with a population of 20,000. Its main attraction is the 60-metre long, bustling Burke Road strip of shops and cafés. The railway station can be found and various tram routes (centrally including the 70, 72 and 75) meet here, making it easy to travel to the city.

Other local attractions include the historic Rivoli Cinemas, (found in the adjacent suburb of Hawthorn East) and the atmospheric Camberwell weekly market. This market is a hotspot for locals and visitors to swap or sell anything from clothes to car parts. It is also home to a good choice of both state and private schools and sits on the edge of the pricey 'private school belt' – suburbs close to the city's top private schools.

Its allure as a suburb has attracted such famous neighbours as Geoffrey Rush, Barry Humphries a.ka. Dame Edna Everage (who grew up in this suburb), Flea from the Red Hot Chilli Peppers, and Australia's very own singing budgie Kylie Minogue.

Housing is reasonably priced (at least for rentals) and consists of both apartments and houses, although large houses built in the 1920s and 1930s dominate the suburb. A three- bedroom apartment will cost between A$300–A$400 per week.

Surrey Hills is a quaint suburb, located 14km outside Melbourne's CBD. It is the perfect place to settle if you want the convenience of living close to the CBD, but don't want to pay overly inflated prices. Prices here, however, do vary from A$350–A$800 per week, for a three-bedroom house. Its current population is 13,300, and the suburb is firmly upper middle-class and family oriented. In between Canterbury and Riversdale roads you will find the 'English Counties district', where the streets are named after English counties, including Kent, Middlesex, Essex, Suffolk and Durham.

It is well serviced by all modes of transport and has its own small shopping district (250m long) along Union road. It also has its own primary school 'Surrey Hills primary'.

Outer suburbs

Craigieburn

A suburb of outer Melbourne (in the city of Hume) which is growing in population (currently 21,000) due to its affordable housing, urbanisation and new development areas. Popular with young families, the council is currently developing new schools and many more parks. Most of the area is more than 200 metres above sea level (with Mount Ridley being the

FACT

■ Australian singers Kylie Minogue and Dannii Minogue were raised in nearby Burwood and attended Camberwell High School. Famous Aussie comedian Dame Edna spent his/her childhood years in the Golf Links Estate at 36 Christowel street. Check out the gladiolis in the front garden!

northernmost hill in north-western metropolitan Melbourne), which gives the area clear views of Melbourne's CBD, some 25km away. There are adequate transport links to this suburb via the main highways and the electrified railway service, which now links Craigieburn Station (opened in September of 2007) to the CBD. However, commuting to the CBD is a slow journey of over an hour on the train, and more if driving in congested peak hour traffic.

Housing is plentiful in the new and existing estates and is some of the most affordable throughout Melbourne. A three–four-bedroom house with a driveway, front and back garden will cost A$300–A$400 per week.

Pakenham

Pakenham is an outer Melbourne suburb, found 56km south-east of the CBD. New housing estates are boosting its population (which is currently 21,000), is with the property company Delfin responsible for the most prominent estate, Lakeside. Local attractions include a sports/aquatic centre, horse racing track and a civic centre. Pakenham transport links are adequate but commuting to the CBD takes over an hour on the train, and can be more if you drive in heavy traffic. It is located on the main railway line between Melbourne and Gippsland, and its railway station marks the end of the suburban electrified service. It is a very popular suburb for families.

Housing is extremely affordable in this suburb with a three–four-bedroom large house with gardens and driveways costing around A$240–A$280 per week.

Park Orchards

With a population of only 3,900, this is an affluent outer eastern suburb of Melbourne, characterised by its natural bushland feel. If you are looking for a suburb where you can get away from your neighbours and enjoy Australian nature and wildlife, only 25km from the CBD, this may be the one for you. Most houses sit on at least an acre of land.

Park Orchards is also known locally as the 'sporty suburb', as it houses the Park Orchards Tennis Club, Basketball Club, Netball Club, Domeney sporting facility (which hosts the home games of the Park Orchids cricket club), is home to the 'Sharks' which is the Park Orchids North parish junior football club (quite a mouthful), the BMX club and the Yarra Valley Old Boys football club.

Houses are immaculately well looked after and often cost in excess of A$1m. It is often seen as a more affordable option for large families as there are two local primary schools and a number of private and state secondary schools located in this area. It is close to the Eastern freeway which will take you quickly by car to the CBD (at least in non-peak times), but is not well serviced by public transport.

Other local attractions include 'The 100 Acres' which can be found adjacent to Domeney. It is an area of natural bushland and home to

hundreds of local indigenous plants, birds and animals, such as echidnas and sugar gliders.

Nearby suburb Kangaroo Ground is reputed to have the only post office in Australia that is also a winery. This could be the answer to the other countries' closure of many of their post offices! The surrounding bushland contains kangaroos, koalas, kookaburras, deer, snakes, lizards and many other species.

Warrandyte

This is a semi-rural suburb in Melbourne, which can be found 27km east-north-east of the CBD, on the southern banks of the Yarra River. The suburb was founded during the gold rush era (gold was first discovered here in 1851) as the surrounding hills and river were once rich in gold. It has grown in popularity over the past decade, for people with families who wish to spread their wings and own an acreage, close to the beautiful river ways and hills.

Many of the surviving houses retain evidence of its colonial past and you will find a large three–four-bedroom house with plenty of room in the front and backyard for as little as A$300–A$600 per week. The area is also known for its environmentally friendly conservation programs and its annual Volunteer-run Warrandyte Festival held in March.

Park Orchards is also known locally as the 'sporty suburb', as it houses the Park Orchards Tennis Club, Basketball Club, Netball Club, Domeney sporting facility (which hosts the home games of the Park Orchids cricket club), is home to the 'Sharks' which is the Park Orchids North parish junior football club (quite a mouthful), the BMX club and the Yarra Valley Old Boys football club.

Tip: One thing to consider before buying or renting here, is the suburb's history of bushfires. Major bushfires have swept through Warrandyte throughout history, and the town was at the centre of the Black Friday bushfires in 1939, in which 71 people lost their lives.

◼ HOUSING

Australians are proud to note that they have one of the highest levels of home-ownership in the world, with more than 67% of Australian households either mortgaged or owner-occupied, and 28% rented on the private market. Most Australians live in single-storey houses with a garden at both the front and the back of the house. Gardens are usually designed to take advantage of the weather and will generally have at least one shaded patio to create an external living area. Most will have a semi-detached lockable garage, or at the very least, a carport (covered hard-standing). A basic family home is expected to comprise three bedrooms, an open-plan living and dining area, fitted kitchen, at least one bathroom, and a separate laundry (including a large sink known as a trough, and fitted plumbing for a washing machine). Every home without exception (indeed, by law) will have a laundry, and it is unheard of to install a washing machine in a kitchen. Four-bedroom houses are also very common, but there are very few, if any, two-bedroom houses built nowadays. Every so often, in areas such as Darlinghurst in Sydney and Richmond in Melbourne, you will find loft conversions and studios for

Bunyip Day

The Black Friday Fires robbed Warrandyte of precious trees and wildlife. After the fire was over, a local man affectionately known as 'Homeless Harry', emerged from Whipstick Gully. He was adamant that he had, in fact, seen the infamous Warrandyte Bunyip. January 14, the day Harry sighted the Bunyip is now celebrated in Warrandyte as 'Bunyip Day'

Just as the Scots embrace Nessie (the Loch Ness Monster), Australians are brought up to believe in the mythical Bunyip (which has been sighted various times throughout Australian history). It has through the ages been depicted as a lake monster with flippers and walrus-like tusks and horns. Sometimes it has been described as pink in colour and lurking in billabongs, creeks and swamps.

compact city living. Older built Victorian terrace houses in the city centres will also still offer two–three-bedroom units.

Most houses are likely to have a family room (informal living area) in addition to the usual two reception rooms and will generally have two bathrooms, one of which is usually *en suite*. The focus of the bathroom is always the shower, which is never located over the bath (as most states have water restrictions in place at any given time). Australian showers come on hot and strong from the mains, and electric showers and booster pumps are not required; bathrooms are always tiled, thus a carpeted bathroom is a source of amusement to Australians visiting Britain. Kitchens always include a cooker (known as a stove) and fitted cupboards, which, in modern houses, will include a large pantry cupboard. Carpets, curtains and light fittings are always included in the price unless stated otherwise. Wooden floors are gaining popularity, as are renovating old warehouse spaces and turning them into units.

Many homes based in the suburbs of Australia have a swimming pool and these must be secured with childproof fences and gates. Local councils inspect swimming pools annually (via helicopter) to ensure that they comply with legal requirements in terms of safety and security, and regulations are strictly enforced: fences must be unclimbable and more than 5 feet (1.5m) in height, and pool gates must be locked and on a self-closing spring.

Pool cleaning equipment (vacuum, hoses, and leaf rake) should be included among the house fixtures and fittings. Most home pools are chlorinated, which means that you will need to add chemicals daily. Increasingly however, people are choosing either to install saltwater pools or to convert existing pools to saltwater technology. If you are lucky enough to have a saltwater pool you will only need to add salt once a year, and then leave the converter to do the rest. Saltwater pools also maintain a higher water temperature than chlorinated pools.

Australian houses are usually built either of double brick or of brick veneer (an external brick 'skin' over a timber-framed dwelling). Building regulations in Western Australia require double brick construction, however, in the eastern states, where the topography is more inclined towards earth movement as brick veneer is more structurally sound. Roofs are generally tiled with terracotta or, in cheaper construction, (indistinguishable) coloured cement tiles, but colour bonded steel sheeting is currently fashionable, mimicking the traditional Australian tin-roof. Most Australian homes are fitted with insulation in the roof space and, often in the walls. This insulation, made from fibreglass or wool fibre compacted to the size of a hay bale, helps to keep the house cool in summer and warm in winter. Most homes are fitted with fly-screens over the doors and windows, so that doors and windows can be left open without admitting insects.

Shady verandah – a must in summer

Property glossary

Duplex/ triplex	Property development in which two or three compact, single-storey houses in a unified architectural style are built on a large suburban block
Freehold	Most Australian houses and land are held on a freehold title
House	In Australia, a house is usually of the 'bungalow' type, i.e., it is likely to be single-storied, unless stated otherwise
Strata title	Flats, townhouses, villas, duplexes and triplexes are usually held on a strata title. Under this system a property owner owns absolutely all the space enclosed by the exterior walls of the property, as well as a pro-rata percentage share of all the communal space of the development in its entirety. Strata fees are payable quarterly to a 'body corporate', which is a democratically constituted management authority, and cover the maintenance of the fabric of the structure and communal garden areas
Terrace	A terraced house, with party walls on both sides. This type of housing is only found in old, inner-city areas and is often sought after for its 'character and charm'
Town house	A compact house of two or more stories in a small development. It will usually share one or more party walls with neighbouring townhouses
Unit	A term in common use to describe a flat or apartment. A unit can be located either in a high or low-rise development
Villa	A compact bungalow-style house in a small, unified development, usually with one or more party walls and a shared driveway

Finding rental accommodation

You have made your decision to emigrate, told your parents and friends and have booked your flights. Next step is finding somewhere to send your boxes of worldly possessions to; namely a home!

If you are visiting Australia before moving over, be sure to take down a note of any suburbs you like the look of and, in turn, keep your eyes peeled for any suitable estate agents you could contact.

Luckily, these days most estate agents (the top real estate agents in Australia are Professionals and Ray White) have their own websites, many with interactive virtual tours on them. These should provide you with a list of suitable properties, which you can arrange to either visit by appointment or view at 'open inspection' or 'open home'.

 Professionals real estate: www.professionals.com.au/
Ray White: www.raywhite.com/

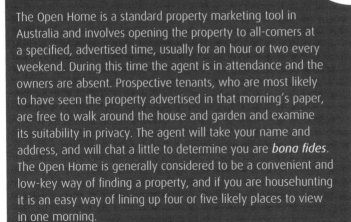

The Open Home

The Open Home is a standard property marketing tool in Australia and involves opening the property to all-comers at a specified, advertised time, usually for an hour or two every weekend. During this time the agent is in attendance and the owners are absent. Prospective tenants, who are most likely to have seen the property advertised in that morning's paper, are free to walk around the house and garden and examine its suitability in privacy. The agent will take your name and address, and will chat a little to determine you are *bona fides*. The Open Home is generally considered to be a convenient and low-key way of finding a property, and if you are househunting it is an easy way of lining up four or five likely places to view in one morning.

Online rental sites

 Online rental sites: www.online rental sites realestate.com.au
www.domain.com.au
www.rent-a-home.com.au

These sites are not exclusive to any one estate agent and can offer the most comprehensive way to monitor prices, availability and location. Most offer a registration service as well, so you can receive regular updates and advice. This may help nudge you to the front of the queue when your favourite property crops up.

 If you are thinking about sharing accommodation when you first arrive: check out www.gumtree.com.au

If you haven't found your dream apartment/house before moving out to Australia, you can walk in and see the real estate agent personally, and ask to see some of the properties either on their weekly printed list or pictured in their window. Unfortunately, their main concern will be reaping in the commission on property sales rather than rentals, so it may take a while. If this is the case, you can opt to rent a serviced apartment, hotel, apartment hotel (one which contains a kitchen and amenities) or stay temporarily in a hostel (the cheapest option).

Rental properties are advertised in the real estate supplements of all capital city newspapers, often on Wednesdays and Saturdays. If you have already decided in what suburb you'd like to be based, then you can also try the local papers, including weekly freesheets, which also carry extensive advertisements.

Australia's leading newspaper for real estate is *The Age* (www.theage.com.au) with the main days for rental property advertising being Saturday, Sunday and Wednesday.

The states of Australia, all have their own independent papers with real estate sections. In Victoria, for example, whether you are renting or buying, it is a good idea to subscribe to www.leadernewspapers. com.au. They produce weekly papers for each suburb. Ask them for a copy of all the local newspapers, or just the ones in the areas you are interested in (there is a

small charge for each newspaper if you purchase one, but if you live in an area, you will receive one free of charge). These local newspapers contain listings of many of the properties for lease and sale, and also give you the names and phone numbers of real estate agents in each area.

 To find newspapers in your state: www.yellowpages.com.au

Renting property

Australians have a strong home-owning ethos. Most people prefer not to rent if at all possible, but many have no choice as they stay in their current rentals to save for the deposit on their house.

Rented housing in Australia is still relatively less expensive than in Europe, and both tenant and landlord rights are well protected. Among other things, tenancies are always covered by leases and there is no indefinite security of tenure. Renting out a property is not a risky venture for a landlord, who can easily have unsuitable tenants evicted, so people are very willing to place their investment properties and homes on the rental market. Changes in taxation law have meant that it is no longer as financially advantageous as it once was to buy property for the purposes of renting it out, and as a result the amount of property available to rent has declined, with a concomitant rise in rentals.

The Australian Institute's 2007 *Real Estate Market Outlook* report, published in January 2007, states that:

'The average weekly rental for a two to three bedroom house in Melbourne, which is generally considered an expensive city in terms of property prices, is A$380 per week (for a two–three-bedroom property), clearly far less than in most major European cities. This a state average. Places that are more desirable and close to the city can cost more than A$600 a week.'

> 'The proportion of rental properties that were vacant had fallen to a relatively low level last year, and rents nationwide rose by an average 9.8% in the year to September.'

Rents are not subject to state control in Australia, but are set by the lease agreement signed by both tenant and landlord. Usually, such an agreement will set the rent for a six-month period, with a reassessment at the end of the lease period. In some states residential rents may be controlled, but only on properties which were tenanted before changes in the law. The Federal Discrimination Act prohibits discrimination by landlords against prospective tenants, and it is illegal to refuse a tenant on the grounds of sex or marital status, pregnancy, or ethnic origin. If you suspect that a landlord or agent has made an illegal refusal of your application to rent his or her property, you should contact the nearest Office of Consumer Affairs, which will be able to advise you further. In general, however, landlords are interested in having their property occupied by rent-paying tenants, and you are unlikely to have your application for tenancy turned down if you can provide good references and evidence of sufficient financial means.

Properties for rent are advertised in the 'To Let' section of the property pages in city and state newspapers and in weekly, free community newspapers. Real estate agents also usually have a specialist property management division, which will also have listings of available properties, and you can approach agents directly in the areas in which you hope to find accommodation.

 To find your nearest office of consumer affairs: www.consumersonline.gov.au

Tenancy agreements

Very short-term rented accommodation can be difficult to find in Australia as most property owners will only accept tenants prepared to sign a tenancy agreement valid for six months. It is occasionally possible to find an owner who is prepared to make a short-term lease available, and in such cases the lease may later be extended by private agreement, allowing you to remain on a weekly or monthly basis after the expiry of the lease. Although this can be convenient for travellers, it does not give much security to longer-term visitors, and you will need to be willing to move at short notice should the owner decide to make other arrangements. In general, a first lease is given for six months and can be extended, provided that you and the owner both agree to any change of conditions, including a rent rise (most landlords do not automatically raise the rent every six months). Properties are almost invariably let unfurnished, but will include a cooker and, often, a fridge. Lease agreements in Australia usually conform to a standard format, and the contract can be purchased for a couple of dollars at any newsagent. They are simple to understand and offer fair and equal protection to both landlord and tenant. The underlying assumption in Australian rent law, however, is that the property belongs to the landlord, who has greater rights in terms of protecting and enjoying the benefits of his or her investment. There is, therefore, no concept of the 'sitting tenant' or of 'squatting', and unruly, destructive or non-paying tenants can be swiftly and effectively evicted.

Letting agents or property owners generally require tenants to pay a bond or deposit of four weeks rental, in addition to a month's rent in advance. The bond can sometimes be as much as six weeks' rent, and owners may occasionally ask for up to two months' rent in advance. You should, therefore, allow for several thousand dollars to establish yourself in a rented property. This bond will be held by a third party, so its release will be fair to both the landlord and tenant. The bond cannot have amounts subtracted from it by the landlord until he has proven the damage/wear to the third party. The bond can be entirely or partly forfeited if the tenant defaults on payment or conditions of the lease. If you leave the premises and any provided furniture and fittings in a good condition, allowing for reasonable wear and tear, your landlord will refund your bond at the end of your tenancy.

Most landlords will provide an inventory of the property, and this will detail the condition of the house at the start of the lease (it might list, for example, existing scuff marks or cigarette burns). You should read and assess this inventory before you sign your lease, as signing will imply your agreement with its contents. The property will be inspected at the end of your lease, and may be inspected at any time during the period of the tenancy, providing the owner or agent gives 48 hours' notice of their intention to enter. They must, however, by law, have good cause to affect entry, for example, if neighbours report obvious signs of neglect; and you have the right to be present during any inspection. End-of-lease inspections are usually very thorough indeed: expect to have extractor fan covers removed and inspected for dirt and grease, pictures moved, and carpets lifted. You will need to seek permission under the terms of a standard lease to effect any change to the fabric of the property, even if it is just to put up a picture hook.

The owner of a rented property is responsible for all council and water rates, as well as strata and management fees, but the tenant pays costs for all utilities such as electricity, gas and telephone.

Rental costs

In Australia there is very little 'social housing' of the type provided by councils and district authorities in Europe. For example the United Kingdom has brought in procedures that delegate 20% of all new housing complexes to include affordable housing to key workers.

Traditionally, the 'Great Australian Dream' has meant that even in the lowest socioeconomic groups there has been a high expectation of home ownership, and accordingly, that to be housed by the state 'Housing Commission' has been an object of shame. In addition, rent laws, as outlined above, have kept the private rental sector competitive and stable, so that few people have needed to fall back on the state to provide them with accommodation. Most commonly, state housing is available to socially marginalised groups, such as Aborigines and refugees. The criterion

Simon Bloom found that accommodation can be difficult to find, and expensive in major cities:

'It can be tricky to rent. I'm fortunate that I've been renting the same place for four years. There are a lot of people competing for rental property. A decent place will be upwards of A$500 per week. Buying is probably easier but the majority of properties are sold at auction so you never know how much it'll sell for. House prices are pretty steep in Melbourne. In a reasonable/nice location a two bedroom apartment will start at A$450,000'.

for eligibility is that the applicant must demonstrate an inability to secure decent accommodation in the private sector at a rent, which is in their capacity to pay. However, given that rent assistance for private tenants, whether unemployed or on a low income, is available from Centrelink (the Government agency responsible for social security payments), there are very few people to whom this might apply.

In the private sector, there is almost always a good variety of properties available to rent, although this is becoming harder in sought after places such as the Sydney Eastern Suburbs and parts of Melbourne and Perth. The current economic climate has seen many first-time buyers remaining in their rentals instead of purchasing, thus congesting the rentals market.

 Guide to current weekly rentals:
www.realestate.com.au
www.theprofessionals.com.au
www.domain.com.au

Local references and credit history

When you finally decide on the right property, you will be asked to fill out an application form and a lease. So you don't miss out on the apartment/house it is wise to take these documents with you:

- driving licence
- passport number
- business reference
- employer reference
- personal reference
- rental and/or sales reference (if you have never rented but have sold a property, the selling agent is also a good reference).

Some agents will ask for written references, but in most cases you will just need to supply contact telephone numbers and names of the relevant people.

If you don't have local references, you may encounter a few problems. Ensure that your new employer (if you are walking straight into a job) writes you a reference immediately and try and set up a bank account from your home town before heading off (see page 74 on banking).

The last alternative might be that you have to pay up to six months of rent up front.

Local taxes

Council rates are levied annually and are the responsibility of the property owner. They are a tax on property and not on the individual. Tenants do not have to meet any council rates charges, which include a refuse charge for the collection of domestic rubbish, and charges for amenities provided by the council. Council rates are determined by the location and size of

FACT

It is a legal requirement for a house to have a laundry room separate from the kitchen in Australia.

the property, and are calculated by the Valuer-General on its gross rental value. Property valuations are made approximately every two years. Rates will be higher if you buy a house in a high demand area with excellent services and amenities. For an average, middle-class Australian suburban family home, you can expect a general rates charge of around A$650 per quarter, as well as an additional levy for refuse collection.

Rates and charges are payable to the local or shire council. A discount is sometimes given for prompt payment, but more often prompt payers are rewarded by entry into a council draw which will offer a substantial prize, such as an international holiday or free rates for a year. Details of the council raffle will be published in the local newspaper in addition to being supplied with the rates notice.

Hazards. Apart from the climate, and bushfires, the greatest threat to buildings with structural timbers is white ants (termites).

■ BUYING PROPERTY

Buying a home or land

Properties and vacant land are advertised for sale in the Real Estate supplements of all capital city newspapers, often on Wednesdays and Saturdays. Most local papers, including weekly freesheets, also carry extensive advertisements and are a good place to start if you have decided on a particular area. Government or 'Crown' land is also occasionally advertised for sale, especially in outer suburban areas undergoing new development. If you are interested in building a new home at an economical cost (that is, *not* by subcontracting your own architect and builder), you should look at the newspaper section headed 'Display Homes' or 'Project Homes'. A

A typical real estate office in Australia has lots of ads in the windows

project home is an off-the-peg architectural design offered by a builder and built especially for you, either on your own land, or on land supplied by the builder and offered as part of a package. Once you have selected a suitable design, you are free to customise it to a certain extent, choosing internal finishes, bricks, tiles, and landscaping. Many people choose to have the ceiling heights raised in project homes (they are usually designed to the legal minimum of eight courses of brickwork), and this will add a few thousand dollars per course to the cost of the design. Project homes are an extremely popular choice in Australia, and rather than simply buying a new home in a development, most people prefer this more individual option. A project home package for a home comprising four bedrooms, two bathrooms, and two or three reception rooms, including plans, building and land, in an outer suburban area of Brisbane can cost as little as A$110,000. If you choose to build on your own land, your new home can be built for around A$70,000. Examples of builders' project homes, known as 'display homes', can be viewed at various 'display villages', the locations of which are advertised alongside the relevant floor plans. Over 30% of houses are sold at auction in the most sought-after areas.

■ Real estate and house prices in Adelaide from the July 2006 to September 2006 have grown by an average of 0.6%. Housing prices in Adelaide from September 2005 to September 2006 have grown by an average of 6.4%. Average price A$350,000.

Guidance prices:
www.realestate.com.au
www.domain.com.au

Average cost of housing

The average (three–four-bedroom) house price in Melbourne is A$420,000, compared to A$560,000 in Sydney and A$380,000 in Brisbane. Prices in Melbourne and Sydney continue to increase and Perth has recently had a leap in the property market, due to the recent commodities boom. This has taken Australian real estate by surprise, as until fairly recently, Perth housing was comparatively cheaper than the Eastern States. Perth is now second only to Sydney in housing costs and continues to grow. The site www.homepriceguide.com.au, recently stated that Perth's median house price for the June 2006 quarter was A$455,000.

If you are moving to the Australian Capital Territory (ACT), you should note that there is no freehold land available in Canberra. Instead, the Commonwealth Government grants 99-year leases on blocks of land for residential purposes, and these are released for sale to keep pace with demand. All residential land is sold at public auction, and unsold sites are available after auction at the Land Sales Office. Reserve prices are set at 80% of the assessed market value. Leaseholders are obliged to commence construction in 12 months and to complete construction in 24 months. All land released for sale under this system is within 19 miles (30km) of the city centre, and all sites are fully serviced, with social amenities added as the suburb develops.

Finance

FACT

■ *Mortgages.* Almost half the home loans in Australia are arranged through a broker.

The home loan market in Australia has been highly competitive in recent years with a number of new players entering the fray and a myriad of options available. Having negotiated the maze, however, borrowers can enjoy exceptional value for money in their choice of investment. Non-bank lenders are now offering more flexible features, including the option to redraw on extra payments, and loans are being offered at competitive rates by established banks, credit unions, building societies, and new-style mortgage originators. Lenders will consider loans of up to 95% of the property value, and mortgage eligibility is calculated on a formula based on the income level of the applicant, or of the applicant and partner in combination (usually three times one salary or two and a half times both salaries). There are an increasing number of lenders offering no-deposit home loan packages to encourage potential buyers into the market, including builders who will supply no-deposit finance for buyers to purchase their project homes. Usually such offers will have hidden (or not-so-hidden) costs – such as higher interest rates.

Application or establishment fees are charged by both banks and other lenders to cover the cost of setting up a loan agreement, including legal and valuation fees, and disbursements such as mortgage registration and stamp duty. The amount of these initial fees varies widely between lenders: some simply pass on their costs, others absorb them (a no-fees mortgage), while some of the bigger players, who have less to fear from competition, may charge as much as A$900.

Lending terms and conditions can vary considerably between lenders, and as of January 2008, Australia's eight major lenders (along with many others) shifted their standard variable rates and they are now no longer set at a state average. With the Royal Bank of Australia's announcement of further rate rises in March 2008, standard variable rates among the major banks and lenders are now: AMP Banking 9.32%; ANZ 9.37%; CBA 9.32%; Homeside (NAB) 9.27%; St George 9.37% Suncorp 9.32%; Westpac 9.27%. For individual lender comparison rates, you will need to either check with the relevant lender or discuss with your individual mortgage broker.

This is a massive increase, as in late 2004 the interest rate stood at around 5.38% per annum for standard variable home loans. The maximum term for a standard home loan is 25 years, with a few lenders offering 30-year terms, depending on the age of the applicant. Fixed loans are popular as they provide security against interest rate rises, and such loans are now more flexible than they have been, with lenders offering the facility of extra repayments without penalty.

Pros and cons of lending with standard variable rates

Pros
- If interest rates drop, repayments might drop.
- Generally, additional or extra payments reducing the principle can be made without penalty, allowing the home loan to be paid off faster.
- Additional repayments can usually be taken back by you.
- This product is flexible and often has more features.

Cons
- If interest rates rise, repayments might rise along with the amount of interest paid. The borrower is then required to make larger repayments.
- These generally attract a higher interest rate than basic home loans.

Australia's four largest banks are the Commonwealth, the ANZ, Westpac, and the National Australia Bank. All offer mortgage products and applications for a home loan can be lodged at any branch. Increasingly, suburban branches operate as little more than shop-fronts, with management and lending decisions taken at head office, so you need not necessarily approach your own branch for information. The Commonwealth Bank and the ANZ both have excellent websites, which describe their full range of products, and by entering your details online, you can receive an instant assessment of your eligibility for a mortgage.

Commonwealth Bank (from UK): www.migrantbanking.co.uk
Commonwealth Bank (from Australia): www.commbank.com.au
ANZ: www.anz.com.au

Non-bank lenders are playing an increasingly important role in the mortgage market and are known as mortgage originators or mortgage managers. Such lenders, who include insurance companies and credit unions, act as intermediaries between borrowers and larger institutions. These big institutions are the real lenders behind mortgage originator loans, and are usually organisations that do not wish to participate in the market directly. Other funds are obtained from securitisers, who raise funds on the financial markets and then redistribute them to originators. Industry standards require that independent trustees oversee originators and the loan monies that they collect to protect the interests of the borrower. Aussie Home Loans is the most aggressive of the mortgage originators and advertises extensively on radio and in newspapers.

Aussie Home Loans: www.eaussie.com.au
Macquarie Mortgages www.macquarie.com.au
Aussie Mortgage Masters: www.beatthebanks.com.au
AMP Home Loans: www.amp.com.au

Mortgage brokers

In such a complex environment, borrowers are increasingly seeking the services of mortgage brokers, who are able to source the most suitable and least expensive loan for your needs. A good broker will be able to find you the best loan, explain it in detail, help complete the loan documents, and guide the application through to acceptance. Brokers make their money on commission from the lender, and there are no fees charged to the borrower. Almost half the home loans in Western Australia are now written by brokers and the trend is steadily increasing in the eastern states. Mortgage brokers advertise widely in the press and Yellow Pages, and some of the franchise real estate chains, such as Ray White Real Estate and LJ Hooker also offer broking services. 1st Australian Mortgage is an independent mortgage broker, associated with a national network of mortgage lenders and claim to be able to provide you with the finance that suits best depending on your needs.

Ray White Real Estate: www.raywhite.com.au
LJ Hooker: www.ljhooker.com.au
1st Australian Mortgage: www.1stam.com.au

Useful resources
Australian and New Zealand Bank (ANZ): 020 7378 2121; www.anz.com
Commonwealth Bank of Australia: Financial and Migrant Information Service, 020 7710 3999; www.migrantbanking.co.uk
Westpac Banking Corporation: 020 7621 7000; www.westpac.com.au

Purchasing

Every state in Australia has its own laws pertaining to real estate transactions, and its own licensing laws for real estate agents. In general, you should expect your real estate agent to hold certification from the appropriate state government authority, and preferably, that they or their agency should be a member of the Real Estate Institute of Australia (REIA) or state-affiliated branch. If your agent is a member of the REIA or its affiliates, such as REIWA (the Real Estate Institute of Western Australia), you will be protected in the case of any malpractice. Estate agents who are the Principals (proprietors) of an agency must be certified at a higher level, and any agent intending to conduct a sale by auction must hold a separate licence to do so.

There are five types of fees for which you must budget for when purchasing a property in Australia:

- **Solicitors'/Settlement Agents' Professional Fees.** These are fees charged by a solicitor or settlement agent for conducting the legal business of the purchase on your behalf.
- **Search Fees and Outlays.** These fees cover the cost of the searches undertaken to ensure that the property is free from encumbrances.
- **Stamp Duty.** Stamp duty is a state government tax on the purchase price of the property. It is calculated as a percentage of the value of the transaction, and is affected by the area of land purchased and whether the purchasers intend to reside in the property. Concessions apply in some states (for example, Queensland) to first time buyers who will reside in the property. Stamp duty varies considerably and is calculated on *ad valorem*, nominal or concessional rates of duty depending on the state or territory.
- **Registration Fees.** Fees are charged by the state department of land management or natural resources to effect the registration of transfer of ownership and related mortgage documents.

■ **Lender Fees.** It is common practice for lenders to charge administration fees for setting up a mortgage. As the home loan market becomes increasingly competitive, however, such fees (which can be as high as A$900) have become more negotiable, and can be avoided completely if you shop around.

Settlement

The process of exchanging contracts to complete a property transaction is known in Australia as 'settlement'. Settlement is a far easier process in Australia than the UK and the concept of the 'chain' does not exist. Once a vendor agrees to an offer on a property, a contract is signed stipulating a date for settlement, which will usually be 30–90 days from the date of offer. During this period, the purchaser arranges finance and completes all the legal formalities. Settlement **must** take place on the nominated date, and if it cannot, the party at fault becomes liable for the payment of penalty interest.

Conveyancing

The conveyancing market has been deregulated in recent years and is no longer the exclusive province of solicitors. Most people now turn to specialist 'settlement agents' instead, who are trained in conveyancing and property law, but who are not lawyers. Settlement agents' fees are almost always much lower than those charged by solicitors for an identical service, and are generally in the region of A$500–A$1,100, depending on the value of the property and the state in which you reside. In South Australia the legal legwork on most property transactions is handled by a land broker. It is possible to do your own conveyancing, but it is not recommended: the risk of steep penalty interest payments in the case of delay through error or lack of expertise can outweigh the saving of a few hundred dollars.

Buying without residency status

If you have not been granted permanent residency in Australia, any residential property purchase will require the prior approval of the Foreign Investment Review Board. Generally speaking, the Board will *not* approve the purchase of second-hand residential real estate by non-residents; however, if you are a temporary resident wanting to acquire a home for your stay in Australia, you may be granted foreign investment approval, subject to meeting certain conditions. If you are an overseas investor hoping to buy a holiday home or invest in residential real estate in Australia, you should seek advice from the Foreign Investment Review Board. Additionally you could obtain advice from a solicitor specialising in Australian property law.

 Foreign Investment Review Board: 02 6263 3795 ; firb@treasury.gov.au ; www.firb.gov.au

Real estate agencies

Most people buy and sell their property with the services of a local real estate agent, and few owners market their own properties. Agents act on behalf of the vendor and not the purchaser, and their responsibilities include advertising and contract negotiation to obtain the best possible price for their client (who, you should always bear in mind when you are buying, is *not* you). Homes for sale will be advertised in the local press, and the larger statewide newspapers will generally publish a property section at the weekend (often on Saturday). In addition, most agents will have extensive photo displays in their office window. The distribution of detailed description sheets giving measurements of each room, location of power points and other features is not an Australian practice, although top-of-the-range homes are often marketed through glossy, descriptive brochures. Instead, when you approach an agent about a property, you can expect to be told only the price (or, increasingly, an acceptable price range), the number and types of rooms and any other facilities, swimming pool, reticulation, and air conditioning. If the property is still of interest, the agent will arrange to accompany you on a private inspection, or you may be asked to attend the next 'Open Home' (see page 135).

Listing a property with an estate agent

There are three different methods of listing a property with an estate agent, and you will often see one of the following terms somewhere in an advertisement:

Converted warehouses are popular within the central areas of Melbourne and Sydney

- **Sole/Exclusive Agency.** This means that the property is being offered by one agent only, and can be viewed only by contacting the specified office. Advertisements for sole agency properties will carry the name of the particular agent (for example, Mike Jones of Smith White Realty) who has obtained the listing. All contact and requests for information must be directed to the named agent.

- **Open Listing.** Under an 'open listing', any number of agencies can offer the property to buyers. This method is common in some states (Queensland) and unusual in others. In some states (e.g. Western Australia) it is common for more downmarket properties or areas, and unusual at the middle and upper end of the market. It is not generally considered to be an effective way to sell, as there is no single agent with a keen incentive to make the sale.

- **Multilisting.** Multilisting is very similar to the American 'Multiple Listing Service' (MLS), and means that a property is listed by a number of specified agencies. Multilisting is the least common method of marketing a property.

If you are looking for a property to buy, you can approach an agent to act on your behalf in the search. The agent will then obtain lists of all the properties for sale in your price range and desired area, and will arrange for you to view them. There is no fee to the purchaser for this service; it can be a good way for a newcomer to find a suitable property, as the agent will have detailed local knowledge about shops, schools and amenities, which you may lack. Your agent makes his or her money, once you decide on a property, by negotiating a conjunctional sale: the vendor's agent splits the sale commission 50/50 with the introducing agent. Conjunctional sales apply to properties marketed under sole agency as well as by other methods, and there are very few agents who will refuse to conjunct.

> Real estate agents:
> www.professionals.com.au (Australia-wide real estate)
> www.professionalsnewfarm.com.au (Brisbane property)
> www.primelocation.com.au (Australia wide)
> www.domain.com.au
> www.realestate.com.au
> www.ljhooker.com.au

Buying at auction

Many Australian properties at every level of the market are sold by auction. Auctions, and attitudes to sale by auction, vary from state to state. Some franchise groups push vendors to sell by auction, but they are not universally popular: some agents consider them to be most suitable for distress sales (in which case, they can result in bargains), while others use them only in a competitive, rising market (in which case, you can end up paying too much). Vendors who sell by auction are responsible for the advertising costs of the agent.

Buying at auction can be an intimidating experience, and it is advisable to attend a few as a kind of 'dry run', to get the feel for what you will be up against. In some states, auctions are conducted in the front garden of the property for sale, so it is easy to wander up and listen. In other states they are usually held in auction rooms.

Success at auction depends on doing your homework:

- Know your financial limits by visiting your bank manager beforehand, and *never* bid above that limit, no matter how persuasive the auctioneer's patter
- Know the market, so that you have a clear idea of the true worth of the property; shop around, comparing prices of similar houses. Once you have identified the house you want, spend several weeks before the auction date visiting other auctions in the area to evaluate the level of bidding
- Make prior enquiries about the contract, establishing what the property includes, and making sure it is free from any important defects. Examine the building report and pest certificates, and ascertain the level of deposit that will be required in cash on the fall of the hammer (it is likely to be 10%)

> **Here are some valued tips on succeeding at auctions, from one of Australia's leading property auctioneer experts, Paul Liddy (The Professionals, New Farm, QLD):**
>
> 'The Auction Process is widely supported as an effective method of sale of property in all states of Australia, particularly along the eastern seaboard, although the legislation that applies varies in each. Primarily, bidders need to be aware that buying at auction requires the winning bidder to sign an unconditional contract, usually 30–90 days long, and pay a deposit forthwith. This deposit has traditionally been 10% of the bidding price, however is some states and circumstances a lower deposit can be negotiated through the agent, before the Auction begins.
>
> If considering buying at auction any prudent purchaser would be well advised to do their research with regards to comparable recent sales, and set themselves a limit before getting carried away in the excitement of the event. While the legislation varies, there is no 'Cooling Off' period associated with Auction sales so, particularly with older and timber homes it is well worth considering commissioning a Pest and Building inspection of the property before the Auction Day.'

On auction day, you should check the contracts again, to ensure that no changes have been made. Arrive early, and have a last look around if possible. At this point you should introduce yourself to the auctioneer and let them know that you are interested in buying. Sit in easy view of the auctioneer, preferably near the front or at the sides, where you can observe competing bidders. The auctioneer will then commence the patter and ask if there are any questions: bidders who play tough like to take this opportunity to unsettle the opposition by fielding queries about six-lane highways or high-rise tower blocks. Try and ignore such strategies and bid with confidence; bidding low and often is the approach recommended by experienced agents. Properties are always auctioned with an undisclosed reserve price, and if it is eventually passed in, you will be able to try and negotiate privately after the auction. Auctioneers also have to state when the reserve is reached.

Finally, some agents advise that if you really want the house, you could try making an offer in advance: the vendor may be as nervous as you are, and only too glad to tie it up without going through with the whole ordeal.

Contracts

Most property sales are concluded through the exchange of a simple standard contract issued by the state Real Estate Institute. This contract will specify the sale price and deposit (notionally 10%, but in practice, highly negotiable), the date of settlement, and the fixtures and fittings to be included in the sale. You should note that it is expected that fixtures and fittings will be included in a sale and, if you are selling, you will be in breach of contract if you so much as remove a light bulb without specifying your intentions. Cookers and dishwashers are considered fixtures and must remain in the property. The contract will also require that all appliances are in good working order, and this includes external appliances such as swimming pool filters, air conditioning, and ducted vacuum systems. At the time of making an offer, conditions are usually appended to the standard contract, and the failure of either party to meet the stated conditions will invalidate the sale.

Usually a contract is signed subject to two main conditions: firstly, that the purchaser provide proof of mortgage finance or cash resources in 48 hours; and secondly, that the vendor provide a current white ant certificate in one week. White ants are a type of termite, which can cause havoc with a building's structural timbers; they are a serious concern and their control is monitored by law. A white ant inspection certificate ensures that your property is free from infestation or, if white ants have been found, that they have been destroyed by chemical treatment. Evidence of previous, treated white ant infestation is not an impediment to the sale of a property. A white ant inspection certificate costs around A$250 and this cost is borne by the vendor. If these conditions and any others particular to your property are met, the contract becomes binding. Should you change your mind for any reason, you will forfeit your deposit. Similarly, should the vendor break the contract, your deposit will be refunded plus the same amount again as a penalty payment.

Useful resources

Foreign Investment Review Board: 02 6263 3795;
firb@treasury.gov.au; www.firb.gov.au
LJHooker is one of Australia's largest real estate groups with offices throughout the country. Their customer service centre (1800 621 212) will be able to recommend an office in your intended area as well as provide local information. They also have an excellent website at www.ljhooker.com.au which provides useful advice on all aspects of buying and selling, and online property information.
Realestate.com.au: 03 9897 1121 (1300 134 174); email propertycustomers@realestate.com.au; www.realestate.com.au.
Reale state.com.au, exclusively endorsed by the Real Estate Institute of New South Wales (REINSW) and the Real Estate Institute of Tasmania (REIT), provides a medium for real estate agents to advertise their listings and for potential buyers to search for properties.

Street art is common in the major Australian cities

Consyl Publishing Ltd: (UK) 01424 223111; www.consylpublishing.co.uk, distributes the Australian magazines, *Real Estate Weekly* and *The Homebuyer*, which contain illustrated for-sale advertisements for property around Australia.

■ CONNECTING UTILITIES

Electricity, gas and water supplies are controlled throughout Australia by regional state authorities and costs vary to some extent between states, and between urban and rural areas. Remote outback areas may attract particularly high charges, especially for water.

When you first move in, it is your responsibility to connect all the services to the premises, such as the water, gas and electricity. For all connection details concerning these utilities, see the following chapter.

If you would like a telephone line you will need to arrange for this to be connected and pay the relevant connection fee. Telstra, Virgin and Optus are Australia's main phone and internet providers. Contact them on either the phone number or web addresses on page 162, or simply go in person to one of their many shops, located in most large shopping malls. You will need ID, such as your passport, and current bank/utility bills with your address. They will charge you an installation fee and talk you through the various monthly price plans.

Electricity and gas

Most new homes in Australia are connected to both gas and electricity supplies. Australia's plentiful supplies of natural gas mean that this energy source is relatively cheap, and savings are passed on to domestic consumers; thus most people choose to use gas in preference to electricity wherever possible. Many older homes, however, are not connected to the gas supply, and although this can easily be arranged by contacting the local state gas authority, it is likely to cost several hundred dollars for the service to be installed. Some remote areas do not have a natural gas supply, and in these regions, LPG (liquid petroleum gas) is commonly used, obtained in bottled form, usually from the local garage.

Energy companies

Australian Gas Limited: www.agl.com.au

Origin Energy: 13 24 63; www.originenergy.com.au/movers

Energy Australia: 13 15 35 www.energy.com.au

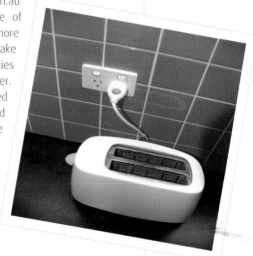

Electricity is the most important source of domestic energy, but is considerably more expensive than gas. In an effort to make electricity more competitive, state authorities such as Western Power (www.westernpower.com.au), in Western Australia, have introduced 'SmartPower'. SmartPower is a demand management system which relates the price paid for electricity to the cost of producing it, which is greater at times of peak demand. To take advantage of this system, a SmartPower Meter must be installed. Prices range from A$200 to A$600, depending on what type of meter you need and whether you are in an existing property or a new build.

 SmartPower Meter: 13 13 53 www.synergyenergy.com.au

The Smart Meter records the amount of electricity used in your home during different charging periods, enabling you to monitor your appliance usage and thus shift the times you run your appliances (washing machines and swimming pool filters, for example) to lower your electricity costs. In general, a family with a swimming pool will recoup the cost of the Smart Meter in a short time, and will make ongoing savings of at least 30% on their previous power bills.

The voltage in Australia is 240/250V and the current is alternating at 50 Hz. The power points take three-pin plugs, which have two diagonally slanting pins above one straight pin. Appliances brought from the UK will work throughout Australia, after changing the plugs, but those brought from the USA will not.

 To connect a supplier:
Energy Australia: www.energy.com.au (read the meter before you contact them)
Integral Energy: www.integral.com.au
Or look in www.yellowpages.com.au for electricity suppliers

Solar Power

Australia is a world leader in solar technology, and Australian homes first began using solar power back in 1953. Today, many homes in areas with enough sunshine use solar power to heat water. A solar hot water heater provides around 95% of hot water energy needs (for washing and home heating) free of charge from the sun, resulting in enormous savings on traditional energy costs. The capital cost of a solar hot water heater is high, but once installed they are maintenance-free and have a very long lifetime, so that the initial high cost is soon outweighed by the benefits. A solar hot water system looks like a large, flat, black rectangle, with a cylinder at the top; it is installed on the roof, usually on the western side of the house where it will receive the most sun, and is aesthetically unobtrusive.

 Solar hot water systems: www.solahart.com.au.

Domestic climate control

Australian homes are very seldom centrally heated, except in those few areas where the climate is sufficiently cold to require it. Instead, most homes are heated on a fairly *ad hoc* basis, usually by a combination of portable electric fan heaters or radiators, reverse-cycle air conditioning, and slow combustion stoves. Pot-belly stoves or other solid fuel enclosed fires are becoming increasingly popular as a means of heating the main living areas of the home, and can even be installed so that they heat the water supply as well. Coal fires are banned by law, and coal-substitute fires are extremely unusual; open fires and slow combustion stoves are wood-fuelled, though in Adelaide mallee roots (very dense knots of gnarled wood which do not need chopping), which can be bought by the tonne, dominate the fuel market. Wood suppliers (who are often farmers clearing their fields) advertise in the classifieds columns of local newspapers.

Only about 50% of residents using firewood for heating actually buy their wood, and thousands of Australians (most of them in metropolitan areas) collect their wood from roadsides, stock routes, private property and reserves. Of the six million tonnes of wood consumed in Australia each year, two-thirds is used for domestic heating. However, the extent to which most people warm themselves in the Australian winter is via the trusty electric blanket (a toasty blanket which contains electric coils and is placed under your sheets and controlled via a switch).

Home cooling rather than heating is the focus of most Australian climate control, and almost every home will have some method of lowering the internal temperature. Electric ceiling fans are popular and very effective, as well as being cheap to install and to run. There are several different types of air-conditioning in common use: the evaporative type is the cheapest and is generally portable, but requires an open window to work effectively; reverse-cycle is more effective, and can also be used to heat the room in winter. The unit for reverse-cycle air-conditioning is installed in an external wall. Homes in the upper end of the market will often have ducted air-conditioning, which is run from a central plant in the roof or garage, distributing cold air through vents to every room. Air-conditioning is essential in the northern regions of Australia, both in the home and the car, and all offices and shops throughout Australia are air-conditioned.

Keeping cool on the cheap

Australian architects are very aware of the need to design for the climate and new houses will, for example, have few or very small windows on the hot, western side. Large windows and patio doors will always be shaded by a pergola, often covered with ultraviolet-resistant plastic. Solar films, which allow in light but not heat, can be applied to windows, and are a cost effective way of keeping homes cool. Climate management in Australia is second nature to locals, but methods may surprise those brought up in a cooler climate. The British response to the sun is to throw open all the windows and enjoy; in Australia, this would be considered eccentric, if not completely mad.

If you want to keep your home cooling costs down in summer, you should do as the locals do:

- At sunrise, get up and close every single window in the house. Pull down all blinds and close all curtains; if there are awnings or shutters on outside windows, pull them into place. Close any vent that allows the entry of external air.
- When entering and leaving your home during the day, make sure that any door is open for as brief a time as possible. The aim at all times should be to prevent the hot external air from coming inside.

- When the exterior temperature drops below the interior temperature (usually at sunset), it is time to open up. Throw open everything that has been closed; windows and doors will have lockable screens which will allow you to do this in safety. Leave everything open all night, to allow the house to cool down before the next day's onslaught.
- On really extreme days, try 'hosing down' (but not if there are water restrictions in operation). This method involves soaking the exterior walls and patio areas with water from the garden hose, and should be done after dark to avoid instant evaporation.

Water

Water is a scarce and valuable commodity in Australia, and is treated with respect by most people. All urban areas are well served by high quality, clean water supplies from reservoirs, but extreme summer conditions and drought can mean the frequent imposition of water restrictions on non-essential water use. Most states often impose such bans and can often mean that in the peak of summer, residents may only have one shower a day, refrain from watering their garden or washing their car and have to limit their washing of clothes. For example, January and February of 2008 were the wettest summer months known to Queensland in over 150 years, yet the government decided not to lift the restrictions, so they would have enough water in their reservoirs to last the year. Public education campaigns encourage water-saving measures, such as shorter showers (the Queensland government recently sent residents stick-on shower egg timers set for four minutes, so that they could monitor their shower times) and water recycling (using washing-up water on the garden, for example). Garden watering is generally done after dusk to avoid evaporation.

Water is supplied to homes and businesses by state authorities who build and maintain reservoirs, and ensure the safety and management of the water supply. Water provision charges are imposed to fund these services and are paid annually or quarterly by consumers. Water and sewerage service charges apply to every connected residential property, along with a metered water usage charge, currently 74 cents per kilolitre (1,000 litres) in Melbourne and 97 cents per kilolitre in Sydney. A sewerage disposal charge is also levied and takes into account seasonal factors affecting water usage. Other charges may be applied depending on the state water authority, for example, in Melbourne a Parks Charge and a Water Drainage Charge is levied on all rateable properties. Depending on your circumstances, rebates and concessions on water charges may be available and families suffering financial hardship can apply to make payments under pre-payment budget schemes.

High water charges mean that it is expensive to keep domestic gardens green during the summer months using mains water. Many Australian homes, therefore, have irrigation/sprinkler systems, known as 'reticulation', which water the garden automatically from a private artesian bore. Homeowners frequently pay to have a bore sunk in their garden, sometimes to a depth of up to 492 feet (150m), to tap into the water table. The cost of the bore can be very high (around A$4,500) and is determined by its depth and the geographical structure of the land. However, in the long term, a bore enables enormous savings on water bills. Bore water can only be used for gardening, as it is unsuitable for drinking and its high mineral content means that it will stain swimming pool surfaces. During periods of water restriction, bore owners are the only people who are able to water their gardens sufficiently to maintain them. All mains garden watering must be done before dawn or after dusk to reduce wastage due to evaporation and even homes with bore reticulation usually follow this method to avoid scorching leaves and grass.

Most new Australian gardens have moved away from the traditional British garden towards gardens in which native Australian plants predominate. Native plants have adapted to dry conditions over the millennia and require very little water to stay alive; their cultivation also encourages native bird life. Wood chips and extensive patio areas are also popular, reducing the area of garden devoted to lawn, which is expensive and time-consuming to maintain in Australia.

In rural areas, domestic rainwater tanks are frequently used to collect precipitation for drinking, washing, and gardening. If your home or holiday cottage has a rainwater tank, make sure that it has a cover to prevent rodents and native marsupials drowning in it and contaminating the water.

Australian mains water is completely safe, and the taste is generally good. In most areas the supply is fluoridated to promote dental health. Unlike the water supply in most British areas, Australian water is 'soft', that is, it does not contain limescale. This means that soaps lather easily, tap fittings and appliances do not require the same maintenance, your hair is softer after washing and dishwashers do not need the addition of salt. During the summer months, however, garden hoses and domestic swimming pools can be the site of the bacteria which cause amoebic meningitis, and it is extremely important to maintain chemical levels in pools, and to let the water run for a while before allowing children to play with or drink from garden hoses.

Telecommunications

Until the late 1980s, Australia's telecommunications were controlled by a state monopoly, Telecom Australia. Since then, the market has gradually been deregulated, allowing at first just a single competitor, Optus. In 1997, however, full deregulation was achieved, and there are now a host of options in the telecommunications market, resulting in vastly reduced costs and, in general, a much more competitive service. Today, there are more than 100 telecommunication providers. Telstra (formerly known as

Telecom Australia and 51% government owned) still dominates the local and domestic market, although Optus and Virgin have a significant share of the interstate and international long-distance market. Telephone lines are mostly land-based and reach about 96% of all households. There are about eight million mobile phone subscribers (42% of the population and one of the highest user rates in the world) and over seven million internet users in Australia. International telecommunications links are provided by the Overseas Telecommunication Commission (OTC). Since deregulation, digital suppliers have multiplied exponentially, and it is now possible to call abroad very cheaply by subscribing to one of these services, such as Primus or DigiPlus. Services and special offers are advertised in daily newspapers, and after subscribing, you simply prefix a special call-code to the number you want to dial. You will receive a separate bill from your supplier, and the service can be run concurrently with your Telstra or Optus account. International call rates are falling almost daily due to competition among phone companies. Calls to the UK and the USA are currently around 21 cents per minute – compared with a charge of around A$1.60 per minute 10 years ago.

 Connect to Skype: www.skype.com/useskype

Internet phone

One of the best things to come out of the broadband revolution is internet telephony such as Skype. Skype means you can now call internationally or nationally for free if the person you are calling has Skype downloaded to their computer or mobile. If they don't have Skype, it will cost you as little as US$0.019 per minute to call their landline or mobile (for most developed countries).

- **SkypeIn** is receiving calls on your own SkypeIn number. Those calling you only have to pay the cost of calling the local number and you can receive the call wherever you are in the world. (Most countries connect to Skype).
- **SkypeOut** is when you place a call from either your computer or Skype mobile (3 network currently have this service) to a landline/mobile – this will cost a small fee, but is much cheaper than using your network provider).

To sign up for Skype you need a headset and microphone for your computer (or Skype mobile), a credit card to top up your account and a witty username.

Landline

All Australian homes are fitted with a telephone line, and a second line with a different number can be installed from A$125–A$299 (depending

on whether you have a line already installed) from Telstra, but there are special deals and packages available from all suppliers and it is a good idea to shop around. Telephone bills are issued quarterly or monthly by each of the suppliers whose services you use. Telstra and Optus bills include local metered calls, subscriber trunk dialling (STD), interstate/long distance national calls, and international direct dialling (IDD) calls, as well as service fees, equipment and any other charges. Service charges are around A\$25 a month, and customers can choose either to buy their own telephone handsets (in which case there are no equipment charges), or to rent handsets from Telstra or Optus for around A\$7 per quarter per phone. Fax machines operate via the standard phone line, and their use is charged in the same way as a phone call.

In Australia, local calls are charged at a flat rate of 25 cents (or free depending on what package you sign up for) from a domestic phone (on a payphone, 40 cents), regardless of the length of the call. Whether you are on the phone for three seconds or three hours, the cost of the call is always the same, and you never need to worry about running up your phone bill or calling during economy periods if you are phoning in the suburban boundaries of your city or town. Flat rate local calling is of particular significance in the electronic communications sector and is one reason why Australia leads the world in domestic internet access: for the cost of a 25-cent call to your internet service provider, you can surf the net for as long as you wish without incurring any further calling charges. Long-distance national and international calls are, however, charged according to the distance and the length of the call, as well as by time zone: day rate (8am–6pm) is the most expensive, economy rate (7am–9am, 6pm–9pm) is somewhat cheaper, and night rate (9pm–7am and all weekend) the most economical for national calls.

Dialling codes

The codes for dialling Australia direct from abroad are:

Adelaide	00 61 8
Brisbane	00 61 7
Canberra	00 61 6
Darwin	00 61 8
Hobart	00 61 3
Perth	00 61 8
Melbourne	00 61 3
Sydney	00 61 2

The code should prefix the local number, which will be eight digits long in most capital cities, and six digits long in more rural areas. If you are dialling a number in Australia you must place a zero before the area prefix above before dialling. International directory assistance (from the UK, call 118 505) can advise on changes should you have any out-of-date contact numbers.

To dial overseas from Australia, prefix the number you require firstly with your international call supplier override number, and then add the international dialling code 0011. International faxes are sent using the code 0015.

Phone and broadband companies

Telstra: www.telstra.com.au. Telstra's broadband company is known as Bigpond, and they also do pay TV, which includes the Foxtel and Austar channels. To connect all services at the same time contact 13 76 63 www.bigpond.com

Virgin: 1300 555 100; www.virginbroadband.com.au

Optus: www.optus.com.au

AAPT: www.aapt.com.au

Gotalk Australia: www.gotalk.com.au

Omniplus: www.omniplus.com.au

Primus Telecommunications: www.primus.com.au

3 network: www.three.com.au

Mobile phone

Mobile phone services are run by various cellnet providers, such as Vodaphone, 3 Network, Virgin and Optus and offer much the same range of contract options as available in the UK and USA. They are billed separately

from the main phone number. Most mobile phone providers now have shops set up in shopping malls and also have self-explanatory websites and numbers you can call. If you are after a mobile phone with a monthly contract, you will need a credit history and ID, such as passport, driving licence and utility bills with your address.

An easier option (until you gain a credit history) may be the 'pay as you go' SIM card, which can cost as little as A$20 (including some talk time) and are simply placed into the back of your existing mobile (which may need to have unlocked). If you are taking your phone from the UK with you, check to see if Australia has the same provider (such as Vodaphone and 3) and nine times out of ten, the SIM card will be right for your mobile. If it isn't and the phone has a network lock placed on it, this can easily be removed at phone shops for a nominal charge (usually around A$20). Once you have the new SIM card in your mobile, you must call the network provider and inform them of your address and name – they will then connect you. To top up, you can then either pay online, buy credit vouchers from news agencies or grocery stores or by calling the provider.

FACT

The emergency services number in Australia is 000.

Mobile phone providers

Virgin Mobile: www.virginmobile.com.au

3 Mobile: www.three.com.au Also do broadband and internet connection, as well as Skype – so you may be able to connect everything with the one call to 13 33 20;

Vodaphone: 13 00 65 0410; www.vodaphone.com.au

Optus: 13 00 301 937; www.optus.com.au

The emergency services number in Australia is 000.

Furniture

As most Australian units and houses are leased out as unfurnished (besides a fridge, washing machine and stove if you're lucky), you may have to decide whether to rent all of the bits and bobs required to fill the space, or whether to take the plunge and head for the dizzy heights of the furniture mecca that is IKEA.

First you must factor in the duration of your stay, as if you are only planning on living in Oz for six months, you may want to opt for the rental side of things, as lugging heavy furniture home is never a good idea. Or it may be style you are after, and as styles are constantly changing and designer ware extremely expensive, you may want to rent so you can constantly update your look. Rental companies rent from periods of one week to 24 months and rental can be extended if needed. Appliances such as plasma televisions, fridges, freezers, washers, dryers as well as lounges (sofas), dining tables, television cabinets and beds are all things you must plan to rent or buy. Most expats either have their existing furniture shipped out (see *Relocation*, page 91) or opt for the likes of IKEA or other local furniture stores. Some of the weekend flea markets do a great trade in second hand furniture and you can also pick up some great deals (often freebies) on www.gumtree.com.au or at your local charity store.

Furniture stores

PABS: Designer furniture stores in Sydney, Melbourne, Brisbane and Adelaide; 1800 20 10 20 (free call); www.pabs.com.au

PHD Rentals: Furniture rentals and electrical appliance hire in Brisbane and Sydney. They also sell factory seconds; nsw free call: 1800 68 25 35 and Queensland free call 1800 68 24 35; www.phdrentals.com.au

Expat Matthew Morrison talks about his move to Oz:

'Rent is cheaper here and you can live in your first-choice location. Flats tend to be unfurnished, so you need to either buy/rent furniture, flat-share or pay a premium for furnished. People tend to continue flat sharing well into their 40s and 50s here!'

IKEA: You can pick up a basic bed for as little as A$139, sofas, glasses, picture frames, rugs, cushions, and more than likely a whole shopping trolley full of bric-a-brac you never knew you needed. Be aware, however, that once you get your day's shopping home, you then have to assemble it from a flat pack. Good temperament is a must! www.ikea.com/au

Deals Direct: Have a large range of budget furniture to choose from and can deliver in two days; www.dealsdirect.com.au/

Daily Life

■ CULTURE SHOCK

You may have been looking forward to this monumental change of lifestyle and have spent months fine tuning your move; from finding a new job in Australia to searching for somewhere to live and saying your goodbyes to friends and family. When you step off the plane you may feel a little anxious, as nothing is familiar. The weather may be different to what you are used to, the transport and accents are similar but very different, and the way of doing things seems confusing and upsetting.

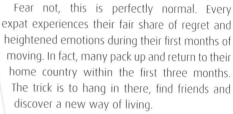

Fear not, this is perfectly normal. Every expat experiences their fair share of regret and heightened emotions during their first months of moving. In fact, many pack up and return to their home country within the first three months. The trick is to hang in there, find friends and discover a new way of living.

Australia is a large island, which is incredibly expensive to leave (especially if you want to return to Europe or the USA). So you must find ways to acclimatise yourself to your surroundings, introduce yourself to your neighbours, accept work drink invites and remember, while nothing will replace what you have at home, it will all still be there when you return for a holiday. It's time to get excited and think about the new friends and experiences you are about to embark on. This chapter will focus on how to settle into a new life as well as how to stay in contact with your old.

> **Expat Joanna Davies remembers how she felt when first arriving in Australia:**
>
> We found Australia to be brighter, more vivid, warmer and friendlier than the UK. We were excited but easily tired by absorbing so much information. We did a lot of research and reading about setting up a new life which I think helped. Relocating to a new country is vastly different to holidaying there and often once the shine of the move has worn off, many expats and family who accompany them feel isolated and depressed.

Settling in

Meeting new people seems like an easy enough challenge, until you actually have to do it. This is particularly true if you are in your late twenties or early thirties, as your peers will have already formed their base friends and don't go out as often as they did when they were younger. If you have a job to walk into when you first arrive in Australia, keep your ears open for office drinks, leaving parties and team building weekends. Australians are for the most part a friendly and welcoming lot, so don't be afraid to speak up and invite yourself along to these events. Another difference in living in Australia is that people will often come up and speak to you on the street, in shops and on public transport. They are not deranged or seeking anything from you, they are just being friendly.

> **British resident Ivan writes about such an event on www.pomsinoz.com:**
>
> 'We visited Western Australia for a 'recky'. We rented a house, which was lovely, and in two days we had met a family from next door. Their kids played with our daughter, we got tipsy by the pool and we never stopped talking about every conceivable topic you could think of, it was great. On our first night there, we decided to walk down to the shops and get a pizza, approximately half a mile away. A family stopped in their 4 × 4 and asked if we wanted a lift. They didn't just give us a lift there; they actually waited and gave us a lift back. Being in a different country, we thought maybe something was going to happen, but they were the nicest people walking the planet. My advice is to talk to everyone, don't be shy and don't think people are after something because they are being nice to you. We found Western Australia very friendly and the people help you as much as they can.'

Expat clubs

There are plenty of expat communities and clubs in each city and they often post their events online. Here are a few:

Poms in Oz

www.pomsinoz.com: This site is useful for both those who have migrated already and those who are still in the UK making their final decisions. It has a live chat room and a friendly community of both Brits and Aussies who are willing to give advice and act as a sounding board for you.

Other places to meet new people include the gym, backpackers' bars (such as Victoria Street in Kings Cross, and cafés/bars; Sydney has quite a few cafés and hostels with most people on their own).

It is always easier to meet new people when you have children. It is a common thread and you can meet other parents through the school community and through the parents of your child's new friends. Children seem to settle better into their new environment and their ease will make you feel more at home.

Melbourne Starter Kit

If you are moving to Melbourne, the government has a 'street party' starter kit that details how to go about organising your very own 'welcome to the neighbourhood' bash. This kit and general information is available on the City of Melbourne website at www.melbourne.vic.gov.au

This website states:

The City of Melbourne wants to encourage people to get out and meet their neighbours and get to know each other better and promote friendly and safe neighbourhoods.

The kit includes:

- free public liability insurance for the local organiser/s
- free access to two mobile gas barbeques
- free traffic plan and management with warden/s and barriers from Citywide paid by the City of Melbourne
- street party kit including a first aid kit, incident book and fire extinguisher
- portable marquee (6m or 3m)
- car trailer for assistance with transporting equipment
- simplified event permit with the City of Melbourne and listing with the local police station
- advice from the City of Melbourne, Place Management team who will be able to provide you with assistance preparing for a street party
- if your party is on the street, the Council will provide a free street closure permit

Australians really do this, and many streets often have barbeques and street parties, erecting trestle tables and marquees on their front lawn, with everyone bringing food and wine to share. If this all seems a little too 'Ramsay Street in Neighbours' for you, then perhaps you should start by socialising with your fellow countrymen.

Parents often opt to migrate with their grown children, as Australia is a long way to go for a visit. Settling in as an older parent can also be troublesome at first, but if you take the plunge and join the local sports club, book club, offer your time by volunteering, or knock on your neighbour's do or you will find there are new friendships to be made.

Canadian Australian Club (CAC)

(www.canadianaustralianclub.com)
All you need to do is to sign up, and they will email you newsletters and upcoming events such as this one found on their website:

7th March 2008 Time: 6pm
CAC Monthly Mixer
    Location : Novotel Liquid Bar, Darling Harbour, 100 Murray St. Come and join us for some fun and laughs at the Liquid Bar, Novotel, Darling Harbour. This is our monthly get together – a chance to meet some new people and catch up with those you know. Children are allowed in our private area so feel free to bring them if you don't have a sitter. There will be some nibbles served compliments of the Novotel. Present your CAC card to obtain the club discount of 25% on beverages and food.

> 'Investing in relationships requires a degree of effort and risk taking. Smile and say hello to as many people as you can each day; you can then practice with ease, your well-versed social skills when you want to invest in a new friendship. If you feel shy, think of some useful phrases to get a conversation going. No one really minds small talk; we all know it's a gambit to open up a dialogue.'
>
> **from 'How to be Happy' by Dr Cecilia D'felice – The Independent, 23/3/08.**

Keeping in touch with family and friends

It's never easy to be far away from childhood friends and close family, but at least you live in an age where you are only a phone or web cam away. Keeping in touch has never been easier or cheaper. Telstra (which is one of the leading phone companies in Australia) as well as Optus have special phone packages which let you dial home (usually in off peak periods such as after 7pm at night) for less than 21 cents a minute, or are often capped at A$4 for the entire call. See *Telecommunications*, page 159.

> **Ali, who is South African, has been a member of CAC since January 2006 and had the following to say in the forum about moving to Western Australia and making friends:**
>
> 'Neighbours were great – we're essentially an Aussie neighbourhood where I live and a South African family, the Poms that live in our street came over as young children and don't consider themselves English. There's a great mix of young and old and at Christmas they have a street party (been going on for years), and Father Christmas comes on the back of a ute. Work is mixed Aussies and English people, and we socialise with a mixture of the two. We've made some great friends through this site too which has been great to share experiences while we all find our feet.'

Even better than these phone packages is making calls via the internet. If you have a web camera, you can also see your loved ones while you speak to them. Skype (see page 160) is another brilliant and inexpensive way of keeping in touch, as it allows users to call traditional telephone numbers, including mobile telephones, for a small fee. This fee is as low as USA$0.019 per minute for most developed countries.

Religious organisations

Many people find that the common bond of faith is an excellent opening to new friendships, and that their co-parishioners are a useful source of assistance in settling in to a new environment. The Council of Christian Unity forms part of the World Division of the Archbishops' Council of the Church of England and helps those looking to explore ways of working with other Christian churches. The World Council of Churches is an ecumenical organisation promoting Christian unity in faith, witness, and service to the world.

> Council of Christian Unity: (London) 020 7898 1000;
> www.cofe.anglican.org/info/ccu
> World Council of Churches: (based in Switzerland) +41 22 791 6111;
> www.wcc-coe.org
> Anglican Church of Australia: 02 9265 1525; email qsoffice@anglican.org.au;
> www.anglican.org.au
> National Council of Churches in Australia: 02 9299 2215; gensec@ncca.org.au;
> www.ncca.org.au

Linda and Keith migrated from Essex in the UK to Newcastle in New South Wales a year ago on a Contributory Parent visa and had this to say on the www.pomsinoz.com website:

'Hi, my husband and I arrived here January 07 on Contributory Parent visas and of course were a bit apprehensive about how we would make new friends but so far it has been great. We have made many Aussie friends (younger and older) through voluntary community work and through bowls and have also made some good expat friends with whom we share experiences etc. We feel that you have to make the effort to go out and make new acquaintances and have found all of those with whom we have made contact very friendly and welcoming and interested in us without being nosy. We have good neighbours too which has made our settling-in period so much easier. Obviously have had a few pangs of homesickness and after 60 plus years miss many things in the old country but overall we are happy with the way things have worked out. We just appreciate that you can't keep comparing, as both countries have their own attractions and are in some ways very different and some ways quite similar. The grass on the other side is not necessarily greener and I think that this must be considered when making a big move. You need to be prepared for the differences.'

Members of other denominations or religions should contact the organisational headquarters of their religious group in their present country to obtain a list of religious contacts in Australia.

■ FOOD AND DRINK

Food

Australian food and eating habits have changed enormously in current decades. The practically cuisine-less country has become one of the trendy food meccas of the world. As recently as the 1980s, Australian cooking was known only for its meat pies, slabs of steak, lamingtons, pavlovas, and pumpkin scones. Since the 1950s, however, the gradual influx of immigrants from Italy, Greece, Yugoslavia, Turkey, Lebanon, India, Thailand, China, Malaysia, Indonesia and Vietnam has meant the enrichment of the longer-standing Anglo-Irish eating style. The sunny climate and outstanding fresh produce and seafood provided the perfect seedbed for the cuisines of the Mediterranean and South-East Asia, so that now chefs are renowned for their 'fusion food', mixing traditions from around the world.

WE TRADITIONALLY "CRUMB" OUR FISH — PLEASE ASK IF YOU WOULD LIKE "BATTERED" OR "GRILLED"

FISH Mongers M

| COD | MEDIUM NO / LARGE BONES | 4.50 / 5.50 |
| SEA PERCH NO BONES ("NO GRILLING") | 6.50 |
| TODAYS SPECIAL INC SAUCE & LEMON — REEF FISH & CHIPS "FIJI SNAPPER" $8.50 SOLD OUT |

FLAKE NO BONES "NO GRILLING" — N/A
ATLANTIC SALMON NO BONES WEIGHED — N/A

NILE PERCH NO BONES — 5.50
SNAPPER NO BONES — Sold out

DORY MEDIUM NO / LARGE BONES — 4.50 / 6.00
REEF FISH "FIJI SNAPPER" NO BONES — 6.00
(6) CALAMARI — 3.00

(IMPORTED) BARRAMUNDI NO BONES — 6.00 / N/A
"AUSSIE" BARRAMUNDI NO BONES WEIGHED — N/A
(6) FISH COCKTAILS — 5.00 OR 1.00 EA

(6) DIVER WHITING NO GRILLING — 5.00 OR 1.00 EA
BATTERED OYSTERS 6 FOR / 12 FOR — N/A
(6) PRAWN CUTLETS — 11.00 OR 2.00 EA

SEA MULLET NO BONES WEIGHED — N/A
COOKING CHARGE ON WEIGHED FISH $1.00 PER 100GM + GST
(6) SEA SCALLOPS — 11.00 OR 2.00 EA

Meat still plays an important part in the Australian diet, and the choice and quality is impressive by European standards. It is also largely inexpensive. Beef, lamb, pork and poultry of all cuts and types are available, as are more unusual 'bush meat' options, such as kangaroo, emu and crocodile. These latter items are speciality fare, but are beginning to be farmed for both the export and domestic markets. In current years 'bush tucker' has become popular, at least as a concept, and in each state there are a number of restaurants offering native aboriginal foods elevated from the campfire to the table. If you have a strong stomach, you may like to try witchetty grubs, usually served, amusingly, poking out of a bush apple.

More appetisingly, Australia has a superb range of delicious seafood, including prawns, lobsters, crayfish, octopus, oysters, mussels, mud crabs and Balmain bugs (a type of crustacean). A huge variety of fresh fish, mostly unfamiliar to European visitors, is available: try dhufish in Western Australia, or barramundi in Sydney for example. If you buy fish from a fish and chip shop you are most likely to be served either shark or snapper; don't be put off by the idea of shark, as it is considered to be a good quality eating fish. The menu of the average fish and chip shop will also offer crab, prawns, squid (calamari), oysters or mussels, deep fried Mars Bars, chicko rolls (a 50-year-old Australian invention designed to be eaten with one hand while drinking a beer with the other, containing a mix of boned mutton, celery, cabbage, barley, rice, carrot and spices in a tube of egg, flour and dough which is then deep-fried), battered savs/Pluto pups (these are basically saveloy sausages with a fried batter on a stick, dipped in tomato ketchup) as well as a choice of homemade marinated pickles.

Fruit and vegetables are all grown locally, and include many tropical varieties, such as mangoes, lychees, avocados, and papayas.

Barbecues continue to be an integral part of Australian social life, but the menu has broadened. A respectable barbecue will be laden with tiger prawns, marinated rump steak and chicken fillets, or perhaps a whole fish garnished with ginger and spring onions. Even without the spectacular beaches, Finlay's Fresh Fish BBQ in Kalbarri, Western Australia, makes the six-hour drive north from Perth worthwhile. This little shack in the sand will cook you up unbelievable prawns fresh out of the water, as well as

FACT

■ Chicko rolls: a 50-year-old Australian invention designed to be eaten with one hand while drinking a beer with the other, containing a mix of boned mutton, celery, cabbage, barley, rice, carrot and spices in a tube of egg, flour and dough which is then deep-fried

A public barbeque with a view

fish and enormous steaks, barbecued for you by Mr Finlay himself. Finlay's mother takes your cash (about A$15–A$20 depending on what you are having) and prepares a range of about six salads, and as many sauces, for your meal, from which you help yourself as you sit on the benches with a drink and watch the sun set the vast sky, your prawns sizzling next to you on the barbecue.

Another must for fish and chip connoisseurs is Doyle's restaurant at Watsons Bay, Sydney. You get beautiful views of one of Sydney's most picturesque beaches from here.

Whether you have a barbie prepared by professionals like the Finlays, or one in your own backyard, or you grill-up on coin-operated gas barbecues provided by the local council, the food is likely to be great and the company congenial.

Australians are renowned for their love of a Barbie! So much so, that many local governments provide beachside/parkside

BBQ's –either free of charge or for a small fee. On sunny days it's best to grab your esky (food cooler), BBQ utensils and BBQ food (seafood, meat and salad) and head down to the beach early, as often queues form and you could be waiting a while to throw that prawn on the barbie.

Restaurants

Australian food is distinguished by the outstanding quality and freshness of the produce. You can expect to eat at a cheap-and-cheerful restaurant for between A$20–A$30 for a two-course evening meal and coffee, excluding wine. Portions are usually extremely generous. In cities with big multicultural populations (such as most of the capitals, and many larger regional towns), you will usually find family-run restaurants which offer great food at incredible prices: in Sydney, No Names used to be famous for serving up giant plates of spaghetti with a hunk of ciabatta and olive oil for just A$2, and in Perth, The Roma, run by the same Italian family for 30 years, still has queues outside on a Friday night for a plate of Mama's pasta. You can eat at The Roma, and dozens of places like it, for under A$15 a head. The decor is basic, but the service is good, and children are welcomed. In Double Bay, Sydney you will also find the most mouthwatering Thai food at Spice Market, where you will have to share a table with other diners while you inhale some of the finest cuisine this side of Bangkok.

In Darlinghurst, Sydney you will find one of the local's best-kept secrets – 'Café Roma', which is hidden in leafy Kellet Street and offers outdoor dining with delicious home made, reasonably priced Italian food in an atmosphere that is entertaining and homely. In Northbridge, there are very similar restaurants run by Vietnamese families, serving up dozens of hot and spicy specialties. The variety of restaurants available in all major Australian cities is enormous, and is at least as varied as in London or New York. Greek, Vietnamese, Mongolian, ethnic Chinese and Indian, Mexican, Lebanese, Portuguese, Italian, Russian, Thai and Polish are all available Australia-wide. Japanese food is very popular, and ramen shops and sushi bars are found in most suburban areas.

Most restaurants in Australia serve cold tap water (usually without you having to ask for it) with your meal, as the heat calls for constant refreshments. Street markets, like shopping centres, will often have a food hall (in Perth, try Subiaco Markets), where you can buy a good Japanese, Thai, or Italian meal for as little as A$10.

Australians are generally very accommodating towards families who bring their children to eat in restaurants, and you will usually be treated with consideration and respect if you choose to introduce your offspring to fine dining at an early age.

At the top end of the market, there are many first-class restaurants, offering the finest food and wines. Modern Australian cuisine emphasises the quality of the ingredients rather than fanciful techniques, so you will taste some of the freshest ingredients without the heavy taste of rich sauces. Service is discreet, and there will usually be a qualified sommelier to advise on appropriate wines (which will be predominantly Australian). Expect to pay up to A$180 a head in the best restaurants, but it will be worth it, especially if, as many do, the restaurant comes with spectacular views over a river, harbour or ocean. The area around Circular Quay houses some of Sydney's finest restaurants; try Aria, which has modern Australian cuisine, with views of the sparkling Harbour and Opera House. Or perhaps you would like to dine at Australia's leading seafood restaurant with the added bonus of a killer view; Doyle's has two remarkable restaurants in Sydney, one at Circular Quay, and the other at Watsons Bay (you can catch a ferry to either).

Café culture is firmly established in Australia. You can be sure of a really good cup of coffee in most establishments. The Dome, a national franchise of coffee vendors, takes its coffee very seriously indeed, and even casual staff spend a week in training, learning how to make cappuccino, macchiato, and espresso coffees as they are made in Italy. As is the case in most countries, Starbucks reigns supreme, and can be found in many a shopping

Aussie coffee	
Short black	Australian idiom for espresso
Long black	1 ml of espresso with 120ml of hot water added after brewing (or an Americano elsewhere in the world)
Flat white	Black coffee with warm milk added (also known as a latte)
Cappuccino	frothy milk on top of coffee with chocolate sprinkled on top

Tipping is discretionary in Australia; however, if you should decide to tip your waiter, it is customary to leave between 10% and 15%. Some restaurants include a service charge, but this is unusual.

mall. If your preferred cuppa is a latte, you should ask for a 'flat white' (or with low-fat milk, a 'skinny flat white') or, confusingly, if you like black coffee/Americano then you must ask for a long black. Any decent café will sell all its various coffees in decaffeinated style as well. As mentioned earlier, Aussies have a love affair with their breakfast culture and you will often be invited out for breakfast meetings and catch-ups. There is nothing quite like sipping your coffee, while taking in the shimmering waters of the harbour before you begin your work day – the only things hampering your enjoyment are the flies who insist on joining you for breakfast.

Traditional Australian food

Australians are particularly fond of fruit and vegetables, and an Australian fruit salad is likely to surpass anything you have previously eaten. Fruit salad is the traditional dessert to accompany a barbecue, and you may be asked to bring one if you are invited as a guest. Be imaginative and include all the various fresh and exotic fruits on display in your greengrocers. Another favourite, the pavlova, is an Australian invention, also most often seen at barbecues. It was created for the ballerina, Anna Pavlova, on an Australian tour, and consists of a meringue base covered with whipped cream and seasonal fruits.

The lamington is another Australian institution, and consists of a cube of extremely light sponge, which has been dipped in a special chocolate sauce and then rolled in coconut. School parents' associations invariably have 'Lamington Drives' as a way of fundraising; school members take orders from students, parents, friends and relatives for at least one dozen lamingtons each, and then a battalion of parents get together to prepare this delicacy. Everybody loves lamingtons, and there are few more effective fund-raising endeavours.

Many Australians grow passion fruit vines in their gardens, and passion fruit icing is very popular for sponge cakes. If you are lucky enough to have a passion fruit vine, make sure that you give it plenty of water and you will be rewarded with the world's most heavenly fruit right through the summer months.

The most famous Australian takeaway food is the meat pie. This is traditionally eaten at Aussie Rules football matches, and by schoolchildren, and always served with tomato sauce. In the past these were pretty ordinary culinary choices, but there are some exceptional meat pie vendors now, with the Daddy of them all being Harry's Café de Wheels in Sydney, a pie cart in Woolloomooloo, on Cowper Wharf Road. Open since 1938, Harry's has served numerous celebrities, who have had their pictures taken and stuck on every conceivable wall, and includes one of Kentucky Fried Chicken's Colonel Sanders and Brooke Shields. You can have your choice of

Australian coffee: be sure you learn the lingo

Chips and the infamous Chiko roll

an array of designer pies with a floater of mashed potato, gravy or mushy peas on top. There are queues for this Aussie institution well into the early hours of the morning and it certainly beats a kebab on the way home from a night of excess.

Wine

Viticulture is one of Australia's leading primary industries, and wine drinking has enjoyed enormous growth over the years as wine production has become more sophisticated and eating habits have changed. Australia's climate and coastal fringe landscape is conducive to wine-growing, and all states have extensive wine producing areas. The diverse climate, topography and soil types mean, however, that Australia is able to produce a wide range of wine styles, from delicate sparkling whites, to full-bodied reds and exceptionally rich fortified wines. There are currently 44 regions of significance to the wine industry, each of which produces distinctive wine varieties. Australia has around 60 different varieties, although most wine drinkers will be familiar with around only 20 names, including Chardonnay, Semillon, Sauvignon, and Shiraz. Lesser-known

types, such as Palomino and Pedro Ximenes, which do not appear on wine labels, are used for making sherry, and Pinot Meunier is used in the production of sparkling wine. Every variety has a specific aroma and taste, known as the primary fruit characters, and many wines will use a blend of these different types. There are more than 1,300 vineyards in Australia, and 366,395 acres (148,275 ha) of land under vines. The top export markets for Australian wines are the UK and USA; wine exports exceed wine imports by ten to one. The top six wine grape varieties currently under cultivation are Shiraz, Cabernet Sauvignon, Chardonnay, Semillon, Merlot and Colombard.

Regional varieties

Most Australian wine production is located in the more highly inhabited south-eastern provinces of New South Wales, Victoria and South Australia – the latter produces approximately 55% of Australian wine. The climate of much of South Australia is a lot like California, with a range of microclimates and a low to moderate rainfall. Inland, the weather gets hotter, and varieties of red wine can be made in almost all of the regions. Some of the best-known regional wine-growing areas are described below.

▨ Margaret River (WA)

Western Australia produces about 3% of Australia's wine – but the grape harvests here account for approximately 20% to 30% of Australia's premium bottled wines. The wine industry in Western Australia was founded even before those of South Australia and Victoria, and for the next 135 years commercial viticulture was confined to the Swan Valley, around Perth. In the mid-1960s, the wine industry began to move south, with the first plantings at Margaret River and Mount Barker. Margaret River has grown to be one of Australia's finest and most vibrant wine producing regions, known for its Chardonnay, Sauvignon Blanc and Cabernet Sauvignon.

▨ The climate of the Margaret River area is strongly maritime, more so than any other Australian wine region, and is the most Mediterranean in style. Overall, the climate is similar to that of a Pomerol or St. Emilion in a dry vintage, which accounts for the quality of its Cabernet, Sauvignon and Merlot varieties. Margaret River's reputation was founded on its Cabernet Sauvignon, and sitll rests on it today. Virtually every winery produces one of these blends, and the style has evolved over the last few decades. The common threads of this wine are ripe grapes, which produce a sweet core, and a slightly earthy tannin. The Chardonnay variety was pioneered by the Leeuwin Estate, and is probably Australia's greatest example of the type. It tends towards a concentrated, complex, viscous and tangy taste, which does not cloy or become heavy. Permutations of Semillon and Sauvignon Blanc are combined to produce a regional speciality known as the Classic Dry White. This wine has a pleasantly herbal or grassy flavour.

- There are many fine restaurants in the Margaret River region, a number of which are attached to vineyards: the most outstanding (and expensive) is without doubt the one on the Leeuwin Estate. Important regional events include the annual Leeuwin Concert, and the Porongorup Wine Festival.

Barossa Valley (SA)

Vines arrived with the first settlers to South Australia and, in the early days, suburban Adelaide was the site of extensive vineyards. The Barossa Valley (including the Eden Valley), Clare Valley, and McLaren Vale were all established in the middle of the 19th century by German immigrants, and wine-growing continues to play a central role in the state's economy. In 2007, South Australia produced just over half of all Australia's wine exports. The climate of the Barossa Valley is almost identical with that of Bordeaux, and is ideal for full-bodied red wines, excellent fortified wine, and robust whites. Shiraz is the most important local variety, and the Barossa Valley is the home of Penfolds Grange, the greatest Shiraz wine made outside the Rhone Valley. Almost every Barossa winery will include a Shiraz or Shiraz blend among its offerings. The style is full bodied, rich in colour, with a touch of chocolate, and a hint of roasted flavour; the wines are long lived. Old vine Grenache and Mourvedre are currently in as much demand as old vine Shiraz, with intense competition between fortified and table wine makers for the available harvest. The Barossa Valley Reisling has a quintessentially Australian style, with strong passion fruit/tropical fruit/lime flavours, which build beautifully with bottle age. Semillon has had a renaissance in current years, and is frequently given a toasting of American oak; it develops quickly into a robust, full-bodied wine.

- Important local events include 'Barossa Under the Stars' (attracting performers such as Julio Iglesias, Rod Stewart, Joe Cocker and Aussie rocker Jimmy Barnes), the Barossa Vintage Festival, and the Barossa Wine Show.

Clare Valley (SA)

The Clare Valley has a continuous history of winemaking that dates back over 150 years. It is a high quality producer of long lived, intensely flavoured, and strongly structured table wines, which are all made in strictly limited quantities. The climate of the Clare Valley, in terms of its viticulture, is strongly dependent on its cool afternoon breezes, which play an important role in slowing ripening on the vines. It is moderately continental, and irrigation is essential due to the winter-spring dominance of the rainfall.

▥ Much of Australia's finest Riesling is grown in the Clare Valley. Typically, it is an austere wine at first, with hints of passion fruit and lime, which quickly develops a touch of lightly browned toast. These wines are long lived and will improve in the bottle for up to 10 years. Cabernet Sauvignon is the other great wine of the region, and is always full-bodied, or even dense. Chardonnay, Semillon, Sauvignon Blanc and Grenache, either singly or in blends, contribute the other main wines of the region.

▥ Important regional events include the Clare Valley Spring Garden Festival, and the Clare Valley Regional Wine Show.

▥ Hunter Valley (NSW)

The Hunter Valley, and particularly its upper region, was reborn in the 1960s and has become one of Australia's premier white wine areas. Typically, it produces soft, rich Chardonnays and quick maturing Semillons from its highly productive vineyards. Chardonnay is regarded as the outstanding wine of the region, with all wine-makers producing examples of real merit. Rosemount Roxburgh is considered Australia's greatest example of the style, and is rich, complex, toasty and creamy, with a strong charred oak overlay. Hunter Valley Semillons are usually fleshy, soft, and likely to be oak-influenced, although in current years there has been a strong move towards traditional, unwooded Semillon styles. These wines peak at around two to four years of age.

▥ In February, March and April annually, the Hunter Valley hosts the Hunter Valley Harvest Festival (www.winecountry.com.au) in October, a jazz festival (www.jazzinthevines.com.au), and an opera (www.4-d.com.au).

▥ Yarra Valley

This is Victoria's oldest wine producing region, with over 3,600 hectares under vine. Located close to Melbourne's CBD (one hour's drive away) it is popular with tourists and locals wanting to sample some of its finest; such as the Yarra Valley Chardonnay. It is also known as Australia's leading cool climate wine region.

▥ Other locally produced wine of international note are the Yarra Valley's elegant sparkling, complex Pinot Noir and rich Cabernet Sauvignons. While the wineries provide the main attraction, other local places of interest include art galleries, accommodation, restaurants, cafés, antique stores,

> *Yarra Valley is Australia's most interesting wine tourist destination, closely followed by (in random order) Margaret River, Barossa Valley and the Hunter.'*
>
> **Tim White, Australian Financial Review, May 11–13 2007.**

markets, nature walks and family attractions such as the Healesville Sanctuary.

ⓘ National Wine Centre of Australia: www.wineaustralia.com.au;
Location of all vineyards, and events listings for the whole country

Beer

A couple of decades ago adverts for the' amber nectar' declared it to be Australia's favourite drink; something that many Australians would not dispute. Every state has its own local beers, which are available nationally; the best known of these are Swan and Emu from WA, Tooheys and Fosters (NSW), Victorian Bitter, or VB, from Victoria, and Castlemaine XXXX (their slogan is 'Australians wouldn't give a XXXX for anything else') from Queensland. Australians drink 'stubbies' – 375ml bottles of beer a little shorter and fatter than the American 12 ounce beer. These bottles fit perfectly in stubby holders foam cooling devices that allow you to drink your beer before it gets warm. You will find that most Australians also drink international lagers, and Mexican beers like Sol and Corona are particularly popular. Beer in pubs is always served ice-cold. Bitter beer or stout is not generally available on tap (draught) in pubs as Australia is an almost exclusively lager-drinking nation, and most Australians find the idea of 'warm beer' pretty disgusting. You should, however, be able to find Guinness on tap in most pubs. Ciders such as Strongbow (dry, sweet or draught) or Woodpeckers are also available.

Boutique beers are now an important part of the market: Redback, Coopers and Cascade are major players in this field, but are expensive compared with mass-produced beers. Ice-brewed beers such as Hahn Ice are also popular. Older generations of Australians also brew their own beer at home and you will often go to the home of a friend's father and be offered some 'home brew' – which is usually as strong as rocket fuel, but tastes OK. There are plenty of pubs and bars all over Australia (serving beer in schooners – 425ml or middies/pots –285ml), and if you don't fancy these you can drink in wine bars, pleasant beer gardens, or with friends at home.

Beer measures in different states

Ordering a beer sounds like an easy enough task, until you have to do it in a different state of Australia. From Schooners to slabs, here's a list to guide you.

State/Measure	Pony	Five	6 oz Beer	A Beer	Butcher	Seven	8oz beer	Pot	10oz beer	Middie	Handle	Stubbie	Can	Schooner	Jug
Victoria	140	-	-	200	-	-	-	285	-	-	-	-	-	485	1140
South Australia	140	-	-	-	200	-	-	-	-	-	-	-	-	285	1140
New South Wales	-	140	-	-	-	200	-	-	-	285	-	-	-	425	1140
Queensland	-	-	-	200	-	-	-	285	-	-	-	-	-	425	1140
Northern Territory	-	-	-	285	-	200	-	285	-	-	285	375/345	375	425	1140
Tasmania	-	-	170	-	-	-	225	-	285	-	-	-	-	-	1140
Western Australia	140	-	-	200	-	-	-	285	-	285	-	-	-	-	1140

Pubs often have a 'sundowner', or happy hour, with cheaper drinks and sometimes entertainment, usually around the hours of summer sunset. The 'Sunday Session' is a similar occasion, held on a Sunday afternoon. For older Australians, the sundowner or the Sunday session is an important part of leisure and social life.

Last but not least, you will need to be updated on the 'lingo'. In certain cities when you buy 12–24 beers you are buying a 'slab' of beer, while in others you will be asking for a 'crate' of beer.

 Tip: Some states of Australia, such as Queensland offer mid-strength beer (which is halfway between full and light-strength beer). The thought behind this phenomenon is that in hotter climates you are going to want to drink more, but you don't want to get drunk before the night has started –mid-strength beer solves the dilemma!

■ SHOPS AND SHOPPING

Shopping in Australia's metropolitan centres is generally excellent. In suburban areas, large American style shopping malls (the largest being the Westfield's chain) offer speciality shops for clothing and goods, as well as supermarkets. Bigger shopping centres often also have a food hall, offering a wide variety of economical cuisines from around the world. Many also have cinema complexes. Most of the older suburbs will have a 'high street' (although it will never be known by this name) very similar to a British high street, with smaller retailers, chain stores, and service outlets. Newer suburbs tend to be planned around the shopping mall, and do not usually have the convenience of a 'corner shop' – known in Australia as a 'deli' or 'milk bar'. In areas with large immigrant populations, delis often stock a wide range of exotic foods in addition to essential items. Shops are generally open from 8.30am–5.30pm, Monday to Friday, 8.30am–4.40pm on Saturdays; with 'late night trading' until 9pm one or two nights a week (usually a Thursday).

Most shops now open on a Sunday, especially in tourist and city centre areas, but Sunday trading is frowned upon in some states, such as Adelaide. Delis/milk bars are usually open from 8am–8pm and every city will have a number of chemists that are open 24 hours a day, 365 days a year. There are an increasing number of 24-hour shops in Australia, (for example Night Owl), and most cities have a handful of these scattered throughout the suburbs.

The quality of Australian produce and goods is generally good. Items bearing a green and gold kangaroo trade mark symbol have been manufactured in Australia, and these are generally more expensive than equivalent goods manufactured in South-East Asia, due to the higher cost of Australian labour. The high quality of Australian-made products is also reflected in their higher prices. In general, however, Japanese, Taiwanese and Korean products, particularly vehicles and electrical goods, conform to Australia's strict quality standards and are usually very competitively priced.

Trendy Brunswick St Fitzroy for shopping in Melbourne

Shopping in Australia can be an enjoyable experience, with a wide range of products available in modern, well-equipped shopping centres, as well as ample car parking, although you could spend days trying to locate your parked car once again. In the rural and more remote areas, however, the situation can be very different. Choice is likely to be limited as shopping centres service much smaller populations, and prices may be significantly higher because of freight costs. Most country dwellers prefer to wait until a trip to the city before shopping for electrical goods or clothing.

Supermarkets

All supermarkets use the barcode shopping system, and groceries are electronically scanned at the tills. Under the ruling of voluntary Code of Practice for Computerised Checkout Systems in Supermarkets, if an incorrect price registers on the supermarket scanner – and you are quick enough to spot the mistake – the price of the item is voided from your receipt and by law you are given the item for free. Supermarkets thus have a keen incentive to keep their barcodes accurate.

Loyalty cards have not been introduced in Australian supermarkets on a wholesale basis yet (although some small boutiques and restaurants operate similar schemes). Many of the larger supermarkets, such as Coles and Woolworths, print vouchers on the back of their itemised receipts

offering free meal deals (on a buy-one-get-one-free basis) at local restaurants and chains, and 4 cents per litre discounts at the fuel pumps if you buy petrol at their sister companies. This promotes consumer loyalty and often these service stations will have all customers brandishing their till receipts. You will also find discounts on anything from carpet cleaning to photo processing.

Edge-of-town superstores are rare, and most people shop in either a large supermarket located in a shopping mall, or in one of the many smaller franchised supermarkets, such as Supa-Valu or Foodland, in the local high street. Supermarkets large and small advertise pages of weekly 'specials' in the local papers and prices are very competitive. For the average price of weekly shopping items, see *Cost of living*, page 79.

Most shops accept major credit and debit cards. Chip and pin hasn't yet been made compulsory in Australia so you will be asked to sign your credit card receipt at the tills and you will need to verify whether your account is credit or savings.

Bottle shops

The biggest difference you will notice when shopping in Australian supermarkets is the absence of liquor in the main store. By law, alcohol may not be sold in the grocery section of Australian supermarkets. Alcoholic drinks can only be bought from licensed liquor stores, also known as 'bottle shops' or 'bottle-oh's'. However, these days many states have allowed liquor stores to be adjoined to the supermarket. You simply pop in there after you finish your grocery shopping.

Drive-in bottle shops are very common and provide the convenience of allowing you to drive up to a shop, roll down the car window and give your order and money to an attendant in exchange for cartons (slabs or crates) of beer or casks or bottles of wine. If you want to sample the delights of drive-in 'bottle-oh', remember that in Australia, you can not drink and drive. Save it till you get to the barbeque!

Bottle shops are usually open from 10am–10pm, Monday to Saturday, and until 8pm on Sunday. They generally stock an extensive range of quality wines, as well as the usual beers and spirits. Most will have a giant walk-in cool room, where all white wines and beer are kept chilled so you need never visit a bottle shop in summer and come home with a warm bottle of white wine. Australians visiting the UK can't believe the lack of refrigeration in off-licences. Larger alcohol-retailing chains, such as Vintage Cellars, hold regular wine tastings, wine discussion evenings for regular customers, and publish monthly newsletters analysing the latest releases and the grape harvests. If you are having a party, most shops will accept the return of unopened bottles purchased from them in a bulk order (as long as labels and seals are not water-damaged from immersion in ice).

Clothes

Australian fashion used to be considerably backward, in fact you could almost guarantee what was big in London, would come into fashion in Australia some six months later, although to be fair this had to do with the seasons, weather wise. Nowadays, however they produce some of the hottest designer names in the fashion world; such as Wayne Cooper, Sass and Bide and Collette Dinnigan. Double Bay's shopping district in Sydney is a fine example of how far Australia's fashion has advanced. Having said that, just because it is made by an Australian designer doesn't mean it is any less expensive. Another noteworthy shopping district is in Melbourne. People come from all over Australia to window shop on Chapel and Brunswick Street. These are the streets that house some of Australia's top designers, quirky boutiques and alternative fashions. You will also find some big names and unusual designer shops in the Central Business District (CBD) of Melbourne and down one of its many laneways and side streets.

For the general fashion wearing population, the attire is very casual, the Australians really dress for the climate. Women wear dresses, cropped trousers and vests with lightweight linen jackets and you will find men in anything from a business suit to a pair of stubbies (very short shorts) and a singlet top (white vest) or knee-length cargo trousers. Also in beachside areas don't be too alarmed if you see a man in a store without a top

> 'Paddington and Woollahra are the first port of call for any visiting fashion victim. At the Paddington end of Oxford Street are established Australian designers such as Lisa Ho, Dinosaur Designs, Calibre, Aquilla and many more. Pop around the corner into William Street for Belinda and Collette Dinnigan.
> For luxury European brands, head back into town. The likes of Chanel, Bulgari, Gucci, Tiffany and George Jensen are conveniently grouped along Castlereagh Street – a short stroll from Sydney's two major department stores David Jones and Myer'

on, this is normal practice, he is probably just cooling down. To give you an indication of how casual the dress sense is, in the 2007 Government elections, voters were allowed to cast their votes in their Speedos and bikinis.

European clothes are usually made from better quality materials and to higher standards than the same kind of clothing in Australian stores, which are largely imported from South-East Asia. Having said this, the cost of clothing from a budget-priced Australian store such as Kmart or Target and other mid-range chain boutiques, is, depending on the current exchange rate, as much as 50% less than clothing from UK stores of a comparable standard. Target has currently had celebrity designer ranges brought in such as Stella McCartney, Zac Posen, Collette Dinnigan – even Posh Spice has been known to shop in Target. Classic Aussie 'clobber' such as Bond's underwear, Ugg boots (highly sought after in winter 2007–08), moleskins, Driza-Bone coats, RM Williams boots, and Akubra hats are all going to be cheaper if bought in Australia. European designer label fashions can be bought in all the capital cities, but at a price. Leather goods, especially shoes and bags, tend to be expensive in Australia, to the extent that it may be worth investing in a few good quality items before you leave home.

 www.on-shopping.com.au/australia/Clothes

Department stores and fashion outlets

David Jones: www.davidjones.com.au Australia-wide
Myer: www.myer.com.au
Country Road: www.countryroad.com.au
Target: www.target.com.au
Kmart: www.kmart.com.au
Sportsgirl: www.sportsgirl.com.au
Lucid Laundry: (Brisbane only, but worth a visit if you're in the area): www.lucidlaundry.com

Witchery: www.witchery.com.au
Collette Dinnigan: www.collettedinnigan.com.au
Bonds: www.bonds.com.au
R M Williams: www.rmwilliams.com.au
Westfield shopping centres: www.westfield.com

■ POST

The Australia postal service is owned and run by the Australian Government, and in general provides excellent services. Post offices and Post Shops are open from 9am–5pm Monday to Friday, and 9am–11am or 12pm on Saturdays, but are closed on Sundays and public holidays. Airmail letters between Australia and the UK and the USA take between three to 10 days to arrive, and parcels take between seven and 10 days. The cost of postage for a letter (up to 50g) to Britain or the USA is A$1.95. Sea mail and Surface Air Lifted (SAL) mail services are also available at a significantly cheaper cost, but are, naturally, much slower services.

Most people send parcels SAL or Sea mail, particularly Christmas parcels, and Australia Post issues a list of send-by dates for guaranteed pre-Christmas delivery all over the world. To send parcels back home in time for Christmas, the send-by date is usually at the beginning of October. Australia Post also offers a cheaper rate for Christmas cards, which should be in unsealed envelopes marked 'card only', and there is a different

send-by date for international cards, usually four weeks before Christmas. There is no division between first and second-class services for local letters, only one standard service and cost. Local letters cost 50 cents and it usually takes one working day to deliver letters posted in the same metropolitan area, or two working days if the letter is from outside the metropolitan region or from interstate.

Australia Post deals with around 5.3bn letters per year and seeks to maintain a uniform standard letter service at a uniform price. It has a 'community service obligation' to fulfil this mandate. As well as letter services, Australia Post offers a telephone bill paying service. It has a website at www.auspost.com.au where you can assess your postage costs, locate postcode numbers, find out about services and special offers, and check the location of your nearest office or agency.

Mail is usually delivered once a day from Monday to Friday in metropolitan regions, but in remote and/or rural regions the mail may only be delivered once a week and can also often be delayed by adverse conditions such as flooding, torrential rain or even snow. There is no Saturday delivery. Mailboxes are located at the front of properties, and mail is never delivered through a slot in the front door. In the case of blocks of flats, there is usually a structure containing one letterbox for every flat, at the front entrance to the property. In some urban areas, it can be wise to lock your mailbox with a small padlock if it is in a communal block, otherwise your mail is not secure.

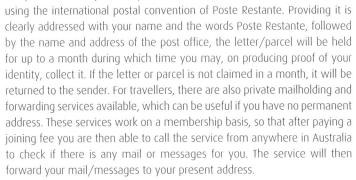

One big difference with the delivery of post compared to other countries is the fact that it's delivered by motorbike in most cities. Australia Post has currently lifted its ban on postman/women weighing more than 90kg, as that's all the motorbike could take (combined with the weight of mail/parcels).

If you intend to travel extensively through Australia during your stay, it is possible to have letters and parcels sent to you at any office of Australia Post using the international postal convention of Poste Restante. Providing it is clearly addressed with your name and the words Poste Restante, followed by the name and address of the post office, the letter/parcel will be held for up to a month during which time you may, on producing proof of your identity, collect it. If the letter or parcel is not claimed in a month, it will be returned to the sender. For travellers, there are also private mailholding and forwarding services available, which can be useful if you have no permanent address. These services work on a membership basis, so that after paying a joining fee you are then able to call the service from anywhere in Australia to check if there is any mail or messages for you. The service will then forward your mail/messages to your present address.

Travellers' Contact Point
A privately owned travellers' mail service. Level 7, Dymocks Building, 428 George Street, Sydney, NSW 2000; 02 9221 8744; info@travellers.com.au; www.travellers.com.au. Open Monday to Friday 9am–6pm; Saturday 10am–4pm. Also at 2–6 Inverness Terrace, Bayswater, London W2 3HX; 020 7243 7884; enquiries@travellersuk.com. Open Monday to Friday 9am–5.30pm; Saturday 10am–4pm.

Main Australian post offices (known as GPOs)
ACT: King George Terrace, Canberra, ACT 2600
NSW: 1 Martin Place, Sydney, NSW 2000

NT: 31–33 Hartley Street, Alice Springs, NT 0870

NT: 48 Cavenagh Street, Darwin, NT 0800

QLD: Shop 6A, 366-370 Shute Harbour Road, Airlie Beach, QLD 4802

QLD: 261 Queen Street, Brisbane, QLD 4000

QLD: 13 Grafton Street, Cairns, QLD 4870

QLD: Paradise Centre Shop 165, 2–10 Cavill Avenue, Surfers Paradise, QLD 4217

QLD: Post Office Plaza Shop, Sturt Street, Townsville, QLD 4810

SA: 141 King William Street, Adelaide, SA 5000

TAS: 9 Elizabeth Street, Hobart, TAS 7000

TAS: 3/25 Wellington Street, Launceston, TAS 7250

VIC: 250 Elizabeth Street, Melbourne, VIC 3000

■ WASTE COLLECTION AND RECYCLING

Australians take recycling very seriously, in fact there are laws in some cities which fine you for throwing out plastics, glass and paper with your everyday garbage. You may wonder how they get caught. The culprit is a tiny camera found in many garbage bins. Australian garbage bins are extremely large and are called Otto bins in some states and wheelie bins in others. The bin has to be so big as it is only collected once a week and the trucks have gigantic claws on the side, which pick the 'wheelie bin' up and pour it inside the garbage truck. You need to be aware of what side to park your bin to the curb, as this can also get you in trouble (the smelly kind, because if you don't park your Otto correctly, they will often leave it behind).

The local government will provide you with separate bins for paper, glass and plastic and they are usually collected on alternate weeks. However, this varies from council to council and from state to state. Some require you to separate your glass from your paper and others will collect it as a mixed bag. They also urge residents to build compost heaps in their sprawling gardens, but if you do not have a garden, you can organise a regular collection by your council.

ℹ Find your local council: www.yellowpages.com.au

The Australians have also found a way to profit from their discarded rubbish. By building the southern hemisphere's biggest waste facility in Eastern Creek Sydney they have worked out that by separating the reusable materials, they can then recycle nearly everything and sell it on. They are doing the environment the world of good, as they incinerate none of it, nor do they ship it to China as other countries do. Environmentalists consider this to be a groundbreaking scheme, as they view waste as a mineable resource rather than something to be wasted or destroyed.

■ HEALTHCARE

In 2007 Australia's mortality rate was 7.56 per 1,000 people per year (compared with 5.87 in 1999) although Aboriginal people continued to have a mortality rate far higher than the national average.

This report also compared the mortality rates of migrants and Australian-born residents and found that most migrant groups had death rates significantly lower than the Australian average. Greeks, Italians, Central and South Americans, Vietnamese and Yugoslavs had the lowest rate. In addition, among Australians aged 25–64, the death rate was 15% higher for men living in rural regions, and 9% higher for women in rural areas.

The report also noted an increase in the rate of multiple births with improving technology in the field of artificial conception, such as IVF treatment, and that dental health has improved dramatically over current years to an extent where few people under 35 years of age have lost all their teeth. Despite the large number of people on hospital waiting lists, the report also indicated that trends showed a continued decline in basic and supplementary private hospital insurance, and government measures have been put in place to offset this decline, by offering incentives to insure privately. These measures now mean that most people over the age of 30 opt for private insurance, as if they do not have it they will have to pay a surcharge (see information below).

Since universal healthcare was introduced in 1972, Australians have come to see it as a right, and both sides of politics are publicly committed to maintaining it. However, the costs to Government are enormous. According to the Bureau of Statistics, Australia spends about A$50bn a year on health, about 8–9% of its gross national product. The revenue gained from the basic 1.5% Medicare tax levy represents only about 11% of this spending. Most of the rest comes from regular taxes.

M M C / MUDGEERABA MEDICAL CENTRE
EST. 1983

Measures designed to attract people back into the private health system

- A 30% rebate on annual health fund premiums, regardless of income. The rebate increases to 35% for those aged between 65 and 69, and to 40% for those aged 70 or older.
- A 1% levy on the total taxable income of higher-income earners without private hospital cover, over and above the 1.5% Medicare levy. The surcharge applies to individuals without health insurance earning more than A$50,000, and to couples or families earning more than A$100,000, with the threshold rising by A$1500 for each child after the first. (To avoid the Medicare surcharge, many higher-income earners take out cheap hospital cover. They may never make a claim. But this cover can be bought for about A$1,000 a year, less than the surcharge the person would otherwise have to pay.)
- The 'Lifetime Health Cover' scheme means people aged 30 or under who take out (and keep) hospital cover pay lower premiums throughout their lifetime than those who don't. Those who join from age 31 on pay a higher premium on the basic private hospital insurance rate (2%) for each year that they were over 30 on joining. For example someone joining private health insurance at age 35 would have to pay an extra 10% more than someone who joined at age 30. (There are no age penalties for ancillary cover.)

In 1998, the percentage of Australians covered by private healthcare fell to an all-time low of 30%. So over the past few years, the Federal Government, concerned about the growing costs of health, has introduced a series of measures designed to attract people back into the private health system.

 Government private health insurance database and information site: www.privatehealth.gov.au

The report also showed that the nation's health was dogged by a rising suicide rate, with more Australians dying by their own hands than in traffic accidents. For the most part, victims were males between 15 and 24 years old, but women of the same age were also at risk. The survey indicated strong links between suicide and the socially disadvantaged and the unemployed, particularly in the Aboriginal population. The number of Aboriginal deaths in custody in the 1990s, which were statistically disproportionate when compared to the average rate of suicides in prison, was so alarming that the Government ordered a Royal Commission to investigate. Despite the Royal Commission's findings (released in May 1991) and its 339 recommendations, indigenous people are still 14 times more likely to be imprisoned than non-indigenous Australians; in the Northern Territory for instance, 72.8% of the prison population is indigenous.

High cholesterol levels are a major contributor to health problems in Australia, affecting nearly three million people nationwide and killing 50,000 each year. Public health concern over this issue is reflected in the amount spent on drugs. Between 1998 and 2000 the cost of the cholesterol-lowering drug subsidy paid by the Federal Government rose by more than A$110m. The number of prescriptions for these drugs increased by nearly two million and now tops the Pharmaceutical Benefit Scheme (PBS) in cost, amounting to over half a billion dollars in 2000 and rising by around 25% each year.

Cancer rates also appear to be on the increase, currently accounting for more than 30% of male deaths and 25% female deaths each year. Breast, lung and skin cancers are the most common killers. As a result of increased public awareness of these health risks, most Australian buildings, including restaurants, are now completely smoke-free. Australians are highly educated about the risk of skin cancer and the dangers of the sun, and now almost universally take thorough protective measures when outdoors.

The perception that Australians have apparently healthy lifestyles was challenged currently, by a National Nutrition Survey, which showed that some 56% of the adult population (18 years and over) was overweight, with 19% of these classified as obese.

Six priority areas of concern have been endorsed by Australian Health Ministers:

- cardiovascular health
- cancer control
- injury prevention and control
- mental health
- diabetes mellitus
- asthma

A range of programme initiatives has been established, aimed at improving health in these areas, which together account for approximately 70% of the burden of disease and cost in Australia – a high demand on the nation's health services.

General practitioner

The first point of contact in obtaining healthcare in Australia is the local General Practitioner (GP), whom you are free to choose yourself. While most people will have a preferred doctor, it is not necessary to register

FACT

- The Australian Government has signed Reciprocal Healthcare Agreements with New Zealand, the United Kingdom, the Republic of Ireland, Sweden, the Netherlands, Finland, Italy, Malta and Norway.

Medicare benefits

If your doctor charges you a fee, you can:
- pay the account and then claim the benefit from Medicare
- claim your unpaid account from Medicare and receive a cheque made out in the doctor's name which you give to your doctor along with any outstanding balance.

Medicare usually pays:
- the full Schedule fee for GP services
- 85% of the Schedule fee for other out-of-hospital services
- 75% of the Schedule fee for in-hospital services

The Schedule fee is a fee for service set by the Australian Government and not what your doctor charges you.

with a doctor, and you are able to go to a different practice for every visit, should you wish. Depending on the doctor, you will either be billed for the consultation, for which you will be reimbursed by Medicare, the Australian national health system, or the doctor will 'bulk-bill' which means they will claim reimbursement directly from Medicare. Doctors who practise in low-income areas generally bulk-bill to avoid asking their patients for payment, however, this is largely a gesture of goodwill on behalf of the GP. The benefits that you get from Medicare are based on a Schedule of fees (index linked) set by the Commonwealth Government.

GPs are able to charge fees they consider suitable for the services they provide. These are usually more than the Medicare schedule fee and this extra amount will not be included in the calculation of Medicare benefits. Thus the patient is liable for any amount in excess, which is known as the 'gap'. For a general visit to your local GP, the gap is normally around A$20 A$30.

 Medicare Australia: www.medicareaustralia.gov.au

Second opinions and specialists

If you wish to have a second medical opinion, you simply make an appointment with another doctor. Generally, appointments are made over the telephone, and you can usually see your GP in two days of your call.

If a GP refers you to a consultant or specialist, you will be given a letter and required to make the necessary arrangements yourself. Even specialists seeing public patients consult in their own rooms, and there is no system

Australian diabetes statistics

- Type 2 diabetes is Australia's fastest growing chronic disease
- Almost 1,500 people are diagnosed every week, 214 people every day
- An average of almost 74,000 people have been diagnosed in the past twelve months
- 599,259 Australians are diagnosed with diabetes. For every one who knows they have it, another has it but doesn't know it – yet
- That is a total of 1.2 million people including those who are unaware they have diabetes
- By 2010, Diabetes Australia expects the number to reach 1.8 million

of attendance at hospital outpatients' clinics. There may be a waiting period before you are seen, although it is usually not long, and once again you will be billed and reimbursed through Medicare. You may choose to see a consultant on a private basis, without referral, for which you will be unable to obtain a refund either from Medicare or from your private insurer.

An increasing number of clinics and medical centres are opening in suburban areas. Most large practices will provide a well woman clinic, minor surgery, and other services. There may also be a pharmacy housed in the centre, from which you can purchase your prescriptions immediately.

Keep your address current
f you change your address, please let Medicare know imme
ocal Medicare office.

Prescriptions

Prescription charges are subsidised under the Pharmaceutical Benefits Scheme (PBS). Patients pay the full cost of medication up to the value of approximately A$31.30 (as of January 2008), and the PBS meets the balance up to the list price; patients on benefits of any kind pay only A$5.00. Contraception is not free in Australia, but is covered by the PBS. The PBS covered around 170 million prescriptions in the year to June 2007. This equates to about eight prescriptions per person in Australia for the year. Most big cities throughout Australia, offer late night and Saturday opening times for medical clinics. Check with your local GP or clinic when arriving.

Hospitals

Patients who require hospital attention or surgery can also choose to be treated either publicly or privately. If you opt for private treatment, you can choose both your attending consultant and the hospital, but will pay a considerable amount for this privilege. On the other hand, you can expect a great deal of luxury for your money, including five-star food chosen from a daily menu, as well as immediate treatment. If you choose to be treated under Medicare, you do not have a choice of hospital or doctor (although you will have had some say in choosing your specialist during discussions with your GP in the early stages), and you may face a long wait for a bed, but, your treatment will be completely free. In the event of an emergency, all patients will be taken directly to a public hospital, and once their condition has stabilised may be transferred if they wish. Ambulance transport is not free, and many people choose to pay a small insurance premium annually to the St. John's Ambulance Brigade to cover them in case they or their family need to call on this service.

Health insurance contributions

Every Australian is covered by Medicare, which is financed through progressive income tax and an income-related Medicare levy. There is no additional charge equivalent to National Insurance in the UK. The Medicare levy is paid at a rate of 1.5% of taxable income above an earning threshold of around A$13,807, or A$23,299 for couples. In the 1996–97 budget the Federal Government announced that a 1% Medicare levy surcharge, in addition to the 1.5% levy, would be introduced for higher income earners (A$50,000 per year for single earners, A$100,000 per year for couples) who do not have private patient hospital cover through private health insurance and all earners (regardless of your income) over the age of 30. This surcharge is part of a package of measures designed to encourage people to retain or take up private health insurance. People receiving state benefits fall below the earning threshold of the Medicare levy, and payments are made on their behalf by the Government. If you choose to be privately insured, you are not exempt from the Medicare levy, but you won't be charged the Medicare surcharge.

Medicare, the Australian national health system

Australia's national health system, Medicare, is outstandingly good but its services are becoming increasingly oversubscribed with the increasing population of Australia and the fact that the population is a 'greying' one. Many Australians, however, do choose to take out additional private medical cover (see surcharge section above) There has been a current surge in so-called 'medical tourism', whereby people in need of major treatment, such as a hip replacement or heart surgery, visit Australia specifically to take advantage of the good facilities, medical expertise and reasonable costs. Medicare is funded by the Australian Government, and administered by the Health Insurance Commission (02 6124 6333, hic. info@hic.gov.au; www.hic.gov.au). Hospitals and other facilities are built and run by the various state health departments who are responsible by law for maintaining a minimum standard of care.

To be eligible for Medicare, you must first register by completing an application form obtainable from a Medicare regional office – call 132 011 to find your nearest office or go to: www.medicareaustralia.gov.au and register online.

You need not necessarily have registered with Medicare before you receive any medical treatment, but will be required to do so before you can make any claim. After you have registered, you will be sent a Medicare card, which looks like a credit card, and this should be carried with you at all times. You will need to present this card on arriving at a hospital for treatment and every time you visit the doctor's surgery. Any children under 15 years old will be listed on the card of one or other of their parents. When you lodge a claim for a Medicare rebate, you will be required to quote your number or present your card; rebates can be made in cash over the counter, and the process is straightforward. You can also lodge claims by post, which takes considerably longer, and forms are available in chemists, doctors' surgeries post offices, and in some states at the actual doctors surgeries – if you present your Medicare card and debit card after your appointment, they may be able to process your claim immediately. This way you pay the doctor the total amount and they automatically apply for any refund due. This is by far the easiest way to claim, but you must first check with your individual GP to see if they have signed up to the scheme.

All immigrants are covered by Medicare, provided they pay the Medicare levy (included in general taxes), and temporary residents who stay in the country longer than six months may be covered by Medicare without having to pay the levy. Medicare covers inpatient and outpatient treatment at public hospitals, as well as hospital accommodation costs in public hospitals and visits to the doctors. If you need regular, expensive treatment, Medicare will cover all of the scheduled fees incurred over the rest of the year once the gap has reached a total of A$365.70 for any financial year (see Medicare benefits, page 200). Most medicines available on prescription are subsidised under the Pharmaceutical Benefits Scheme (PBS). Most PBS-listed medicines cost the consumer a maximum of A$31.30, or A$5.00 for relevant concession cardholders. If you have a record of spending A$716.10 on PBS medicines for yourself and your family in a calendar year you will be entitled to any further PBS medicines for only A$3.63 for each item for the rest of the calendar year.

FACT

■ Medicare does not cover physiotherapy, chiropractic or dental treatment, although some orthodontic treatment is refundable, particularly if surgery is involved. Neither medical repatriation nor funeral costs are covered, and ambulance costs (including transport and treatment) cannot be refunded through Medicare.

Medicare does not cover physiotherapy, chiropractic or dental treatment, although some orthodontic treatment is refundable, particularly if surgery is involved. Neither medical repatriation nor funeral costs are covered, and ambulance costs (including transport and treatment) cannot be refunded through Medicare.

Visitors to Australia from the UK, Republic of Ireland, Malta, Italy, New Zealand, Finland, Norway, Sweden and the Netherlands are also covered by Medicare under reciprocal arrangements (RHCA scheme), and can receive limited subsidised health services for immediately necessary treatment. If you are from the UK, Finland, the Netherlands, Norway or Sweden you are covered for the duration of your approved visit to Australia. As a resident of Italy or Malta you are covered for six months from the date of your arrival. You are not, however, entitled to claim health benefits for a medical condition that existed before your arrival in Australia, including any illness caught on your journey to Australia, or for any on-going medication. Travellers from the countries listed above should enrol at a Medicare office, presenting a passport containing an appropriate visa, and proof that you are enrolled in the national healthcare scheme of your home country. If you are a short-term visitor and you do not come from a country that has reciprocal health agreements with Australia, it is advisable to take out private medical insurance, which is usually available through your travel agent and is likely to be included in any travel insurance policy. Students are not covered by Medicare and you should therefore take out your own health insurance cover.

Retirees need to take out travel insurance and private medical insurance (either in their country of origin or in Australia), as they are liable for all expenses incurred in the case of medical and hospital treatment, including the cost of hospital accommodation. In the case of migrants on a Parent visa application, any medical or hospital expenses incurred by the migrant parent (over the stipulated age limit) will be the responsibility of

Medicare exclusions

There are three categories of new settler that are exempt from eligibility for Medicare. These are:

- people entering Australia to retire
- those who have been granted permanent residence in the Family Stream migration category, who are the parents of their sponsor and are more than 55 years old (men) or 50 years old (women)
- people entering Australia as a foreign diplomat or as a member of a foreign diplomat's family

the sponsor; unless the migrant has private insurance. If only one of the sponsor's parents is over the age limit, then the sponsor is only responsible for the medical expenses incurred by that parent.

Diplomats and their families are advised to take out private medical insurance either before you leave your home country or take out a policy in Australia immediately upon your arrival.

Private health insurance

Private health insurance is widespread in Australia, with around 70% of the population choosing to take out additional cover. Without the private health insurance, they would have to pay the surcharge (gap costs between Medicare supplements and total cost of treatment). Private health cover is much cheaper in Australia than in Britain, and premiums are not indexed for age or gender.

In 2007 there were 39 registered health insurers in Australia.

This gives Australians the option for private funding of their hospital and ancillary health treatment. Most people enjoy the security of knowing that they have the right to choose both the hospital where they will be treated and their specialist who will treat them. In addition, private cover offers refunds for medical services not covered by Medicare, such as physiotherapy, prescription glasses and sunglasses, and dental work. Different levels of cover are available, from basic rates (shared-room) through to a fully comprehensive, deluxe rates. Costs vary from around one dollar a week, up to around five dollars per week for the ultimate in hospital care. Premiums are usually payable in monthly, quarterly or annual instalments and discounts are sometimes given for prompt payment or for payments made annually. Children and dependants are normally covered by their parents' private medical insurance.

The Private Health Insurance Incentives Scheme, developed to make private insurance a more attractive proposition, especially to the young and healthy, was replaced by the Federal Government 30% Rebate on 1 January 1999. The 30% Rebate means that for every dollar you contribute to your private health insurance premium, the Government will give you back 30 cents. For example, if your premium is A$2000 a year you will get A$600 back. All those who are eligible for Medicare and who are members of a registered health fund are eligible for the Rebate – no matter what their level of cover, income or type of membership.

 Federal Government 30% Rebate: 1800 676 296; www.health.gov.au

When choosing a health fund, points to consider should include whether there are any exemptions for previously known illness or for AIDS, what the waiting period is before you can make a claim, and what the benefit limits are for each service covered. Private health insurance companies advertise widely in the local newspapers and on radio and television. Some smaller funds now offer rebates for alternative medical treatments, such as homeopathy and acupuncture, so if you use these services, it will be worth shopping around quite carefully.

Private health insurance

In Australia

Medibank Private: www.medibank.com.au

MBF Health: www.mbf.com.au

Hospital Benefits Fund: www.hbf.com.au

Manchester Unity: www.manchesterunity.com.au

Nib: www.nib.com.au

HCF: www.hcf.com.au

Ahm: www.ahm.com.au

RT Health: www.rthealthfund.com.au

www.iselect.com.au: A useful site for comparing the different private health companies online

In the UK

BUPA International: 01273 208181; www.bupa-intl.com

Columbus Travel Insurance: 020 7375 0011; www.columbusdirect.net

Department for Work and Pensions, Overseas Branch: 0191 218 7777.

Travel Insurance Agency: 020 8446 5414; email info@travelinsurers.com; www.travelinsurers.com

The emergency services

The national telephone number for all emergency services in Australia including ambulance, fire, and police is 000.

Dialling 000 from your mobile phone

Ensure you consult your phone network provider when purchasing a contract on how to access the emergency services from your handset. They should be free on all mobile phones. On some older model/ analogue phones, 000 will connect callers, although many newer digital phones may require the user to dial 112 instead, which is the international standard

FACT

■ The national telephone number for all emergency services in Australia including ambulance, fire, and police is 000.

What happens when you dial 000

■ 000 calls are answered by a Telstra operator who will ask which service you require – Police, Fire or Ambulance.

■ The operator will then ask relevant questions, and arrange an appropriate response from the local Police, Ambulance or Fire Service.

emergency number. To play it safe, have both numbers available on speed dial and check which number connects you, before you actually need to use it.

Non emergencies

Other useful numbers can be found in your household copy of the Yellow Pages (www.yellowpages.com.au) or check online (www.google.com. au). Make sure you make a list of your local police station, hospital and electricity and gas services to keep near your home phone.

Useful websites
Australian Federal Police: www.afp.gov.au
Emergency Management Australia: www.ema.gov.au

Australian Capital Territory
Police Service: www.afp.gov.au
Ambulance Service: www.esb.act.gov.au/as/as.htm
Fire Service: www.esb.act.gov.au/fb/fb.htm

New South Wales
Police Service: www.police.nsw.gov.au
Ambulance Service: www.asnsw.health.nsw.gov.au
Fire Brigade: www.nswfb.nsw.gov.au
Rural Fire Service: www.bushfire.nsw.gov.au/main.htm

Northern Territory
Police, Fire and Emergency Services: www.nt.gov.au/pfes/
Bush Fires Council of the Northern Territory: www.nt.gov.au/bfc/

Queensland
Police Service: www.police.qld.gov.au
Ambulance Service: www.ambulance.qld.gov.au
Fire and Rescue Authority: www.fire.qld.gov.au
Department of Emergency Services: www.emergency.qld.gov.au/

South Australia
Police Service: www.sapolice.sa.gov.au/index.html
Ambulance Service: www.saambulance.com.au
Metropolitan Fire Service: www.samfs.sa.gov.au
State Emergency Service: www.sessa.asn.au
Country Fire Service: www.cfs.org.au
St John Ambulance Service: www.sa.stjohn.org.au/

Victoria
Police Service: www.police.vic.gov.au
Fire Service: www.mfbb.vic.gov.au
Ambulance Service: www.ambulance-vic.com.au
State Emergency Service: www.ses.vic.gov.au
St John Ambulance Service: www.sjaa.com.au/

Western Australia

Police Service: www.police.wa.gov.au
Fire and Emergency Services Authority: www.fesa.wa.gov.au
St John Ambulance Service: www.ambulance.net.au/

Tasmania

Police Department: www.police.tas.gov.au
Fire Service: www.fire.tas.gov.au/
State Emergency Service: www.ses.tas.gov.au/

■ SCHOOLS AND EDUCATION

Australian education is internationally regarded as being of a high standard, particularly in tertiary institutions. An Australian honours degree holds a higher status than a UK honours degree in the UK university system, and holders of such degrees on scholarships to premier universities, such as Oxford and Cambridge, are exempted from one year of study at postgraduate level. International surveys of educational standards recognise Australia scoring at the top of the list, along with Germany and Japan, in terms of science education. Early education practice in Australia is significantly different to that of the UK or USA. Many experts attribute later academic success to the different emphasis in methods of teaching young children, where emphasis is put on self-discipline, on learning by finding out, by questioning and by encouraging a child's interest and enthusiasm for learning.

Education is the responsibility of state governments, and is compulsory between the ages of five and 15. Upper secondary schooling begins at 12 or 13 years old and continues on to age 17 or 18; these extra years are mandatory for students considering further education and school retention rates are very high, averaging around 78%. Around 70% of Australian children attend free, public state-funded schools, which are mostly co-educational and non-religious. A parallel fee-paying, private sector also exists, most of these schools are run by religious institutions, and many are single sex institutions. Children who need to attend boarding school in their secondary school years because of rural isolation will usually attend schools of this type, and their boarding costs are subsidised by the Government. In the primary years, children in the outback are educated by the School of the Air, which provides distance learning by radio and correspondence. There are now a number of schools offering the International Baccalaureate programme to those in their final years of schooling. For children of parents who might be on short-term work contracts in Australia, the International Baccalaureate programme allows them to gain entry into universities in their home country, and into some universities in the USA.

Two magazines for emigrants to Victoria and New South Wales, *Choosing a School for your Child in Victoria* and *Choosing a School for your Child in*

NSW, are available by subscription from Consyl Publishing, details of which are given on page 225. These publications give useful information about the kinds of schools available in these states and answer many of the questions that arise when choosing a new school in an unfamiliar country. The New South Wales version of the magazine also covers boarding schools in NSW, Victoria, Queensland and Canberra.

Australia's academic year of three or four terms, depending on the state, follows the calendar year, running from January to December, so that the long summer holidays of around seven weeks coincide with the Christmas period.

The education system

The educational system is uniform in Australia and both the private and state sectors operate on the same patterns and curricula. Primary education in Australia takes six or seven years, and secondary education either five or six years, depending on the state. Wherever you live in Australia, the combined length of primary and secondary education is 12 years, and school years are numbered Years 1 to 12. Children can opt to finish their schooling in year 10 or to continue for another two years, allowing them potential entry into university.

Preschool

Preschooling is available for children aged three to five years old, and provides educational programmes in which young children are encouraged to develop their abilities, skills and knowledge of the world. Preschool centres often operate in association with local primary schools, and in WA and Queensland are located in the same grounds. Preschools are usually run by local councils, community groups or private organisations except in the Northern Territory and Queensland, where they are run by the Territory and State Governments respectively.

In Western Australia and some of the eastern states, there is an early learning continuum, which covers children aged three to eight years (K-3). The principles of this system recognise the distinctive learning patterns of young children, the nature of children's growth and development, and the value of home and community in learning. Children are encouraged to learn through play, experimentation, and interaction with other children and adults, learning to explore, manipulate objects, materials and technologies. Early reading is neither required nor pushed, and most children enter school in the year they turn six without any reading skills. Current research suggests that this is in fact more effective in encouraging later literacy than enforced early reading in the nursery years, and Australian results bear this out. Instead, preschools focus heavily on creativity and thinking skills, which can be applied later to more academic purposes. Children attend preschool mornings only in their first year, and from 9am–3pm in their second year.

Primary education

In New South Wales, Tasmania and ACT, kindergarten is the word used to describe the first year of compulsory education. Children enter primary school in the year they either turn five or six, (this depends on the state they are living in – see the table below) and there is no concept of 'rising fives' or term-by-term age-group entry. There is very little multi-age teaching in primary classrooms, except where numbers and resources require combined classes (in some rural areas, and in suburbs with falling rolls). Classes in state schools have a maximum of 30 students and many are smaller, depending on the area. State primary schools are almost invariably co-educational. However, many private schools offer single-sex education at this level. Each state sets its own curriculum, but all have common elements, emphasising English language, mathematics, social studies, health education, and physical education.

Many primary schools offer foreign languages from year three and there is a much greater focus on Asian languages – example, Mandarin Chinese, Japanese and Indonesian – than on European. It is less common for children to study French or German, and Latin is not a commonly taught subject. Philosophy and thinking skills are now taught in most schools from year five, and there is a strong emphasis on creative work from the earliest years. Oral communication skills are developed early and children as young as five will be expected to speak to the class regularly on topics of interest. A common practice is 'show and tell' day where children bring in an item from home that has a special value/interest to them and give a speech on it to the classroom.

Sports are an important part of the school day, and in summer many children will have daily or weekly swimming lessons (many schools have swimming pools or access to the local municipality pool/leisure centre). School assemblies provide an opportunity for classes to make drama presentations and are largely the responsibility of the students. Parents are encouraged to attend these weekly occasions. The school day usually runs from 8.50am–3.15pm, but this will vary slightly from state to state.

Secondary education

After finishing either year six or seven, depending on the state, children progress on to secondary school, which is known as 'high school'. In the state sector these are usually of the comprehensive variety, although some states still run a streamed, grammar school system, and others offer special programmes to children gifted in certain fields. These specialist programmes in music, theatre studies, art or sport offer scholarships to talented students from all over the state or territory, and entry is highly

State by state starting age

State or Territory	Minimum age	Age in the year before year 1	Compulsory age	Year before school is called
ACT	4.8	Age 5 on 30 April	Year in which child turns 6	Preschool
NT	4.6	Age 5 on 30 June	Year in which child turns 6	Preschool
NSW	4.5	Age 5 on 31 July	Year in which child turns 6	Preschool
QLD	4.6	Age 5 on 30 June	Year in which child turns 6	Kindergarten/ Preschool
SA	4.5	Continuous entry in the term after 5th birthday	Year in which child turns 6	Kindergarten
TAS	5.0	Age 5 on 1 January	Year after turning 5	Kindergarten
VIC	4.8	Age 5 on 30 April	Year in which child turns 6	Kindergarten
WA	4.6	Age 5 on 30 June	Year in which child turns 6	Kindergarten

competitive. High school students enjoy modern facilities, and are taught a variety of subjects, which include the core studies of English, maths, science and social studies (history and geography), as well as art, home economics and languages.

In many high schools, students in the first year must take the whole range of subjects available, despite personal preferences, to try and help them develop wider interests or recognise previously undiscovered talents. This means that regardless of gender, all students will have to study cooking, sewing, woodwork, metalwork, art, music, drama and sport, as required by the school. As students progress through the high school system, they are allowed to specialise in subjects of their own choosing, until they reach the final two years of school, where subject choices will be determined by future career preferences.

Children with special needs

Special schools are provided for physically and mentally disabled children. In the state system, children with learning disabilities are provided with special tuition inside the regular primary or high school structure. Individualised programmes are delivered by specialist teachers or a team of special educators. Provision is made for children with dyslexia and dyspraxia in most schools.

Gifted and talented children

State education departments recognise the needs of gifted and talented children, and provide special programmes for them. All schools are responsible for the ongoing identification of gifted and talented children, and monitor their progress carefully. Such children are offered a 'differentiated curriculum', the guiding principles of which are: a stimulating and interactive environment, an acceptance of individual differences and potential, a willingness to provide appropriate teaching methods and materials to match those differences, and flexibility. Teachers must, by law, provide for gifted and talented children at all times.

Technology in schools

The various state education systems place a high priority on educating students to take advantage of new technologies. The present Government has promised A$130m over four years to government schools for the purposes of achieving better scientific and technological literacy, to develop school based innovation and build supportive school environments. It has also promised A$34.1m over five years towards the development of online curriculum resources, services and applications. Most schools are well equipped with information technology facilities and offer teaching in this field to even the youngest students. Most schools are also on the internet and provide every class or student with an email address. In many private schools students are provided with their own laptop.

Vocational education

There has been significant change in post-compulsory schooling in current years, with an increasing emphasis on work-based learning. Work experience has been an important part of school programmes for many years, and this has now been expanded into structured work-based learning programmes that combine school and industry-based learning. A number of initiatives have been introduced including VET (Vocational Education and Training in schools programme), school-based new apprenticeships, vocational programmes, fast track programmes, and several others. Approval and certification arrangements provide a means of recognising students' achievements in work-based programmes.

Distance education

Australia's vast size means that many students in rural areas are hundreds of miles from the nearest schools. Every state, therefore, runs an active distance education programme, which caters not only for students who are unable to attend school by reason of their location, but also for ill or otherwise isolated children. State Governments provide professional staff, resources, and support, as well as radio broadcasts and internet services, to children of all ages.

Post-compulsory education

The compulsory years of secondary education finish at the end of year 10 (age 15–16). Secondary Education Authorities in each state issue School Leaving Certificates of achievement (based on coursework and exams and roughly equivalent to the British GCSEs) to students leaving school at this stage. Students who leave after year 10 tend to be less academically inclined and will generally seek an apprenticeship or some other form of vocational training. Retention rates for years 11 and 12 are high, with between 70% and 90% of students staying on, depending on the state and prevailing economic conditions. The retention rate of those students who went on to attend Year 12 increased from 72% in 1997 to 74% in 2007. Students who hope to enter tertiary education take public examinations at the end of year 12. These go by different names in each state; for example in WA, it is the TEE, or Tertiary Entrance Examination; in NSW, the HSC, or Higher School Certificate, and in Victoria the VCE or Victorian Certificate of Education. Students study between five and seven subjects at this level, and these grades are combined to form a tertiary entrance aggregate, which is the sole criterion for entry to university. If your children are likely to be transferring to an Australian University course at this crucial stage, it may be worth them considering the International Baccalaureate as a post-high school qualification as this is accepted internationally as an appropriate level for entry by most universities.

The academic year

Most schools begin their academic year at either the end of January or the beginning of February, and the year ends before Christmas in December. The year is divided into four 10-week terms, with holidays of approximately two weeks interspersing the middle terms. There are no mid-term breaks or 'half-terms'. Public and religious holidays are observed – students and teachers are given the day off along with the rest of the workforce.

Uniforms

State school education is free from kindergarten to year 12. Parents do have to pay the costs of books and uniforms for state schools, but these are kept at a very low level. Uniform may or may not be compulsory, but is generally favoured by both pupils and parents. Schools try to keep it simple: in summer, shorts and a polo shirt for boys, a cotton dress for girls; in winter, trousers for boys and either trousers for girls or woollen tights with thicker skirts. In primary schools, a tracksuit in school colours with a crest on the sweatshirt is most common for the colder winter months. Sunhats, usually of the legionnaire type, are compulsory in years one, two, three and four, and this policy is strictly enforced. The motto learned by all small children is 'no hat, no play', and anyone who comes to school without a hat will be kept indoors. Uniform shops are run by school parents' and friends' associations, and the cost of a complete uniform shouldn't break the bank. Trainers or leather-soled shoes are usually worn with both winter and summer uniforms. In warmer states such as Perth and Brisbane, children are often allowed to wear sandals in the sweltering summer months. Flip-flops (known in Australia as thongs) are forbidden. Secondary school students tend to prefer the Australian Akubra-style hats

(wide-brimmed and made of felt) or straw hats. Factor 15+ sunscreen is provided free to all primary school students, and you should make sure your child goes to school with some on. It will be re-applied during the day by teachers.

Independent and private education

Australia's 900-odd independent, or private, schools account for more than 300,000 pupils, approximately 10% of enrolments in Australia. Around two-thirds of overseas students in Australian schools are enrolled in private schools. Such schools are becoming an increasingly popular choice, despite the considerable expenses involved. Private school fees usually begin at around A$4,500 per year per child, but may go up to as much as A$15,000. Independent schools are usually associated with the various Christian denominations, especially the Catholic Church and the Church of England, and these Christian and Catholic schools tend to charge lower fees than the big independent schools. There are also a number of schools in each state associated with the Baptist Church and non-denominational churches, as well as Jewish and Islamic Schools. The Australian Bureau of Statistics surveys have shown that in 2007 there were 3,441,026 full-time school students enrolled in government and non-government schools combined.

Extracurricular activities

Australian students generally participate in a number of extracurricular school activities, which typically include camps, excursions, environmental groups and sports. Most schools have a concert band or orchestra, a choir, a dance troupe and drama society, which rehearse and perform throughout the year. Government schools provide free music tuition to some children who have been recognised as talented after testing in years three, four, and six. Once selected, children receive tuition and an instrument through to year 12, as well as specialist ensemble opportunities.

Many parents believe that their children will receive an enhanced education at private school, as the teacher-student ratio is usually lower. Class sizes in Australian schools average 30 students, but may be higher or lower than this, depending on the state budget and resources. Upper-school classes also tend to be much smaller, and in private schools the upper-school class sizes are often as low as 15–20 students, while in state schools the size is more often around 18–25. There are, however, some outstanding state schools that consistently achieve standards of excellence in academic, sporting and creative fields. Information about special programmes is available from the local Education Authority, via the Department of Education, Science and Training in your state or territory, and rankings of academic excellence are published annually in the press.

Entry of new arrivals

If you have children currently enrolled in the education system at home, you should bring current school reports with you, including a reference from their teacher or head teacher. Samples of their work will also help the school assess the appropriate grade for your child. Ordinarily, children are placed in a year commensurate with the age of their peer group. Children who are significantly in advance of or behind the level of work being done by other children of the same age may be placed according to their ability. It is rare for a child to be placed with children more than a year older or younger. The difference in the commencement of the academic year in Australia can create problems in choosing the right level beginning in January/February.

Parents' and citizens' committees in schools

Parents can expect to be more involved in their children's education than they may have been previously. Every Australian school has its own parents' and citizens' committee (P&C), sometimes known as 'parents' and friends', 'which consists of parents, teachers and student representatives. These committees raise funds for school excursions or tours, school equipment, and assist in the administration of some aspects of school life, such as the canteen. The Australian school canteen is quite different to the school canteen system in the UK, as hot lunches are rarely supplied. Australians do not eat a large meal in the middle of the day due to the heat. Instead, school canteens are more like subsidised sandwich shops, and sell sandwiches, rolls, salads, pies, some sweet items, and drinks. Many P&C committees have designed healthy, economical and tasty lunch menus which have seen chips and crisps banned in favour of less fattening alternatives. P&C committees also decide on issues such as school uniform, homework policies and behaviour management policies.

Student councils

Most schools no longer operate a prefect system in which some children are appointed to school office by the teachers or head. Instead, in primary schools, all year sevens are given special responsibilities, and the student body elects heads of sporting houses. In secondary school, there will usually be a school council, consisting of representatives elected by each year group at the end of the previous year, who meet and advise school staff of student needs and problems, and who carry designated responsibilities. In general, schools try and operate an open and democratic process in the appointment of student officers, who in turn take their responsibilities seriously.

Further education

Universities

The university academic year follows the calendar year, and teaching usually takes place between March and November. The university year is 'semesterised', and both semesters are divided into two halves by a one-week 'study break'. Enrolments usually take place in December of the year before commencement, but application must be made through the student's school to the state tertiary admissions centre by the August before final public examinations are undertaken. Australia's tertiary education sector has been undergoing a process of overhaul during the last decade, mainly for budgetary reasons. The most significant change has been that institutions that were established as technical colleges or colleges of further education have now acquired university status. This has created a divided system:

1. A group of six universities – Sydney, Melbourne, Adelaide, Western Australia, Queensland and Tasmania – acquiring a kind of 'Ivy League' status

2. A prestigious second level of long-established polytechnic-type universities, such as the University of NSW, Curtin and RMIT

3. A group of respectable but lesser institutions such as Murdoch University and the University of New England

4. The ex-technical colleges, like Edith Cowan University

There is a constant scrabble among the various institutions for research funding, and rankings are very important. Although officially all on a par, there is no doubt that in the perception of the public, employers, and overseas institutions considering students for postgraduate research there remain clear differences in the levels of academic excellence attained by these institutions and competition for entry to the top two levels is always intense. Australian universities offer a wide choice of subjects and qualifications. Currently, for a population of almost 21 million, there are 40 universities. Most tertiary institutions are funded by a combination of state and federal grants, however, public investment in university teaching and learning on a per student basis, with the exception of a period in the early 1990s, has been declining since 1983. Nevertheless, in spite of changes in the funding system, Australian tertiary education remains financially accessible to all.

A report by the Organisation for Economic Co-operation and Development (OECD) has ranked Australia fourth behind the USA, Finland and Japan for entry into full-time tertiary education and also fourth, behind Canada, Norway and the USA, in the percentage of graduates produced. The report also found that of all degrees awarded, engineering accounts for approximately 5.3% of degrees conferred by Australian institutions compared with 22.8% in Japan, 18.9% in Germany and 7.1% in the USA (the OECD average is 12.1%). In natural sciences, however, Australia is a world leader with 14.1% compared with 9.1% in Germany, 4.7% in the USA and 2.9% in Japan.

Fees and other costs

Until 1989, tertiary education was absolutely free for all students regardless of means. By 1990, however, budgetary constraints had forced a rethink on this sacred cow of education policy, and the system was changed so that students became liable for fees under the Higher Education Contributions Scheme (HECS). Under HECS, students paid part of the cost of their further education, with the Commonwealth meeting the balance. In 2002, the Australian Government conducted a review of Australia's higher education system. The Government's response to the review was announced in the policy statement *Our Universities: Backing Australia's Future*. Most reforms emanating from the review commenced in 2005. The fundamental principle of HECS, whereby the Australian Government sets the contribution amount for subsidised places, has not changed. The Australian Government has also maintained the principle that eligible students should not be prevented from participating in higher education because of an inability to pay their student contribution upfront. The deferred payment arrangements and discount for upfront payments that were available under HECS are now grouped together as HECS–HELP assistance.

HECS places are now called Commonwealth supported places. From 2005, higher education providers were able to determine student contribution amounts for Commonwealth supported places in ranges from A$0 up to a maximum set by the Australian Government. Student contributions are paid either upfront or deferred and paid later through the tax system. The options available for paying the student contribution depend on students' citizenship or residency status. If a student defers their student contribution, the Australian Government pays the contribution to the higher education provider on behalf of the student. The debt must eventually be repaid once the student's income reaches the minimum repayment threshold. The Australian Government has increased the minimum repayment threshold for compulsory repayment of a HECS debt from A$35,000 in 2004–05, A$36,184 in 2005–06, and A$38,149 in 2006–07 to A$39,825 for the period 2007–08 for a HELP debt. This means you will not be required to start repaying your debt until your income is above A$39,825. Payments are deducted in the form of a tax levy of between 4% and 8%. compulsory repayments increase as the income increases. There is no interest charged on HELP debts, but the debts are indexed annually to bring it in line with the cost of living. The adjustment is made on the first of June each year and applies to the portion of debt that remains unpaid.

 Commonwealth supported places and HELP assistance: www.goingtouni.gov.au

Compulsory repayments increase as the income increases, and the debt is usually painlessly paid off in a few years. Students who opt to complete an additional honours year on top of pass degree may be eligible for HECS exemption for that year, which is known as a HECS scholarship.

In addition to tuition fees, students must meet the costs of their own textbooks, which may be between A$300 and A$1,300 per year depending on the course, however, most institutions have good second-hand bookshops where texts may be purchased more cheaply. Students are also charged fees to join their student organisations, known as unions, associations or guilds. These organisations provide and are involved in the administration of a large number of benefits, including sporting facilities, discounts, the issuing of student identification cards, insurance cover, photocopying, bookshops, catering, social functions such as balls, and student newspapers. Membership costs range from A$65–A$300 per annum. Until currently, membership of a university's student union was compulsory, except for conscientious objectors, who could choose to have their dues paid to a charity instead. However, current Government legislation, aimed at weakening a united student voice in the light of controversial changes in the higher education sector, made it illegal to require compulsory membership. As a result, student unions now battle to attract new members, and are able to provide fewer benefits to students because of their diminished income.

Choosing a university

Selecting a university can be difficult, and most capital cities have a number of different institutions from which to choose. Every institution and department publishes a prospectus, and university libraries will usually hold a number of these from a range of universities across the country. Careful consideration of these will give a good idea of what is on offer. Most universities have an officer who deals with enquiries from prospective students, and schools will always offer careful guidance on appropriate institutions and courses.

The Australian Department of Education, Science and Training runs a website (www.goingtouni.gov.au) outlining all course and university options available in the country. The publication *The Good Universities Guide* (www.thegoodguides.com.au) covers all 45 universities in Australia, giving a brief summary of each, including breadth of course offerings, depth, flexibility of admissions policy, mature-age opportunities, student-staff ratios, gender balance, research track record, affluence, graduate salaries, employment prospects, library quality, popularity with fee paying students and tuition fees. Details of various courses run by the different institutions, the entry marks required for each course, and entry procedures for the various courses are also given as well as a rating of Australia's top 10 universities and details of comparative graduate employment rates and starting salaries. Annual rankings of the nation's university are published in *The Australian*, as well as most city newspapers. Year after year, the top performing institutions include the Universities of Melbourne, Sydney, Western Australia, and NSW, Monash and Macquarie Universities, RMIT, and ANU (the Australian National University in Canberra).

Student funding and loans

Australian university students usually survive financially on scholarships, part-time jobs, their parents (about 50% of all university students still live with their parents throughout their academic careers), the Youth Allowance, or a combination of all of these. Until July 1998, eligible students were funded by a national educational grant system known as Austudy. Only about 33% of students received Austudy, which was designed as an income support scheme rather than a full living allowance. Many students were not eligible for any Austudy allowance whatsoever on the basis of their parents' income, and relatively few were eligible for the full Austudy allowance. Austudy for students aged between 18 and 24 years has now been replaced by the Youth Allowance, a single payment made to all eligible young people and replacing not only Austudy but also the dole and other social security benefits. The Allowance is still subject to parental

2007 THES-QS Top World 200 Ranking Times Higher Education Supplement University Rankings		
University	**Aus Rank**	**(World Rank)**
ANU	1	(16)
Melbourne	2	(27)
Sydney	3	(31)
Queensland	4	(33)
Monash	5	(43)
New South Wales	6	(44)
Adelaide	7	(62)
Western Australia	8	(64)
Macquarie	9	(168)
QUT	10	(195)
Wollongong	11	(199)
RMIT	12	(200)

means test, but offers some advantages to students over the old system, insofar as they are now also eligible for rent assistance (up to the value of A$105.40 per fortnight for a single adult with no dependents). An interest-free loan of A$500 is also available.

A pared-down version of Austudy remains in force for students over the age of 25. Eligibility for Austudy, and the amount which a mature or independent student can receive under the scheme depends upon enrolment in an approved full-time course (almost all university courses are approved), and on the applicant's income and assets, and, if applicable, those of his or her spouse. If you receive Austudy, you are also allowed to earn an income of up to A$6,136 per annum without affecting your allowance. If you earn above this amount, your Austudy payments will be reduced proportionately. The Austudy supplement provides further funding through a Government-sponsored personal loan, the Student Financial Assistance Scheme. Note that while Austudy is a grant, the Austudy Supplement is a loan, and although it can help students in need, many choose not to take it up as repayment conditions are onerous.

Technical and further education centres

Tertiary education is also available at technical and further education centres (TAFEs), which offer vocationally oriented qualifications. There are approximately 250 TAFE institutions in Australia, but many of these have additional affiliated campuses, training centres and ancillary teaching centres. Every state and territory has a large number of TAFE colleges and centres, in both capital cities and major regional areas. More than a million students are enrolled in TAFE courses, though many of these are part-time students. Many school leavers who want to upgrade their skills or adults who wish to retrain or re-enter the workforce study at TAFEs either on a full-time or part-time basis. TAFEs specialise in training and pre-apprenticeships in a diverse range of trades, including building, the vehicle, metal, electrical and automotive trades, electronics, plumbing, printing, catering, gardening, dairy farming, hairdressing, textiles, jewellery and watch-making, and secretarial and business studies. Both evening and day classes are usually available for most courses. School Certificate and Higher School Certificate subjects are also available for mature students who may be aiming for university entrance.

TAFEs also offer literacy and numeracy classes, as well as English as a Foreign Language for migrants and other new arrivals. There are also a number of short-term, part-time courses available in subjects like bar service, typing, commercial floristry and wool classing. In a current survey conducted by the National Centre for Vocational Education, nearly 85% of TAFE graduates rated their general level of satisfaction with the quality of training very highly.

The cost of attending a TAFE is significantly lower than university. Fee-exemptions are given to students in receipt of Youth Allowance or Austudy, and there are concession rates for low-income earners. TAFE students do not pay HECS. Usually TAFE colleges will allow you to pay fees in instalments.

Overseas students at Australian universities

Australian universities rely increasingly on overseas students for a proportion of their funding. South-East Asian students make up a significant proportion of enrolments, and are concentrated in faculties offering business, commerce and economics, with some entering medicine and law.

The number of overseas students attending Australian universities has grown incredibly over the years, and some universities now hold graduation ceremonies in Singapore and Kuala Lumpur to cater for their South-East Asian alumni. The Australian Government requires all institutions that accept overseas students to register with state authorities to assure continuing high standards of management and education.

If you wish to enter Australia to study, you will need to apply for a Student visa, and this cannot be issued until you can provide evidence that you have been accepted for a course of study and have paid half of the first year's annual fee for your course. It is important to note that you cannot change from Visitor status to Student status while you are in Australia, and that application for a Student visa can only be made in your own country of residence. To retain your visa, you must have a satisfactory record of attendance at your institution, and achieve satisfactory academic results. On completion of your course, you must leave Australia before your Student visa expires, and the Australian Government offers no leniency in this area.

Overseas students do not receive the privileges of government-funded education as offered to Australian citizens and permanent residents. Universities vary considerably in the fees that they charge overseas students, and costs are determined by the demand for the course, the location of the institution, and its level of prestige. The government sets a minimum fee structure for each course, but institutions are free to charge above this level, and frequently do. Fees vary considerably between disciplines and are subject to regular revision: as a general rule, you should expect a humanities degree to cost in the region of A$14,000 per annum, a science degree to cost around A$19,000, and professional courses like medicine and engineering anything up to A$45,000 a year. Various grants and scholarships may be available depending on your qualifications and circumstances. Individual institutions will have information about these.

Most universities have student accommodation associated with the campus, and overseas students will receive help in finding housing and settling in generally. Establishment costs have been estimated by the University of Sydney to be around A$900, and annual living costs for a single student to be around A$16,000 taking in rent, food, and travel expenses and 'entertainment' costs. Australian universities are committed to equity policies, and seek to provide an environment of equal opportunity, free from discrimination, for all students and staff.

Useful resources

Australian Education International: International Education Network, Department of Education, Science and Training, GPO Box 9880, Canberra City, ACT 2601; www.studyinaustralia.gov.au. Advice on study in Australia for international students.

Education Network Australia: 08 8334 3210; www.edna.edu.au. Funded by the Australian federal and state governments, Edna provides information about education and training in Australia and a database of internet resources and free online tools useful for teaching and learning.

National Centre for Vocational Education: 08 8230 8400; ncver@ncver.edu.au; www.ncver.edu.au.

Studylink: www.studylink.com.au. An internet-based directory exploring higher and vocational educational courses in Australia.

Commonwealth Department of Education, Science and Training: 02 6240 8111; www.dest.gov.au

State Tertiary Admissions Centres

NSW and ACT: Universities Admissions Centre (UAC) Pty Ltd, UAC, Locked Bag 112, Silverwater, NSW 2128; 02 9752 0200; www.uac.edu.au

Overseas student societies

Most universities have student-run societies that cater for overseas students from specific countries and regions. These associations organise camps, social functions, speakers and orientation programmes, and will also offer assistance if you contact them before you arrive at the institution. Your university will supply you with contact names for appropriate on-campus student organisations. Universities in Australia are completely free from religious discrimination, and those with large overseas student populations, like the University of Western Australia, provide worship facilities for most major religious groups.

NT: Students must apply direct to Charles Darwin University, Uni Info Shop, Ellengowan Drive, Casuarina, Darwin, NT 0909; 08 8946 7766 or 1800 061 963 (toll free); email uni-info@cdu.edu.au; www.ntu.edu.au
QLD: Queensland Tertiary Admissions Centre; Postal address: PO Box 1331, Milton, QLD 4064; 07 3368 1166; www.qtac.edu.au.
SA: South Australian Tertiary Admissions Centre (SATAC), Ground Floor, 104 Frome Street, Adelaide, SA 5000; 08 8224 4000; www.satac.edu.au.
TAS: Students must apply directly to The Admissions Office, University of Tasmania, GPO Box 252 45, Hobart, TAS 7001; 03 6226 7151 or 1800 030 955 (Toll Free); www.utas.edu.au
VIC: Victorian Tertiary Admissions Centre (VTAC), 40 Park Street, South Melbourne, VIC 3205; 03 9954 3220 or 1300 364 133; www.vtac.edu.au
WA: Tertiary Institutions Service Centre (TISC), 100 Royal Street, East Perth, WA 6004; 08 9318 8000; info@tisc.edu.au; www.tisc.edu.au

TAFE

NSW: TAFE Information Centre, 47 York Street, Sydney NSW 2000; 02 8234 2777 or 131 601; www.tafensw.edu.au
QLD/NT: There are no central information centres, but information can be obtained directly from your nearest college. College contact numbers are found in the government section at the beginning of the telephone directory.
SA: TAFE Information Centre, PO Box 320, Adelaide, SA 5001; 1800 882 661; tafe.info@saugov.sa.gov.au; www.tafe.sa.gov.au
TAS: Institute of TAFE Tasmania, PO Box 2015, Hobart, TAS 7001; 03 6233 7019 or 1300 655 307; www.tafe. tas.edu.au
VIC: The TAFE Virtual Campus, PO Box 266D, Melbourne, VIC 3001; 1800 896 122; www.tafevc.com.au

WA: Training Info Centre, 2nd Floor, City Central Building, 166 Murray Street, Perth, WA 6000; 08 9421 1344 or 1800 999 167; www.training.waa.gov.au/tic
Youth Allowance and Austudy: Freecall 132 490 for information.

International schools

International Baccalaureate Schools (headquarters in Geneva, Switzerland) are becoming increasingly common in Australia, and most capitals have at least one. A regional list of the schools offering the IB is given below. A complete list of such schools (71 in Australia) can be found on the International Baccalaureate Organisation's website (www.ibo.org).

ACT: Narrabundah College, Jerrabomberra Avenue, Kingston, ACT 2604; 02 6205 6999; www.narrabundahc. act.edu.au

NSW: SCECGS Redlands, 272 Military Road, Cremorne, NSW 2090; 02 9908 6479; www.redlands.nsw.edu.au.

NT: Kormilda College, PO Box 241, Berrimah, NT 0828; 08 8922 1611; www.kormilda.nt.edu.au

QLD: Mountain Creek State High School, PO Box 827, Mooloolaba, QLD 4557; 07 5477 8555; www.mtncreekshs.qld.edu.au

SA: Glenunga International High School, L'Estrange Street, Gelnunga, SA 5064; 08 8379 5629; www.gihs.sa.edu.au

SA: Mercedes College, 540 Fullarton Road, Springfield, SA 5062; 08 8372 3200; www.mercedes.adl. catholic.edu.au.

SA: Pembroke School, 18 Holden Street, Kensington Park, SA 5068; 08 8366 6245; www.pembroke.sa.edu.au

TAS: The Friends' School, PO Box 42, North Hobart, TAS 7002; 03 6210 2288; www.friends.tas.edu.au.

TAS: Launceston College, 107–119 Paterson Street, Launceston, TAS 7250; 03 6332 7777; www.launc.tased.edu.au

VIC: Lauriston Girls' School, 38 Huntingtower Road, Armadale, VIC 3143; 03 9864 7555; www.lauriston.vic.edu.au

VIC: Wesley College, 620 High Street Road, Glen Waverley, Melbourne, VIC 3150; 03 9881 5394; www.wesleycollege.net

VIC: Presbyterian Ladies' College, 141 Burwood Highway, Burwood, VIC 3125; 03 9808 5811; www.plc.vic.edu.au

VIC: St. Leonard's College, 163 South Road, Brighton East, VIC 3187; 03 9592 2266; www.stleonards.vic.edu.au.

VIC: Tintern Anglican Girls' Grammar School, 90 Alexandra Road, Ringwood East, VIC 3135; 03 9845 7820;www.tintern.vic.edu.au.

WA: Montessori School, PO. Box 194, Landsdale, WA 6065; 08 9409 9151; www.themontessorischool. wa.edu.au

Choosing a School (New South Wales, Victoria, or Queensland's Private Schools) magazines are available from the Subscription Department, Consyl Publishing, 3 Buckhurst Road, Bexhill-on-Sea, East Sussex TN40 1QF; 01424-223111; www.consylpublishing.co.uk

■ SOCIAL SERVICES

Social security and unemployment benefits

Australia has a full cradle-to-grave state welfare system that has, in recent years, been significantly streamlined. However, social security benefits, including unemployment and family benefits, are not available to temporary residents, and migrants are also ineligible to claim any kind of benefit until they have been resident in Australia for a full two years. The two-year 'no-claim' period was introduced by the government in 1997 following public concern that migrants were taking advantage of Australia's social security system; previously, new settlers could start claiming benefits in 26 weeks of arrival.

 Department of Family and Community Services (FACS): www.facs.gov.au
Centrelink: www.centrelink.gov.au

There is a Centrelink office in each capital city and in most major regional centres, where advisers will provide current information and discuss your eligibility for benefits.

■ PUBLIC TRANSPORT

Most Australian cities are well served by public transport. In the city centre, there are frequent and economical buses; trains also service the Central Business District (CBD). In Melbourne, the city transport system also includes trams, which have become both a feature and an attraction of the city, and which are now considered to point the way forward in public transport planning strategies. Trams on some city routes are free. Sydney has an underground and overground rail system. Most trains are double deckers, providing ample space for everyone to sit down and the views from the top deck can be magnificent – particularly on the North Sydney line, which crosses the Harbour Bridge. In Adelaide commuters use the 'O-Bahn', the world's longest and fastest guided bus way. In Perth, the city council provides free bus services in a restricted area of the city. The Central Area Transit System (CATs for short) is a bus service that operates in the city centre and also in Fremantle. Routes are colour-coded and you can catch one of the service buses at any point along its route and stay on as long as you like, without paying a cent. In both Perth and Melbourne, these free transport services are provided to encourage city workers to leave their cars at home, reducing city traffic congestion. Many tourists and shoppers also take advantage of the excellent services.

In many Australian cities, the public transport tickets are valid for a length of time rather than for a single or return journey (this is similar to the London underground for example and the New York subway). If, for example, you buy a ticket (which is priced according to how many zones you need to cover), that ticket will be valid for a specific length of time, and will remain valid regardless of how many times you get on and off any buses or trains in that time period, within the specified zones. Zones are set in concentric circles, so it is possible to travel out from the city centre to the other side of the city without purchasing extra zones. In addition, in Perth and Melbourne it is possible to use bus and train tickets interchangeably, so you can catch the bus into the CBD and then use the same ticket to catch a train to another destination, or vice versa. You usually pay the driver for your ticket as you board, and there are automatic ticket vending machines at stations.

Australian cities are very sprawling and there are often long distances to be crossed between various areas. In Sydney you can get from the Western suburbs to the international/domestic airport in less than 40 minutes and at a cost of only A$10–14.

As a resulst the public transport is perhaps not as frequent or as well established as in European cities. There is, however, considerable new investment in rail services, especially in Perth, which is constantly increasing its track miles. An average single ticket in Sydney, for example, will cost about A$5. Most Australians still like to drive to work, although there are an increasing number of Park and Ride schemes by which you drive to a convenient bus/rail depot and travel into the city centre by public transport.

To view a railway map of either Sydney or Melbourne see page 500.

FACT

■ In Sydney you can get from the Western suburbs to the international/ domestic airport in less than 40 minutes and at a cost of only A$10–14.

Air

Domestic air travel has become considerably more affordable since competition began between the airlines Virgin Blue, Jetstar and Qantas. Tourists will find it is often cheaper to book internal flights from their home country in advance via the internet, often picking up single seats from as little as A$39 (Sydney to the Gold Coast) Many international airlines offer free or discounted internal flights with their tickets, and there are also a number of air passes available which offer more economical travel in Australia.

Rail

Australia has an extensive rail network, although it is impossible to travel the whole country by train. The remote outback of both the Northern Territory and Western Australia is not served by railway lines at all (the intense heat can cause track to buckle), and Tasmania, being both small and seabound, has never developed a rail system. The eastern coast of Australia, however, is well served by trains. One of the great railway lines of the world, The Indian Pacific, runs between Perth and Sydney and operates weekly. This transcontinental journey is 2,704 miles (4,352km) long, takes 65 hours and travels through two time zones. After watching the sunrise over the Pacific Ocean in Sydney, you can enjoy the Perth sunset over the Indian Ocean. Other legendary train journeys include The Ghan (from Adelaide via Alice Springs to Darwin) and The Overland (from Melbourne to Adelaide). Coastal destinations, including the Great Barrier Reef and Whitsunday Islands, are reached aboard The Sunlander or on Australia's most modern train, the Tilt Train. More than 360 New South Wales regional and interstate destinations, including Brisbane, Canberra and Melbourne, are serviced by the CountryLink network. Interstate rail travel is expensive, and most travellers will choose to undertake it for the experience rather than for the convenience.

There are several rail passes available for rail travel in Australia, which can be booked before departure. All passes are valid for travel in Economy/ Kangaroo seating.

Travel agents

Rail Australia: 08 8213 4592; reservations@railaustralia.com.au; www.railaustralia.com.au

International Rail: (UK) 0870 751 5000; info@international-rail.com; www.international-rail.com

Down Under Answers: 1 800 788 6685; www.duatravel.com

As some long-distance rail services operate on a weekly basis, you are well advised to book ahead, particularly if you have a limited travelling time or are travelling in peak season. Tickets may be booked up to six months in advance and there are often discounts on those tickets purchased in

advance. Single tickets are valid for two months and return tickets must be used within six months of using the outbound section of the ticket.

Coach

Travelling by coach around Australia, while time-consuming, is actually one of the best ways to see the country, as well as one of the cheapest. Nearly 80% of independent travellers use coach services to get around Australia. There are a number of independent bus companies and daily services travel to almost anywhere in the country from every major city. Prices are competitive and the standards are very high. Long-distance coaches are usually fitted with video and stereo facilities, and the drivers often consider themselves to be part of the entertainment, maintaining humour levels should passengers begin to flag in the middle of a long trip. Every coach is fitted with air conditioning, a toilet and drinking water fountains, and there are frequent stops at roadhouses for food, drinks, toilets and even showers. All coaches are strictly non-smoking.

Greyhound Australia is Australia's national coach operator providing services to more than 1,100 destinations throughout the country.

 Greyhound Australia (UK) 01424 722152: www.greyhound.com.au;
Redline Coaches (Tasmania): www.tasredline.com

Bus and combined bus/rail passes

There is a range of bus passes available for travellers in Australia and information can be obtained from travel agents in the UK, USA, or

FACT

■ The Society of International Railway Travellers (www.irtsociety.com) lists these routes, in their top 25 iconic rail adventures: The Sunlander (Brisbane to Cairns), The Indian Pacific (which travels between Sydney and Perth) and The Gahn (which makes the treacherous journey between Adelaide and Darwin).

Australia. For example the Aussie Kilometre Pass allows you to travel a certain amount of kilometres over a period of 12 months from the first day of travel in Australia, with the freedom and flexibility to hop on and off the coach as well as changing direction as often as you like. The Aussie Explorer Pass lets you choose a pre-set travel route and you can stop off as often as you like, travelling in one direction. Selected passes include free tours and transfers to destinations such as Kakadu National Park and Ayers Rock. There are 23 preset routes and passes are valid for one to 12 months from the first date of travel, depending on the pass. All passes are cheaper to buy outside Australia by 10% and you will be able to exchange Aussie Passes on the trans-Nullarbor services (Perth-Adelaide, or vice versa) for Red Kangaroos Day/Night seats on the Indian Pacific train.

Another new way of getting to see this amazing country is by hiring a Spaceship. No, Australia hasn't been invaded by ET, it has simply opened its doors to trendy travel company Spaceships. They currently operate between Sydney and Cairns, and will be launching into Melbourne, Brisbane, Adelaide, Darwin and Alice by October 2008. Basically, it is like hiring a good car to drive that is fitted with more useful features than a campervan. Spaceships start with a Toyota people mover – air-conditioned, power steering, automatic with overdrive, economical, belted seating for four. Then they custom fit the vehicle with a double bed, a two-ring cooker, water supply, a fridge, a DVD player and screen, bedding and utensils for four people. This provides a great alternative to coach or train travel as it has the added bonus of built-in accommodation.

Spaceships: 13 0013 2469 www.spaceships.tv;

■ CARS AND MOTORING

The wide roads and the low risk of hazards such as fog and snow make driving in Australia reasonably easy with the exception of a heavy rain downpour, where people literally have to pull over to the hard shoulder and wait for it to pass. City traffic in Australia, is subject to the problems of congestion and tortuous one-way systems, but the suburban and country roads are usually excellent. In more remote areas the roads are often rough dirt or gravel surfaces best suited to rugged four-wheel drive vehicles. These are also the only vehicles suited to the tough conditions of the outback. Even in comparatively populated rural areas, apart from main roads and highways, most roads will be unmetalled. Generally, it is a good idea to keep your speed down on such roads, as vehicles do not respond as quickly as they do on bitumen roads and are likely to slide around a bit. On city and suburban roads, highways and freeways driving is straightforward, and with many of the major interstate and intercity highways hugging the coast, you can often enjoy some outstanding scenery on your travels.

Fuel

Leaded petrol has been phased out in environmentally friendly Australia, and the owners of old cars now use a 'lead replacement petrol' instead. Fuel costs vary from one area to another and, even in the metropolitan area, prices may vary considerably from suburb to suburb. Petrol tends to be more expensive in rural and remote areas due to freight costs. Petrol has seen continued price increases due mainly to record high oil prices (in excess of A$90 a barrel) and in 2008 prices increased from 1.01 cents to A$1.48 per litre. These prices vary from state to state (see *Cost of living*, page 79). Regular (91 octane) and premium (96 octane) grades of unleaded petrol and Diesel are readily available at petrol stations (often the cheapest petrol can be bought at supermarket garages) and two-stroke petrol is available for lawnmowers and boat engines. You can also use the till receipts from supermarkets, which often offer discounts of four cents a litre off your fuel cost. Most garages also sell LPG (liquefied petroleum gas) for taxis and for topping up boats and gas barbies.

Driving regulations

Australians drive on the left of the road, as in Britain. There are, however, significant differences in speed limits, overtaking and other rules. Some of the basic differences between Australian and European driving are therefore worth noting.

Speed limits

Speed is restricted to 50–60km/h in built-up areas (defined as those with kerbs and street lighting) and to 100–110km/h on freeways or in country areas.

Overtaking

It is legal to overtake in the left (or inside) lane of a dual carriageway/ freeway (this is known as undertaking). On a three or more lane freeway (motorway), it is legal to overtake in any lane. The extreme right lane is not established exclusively as a fast lane, but it is courteous to keep to the left. It is not, however, obligatory to do so, so the British custom of driving up behind a car in the right lane, sitting on its tail and flashing your lights until it moves over to let you pass, is completely inappropriate. This kind of driving is likely to be interpreted as aggressive and may be met by an angry response from Australian drivers.

Road etiquette

It is imperative that you give way to your right when entering a freeway or dual carriageway from a slip road. It would be considered bad driving to come onto a freeway and expect cars in the left lane to move over to the right to let you enter the flow of traffic. Courteous drivers may do this, but it is not common practice, and drivers who do not change lanes to let you onto the freeway or dual carriageway are not considered rude.

The practice of flashing your lights also carries a different meaning in Australia. In Britain you may flash your lights to indicate to another car that it may enter your lane, that you wish to overtake them or to warn another driver that their headlights are not on. In Australia, you may also flash your headlights to indicate to another driver that their headlights are not on, but most commonly drivers will flash their lights to warn oncoming drivers that there is a police speed trap ahead. It is, in some states, illegal to warn other cars that they are approaching a speed trap, but the tradition of Australian anti-authoritarianism lives on and most drivers derive satisfaction from helping others avoid a speeding fine.

Highway Code

You can check the rules of the road by obtaining a copy of the Highway Code online or from your local police station, or traffic-licensing centre. The Highway Code varies in its details from state to state, often on minor points, but there are a number of differences on crucial points such as priority at intersections. If you wish to drive interstate, it would also be helpful to obtain the Highway Code relevant to your destination as each state/territory writes its own road laws. It is compulsory to wear seatbelts, both in the front and back, if a passenger is caught not wearing one, the driver receives a sizeable fine and two points from his/her licence.

Hitchhiking

Hitchhiking and picking up hitchhikers have been actively discouraged since serial killer, Ivan Milat, picked up seven hitchhikers and killed them in the Belanglo State Forest back in 1990–92. In Victoria, hitchhiking is illegal.

 Australian Highway Code:
www.rta.nsw.gov.au/rulesregulations/downloads/roadraustr_dl1.html

Drinking and driving

Penalties for drinking and driving in Australia are very severe and may result in a criminal record. Random Breath Testing (RBT) is legal and means that a driver can be pulled over at any time by the police, who will ask you to blow into a breathalyser to check the alcohol level of your blood. RBT vehicles are popularly known as 'Booze Buses' and are found at all times of the day and night, on both major and suburban roads. There is often no way of escaping them – if you see them ahead and try to take a left or right turn into a residential street to avoid testing, you will find they have set up base here to trap you. The permitted blood alcohol level in Australia is currently 0.05%. You will reach 0.05% after only one or two glasses of wine or beer, depending on the individual. For learners or provisional licence holders there is a zero blood alcohol limit, and for drivers of commercial vehicles many states also have a zero limit. Australian drivers take the risk of being caught extremely seriously. Do not drink and drive in

Licence penalty points

For minor driving offences, most States have a system of penalty points. Every driver has 12 points, and points are deducted according to the gravity of the traffic offence. Details of the points allocated to a particular offence are outlined in the Highway Code. If a driver loses all 12 points in a certain period of time, the driver loses his/her licence for a minimum of three months. This can be much longer if there is serious damage to property or persons involved. Serious traffic offences may be punishable by a jail term.

Australia; you are almost certain to get caught, may get a criminal record, will definitely get a very large fine, and will definitely lose your licence for at least three months. These days very few people, even the young and foolish, take the risk.

The Australian Government also put out a very memorable and amusing advert that states 'If you drink and drive you're a bloody idiot!' They have even be known to take out page adverts in the broadsheet newspapers highlighting the latest 'bloody idiots' who have been caught drink-driving. Hilarious and effective!

The positive side of this draconian policy is that statistics now show that the RBT system is successful and the number of alcohol-related road deaths has fallen considerably. In Victoria, random roadside drug tests continue to operate on a trial basis until laws to introduce them permanently are passed in 2008. A drug-affected driver faces a A$700 fine and a three-month licence cancellation. Those who have used amphetamines in the previous eight hours or cannabis in the past three hours are expected to fail the drug tests. So if you wish to go out for a night of drinking in Australia. the best thing to do is nominate a DD (designated driver – bars will often give the DD free soft drinks all night) or book a taxi.

Breakdowns and accidents

Automobile Associations

There are a number of accident and breakdown services in Australia, but the biggest is the NRMA (National Roads and Motorists' Association). All companies offer varying levels of cover, but home-start is part of basic cover rather than an optional extra. Policies change and prices fluctuate, so you will need to contact the companies directly to obtain current details. On the whole, accident and breakdown cover is much cheaper than in

Europe, and it is the car, not the driver, which is covered. In general, you can expect to pay around A$60–A$100 for a year's breakdown cover. If you need a breakdown service and you are not a member, you can join at the roadside, but a premium is charged for this service. The bigger companies also offer national and international accident and/or breakdown cover free (or at a minimal rate) and will cover the cost of towing a car from remote areas or in the event of a fatality, the cost of flying a body home. The standard of cover is excellent and membership is well worth the fee, particularly if your car is over five years old; cars get a raw deal being driven in Australia, as the distance between places is so vast. Up to 75% of Australian motorists are members of an automobile association, twice the European rate of membership. As on European motorways, there are telephones every kilometre on Australian freeways for the purpose of calling for roadside assistance. Automobile associations also offer other benefits such as tourist information, including hotel guides and maps, as well as the facility to have one of their qualified mechanics check over a used car that a member may wish to buy.

Accidents

If you are involved in a motor vehicle accident in Australia, whether as a passenger, pedestrian or driver, it is essential that you record the details of the other parties involved, including their full names, addresses, phone numbers, driver's licence numbers, the name of the is insurance company, the names, addresses and phone numbers of any witnesses, and a list of damage to the vehicles involved. This inventory should be made at the scene of the accident if at all possible. If the total cost of damage caused by the accident is thought to exceed A$500–A$1,000 (depending on the state/territory you are in) you must call the police, and in this case, it is helpful to record the name of any attending officers. If you sustain any physical injury, no matter how minor, you should see your GP and describe how your injuries were caused and their extent, in detail. Medical records will often affect any amount awarded as compensation in any personal injury claim.

Motorists' support services

Australian Council of the Royal Flying Doctor Service: 02 9241 2411; enquiries@rfdsno.com; www.flyingdoctor.net. Contact this office for a list of RFDS bases Australia-wide.

Australian Automobile Association (AAA): 02 6247 7311; aaa@aaa.asn.au; www.aaa.asn.au

Automobile Association of the Northern Territory (AANT): 08 8981 3837; information@aant.com.au; www.aant.com.au

National Roads and Motorists' Association (NRMA): 02 9848 5201; www.nrma.com.au

Royal Automobile Club of Australia: 02 8273 2300; raca@raca.com.au; www.raca.com.au

Driving in the outback

It is very important to never underestimate the danger that exists for wanderers in the outback. If you intend to drive in the outback, or undertake long distance trips, Tourism Australia can provide information detailing city-to-city links, motoring clubs, information on vehicle rental and accommodation, as well as essential rules for outback motoring.

Drivers are advised to prepare thoroughly for a trip through the outback, to notify friends and relatives of expected times of arrival, to inform them on arrival, to check intended routes carefully, to refuel at every opportunity and to keep an additional week's supply of food, water and fuel in case of a breakdown in remote areas. Many people have died of exposure and dehydration after breaking down in the outback. You are advised always to remain with your car if it breaks down in the outback, as the vehicle will provide shelter from the sun and serves as an obvious point of reference for rescue teams.

The Royal Flying Doctor Service of Australia (RFDS) offers a service for outback travellers, which includes advice on touring and emergency procedures, as well as hire of transceiver sets with emergency call buttons. It is advisable to contact the RFDS for information before embarking on a trip into the outback.

Royal Automobile Association of South Australia: 08 8202 4600; www.raa.net
Royal Automobile Club of Queensland (RACQ): 07 3872 8456 or 131 905; www.racq.com.au
Royal Automobile Club of Tasmania (RACT): 03 6232 6300; or 132 722; info@ract.com.au; www.ract.com.au.
Royal Automobile Club of Victoria (RACV): 131 955; www.racv.com.au
Royal Automobile Club of Western Australia: 08 9421 4444; www.rac.com.au

Driving licences

Each of the states and territories of Australia has a separate authority responsible for the issuing of driving licences. The minimum age for holding a licence is either 17 or 18 years, depending on the state or territory. A potential new driver may obtain a Learner's Permit three months before they reach driving age (at either 16 years 9 months or 17 years 9 months of age depending on state/territory), after first passing a written test on the Highway Code. A learner driver may only be accompanied or instructed by someone who has a clean driving licence and who has been driving for at least seven years. Learners must always display 'L' plates attached to the car. Although in practice most learners get at least some driving experience in the presence of a suitably qualified friend or member of the family, it is nonetheless advisable to have lessons with a qualified instructor before attempting the driving test.

Once a learner feels confident with the basic driving skills (in most states, this is after gaining 100 hours of self-assessed driving experience), the driving instructor will make an appointment for the driving test with a police examiner. On passing the test, a driver is granted a 'probationary' licence and is required to display 'P' plates on the car every time they drive for between one and three years. Probationary drivers are subject to restrictions on speed and blood alcohol limits, and face severe penalties if caught exceeding these limits. After one to three years, the probationary driver is considered to be sufficiently experienced to be awarded a full driving licence. Driving licences are not issued for an indefinite period (or until your 70th birthday) and must be renewed periodically, generally every five or ten years.

If you arrive in Australia with a driving licence issued overseas, different regulations apply. If you are considered to be a visiting driver (if you are temporarily in Australia and usually reside outside Australia) you may drive

any vehicle, including a locally registered one, provided you hold a current full driving licence or International Driving Permit (issued in your home country) for the class of vehicle to be driven. In Britain, an International Driving Permit can be obtained from the AA, even if you are not a member, and from most main post offices.

Obtaining an Australian driving licence

If you intend to become a permanent resident of Australia, you must obtain a driving licence issued by the relevant state or territory authority. Although you may be given a period of grace, which varies from state to state (usually three months), you will be required to obtain a driving licence as soon as you take up permanent residence. New settlers holding a current valid British driving licence must take a written test based on knowledge of the state/territory Motor Traffic Handbook (also known as the Highway Code) as well as a practical driving test. In addition, it is necessary in most states to undergo an eyesight test. A driving licence issued in one Australian state or territory is valid across Australia.

Car registration

Registration fees are payable according to the type of vehicle and the expected wear and tear that vehicle will inflict on the state's or territory's roads over the course of a year. In most states or territories, temporary residents and visitors are exempt from registration fees as long as the registration of the vehicle continues to be valid in the country of origin. A vehicle imported from abroad must be inspected on arrival by the nearest registration authority to ensure it is roadworthy immediately after its arrival in Australia. In addition, you will need to provide the following documents: a Carnet de Passage or other evidence that security has been lodged with Australian Customs, evidence that it is covered by third party insurance in Australia, a current registration certificate from the country of origin, and a valid driver's licence from the country of origin. Registration payments include third party injury insurance (CTP) and costs vary between states. The combined cost of registration and CTP of a popular six-cylinder family sedan ranges from A$400–A$600. Fees differ depending on whether the vehicle is intended for business or commercial use (for which standard fees apply) or solely for family or personal purposes (for which family vehicle fees apply). A family vehicle will receive a discount of around A$50 on the annual registration fee.

To register your vehicle, contact your local traffic authority (listed below). In New South Wales you must get an endorsed Compulsory Third Party Certificate (Green Slip) from an insurance company to be able to register your vehicle. Payment of the combined vehicle registration and CTP can be made at any metropolitan Post Office or at the office of the relevant authority, although payment procedures are subject to change and you should check with the proper registration authority. In Western Australia, payment of vehicle registration can only be done by cheque or via the metropolitan Post Office branches, and not at the Police Department. Once registered the vehicle will be fitted with Australian number (registration) plates which vary from state to state; those living on the sunshine coast of Queensland will often have plates decorated with palm trees.

Useful resources

ACT: Road User Services: 02 6207 7000; roaduserservices@act.gov.au; www.transport. act.gov.au
NSW: Roads and Traffic Authority: 02 9218 688; www.rta.nsw.gov.au
NT: Motor Vehicle Registry: 08 8999 3111; www.nt.gov.au
QLD: Queensland Transport: 132 380; www.transport.qld.gov.au. Service Centres are located throughout Queensland.
SA: Transport SA, Registration and Licensing Office, EDS Centre: 131 084; enquiries@transport. sa.gov.au; www.transport. sa.gov.au. 15 customer service centres throughout South Australia that deliver Registration and Licensing services.
TAS: Registrar of Motor Vehicles: 1300 851 225; info@dier.tas.gov.au; www.transport.tas.gov.au
VIC: Vic Roads Vehicle Registration: 03 9854 2666; www.vicroads.vic.gov.au
WA: Licensing Services: 08 9427 6404 or 131 156; call.centre@dpi. wa.gov.au; www.dpi.wa.gov.au/licensing/. Licensing centres throughout Westren Australia.

 TAXATION

Income tax

Australia revised its taxation laws back in July 2000 and a new tax system was introduced, bringing in new measures such as the Goods and Services Tax (GST), Pay-As-You-Go (PAYG) taxation and some business tax reform measures. Australia's Government structure means that each tier imposes its own taxes:

- The Commonwealth Government administers general taxes such as income tax, GST, customs and excise, fringe benefits tax, superannuation guarantee charge and taxes on natural resources projects.
- State and territory governments administer taxes such as payroll and workers' compensation taxes, stamp duties, bank account taxes and land tax.
- Municipal governments levy rates and charges on the owners of real estate.

Income tax in Australia can be quite a complicated business and the completion and lodgement of a tax return is the responsibility of the individual. To help demystify the taxation procedures, Tax Packs containing forms and an information magazine, produced by the Australian Taxation Office, are available free from newsagents and Taxation Offices across Australia. The Tax Pack is reviewed annually, in an effort to make completing a tax return less difficult, but even so, the Tax Pack is a formidable publication with detailed information and instructions. Both format and terminology are quite daunting and for this reason, fewer and fewer Australians are choosing to complete their own taxation returns and are turning to chartered accountants or licensed tax agents to complete the forms for them.

The Australian financial year begins on 1 July and ends on 30 June, and tax returns must usually be lodged by the end of October. Even if you think you are not liable to pay any tax, you are generally required to lodge a tax return in Australia if you are normally resident there, or if you are a non-resident who has derived an income in Australia. Every taxpayer requires a Tax File Number (TFN). To apply for a TFN you will need to contact the Australian Tax Office on arrival in Australia.

Although taxation rules and regulations are subject to continual re-assessment and change, clearly most Australian adults will fall somewhere in these categories and are therefore required to complete and lodge an annual taxation return.

Completing a tax return

To complete a tax return, you need to attach official statements of the amount of tax you have paid over the year. These statements are known as PAYG (Pay As You Go) Payment Summaries and are issued automatically by employers at the end of the financial year. If you do not receive a Payment Summary from your employer you must request one.

If either you or your employer have lost your PAYG Payment Summary, or they have gone missing in the post, you are usually able to get another copy from your employer. If your employer is unable to provide you with a copy, then he/she can give you a letter showing all the details of the original documents. In the unlikely event that you are not able to obtain a letter from your employer, you can fill in a Statutory Declaration of lost or missing Payment Summaries (available from your local Tax Office). If any information on your Payment Summary is wrong, your employer must provide a letter showing your correct income and tax details.

Self-assessment

If you choose to complete your own tax return, the tax office will work out your refund or tax bill based on the information you have provided. The tax office assumes the information you have provided is true and correct, but you should note that after they have calculated your rebate or bill and informed you of their calculations in your Notice of Assessment, their computers continue to check for missing or incorrect information. Your tax return may also be subject to an audit and, should the original assessment be judged incorrect, the tax office will change it and send you an amended assessment. In addition to extra tax you may be liable for a penalty if you fail to show reasonable care in the preparation of your return. Knowing this it is understandable why many Australians simply don't want to take the risk and so pay a professional to shoulder the responsibility.

Self-assessment can now easily be completed online. You cannot do this the first time you complete a return. You must initially do a manual return and then, the following year, you are permitted to complete your return online. Log on to register, then once you are given an internet registration code you can enter your taxable income and expenses and have the system automatically estimate your return or payment (see e-tax below).

 Australian Taxation Office: www.ato.gov.au

Professional assistance

If you would like assistance filling out your own tax return, you will be able to find chartered accountants or other professional taxation assistance services in the Yellow Pages (www.yellowpages.com.au). It is advisable to phone around as the cost of the service can vary greatly. The Tax Office recommends that if you get someone (other than them) to help you complete your return, you should ensure that that person is a registered tax agent. Some agents offer a free initial assessment and discounts to pensioners. Tax return fees charged by a registered tax agent are tax deductible against your next annual tax return. The company Destini Global Financial Services (address below) specialises in helping those emigrating to Australia with their tax and financial matters.

Tax help is available for seniors, people from non-English speaking backgrounds, the disabled and those on low incomes who cannot afford assistance with completing their tax returns. Tax help centres are run by community volunteers, and you should contact your local tax office for details of your nearest one.

There is also a Translating and Interpreting Service (TIS) available specifically to help non- English-speaking people with their tax returns. The TIS offers joint meetings with interpreters and tax officers, and you simply call the TIS to make an appointment. TIS phone numbers are found in the community information pages of your phone directory.

The postal addresses and phone numbers of the various state and regional Tax Offices are listed at the back of Tax Packs and in the Government section of the telephone book.

 Destini Global Financial Services: 020 7611 4777; global@destinifs.co.uk; www.destiniglobal.co.uk. Specialise in offering specialist tax and financial advice and transferring UK pensions to Australia.

Tax returns

It is obligatory to lodge a tax return at the end of the financial year if any of the following apply:

- You had tax deducted from your pay or other income (including Australian Government pensions, allowances or benefits)
- You had tax deducted from interest, dividends or unit trust distributions (applicable only to residents) because you did not quote your TFN or Australian Business Number (ABN) to the investment body
- You were required to lodge an activity statement under the PAYG system and pay an instalment amount during the year
- Your taxable income for the previous year was more than A$6,000 (residents) or A$1 million or more (non-residents)
- You incurred a net taxable loss, or are entitled to a deduction for a prior year loss
- You were entitled to a distribution from a trust, or you had an interest in a partnership and the trust or partnership carried on a business of primary production
- You were an Australian resident for tax purposes and you had exempt overseas employment income and A$1 or more of other income
- You are a special professional covered by income averaging provisions
- You received income from dividends or distributions exceeding A$6,000 and you had imputation credits or amounts withheld because you did not quote your TFN or ABN to the investment body
- You conducted business in Australia
- You paid provisional tax on your previous year's assessment
- You were under 18 years of age as of the 30 June and your total income was not from a salary or wages, and was more than A$1,333
- You are the liable parent under a child support assessment
- You have a reportable fringe benefits amount on your PAYG payment summary
- You are entitled to a tax offset
- You received a pension, allowance or benefits and your assessable income was more than: A$15,970 if you were single, widowed or separated at any time during the year; A$15,164 if you had a spouse but either of you lived in a nursing home or you had to live apart due to illness; A$13,305 if you lived with your spouse for the whole income year

Claiming back tax on expenses

Deductions are generally available for work-related expenses of a non-private or domestic nature, as well as other expenses such as gifts to organisations that are endorsed as deductible gift recipients. If audited, you will have to substantiate your work expenses claims, for example motor vehicle, travel, clothing, tertiary studies, tools of trade, reference books and other expenses. It is therefore necessary to keep records of any work-related expenses to avoid additional tax and a possible penalty.

You can claim for the cost of using your car for work or business purposes, for example travelling directly from one place of work to another, or from one job to another. You cannot, however, generally claim for the cost of travelling from home to work.

If you are an employee and the total of your claims is A$300 or less, you must keep a record of how you worked out each of your claims. If the total of your claims is more than A$300, you must keep records of receipts, invoices and similar documentary evidence supported by or on behalf of the supplier of the goods or services. Cheque stubs are not considered acceptable as evidence. The receipt, invoice or documentary evidence must:

◾ Be in English or the language of the country where the expense was incurred

◾ Have the date on which the expense was incurred

◾ Name the person who (or business which) supplied the goods or services

E-Tax

This service began in October 1998, which is an electronic tax preparation and lodgement software package. It was based on the original hard-copy Tax Pack. The Australian Taxation Office (ATO) has developed high levels of security to ensure that personal income tax information is secure. When you complete your return online, you sign it electronically using the in-built public key technology, and the e-tax software will encrypt your tax return file for transmission over the Internet using a secure link.

- Show the amount of the expense in the currency in which the expense was incurred
- Give details of the nature of the goods or services
- Show the date the document was made out.

A diary may be used to prove your claims for expenses that are no more than A$10 each and which add up to no more than A$200, or for expenses for which it was unreasonable to expect to get a receipt. The diary should contain all the details that would be required on a receipt or invoice. In addition, you must sign each entry in the diary.

The information outlined above should be kept for a period of five years after lodging your tax return. Records of other business-related expenses incurred by self-employed persons should also be retained for five years after lodging their tax return. If you appeal against an assessment, you must retain your records until the dispute has been finalised, if that period exceeds the given record retention period.

If you are to be audited, you will usually receive written notification at the beginning of the audit and you should follow the instructions contained in the letter.

Income tax rates

The following table shows personal income tax rates for those resident in Australia for the financial year 2007-2008. There is currently a tax threshold of A$6,000 in Australia, which means that the first A$6,000 earned is tax-free. The tax rate applicable on earning over this amount is described below:

Taxable income	Tax rate
A$ 0–6,000	Nil
A$ 6,001–30,600	15c for each A$ 1 over A$ 6,000
A$ 30,601–75,000	A$ 3,600 plus 30c for each A$ 1 over A$ 30,000
A$ 75,001–150,000	A$ 17,100 plus 40c for each A$ 1 over A$ 75,000
A$ 150,001 and over	A$ 47,100 plus 45c for each A$ 1 over A$ 150,000

These rates do not include the 1.5% Medicare levy

If you become a resident of Australia during the financial year you are entitled to a *pro rata* amount of the A$6,000 tax threshold. For the tax year you calculate this amount by adding up the number of months from when you became a resident of Australia up to the 30 June. This amount is then divided by 12 to give you the proportion of the year spent in Australia, then multiplied by A$6,000 to give you your tax-free threshold. If, for example, you have only been resident in Australia for two months, your tax threshold is assessed as 2/12 × A$6,000 = A$1,000, but if you have been resident for 11 months, your tax threshold is 11/12 × A$6,000 = A$5,500.

Your assessment can take up to eight weeks after lodging your tax return, or often instantly if you choose to use the e-tax system. If you are required to pay tax, you will be given 30 days' notice. Tax can be paid by cheque or postal money orders made payable to the Deputy Commissioner of Taxation, in cash or cheque at any Post Office (you must take your Notice of Assessment with you), by mail (cheque or postal order only), at Tax Offices (take your Notice of Assessment), or by direct debit/ refund. This last service is available from tax agents who lodge tax returns electronically.

If you cannot pay your tax by the due date, you may be given extra time to pay depending on your circumstances. You will have to provide details of your financial position including assets, liabilities, income and expenditure, and the steps you have taken to obtain funds to pay your debt. If granted additional time, you will have to pay a general interest charge (GIC). The GIC is a commercially linked interest rate that compounds daily and varies every quarter with changes in the money market.

Offsets

There are numerous tax offsets (formerly called tax rebates) that may be available to you, and it is worth being aware of them even if you are not currently eligible. If your tax offsets are greater than the tax on your taxable income, they can only reduce the amount of tax you pay in that year to zero. There are three exceptions to this rule:

- The 30% private health insurance rebate, where any excess is refunded to you
- The land care and water facility tax offset, where any excess is refunded to you
- The franking tax offset, where any excess imputation credits on dividends paid to you on or after 1 July of the tax year are refunded to you

Where you have excess refundable tax offsets available, these can be applied to reduce your tax, including the Medicare levy. Being eligible to claim a tax offset depends on things like maintaining a dependant, living in a remote area, or on how much taxable income you earned. A brief summary of some of the tax offsets available is given below:

Some tax offsets

- You were involved with heritage conservation work
- You were earning interest from government securities
- You were earning interest from the land transport facilities tax offset scheme or infrastructure borrowings scheme
- You were entitled to the land care and water facility
- You were living in a remote or isolated area of Australia
- You were responsible for the maintenance of your parent, spouse's parent or invalid relative
- Your net medical expenses were more than A$1,500 in the tax year. You can claim a tax offset of 20% – 20 cents in the dollar. There is no upper limit on the amount you can claim.
- You were serving overseas as a member of the Defence Force or a United Nations armed force
- You were responsible for superannuation contributions on behalf of your spouse
- Low income tax payers – if you were an Australian resident for tax purposes and your taxable income in the period 2006–07 was less than A$25 000, you will be entitled to a low income tax offset of A$599.96
- You claimed family tax benefit
- You are a low income, aged person

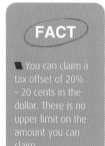

Capital Gains Tax

Many Capital Gains Tax (CGT) assets are easily recognisable – for example, land, shares in a company and units in a unit trust. Other CGT assets are not so well understood – for example, contractual rights, options, foreign currency and goodwill. All assets are subject to the CGT rules, unless they are specifically excluded. CGT assets fall into three categories: Collectables, personal use assets and other assets.

Since 1985, Australia has had a Capital Gains Tax (CGT). You will be liable for this tax if you make capital gains from selling or otherwise disposing of any CGT assets, or if you receive some other capital amounts in a financial year, unless a relevant CGT exemption replies. Examples of capital amounts include a forfeited deposit, premium received for granting a lease, or a capital gain distributed to a beneficiary of a trust. Net capital gains (after offsetting any capital losses you may have) are included in your assessable income and taxed at your applicable income tax rate, subject to the CGT 'discount' rules. Under the CGT discount rules, if you have held the CGT asset for at least 12 months, only one half of the net capital gain is taxable, unless you choose to apply indexation. For assets acquired before 21 September 1999, you may choose to apply indexation to the cost base of the asset (with the cost base being increased by reference to movements in the Consumer Price Index from the quarter in which you acquired the asset up to the quarter ending 30 September 1999) instead of the CGT discount. Any assets you may have acquired before 20 September 1985 are not subject to Capital Gains Tax.

There have currently been changes to the basic eligibility conditions as well as changes to the grouping rules for small businesses applying for capital gains tax concessions from 2007–08 and later income years.

The changes to the basic eligibility conditions include:

- A turnover test as an alternative to the maximum net asset value test
- An increase to the maximum net asset value threshold to A$6m

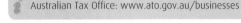
Australian Tax Office: www.ato.gov.au/businesses

Collectables

In your return you should include items that are used or kept mainly for personal use including: paintings, sculptures, drawings, engravings or photographs, reproductions of these items or property of a similar description or use, jewellery, antiques, coins or medallions, rare folios, manuscripts or books, and postage stamps or first day covers. A collectable can also be an interest in, a debt that arises from, or an option or right to acquire any of the above items. Any capital gain or capital loss you make from a collectable acquired for A$500 or less is disregarded. A capital gain or capital loss you make from an interest in a collectable is disregarded if the market value of the collectable when you acquired the interest was A$500 or less. However, if you acquired the interest for A$500 or less before 16 December 1995, a capital gain or capital loss is disregarded. If you dispose of collectables individually that you would usually dispose of as a set, you are exempt from paying capital gains tax only if you acquired the set for A$500 or less. This does not apply to collectables you acquired before 16 December 1995.

Personal use asset

A personal use asset is deemed to be a CGT (Capital Gains Tax) asset, other than a collectable, that is used or kept mainly for personal use including: an option or a right to acquire a CGT asset of this type, a debt resulting from a CGT event involving a CGT asset kept mainly for your personal use and enjoyment, or a debt resulting from you doing something other than gaining or producing your assessable income or carrying on a business. Personal use assets also include such items as boats, furniture, electrical goods and household items. Land and buildings are not personal use assets. Any capital loss you make from a personal use asset is disregarded. If a CGT event happened to a personal use asset during or after the 1998–99 income year, any capital gain you make from the asset or part of the asset is disregarded if you acquired the asset for A$10,000 or less. If you dispose of personal use assets individually that would usually be sold as a set, you obtain the exemption only if you acquired the set for A$10,000 or less.

Other assets

Assets that are not collectables or personal use assets include: land and buildings, shares in a company, rights and options, leases, units in a unit trust, instalment receipts, goodwill, licences, convertible notes, your home (although there is a CGT exemption for your main residence), contractual rights, foreign currency, and any major capital improvement (above the improvement threshold) made to some land or pre-CGT assets.

 For a full explanation of Capital Gains Tax with all its separate clauses go to Australian Taxation Office, www.ato.gov.au

Fringe Benefits Tax

The Fringe Benefits Tax (FBT) was introduced in July 1986 by the Government in an effort to control the amount of non-cash (and therefore often non-taxable) benefits offered by employers as part of a job package. FBT is payable (at the rate of 48.5%) by the employer on the 'grossed up' taxable value of all non-exempt fringe benefits provided by the employer during the FBT year, which runs from 1 April to 31 March. Fringe benefits are not taxable in the hands of the employee. Companies also cannot claim expenses such as business lunches and entertainment costs on behalf of the company. Taxable fringe benefits include company cars, free or low-interest loans, free or subsidised accommodation or board, goods and services sold at a reduced rate or provided free and expenses paid on behalf of an employee.

Cars are probably the most common fringe benefit, and an employer normally pays FBT when a car is owned or leased by a company and made available to an employee (or family member) for private use. FBT on cars does not normally apply to self-employed people or to a partnership if the vehicle is used wholly and exclusively for business. It does not apply to cars owned or leased by an employee, even when the cost of operating the car for business use is claimed as an expense against the taxable income. When FBT is chargeable, it applies to all passenger cars, wagons, minibuses, panel vans and utilities designed to carry less than one tonne or a bus with fewer than nine seats. There are many variations and exemptions to the FBT and probably the safest way of working out whether you are liable or not is to get a professional to do it for you.

The Government has currently announced that from 1 April 2007, the fringe benefits reporting exclusion threshold will increase from A$1,000 to A$2,000.

 Australian Tax Office: www.ato.gov.au/businesses

Goods and Services Tax

The Goods and Services Tax (GST) was introduced on 1 July 2000. Bearing some similarity to the system of VAT in the UK, the GST is a broad-based tax of 10% on the supply of most goods, services and anything else consumed in Australia. You must register for GST if the annual turnover of your business is A$75,000 or more (A$100,000 or more for non-profit organisations). You may choose to register if the annual turnover of your business is less than A$50,000 (less than A$100,000 for non-profit organisations). GST is charged on imported goods, but not on wages or salaries. The amount of GST payable on a taxable supply is 10% of its value. To work out how much GST is included in the price of a taxable supply, you need to divide the price of the goods by 11. Some supplies are not taxable and are called GST-free supplies. These include most food, some exports, most health and childcare services, educational supplies and cars for use by disabled people. The GST has not been greeted too warmly by Australians and in particular women, who are being charged GST on products they purchase regularly from the chemist, such as birth control pills.

Higher education contributions scheme

Higher education contribution scheme (HECS) regulations are described in detail on page 218. The rate of HECS tax varies from 3% to 6% of your taxable income. In addition, since 1994, the Australian Government has instructed employers to deduct additional taxation instalments to cover any possible Higher Education Contributions Assessment Debt in future years.

 HECS, Your Questions Answered: booklet available from tax offices or www.goingtouni.gov.au

Death duties

Currently, there are no death duties in Australia, although Capital Gains Tax (CGT) is widely considered to be death duty by another name and widely resented as such. Capital gains arising when an asset passes to the deceased's estate and then to the beneficiaries are generally disregarded though, although pre-CGT status or an exemption, such as for a main residence may be lost. If you are making a will, you should seek tax advice on the most effective method of disposal of your assets.

■ CRIME AND THE POLICE

Australia has many of the crime problems associated with developed nations and urban life, but on the whole, residents and visitors report feeling relatively safe. In particular, compared with other western countries, Australia's homicide statistics are very low, and, in spite of popular opinion, which seems to indicate an escalation, they have remained fairly static over the last decade. The Australian Bureau of Statistics currently found that the most frequently reported crime is unlawful entry with intent, with motor vehicle theft the next most common crime, followed by robbery and sexual assault. The defining feature of Australian crime is the rarity with which firearms are employed. Australia has very stringent gun laws (which have become even more so, since the tragic Port Arthur massacre in 1996) and only 20% to 25% of homicides in Australia involved the use of a gun, compared to around 70% in the USA.

Crime patterns differ throughout the states and territories: the Northern Territory, for example, has the highest per capita rate for homicide and sexual assaults, but the lowest for armed robberies. Western Australia has the highest number of motor vehicle thefts and burglaries, but its rate of murder and attempted murder are at or below the national average. New South Wales had the highest rate of armed robbery, which is attributed to

the fact that it has the largest heroin-dependent population in Australia. Canberra had the highest rate of kidnapping, attributed to acrimonious marital disputes over custody of children, and South Australia has the highest incidence of robbery and blackmail. The International Crime Victims Survey has noted that urban dwellers in Australia are four times more likely to install security devices than their rural cousins and 62% more likely to feel the need for special locks on exterior doors and windows. These levels are exactly comparable to similar communities in other western industrial nations. Australian crime figures are, in general, much more closely in line with European ones than with US figures, and Australian rates of motor vehicle theft are very low compared with those in the UK.

Police forces are the responsibility of state/territory governments and are headed in each state by a Commissioner for Police. Regulations for each force vary and some may carry guns on duty, depending on the state. There is also a Federal Police Force. This is Australia's international law enforcement and policing representative and the chief source of advice to the Australian Government on policing issues. It enforces Commonwealth criminal law and protects Commonwealth and national interests from crime in Australia and overseas. In recent years, allegations of police corruption in several Australian states have resulted in purges and high public accountability. In general, the police enjoy a good public profile and maintain open communications with the community.

◼ THE LEGAL SYSTEM

Australia's legal system is governed by many aspects, with the majority of laws set out in the voluminous (9 July 1900) Constitution of Australia. This forms the basis for the Australian Government and describes, in detail, Australia's system of constitutional monarchy. Australian law is based on English common law and consists of the Australian common law, federal laws enacted by the Parliament of Australia and laws enacted by the Parliaments of the Australian states and territories. All of the States and territories of Australia that are self-governing are separate jurisdictions and have their own system of courts and parliaments, yet all decisions for the nation as a whole come from the Australian Government. Laws passed by the Parliament of Australia apply to the whole of Australia.

Courts

The Australian Court system can seem quite confusing at first glance, as it is made up of a hierarchy of courts that range from the local to the federal level. To make it clearer it has two distinct divisions – State and Commonwealth. Each court has been granted specific powers to deal with different types of legal matters.

The State court system

In each State the courts are divided into three levels, with the lowest being the local courts (often called the magistrates court), the intermediate courts being the district or county and the highest being the Supreme Courts.

Determining the court in which a case should be heard depends on the seriousness of the offence and its complexities. Thus the more serious and complex cases are heard in the highest courts, which are the Supreme Courts. Decisions that are made by courts at the local and intermediate levels can be appealed against at a higher level. The same procedure for appeals applies at the Commonwealth level.

- **Local courts.** Local or lower courts hear minor civil, criminal and family law cases. The courthouse is overseen by a single judge and his/her jurisdiction is very limited in civil cases (both by monetary awards and penalties they are legally allowed to impose).

- **District and county courts.** More serious offenders are dealt with in the intermediate courts. These usually involve expensive and more complex civil and criminal cases. A single judge presides over civil cases and a full judge and jury decide the more serious criminal offences.

- **Supreme Court of Australia.** Only extremely serious cases are heard at the Supreme Court. This level holds the jurisdiction to hear appeals, thus the Supreme Court hears appeals from the lower State courts or from a decision by the Supreme Court that was made by a single judge. The Supreme Court can implement federal jurisdiction in some cases, and also deals with major civil litigation and serious criminal cases.

Commonwealth courts

The Federal Court of Australia

- The Federal Court has original jurisdiction over all federal matters that are granted to it by the Commonwealth Parliament. This can include laws for bankruptcy, administration, corporations, industrial relations and taxation.

- The Federal Court of Australia can hear appeals from decisions of the Supreme Courts of the Australian territories, and the decisions of state Supreme Courts when exercising federal jurisdiction. It also hears appeals from decisions of single judges of the Federal Court.

Family Court of Australia

- The Family Court of Australia, as the name suggests, deals with all family law matters. This is largely made up of child custody battles between parents, divorce disputes over property and prenuptial agreements.

The High Court

- This is the highest level of all court systems in Australia, and is the supreme federal court. Once you have had your case heard here, there is no turning back – the decision is there to stay

- A Chief Justice and six other judges reside on the High Court Bench. Judges can either hear cases as individuals or as three, five and seven person panels. A final decision must be reached by a majority of judges.

The High Court has original jurisdiction in all matters:

- In which the Commonwealth Government is a party
- Between states, or between residents of different states, or between a state and a resident of another state
- Of interpretation and application of the Australian Federal Constitution. This involves review of laws that have been passed by the state and federal parliaments and review of government actions to determine whether they are constitutionally valid
- That arise under an international treaty or that affect consuls or other representatives of other countries

Weird laws

As Australia is still a relatively new nation they do not have as many amusing and antiquated laws as other countries. They do, however, have a few odd ones, such as these below found on www.dumblaws.com/laws/international/australia:

- Children may not purchase cigarettes, but can smoke them
- You may never leave your car keys in an unattended vehicle
- It is illegal to roam the streets wearing black clothes, felt shoes and black shoe polish on your face as these items are the tools of a cat burglar
- It is illegal to read someone's tarot, or give them a psychic reading, as these are forms of witchcraft
- Under Australian Communications Authority (ACA) regulations, your modem can't pick up on the first ring. If it does the ACA permit for your modem is invalid and there's a A$12,000 fine (Telecommunications Act 1991)
- Until the Port Arthur killings (a horrific massacre in 1996 when a gunman took the lives of 35 innocent people) in Tasmania it was legal to own an AK-47 but illegel to be gay
- The legal age for heterosexual sex is 16, unless the person is in the care/custody of the older person, in which case it is 18

The High Court can hear appeals, by special leave – of decisions of state, federal and territory courts – in all matters.

Wills

If you die without having made a will, your estate will be distributed to your next of kin according to the various statutes of the state that provide for intestacy. These statutes vary from state to state, and distribution of the estate will vary according to the number and relationship of any immediate kin. In cases where there is no traceable family, the estate usually passes to the State Treasury. Clearly, it is preferable to make a will, especially if you have a *de facto* partner: the state of Victoria, for example, does not recognise the automatic right of inheritance of *de fac*to spouses. Estate duties and state death duties have been abolished in Australia, and under the present law, no such taxes are payable on any deceased estate, regardless of its size.

Proper estate planning can be complex, especially where large assets are involved and in many cases can be complicated by the usefulness of family trusts. Professional assistance is highly recommended to maximise an estate's freedom from Capital Gains Tax (CGT) for the beneficiaries. A will must also fulfil formal and legal requirements to be valid, thus it is advisable to seek professional legal advice. Solicitors' costs for this service are likely to be high (around A$150 per hour), although some solicitors now offer will-making 'kits', which guide clients through the process for a much-reduced fee. There are a number of kits available and you can even access these online. However, you should make sure that a kit covers all aspects of will making satisfactorily, including family provision and CGT. The 'Legal Kits of Victoria Will Kit' is recommended for its coverage of all such essential matters. Lawyers are permitted to advertise in Australia, and testamentary services are frequently advertised in newspapers. Most Australian states have, in current years, relaxed many will-making formalities in an attempt to protect the true intentions of testators, but there are still important obligations that must be followed to ensure the validity of your will. A will must be in writing and must be signed by the testator in the presence of two witnesses. If a witness is a beneficiary, or married to a beneficiary of that will, the gift to that beneficiary will fail (although the whole will may not necessarily fail). It is of the utmost importance that beneficiaries are not requested to witness the will. Wills may be revoked by the testator at any time after execution, by destruction, by a later will, or by marriage. Divorce, however, does not automatically revoke a will.

A will made overseas which is valid according to the law of the country where it was made, will be accepted for probate in Australia, even though that will may not be valid according to the law of the particular state in which the deceased lived. Probate is an order or grant by the Supreme Court in favour of the executor, authorising him/her to collect the assets of the deceased and deal with those assets according to the terms of the will. A testator who has already made a valid will overseas can deal with assets acquired in Australia by means of a separate ancillary will.

 Will making and other financial planning: www.moneymanager.com.au.

Working in Australia

■ FINDING A JOB

The employment market

ustralia continues to experience high levels of job optimism, has a booming economy and currently has an unemployment rate which fell to a record low of 4.1% (as of April 2008), its lowest since the early 1970s. This is remarkable considering it was peaking at almost 11% in 1992.

Economic growth in Australia has pushed forward to a remarkable 4.3% during the year 2006–07; this was primarily underpinned by strong household consumption expenditure and robust private business investment. The Department of Employment and Workplace Relations monitors such factors and reports that growth in the natural resource rich states of Western Australia and Queensland continue to outpace activity elsewhere in Australia, mainly because of the impact of the commodity price boom.

As a result of the above conditions, the Australian labour market gained strength and Australian Bureau of Statistics (ABS) figures published on 10 April 2008 state that the labour force grew by 14,800 people to 10,681,600; this remains a record high. ABS states that in the 2006–07 Australian labour force, a quarter were born overseas, compared with 68.4% born in Australia. Full-time employment rose by 3.2% and part-time employment

FACT

■ The volume measure of GDP is an indicator of real growth in Australian production. Between 1997–98 and 2005–06, Australia's real GDP grew by 31%.

grew by a record high of 1.8%. Full-time employment accounted for 81.8% of total employment growth during this period.

The industries that reported strong levels of employment growth during this period were accommodation, cafés and restaurants, property and business services and construction.

With such strong labour market conditions, the level of long-term unemployment also fell significantly by 29.3%, which was the lowest level since the 1980s.

Although employment in manufacturing, the third largest employing industry, fell slightly, future growth is expected. The agricultural sector has shown major job losses owing to the ongoing drought situation. Demand for broadband services should contribute to some growth in communication services. In the years 2010–11, the strongest growth areas will continue to be in property and business and health and community services, followed by accommodation, cafés and restaurants, and cultural and recreational services.

The Australian Capital Territory had the highest employment participation rate (73.6%) and lowest unemployment rate (3.0%) of all the states and territories. Tasmania had the lowest participation rate (60.3%) and the highest unemployment rate (5.7%).

In industry, engineers continue to prosper on the employment market, followed by those working in the construction and property services. Other areas where employees are increasingly being taken on are in utilities, resources, wholesale and distribution. Employment levels in the chemical and oil industry and transport and manufacturing, are all well below national expectations. Western Australia shows the best biggest rise in industrial industry employees. The education sector, followed by non-profit making organisations and government are most optimistic in terms of employment growth in the government and infrastructure sector. In the financial and professional services sector, the legal industry is best off, followed by service industry employees and finance and insurance service employees. Opportunities for full-time staff are better than ever at present, compared with casual contractors and temporary workers.

Current skills shortages

There are currently huge skill shortages in many occupations down under. The Migration Occupations in Demand List (MODL) published by the Department of Immigration and Multicultural and Indigenous Affairs (DIMIA) is shown in Appendix 6 (July 2007). These occupations are coded with an ASCO (Australian standard classification of occupations) code to assist with searches on the skill matching database.

There are many occupations on the MODL to choose from. Skill shortages are caused by many factors, including economic and demographic change, qualified workers deciding not to work in the field in which they trained, and variations in labour demand in the states and territories of Australia.

FACT

■ The Australian Capital Territory had the highest employment participation rate (73.6%) and lowest unemployment rate (3.0%) of all the states and territories. Tasmania had the lowest participation rate (60.3%) and the highest unemployment rate (5.7%).

State by state

ACT: the financial and professional sector is the most optimistic in terms of job opportunities followed by the IT and telecoms sector, and government and social infrastructure.

New South Wales: the finance and professional sector is also thriving, and outstrips the other booming industries such as retail, property, industrial and consumer sectors.

Queensland: shows growth in the financial and professional sector, followed by IT, telecommunications and industry

South Australia: the IT industry continues to stay afloat, closely followed by the government and social infrastructure sector, and the finance and professional sectors.

Victoria: showed continued growth in the government and social infrastructure sector, followed by the consumer, IT and telecommunications sectors

Western Australia: shows the largest employee growth spread over the three sectors of industry, consumer services, and government and social infrastructure.

Shortages often have more to do with the lack of available tradesmen than an increased demand on the trades themselves. Vocational education has increased the number of school leavers going out into the labour market with training and specific job-related skills, but in some trades skill shortages are so severe that employers have applied for special permission from the Commonwealth Government to bring in overseas-trained personnel to fill skilled jobs. Many companies are now using labour hire contractors to fill jobs that would previously have been done by apprentices.

The future

The Government has projected significant changes in the composition of the working population, with long-term trends leaning towards more part-time work, a middle-ageing of the workforce, and an increased proportion of female employees. Prospects for employment vary according to industry sector and the skill level of the occupation. The largest share of new jobs is expected to come from:

- accounting, finance and management (25%)
- sales assistants and storepersons (17%)
- health, fitness, hair and beauty (9%)
- food, hospitality and tourism (8%)

Utes are very handy for picking up goods

Although there are good prospects and career opportunities across all industries, most new jobs are expected to come from a handful of strongly growing service industries, providing more than 80% of new jobs: property and business services, retail trade, health and community services, construction, and accommodation, cafés and restaurants. To offset decline in traditional industries, the new national Labor government is strongly focused on the need for vocational education, skill building, and the multiskilling of the work force. As a result many mature workers now accept the need to retrain or develop their skills, to keep up with the skilled competition.

Unemployment rates for migrants

Unemployment rates for migrants vary depending on skill levels and proficiency in the English language. In February 2008, the trend unemployment rate for Australia was 4.1%. It is estimated that migrants who arrived between 2001 and 2008 had an unemployment rate of 5.9%. Of these migrants born in English-speaking countries had an unemployment rate of 4.6% while those arriving from non-English-speaking countries had a higher rate of 6.8%. Current arrivals generally have a higher unemployment rate than those who have lived in Australia for some time.

i Department of Employment and Workplace Relations:
www.dewrsb.gov.au. Publishes a quarterly magazine called the
Australian Jobs Update, which is intended to give migrants an overview
of the prevailing labour market conditions.
DEWRSB also publishes a monthly skilled vacancy survey:
www.workplace.gov.au.

Job search resources

Start online

If you are jobhunting in Australia from overseas, by far the best, quickest, and most convenient resource is now the internet. There are dozens of Australian recruitment agencies on the internet, all of which advertise frequently updated lists of positions, as well as providing registration and CV lodgement services. Two major Australian media groups, Newscorp and Fairfax (which between them publish the greater part of Australia's mainstream newspapers) also put their classified recruitment sections online, and these are updated daily. The websites of these two corporations together carry around 20,000 job advertisements per week. In addition, the Australian Job Network (AJN) (the government job-finding

organisation, details below) has an excellent site searchable by location, job type and interactive map. In most cases, jobs listed on the AJN site will detail conditions and pay, and although it may be difficult to apply for jobs listed on this site from overseas, it will give you a good idea of the kinds of work available in almost any field.

UK newspapers and directories
Directory of Jobs and Careers Abroad: Published by Vacation Work (£12.95) has a section on Australia including contact details and other sources of employment information. Vacation Work Publications also has a very useful links page at www.vacationwork.co.uk

TNT Group: 020 7373 3377; www.tntmagazine.com/anzguide. Free annual 200-page guide which includes the latest information on working in Australia. Also available from travel agents. www.tntdownunder.com: weekly 'living down under' magazine, which has a jobs section and loads of handy hints for new settlers.

Australian newspapers

Jobs are advertised in community, local, regional and national newspapers. Most major daily newspapers carry a large recruitment section on Saturdays, and many carry advertisements for specialist professional positions on some days (for example, tertiary education sector jobs in *The Australian* on Wednesdays). Professionals and executives are advised to consult *The Australian* in addition to their state newspapers, as most high-status jobs will be advertised in this paper, regardless of location.

Employment wanted advertisements

Placing an advertisement in a local or community newspaper can be a useful way of finding casual work, but is unlikely to land you secure long-term employment. Most people using Situations Wanted classifieds are looking for occasional cash jobs, such as gardening, babysitting, or cleaning. If you are on a working holiday, this may be one of the best ways of picking up occasional work to suit your travel schedule, and will probably pay at least A$12 per hour. For graduates, short-term tutoring, particularly around exam time, can be quite remunerative and most local papers will have a separate column for advertising services of this type. Another location for placing your employment adverts would be the network of Backpackers World outlets throughout Australia. They have a huge cork board in each of their backpacker travel outlets and you are welcome to browse the opportunities pinned on there or place your own wanted advert. Also, it's worth dropping in to any of the backpacker's hostels and local cafés surrounding them as they often have adverts placed in their recreation rooms.

i Backpackers World: www.backpackersworld.com.au

Employment agencies

UK-based Australian employment agency

Bligh Appointments is the largest employer of working holidaymakers in both Sydney and London, and can help in the search for temporary work before you even leave home. They specialise in office support and industrial jobs and offer good rates and an immediate start. Bligh have offices in Sydney (02 9235 3699; www.careerone.com.au/bligh) and London (020 7603 6123).

Recruitment consultancies

Recruitment consultancies generally specialise in placing staff in sales, marketing, finance, accounting, IT, engineering, office administration, and hospitality. While many employment agencies also cover these areas, recruitment consultants deal mainly with executive and upper and middle management placements. They advertise available jobs in major newspapers and usually offer a complete recruitment service. If you are seeking work of this kind, you can contact a recruitment consultancy 'on spec' to discuss your qualifications and experience, and any potentially suitable vacancies. A list of recruitment consultants and contact numbers can be found in the local Yellow Pages.

 Yellow Pages: www.yellowpages.com.au

Employment agencies

Employment agencies deal in both temporary and permanent work, usually in the secretarial, clerical, accounting and IT fields, or in hospitality or heavy industry. Most advertise in the Yellow Pages and are found in prominent locations in the Central Business Districts and other urban centres. The international firms Drake Personnel, Kelly Services, Centacom and Adecco all have agencies in Australia. In addition to the large, generalist agencies, there are many smaller, specialist firms, particularly in fields such as nursing, legal temping, banking, and IT. If you are a registered nurse or teacher looking to work in Australia, it is vital that you take proof of registration and qualifications with you. You can expect to earn around A$14 an hour for clerical work, A$15 for secretarial and A$17 for computer work.

Recruitment consultancies and employment agencies

Adecco: 02 9244 3400; sydney@adecco.com.au; www.adecco.com.au. World's leading employment services company, with more than 5,000 offices in 58 countries. For office locations in other areas call 132 993.

AAA Nannies: 02 9557 6644; www.nanny.net.au. Australia's leading au pair agency with offices Australia-wide.

Bayside Group: 02 9261 5100; www.baysidegrp.com.au. Supply executive recruitment, temporary and contract placements of legal, IT and accountancy staff.

Goldstein and Martens Recruitment Consultants: 02 9262 3088; enquiries@goldsteinmartens.com.au; www.goldsteinmartens.com.au. Pays A$2–3 above the average hourly wage.

Involvement Volunteers Association: 03 9646 9392; ivworldwide@ volunteering.org.au; www.volunteering.org.au

Metro Personnel: 02 9299 5477; www.metropersonnel.com.au

Michael Page International: 02 8292 2000; www.michaelpage.com.au. Temporary and contract work in finance and accounting, legal, sales and marketing, technology, human resources and engineering.

Select Appointments: 02 8258 9999; www.select-appointments.com.au. Specialise in placing professional, motivated travellers. They have positions for receptionists, data entry operators, secretaries, accounts clerks, medical and legal secretaries, WPOs and warehousing staff. Select also have offices in Perth, 08 9321 3133; Brisbane, 07 3243 3900; Melbourne, 03 8663 4700; Adelaide, 08 8468 8000; Canberra, 02 6278 0088.

Labour hire contractors

Labour hire contractors specialise in placing skilled manual workers and tradespeople, labourers, storepersons, process workers and factory staff. These agencies generally do not operate high street offices and are found in industrial areas. Most advertise in the Yellow Pages and it is usually best to visit in person, taking with you any trade or City and Guilds certificates you may have. Qualified tradespeople are paid well in Australia, and in states with booming construction industries there is usually a shortage of such people. Bricklayers are particularly in demand and can expect to earn a high wage, while mine workers can earn more than A$1,200 per week. Mining work is labour-intensive and unskilled workers are often needed. Modern mine sites operate equal opportunities policies, and most employ women in a wide range of capacities. There is also strong demand for skilled mechanics.

i Yellow Pages: www.yellowpages.com.au
Australian and New Zealand Employment Review: 0845 230 2526; www.jobfastrack.co.nz or www.emigration.uk.com. Regular updates on the employment scene in Australia and New Zealand

Professional and trade bodies

Professional associations

Most professions in Australia have a national association or governing body, which is also likely to have state chapters. In some cases, membership of an association is compulsory for practicing members, and in such instances, membership fees are tax deductible. Most professional associations publish a journal, which, in specialist fields, may be the best source of employment information. Specialist publications provide another important source, and will usually report on developments in their field, as well as advertising job vacancies. Conferences and development courses will also be advertised in such publications.

Working Holiday assistance schemes

- **BUNAC.** The British Universities North America Club (BUNAC) has a 'Work Australia' programme, which is designed to help those aged 18–30 deal with all the organisational aspects of a working holiday. The service helps with obtaining flights, insurance etc, and includes comprehensive orientation sessions at home and on arrival in Australia, a group two-day stopover in Bangkok or Hong Kong en route and two free nights' accommodation in Sydney. It also provides ongoing support through BUNAC's subsidiary, International Exchange Programs, including a postal service, voicemail card and the help of the Sydney resource office for general advice throughout your stay.

- **SWAP.** Young Canadians going on a working holiday to Australia can participate in SWAP Working Holiday Programs available through the offices of Travel CUTS, Voyages Campus, the Adventure Travel Company, and Odyssey Travel. SWAP Working Holiday Programs is a non-profit activity of the Canadian Federation of Students.

- **IEP.** International Exchange Programmes (IEP) support working holiday-makers through IEP centres in Sydney, Melbourne, and Auckland.

> *i* BUNAC: 020 7251 3472 www.bunac.org.uk
> SWAP: www.swap.ca
> Canadian Federation of Students: 613 232 7394; info@cfs-fcee.ca;
> www.cfs-fcee.ca
> IEP: 03 9329 3866; www.iep.org.au

Chambers of Commerce

The Australian Chamber of Commerce and affiliated state Chambers of Commerce advise and provide information on employment in Australia. They also produce detailed regional summaries of employment and economic growth, and are particularly useful as a point of contact for small business people. The Australian–British Chamber of Commerce, for example, aims to promote business growth and development in Australia, and to encourage reciprocal trade between the UK and Australia.

Useful resources

Australian British Chamber of Commerce: 02 9247 6271;
www.britishchamber.com

Australia and New Zealand Chamber of Commerce UK:
0870 890 0720; enquiries@anzcc.org.uk; www.anzcc.org.uk

Australian Industry Group: 03 9867 0111; www.aigroup.asn.au. The Australian Industry Group is an independent organisation created to help Australian industry be more competitive domestically and internationally. Aspects of industry covered include the economy and related investment issues, taxation, industrial relations policy, environmental issues, education and training.

Company transfers and job exchanges

If you are currently working for a company that has offices or branches in Australia, opportunities may exist for either permanent or temporary transfer. Outside the multinationals, it may be possible to find work in Australia under an exchange scheme. Such schemes are common in the teaching profession, and you should contact your local education authority for further information. Many exchanges provide not only a job swap, but also all the domestic necessities. You may find yourself minding your exchange colleague's pets for a year, but you'll probably also find yourself minding their pool too!

■ SHORT-TERM WORK

There are many opportunities in Australia for short-term and casual employment. The Australian Government has never felt it necessary to restrict drastically its working holiday-maker scheme, even in times of economic downturn, as it is clear that travellers are prepared to take on the kind of temporary jobs that locals seeking a career or job security shun. Some industries, especially in the primary sector (see agriculture below), rely on itinerant casual workers to fill their labour needs, and the adventurous should find plenty of scope for some once-in-a-lifetime employment experiences.

Agriculture

Primary industry is the backbone of the Australian economy and there is a great variety of work available on farms and stations all year round. These opportunities are not just limited to working the land: mechanics, builders, tractor drivers, welders, domestics, cooks and teachers are all needed. Horse riding skills or a heavy goods vehicle (HGV) licence will improve

your chances of finding work. If you have a farming background, preferably with experience in cereal crops, you will find it easy to get seasonal farm work, especially in heavy tractor soil tillage, drilling, single pass seeding and combine harvesting. Pay varies between a flat rate of A$90–A$130 per day, or A$9–A$14 per hour before tax. You are likely to have to work between 50 and 80 hours per week, seven days a week, particularly during seeding.

Most travellers opt for the outdoor seasonal job of fruit farming. Fruit farmers rely quite heavily on casual labour at harvest time and this kind of work is ideal for travellers as it is of brief duration and offers the opportunity to 'follow the crops' from region to region. The summer months, from October to April, are the prime times for harvest work around Australia. The work can be hard, but once you become proficient you can expect to earn around A$360 per week after tax.

Harvest work opportunities

Month	Crop
Western Australia	
Feb–Mar	Grapes
Mar–May	Apples, pears
Mar–Jun	Crayfish
Mar–Jun	Oats, wheat, barley
Mar–Oct	Prawns, scallops
May–Sep	Squash, rock melon
Apr–Nov	Melons
Jun–Dec	Peppers, tomatoes
Jul–Aug	Bananas
Jul–Dec	Wildflowers
Oct–Jan	Mangoes

Victoria

Jan–Apr	Pears, peaches, apples, tomatoes, tobacco
Feb–Mar	Grapes
Sep–Nov	Asparagus
Oct–Dec	Strawberries
Nov–Feb	Cherries, berries
Nov–Dec	Tomato weeding

New South Wales

Jan–Mar	Stone fruit, grapes, pears, prunes
Feb–Apr	Apples
Mar–Jun	Cotton picking
Sep–Dec	Asparagus
Sep–Apr	Oranges
Nov–Dec	Cherries
Nov–Apr	Oranges
Dec–Jan	Onions
Dec–Mar	Stone fruit
Dec–Apr	Blueberries

Queensland

Feb–Mar	Apples, pears
Feb–Apr	Rock melon, ginger
Mar–Dec	Wide range of vegetables
Apr–Jun	Citrus fruit
Apr–Nov	Beans
Apr–Dec	Tomatoes
May–Oct	Broccoli
May–Dec	Sugar cane
Jul–Sep	Ginger
Jul–Dec	Onions
Sep–Nov	Tobacco
Nov–Jan	Plums, cotton, peaches

South Australia

Jan–Mar	Dried fruits
Feb–Apr	Apples, pears, grapes, peaches
Feb–Aug	Brussels sprouts
Jun–Sep	Pruning
Sep–Jan	Oranges (juicing and packing)
Oct–Feb	Strawberries
Dec–Feb	Apricots

Tasmania

Mar–May	Apples
Dec–Jan	Soft fruit
Feb–Apr	Grapes
Mar–Apr	Hops
Jan–Feb	Scallop splitting

Almost all harvest work is advertised through the Australian Job Network (AJN), and now that all Centrelink offices (under whom the Australian Job Network operates) are linked by the internet, it is no longer necessary to go to the appropriate regional office to find out what work is available. Instead, you can visit the Centrelink office in the city or town where you are currently located and using the computer terminal and interactive map, find out what opportunities are available throughout Australia. Once you have found the kind of work you want, in an area that interests you, you will need to travel to that region to be interviewed by the local AJN officer, however, the online service does make co-ordinating your work and travel much easier.

 Jobsearch online database: www.jobsearch.gov.au

If you intend to do harvest work, you will need to be fit and healthy, and capable of working long hours in hot, dry and dusty conditions. There is usually minimal accommodation available during harvest; however, most orchards have on-site camping facilities if you have your own tent or caravan. Farms can be located as much as 62 miles (100km) from the nearest town, so this kind of work is most practical if you have your own transport.

 Workabout Australia available from www.vacationwork.co.uk

If you are looking for jobs in the cities of Australia, it is also worth popping in to the many hostels and Backpacker travel centres dotted around these districts. Most of them will have a corkboard with notices of cash work, shared travel, cars for sale and accommodation offers.

One such place is Backpackers Travel World, which has offices in Kings Cross, Sydney, Perth, Byron Bay and 30 other locations throughout Australia. You can also book travel with them and ask advice on all matters pertaining to travelling down under.

 www.backpackersworld.com.au

Aquaculture

Aquaculture is a rapidly growing area of primary industry in Australia, and fishing work is available in many coastal areas. Crayfish, prawns, scallops, and abalone are all harvested according to very strict seasonal regulations, and work in these areas can be very highly paid. Many fishing trawlers, especially those with processing facilities, also take on workers. However, this kind of work often requires being at sea for extended periods and is not for the fainthearted. The seas around Australia can be perilous.

Mining

Working in the mining industry in Australia can be both challenging and very rewarding financially. There is plenty of work available for unskilled labourers, and the best way to find such work is usually to visit the human resource offices of large mining companies at their city headquarters. If you strike lucky, you could find yourself on a plane in a few hours – finding mining work really is about being in the right place at the right time. There

are mines and related mining activities all over Australia (with Western Australia in particular, currently experiencing an economic boom and skilled worker shortage), from giant iron-ore projects in the north-west to small family-run gold and precious stone prospecting ventures in the south. Miners usually work a seven-day week, often from dawn to dusk, and sometimes for as many as six weeks straight. The pay is likely to be more than A$1,600 per week, and there is very little to spend it on on-site. If you work above the 26th parallel (the Tropic of Capricorn), you are entitled to extra pay, known as the 'tropical loading' or 'remote area allowance'. Most mining companies are now prepared to employ women on-site, and indeed many prefer to do so, as women are considered to respond less aggressively to the pressure-cooker atmosphere of isolated mine sites.

Nursing

There is a huge demand for supply nurses in Australia, especially during the Australian autumn and winter months from April to september and there is a shortage in every state. Specialist nurses, particularly A&E, intensive care and psychiatric, are always needed and a qualified and experienced nurse is likely to have no difficulty in obtaining work from a nursing agency. The Australian Government helps overseas nurses to emigrate through a new 'fast-track' migration scheme. This applies particularly to those wishing to work in rural and remote areas. Australia recognises overseas qualifications of nurses from the UK, USA, Canada, New Zealand and Singapore, but nurses from non-English-speaking countries must complete a bridging course and 80 hours practical training.

Registering with the Nurses' Registration Board

To work as a nurse in Australia, even on a temporary basis, you will need to be registered with the Nurses' Registration Board of the state in which you hope to work, and many agencies will help you with this procedure. New South Wales is the least expensive state to register in – the fee is currently A$80 for one year. Before you leave home you should apply for your Authority to Practice, which will prevent any delays on arrival.

 Australian Nursing and Midwifery Council (ANMC): 02 6257 7960; www.anmc.org.au. Information about nursing and midwifery in Australia.

Job opportunities for registered nurses

Australia wide: www.nursingaustralia.com

Queensland Health: 07 3234 1544; www.thinknursing.com. A Government department involved in all areas of healthcare across Queensland.

Nurseworldwide: 02 92862800, nww_syd@nurseworldwide.com.au; www.nurseworldwide.com.au. A specialist recruitment agency. Provides comprehensive assistance package including help with registration, visa sponsorship (if required), accommodation and 'meet and greet' at main airports.

Heartbeat Nurses: 02 9891 2255; www.heartbeatnursing.com.au. Agency that supplies all leading public and private hospitals in Sydney. There are also jobs in country and interstate hospitals. Day or three-month contracts, Nurse Work and Travel Programmes around Australia.

Nursing in Melbourne: www.melbournenursing.com.au. Variety of opportunities for travelling nurses or those interested in either extended or permanent placements.

Health Staff Recruitment: (Adelaide) www.healthstaffrecruitment.com.au

Australian Nursing Federation, Tasmanian branch: www.anftas.org/anf_services/service_nursing.html

Nursing and Midwifery Jobs Northern Territory: www.nursing.nt.gov.au

Teaching English as a foreign language (TEFL)

Australia has a flourishing TEFL market, which caters mainly to South-East Asian students. There are large English language schools in every capital city, all of which require casual, short and long-term teachers for their various courses. To teach English as a Foreign Language in Australia you will need a recognised TEFL qualification and some prior teaching experience. Many people on Working Holiday visas now choose to take an appropriate course before they leave home to have this remunerative option on their travel. Casual TEFL teachers can expect to earn between A$15 and A$25 per hour. Perth, Sydney and the Gold Coast have the largest and most active TEFL sectors.

Cactus TEFL: www.cactustefl.com/tefl/australia

Au pair

Au pair work is another standby for working holidaymakers and there is considerable work available for those with experience and good references.

Once confined almost entirely to remote rural families who needed the services of a child-minder cum governess, changing work patterns have led more and more urban families to employ full-or part-time nannies or au pairs. Australian families generally will *not* expect anyone employed as a childminder to undertake household duties other than those required for the immediate well being of their children. Extra work, such as ironing, should be specified by the employer in advance and agreed to by you, and you can negotiate extra pay for these additional duties.

Male au pairs

Australian anti-discrimination laws do permit employers to specify the gender of a childminder; many families prefer to employ women to care for their children, and male applicants can be legally rejected. However, some families might actually prefer a male au pair, especially if the children are boys and like playing sports. There are numerous domestic and specialist au pair agencies supplying staff in this field. References will be checked thoroughly and holding a driving licence will be an asset.

 AAA Nannies: www.nanny.net.au
Find au pair: www.findaupair.com/agencies. asp
Transitions abroad: www.transitionsabroad.com/listings/work/shortterm/au_pair_jobs
Cultural care: www.culturalcare.com/hostfamilies/faq

Tourism and hospitality

Australia's tourist industry is one of the country's largest employers – more than 500,000 are employed across the nation – and there are a wide variety of jobs available. Hotels require porters childminders, and kitchen hands,

in addition to more qualified and experienced employees such as chefs, waiters and bar staff. A silver service or bar attendant qualification acquired before you leave home will equip you to find well paid work in every city.

Croupiers are required by casinos (there are one or two very large ones in most states, including Star City in Darling Harbour, Sydney) and this kind of work is very highly paid; you will, however, require training and experience to be considered.

There is work available for instructor level Professional Association of Diving Instructors (PADI) qualified divers at the major dive spots around the coast, especially on the Great Barrier Reef and off Exmouth, in north-west Western Australia. Divers should note that PADI is the most common certification system in Australia; British Sub Aqua Club (BSAC) qualified divers will find it easier to find work if they convert their qualifications before travelling.

Any working holidaymakers already very experienced in the Australian outback may find work as guides in some of the national parks, particularly Kakadu. Many coach companies also take on tour leaders and coach drivers with an appropriate licence and experience. Queensland offers the greatest opportunities in terms of resort work, but most jobs are found by word of mouth: if you hope to work, say, on the Gold Coast, the most likely way of picking up work is to go there and ask around. The Australian Job Network (AJN) is the best first port of call for work in the tourism and hospitality sector.

 Australian job network: https://jobsearch.gov.au
Tourism and hospitality jobs in Australia: www.seek.com.au/hospitality-tourism-job
www.mycareer.com.au/jobs/-/hospitality-travel-tourism

Office work, telemarketing and sales

Office temps are particularly in demand during the Australian summer months and over major holiday periods such as Christmas and Easter. Most commonly, short-term work is available in secretarial, clerical, word-processing and data entry positions, all of which require some degree of skill and previous experience. The banking, finance, and stockbroking industries always require temps, especially during peak periods such as the end of the financial year (30 June). Unskilled casual work is often also available at this time when large supermarkets and department stores do their annual stocktake. There are innumerable employment agencies supplying both general and specialist short-term staff, and these are listed in the Yellow Pages. The AJN is generally less fruitful as a source of this kind of work, although temporary government and public sector positions will be advertised there.

Telemarketing does not appeal to everyone, but can be financially rewarding if you are successful. Turnover is unusually high in this industry, and telemarketing firms have no hesitation in employing backpackers as it is rare for any staff, whether itinerant or not, to stay the pace for more than a few weeks. Telemarketing jobs are usually advertised in the employment classifieds of local and major city newspapers.

 Australian Job Network: https://jobsearch.gov.au
Telemarketing/customer service jobs: www.seek.com.au/customer-service-jobs
www.mycareer.com.au/jobs/all/customer-service-contact-centre/telemarketing-telesales
Yellow Pages: www.yellowpages.com.au

Voluntary work

Countless charitable organisations throughout Australia rely on volunteers to help run their many aid, development and conservation programmes. Becoming involved in such enterprises offers the working holidaymaker an opportunity to experience a different side of Australian life while gaining new skills and contributing to a worthwhile cause. If you are interested in volunteering in any capacity, contact the Charities' Commission in your state (listed under Government Organisations in the White Pages) who will be able to supply you with a list of all the charities registered with them. Visitors to Australia who are interested in the country's unique landscape are often particularly attracted to conservation work. Volunteers contribute A$40–A$50 per day to cover accommodation, meals and projected travel expenses.

 Conservation Volunteers Australia: 03 5330 2600; info@conservation volunteers.com.au; www.conservationvolunteers.com.au
White Pages: www.whitepages.com.au

■ EMPLOYMENT REGULATIONS AND SKILLS

Residence and work regulations

To work in Australia, you must hold an appropriate temporary or permanent residency visa. The Australian immigration authorities are draconian in their treatment of illegal workers, and anyone caught working without a visa should expect to be deported immediately. A data-matching programme operated by the Department of Immigration and Multicultural and Indigenous Affairs (DIMIA) links the computers of the Australian Taxation Office, Centrelink and the Health Insurance Commission (Medicare), making it almost impossible to get away with flouting immigration laws. DIMIA is focusing its efforts to locate illegal workers in industries that employ large numbers of casual workers, especially in rural areas, where cash payments have traditionally made it easier to work outside the purview of the eagle eye of the tax office.

The eligibility criteria, requirements and procedures for obtaining residency in Australia, whether on a short or long-term basis, are described in detail on page 36.

Skills and qualifications

Successful applicants under the Skilled Stream migration programme are required to have a prescribed level of professional experience and qualification. As explained more fully on page 54, these skills are assessed during the application process by means of the 'Points Test'. Points awarded for skill levels are based on your current occupation and the level of your qualifications, which must be of a standard recognised as industry-appropriate in Australia. Your current occupation is defined as the one which you have performed over the last 12 months and which you regard as your usual occupation. Thus, if you have obtained qualifications in one field (say, a degree in modern languages) but are currently working in a field that does not directly utilise those qualifications, you will, in effect, be assessed as unqualified. This clause creates difficulties for many applicants who are working in areas such as information technology or office management, where in many cases skills have been acquired on-the-job or through graduate programmes. Concessions are made for workplace training, however, and each case is assessed on its individual merits.

Points are awarded for length of professional experience (usually three years is required) and for membership of professional or industrial associations. Trade certificates, diplomas and degrees must be recognised as 'acceptable' (that is equivalent to an Australian qualification) to score any

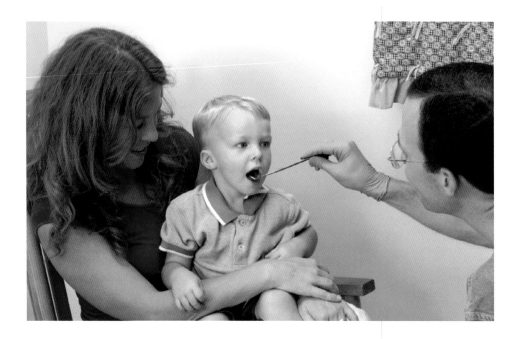

points. DIMIA has Migration Occupation in Demand and Skilled Occupations lists (www.immi.gov.au).

Bridging courses for people trained overseas

Australian Education International (AEI) through the National Office of Overseas Skills Recognition (NOOSR) can provide advice on the acceptability of any qualification you hold. They also offer bridging courses for overseas-qualified professionals whose qualifications have not yet been recognised in Australia, enabling applicants to meet the academic and professional requirements for registration or entry to regulated professions. Government-regulated professions include: dentistry, veterinary science, medicine, law, radiography, pharmacy, architecture, physiotherapy and nursing. Accountancy, dietetics, social work, engineering and surveying are self-regulatory (many are offered as online courses – see below). You will be eligible for partial financial support on a NOOSR course if you have permanent residency in Australia, have overseas professional qualifications at Bachelor's degree level or above and if you have obtained details of the training you require from the professional body which assessed your qualifications.

 AEI-NOOSR: 1800 020 086 (free call) or 02 6211 9334; noosr@dest.gov.au; www.dest.gov.au/noosr

What are bridging courses for overseas-trained professionals?

If you are doing a bridging course as an overseas-trained professional, you are undertaking higher education studies that will enable you to meet specific academic or professional requirements for entry to a professional occupation in Australia. These requirements must be specified in an assessment statement.

An assessment statement is a written statement that lists the studies, examinations/tuition and training programmes that you need to undertake successfully; to meet the requirements for entry to your profession. It is issued by an assessing body for a listed professional occupation.

■ ASPECTS OF EMPLOYMENT

Salaries

Pay rates in Australia fall broadly into four bands: the lowest paid workers earn an average of A$450 or less per week (casual workers can earn from A$12–A$15 per hour), mid-range salaries (which account for two of the four bands) cluster firstly around A$650 and then, in the upper-mid-range, around A$900 per week, and finally, the highest paid employees can expect a weekly pay packet in excess of A$1,690 per week. In 2007, the minimum wage was A$7.65 for a 17-year-old, working part-time or A$9.56 if working casual in a restaurant.

In 2007, the median annual starting salary for new Bachelor degree graduates aged less than 25 and in their first full-time employment was A$43,000. Males earned a starting salary of A$45,000 and females earned A$42,000.

Rates of pay are differentiated between the public and private sector and by gender and age. Men still tend to receive a higher weekly income than women in the same sector, although this can be accounted for by gender divides in industry, rather than in terms of direct discrimination, which is, of course, illegal. The average weekly earnings for men are A$997.10 and A$867.90 for women. Younger people are likely to be paid less than their seniors. Employees earning at the top end of the salary bands are likely to fall into one of two key industries – finance and insurance, and mining – while those at the bottom end are generally found in the retail trade and in the hospitality industry. Earnings are related to skills obtained through education and work experience. Work experience is related to age, especially for those in their 20s and 30s, and therefore wages tend to rise with age. Unskilled workers can expect to earn between A$8–A$20 an hour, depending on location, level of skill, and whether they are paid hourly or are on piece work rates. The traditional working holiday standby, fruit picking, may be easy to find but is poorly paid. Workers are often paid not by the hour but by the quantity of produce harvested. The average harvest picker can expect to earn somewhere in the region of A$300–A$600 for a six-day week.

Bear in mind that a dollar goes a long way in Australia and that although earnings may seem low, the same standard of living that you are used to back home can be had for less in Australia.

The Australian economy currently has a CPI (Consumer Price Index) of around 2.8%, an average inflation rate of 3.0%, and its lowest unemployment rate since the early 1970s, of 4.1%. Industries with a shortage of skilled labour are expected to experience a greater increase in pay rates, while salaries in those areas where there is an oversupply of labour may see wages decline.

Award Rates – recommended minimum wages – are set by both the Federal and State governments for various trades and industries. Many, if not most, employers pay above the Award Rate, but you should find out if there is an Award in place before entering into negotiations with an employer. The appropriate union will be able to advise you on Award Rates and Conditions.

Tax file number

Everyone who works in Australia must have a tax file number (TFN) and you will need to apply for one as soon as you start work or, preferably, even sooner. TFN can take up to six weeks to be issued and until you receive your number and are able to pass it on to your employer, you will be taxed at the maximum rate of 49%. Application forms for a TFN are available from all Centrelink and tax offices and can also be printed and submitted online. Non-residents with a TFN pay tax at a rate of 29 cents in the dollar (29% of all earnings up to A$450 per week).

i Apply for your tax file number online: www.ato.gov.au/individuals

You can apply for your TFN online before you leave if you are a visa holder with work rights, such as:

- a Working Holidaymaker
- a New Zealand citizen
- an overseas student whose course of study is six months or longer

When you apply this way, the electronic system verifies your identity through the Department of Immigration and Citizenship (DIAC) system. Make sure that you keep a record of your receipt number. You will need both a valid passport and a work visa authorised by DIAC.

The Tax Office will mail a letter with your TFN to your nominated address within 28 days of receiving your application. If you have not received it in 28 days, phone the Tax Office on 1300 13 00 25 (8.00am–6.00pm, Monday to Friday). If you applied online, you will need your receipt number.

Tax returns

Before you leave Australia, you should lodge a tax return (also available from the Centrelink offices and inside the Tax Pack). Every employer for whom you have worked should have supplied you with a 'payment summary' on leaving; you will need to keep these and attach them to your tax return as proof of your total earnings. The taxation office will assess your return, usually in a couple of weeks of lodgment, and a refund cheque (if applicable) will be forwarded to your nominated address, either in Australia or overseas. You can have your refund paid directly into your account.

 Fill in your tax form online: www.ato.gov.au

Benefits and perks

Only the most senior positions attract additional benefits in Australia since changes in taxation laws made fringe benefits economically unattractive. Cars, health insurance plans, entertainment expenses and even frequent flyer points are now all taxed as income, so that any benefit is offset by a commensurate loss of salary. Benefits earned under incentive schemes are also taxable. Childcare and workplace crèches, however, are not included in the fringe benefit tax, and indeed, employees using external childcare can claim a rebate on their expenses via the local Medicare office.

All employers pay superannuation (private pension contributions) for their employees at a basic rate of 9% of salary. Many employers also offer an additional percentage or two, up to around 10%, and this is now the most common form of employment incentive.

Most senior executives can still expect to receive a company car, but in general, benefits offered at any other level of employment are likely

to be industry-linked. Thus, if you work for a major bank, you can expect to be eligible for subsidised borrowing, or in health insurance, for free or discounted health cover. Most Australian employees do not expect, or indeed want, any other fringe benefits that may cut into the cash in their pocket.

Maternity benefits and parental leave

Maternity benefits

Australia, along with New Zealand and the United States, is one of the few industrialised nations in which the state does not pay maternity leave benefits. Government sector employees are entitled to three months' paid leave, but few women employed in the private sector receive any paid maternity leave. All women are entitled to unpaid maternity leave of not more than 52 weeks, taken either during or after their pregnancy. On the expiry of the leave, the employee is entitled to return to her previous position or an equivalent, if that position no longer exists. All new mothers who are legal residents of Australia are entitled to receive the Baby Bonus, a one-off lump sum payment of A$4,133 (as of 1 July 2007) made by Centrelink. In cases of multiple birth, the Maternity Allowance payment is paid for each child born (including stillbirths). In addition,

Centrelink offers an incentive payment for immunisation called the Maternity Immunisation Allowance. This allowance is designed to combat falling levels of immunisation and provides parents with a lump sum of A$232.70 on presentation of proof of full immunisation in their 18-month-old child (claims must be made on or before the child's second birthday).

To claim the Baby Bonus, you must fill in the form, either:

- At the hospital
- Online at www.familyassist.gov.au
- By phoning 13 61 50

You need to claim within 26 weeks of the baby's birth or in the case of an adoption within 26 weeks of the baby coming into your care.

Paternity and adoptive leave

All Australian workers, not just mothers, are entitled to parental leave, which, in addition to maternity leave, also comprises paternity and adoptive leave. Paternity leave may be taken in conjunction with the birth of a child to a spouse or *de facto* partner, while adoptive leave may be taken in conjunction with the adoption of a child under the age of five years. For both types of leave, 10 weeks' notice of intention must be given to the employer. Any employee who has completed at least 12 months' continuous service, whether full or part-time (but not casual), is eligible for parental leave. However, paternity leave cannot be taken simultaneously with maternity leave for the same child. Employees are entitled to take up to 52 weeks parental leave, which must be completed before the child's first birthday (or the first anniversary of an adoption). You cannot be dismissed for taking parental leave and your employer cannot legally refuse your application for it. On your return to work, you are entitled to your old job back or, if it no longer exists, to one at an equivalent level, and your seniority and accumulated leave must be preserved in your absence.

Superannuation

Superannuation is Australia's answer to the economic burden of state pensions in the context of an ageing population. In essence, it is a compulsory private pension planning scheme. All employees are required by law to pay a percentage of their salary into a superannuation fund designated by their employer, to which the employer also contributes an additional minimum percentage payment on the employee's behalf. If you move jobs, you are entitled to transfer your superannuation package to your new employer's chosen superannuation fund without incurring any penalty. The transfer of super annuation from one fund to another is known as a 'roll-over'. Alternatively, if you wish to remain with your current fund, you can ask your employer to contribute to that fund instead. Contributions to 'super funds' are of two types: preserved and voluntary. Preserved contributions comprise the minimum compulsory contributions, described above, and these cannot be withdrawn or otherwise utilised until the age of 55. In addition, however, employees are entitled to make ongoing voluntary contributions or occasional lump sum contributions to their fund, and this component is known as non-preserved (it can be withdrawn on leaving a job – see below). Self-employed people are advised to take out a 'self-employed' superannuation policy available from banks and life insurance companies. If you leave the country permanently, your superannuation will remain locked into a fund until you advise which fund you would like it transferred over to.

People under 55 who have non-preserved, unrestricted benefits can withdraw but are taxed 20%, plus (if you are earning enough) the 1.5% Medicare levy. Therefore it is advisable to leave it in the fund until you are of retiring age.

From 1 July 2007, there are significant changes to the tax treatment of superannuation. These include tax-free benefits for people over the age of 60. So, for most of those who receive super benefits from a taxed source, payment of a benefit as a lump sum or income stream (such as a pension) will be tax-free.

If your super comes from a source that is not taxed (such as public service super funds), your benefits will continue to be taxed when you receive them. However, you may be entitled to a tax offset that will reduce the tax payable on these benefits.

As noted above, you can add extra amounts to your superannuation fund. However, since 1 July 2007, concessional contributions made to super will be subject to an annual cap of A$50,000. What is classified as a concessional contribution includes employer contributions (including contributions made under a salary sacrifice arrangement) and personal contributions claimed as a tax deduction by a self-employed person. The age-based limits on deductions that currently exist for these contributions will no longer apply.

If you make concessional contributions, you will be taxed at a rate of 31.5%. This is on top of the 15% tax paid by the fund. You can ask your super fund to release money to pay this excess contributions tax. Between 1 July 2007 and 30 June 2012, a transitional concessional contributions cap will apply.

There are also changes for the self-employed, those without a tax file number (TFN) and those making non-concessional contributions to superannuation.

i Australian Tax Office: www.ato.gov.au

Working hours, overtime and holidays

The Australian working week averages 35–40 hours over a five-day week, with government positions taking the middle road at precisely 37.5 hours. In most jobs, you can expect to work an eight-hour day with an hour for lunch, although some shift-work industries, such as nursing or hospitality, will usually require much greater flexibility. Flexi-time is common, and allows you to set your own working hours around a compulsory 'core time' (usually 10am–4pm). Extra hours worked can be 'banked' against time off on full pay, which is in addition to statutory leave. Flexi-time is very popular, and is in place in almost all government jobs, tertiary education administration and in many private companies. Minimum working pay and conditions are set by either the Commonwealth or State governments.

If you are required to work on a Sunday or a public holiday, you should be paid at twice the normal rate. At any other time, overtime is paid at 1.5 times the normal rate for the first three hours, then at double-time after that. Employees are entitled to a statutory minimum of four weeks' paid leave per annum. Holiday leave is sweetened with a bonus known as 'holiday loading', which means that your salary is increased by an extra 17.5% during the period you are on leave. Many industries and professions offer increasing leave entitlements linked to length of service, and may, in some cases, offer as much as eight weeks' holiday per year. Untaken leave can usually be carried over from year to year, and many people choose to bank up holidays to take extended travel breaks.

After 10 years' consecutive service with a single employer, an employee is entitled to 'long service leave' of up to three months (it varies hugely from state to state) on full pay. For example, in New South Wales, long service leave is two months' paid leave after 10 years' service with the same employer and one month paid leave for each additional five years' service. Some companies break up this leave, so that it works out as two months on full pay and nominated other months on half pay. Long service leave conditions vary considerably between employers, and in many cases additional incentives such as a travel allowance may be offered.

Working entitlements
SA: www.legislation.sa.gov.au
QLD: www.wageline.qld.gov.au/leaveentitlements/longservice_leave.html
NSW: www.industrialrelations.nsw.gov.au/rights/entitlements/longser
VIC: www.det.vic.gov.au/hrweb/employcond/leave/lsl.htm
NT: www.ocpe.nt.gov.au/pay_and_conditions
TAS: www.tic.tas.gov.au/decisions_issued/long_service_leave
WA: www.wairc.wa.gov.au/awards

In addition to annual leave, all employees are granted a period of paid sick leave, the length of which will be specified in their contract. Most employers give between two weeks and three months paid sick leave.

Any absence of more than 48 hours generally requires a medical certificate from a GP to claim payment. Many employers also offer compassionate leave of several days per year, which can be used in times of personal emergency such as bereavement. Compassionate leave and sick leave cannot be carried over from year to year.

Trade unions

The trade union movement in Australia has become very weakened over the past decade, with fewer Australian employees joining unions than ever before. To offset loss of membership, many unions have amalgamated with others in related trades and professions, forming super-unions with increased negotiating power. The unions that have remained strongest are those representing industries in which there is continued unrest, particularly in teaching, nursing, policing, and wharfside occupations. 'Closed shops' are illegal, but the powerful BLF (Builders Labourers Federation) is occasionally known to operate union-only sites. Most workplaces have a union representative, and if you choose to join, dues can be automatically deducted from your salary. Union dues are a tax-deductible expense. The Australian Council of Trade Unions is the national trade union organisation and can provide advice on the union most appropriate to your circumstances and occupation.

 Australian Council of Trade Unions: 03 9663 5266; www.actu.asn.au

Employment contracts

In Australia every employee is covered either by a contract or a 'workplace agreement'. Workplace agreements are signed by both employer and employee, and stipulate the agreed conditions of employment, including hours, leave arrangements, uniform or safety-wear requirements, and notice and termination procedures. Even casual workers must be covered by one of these contracts, which are then lodged with the State Commissioner for Workplace Agreements as a legally binding document. Workplace agreements have not entirely replaced employment contracts, although they are nearly identical in purpose and effect. It is usually only in more senior and permanent positions that employees are covered by a contract.

A contract should specify:
- All leave entitlements (holiday, sick, parental, and compassionate leave)
- Overtime conditions
- Benefits
- Superannuation contribution levels
- Hours (including flexi-time arrangements)

- Long-service leave
- Uniform regulations
- Health and safety observances
- Termination procedures, which will usually follow the form of a first and second verbal warning, written warning, and formal interview (which may be attended, at your request, by a union representative)

If a contract is broken by either party, the injured party is able to sue the other party for breach of contract through an industrial tribunal. Temporary workers and travellers should particularly note that if you fail to give the contractually defined period of notice of resignation, your employer is legally entitled to withhold wages equivalent to that period.

Employment laws and rights

All employees have a basic right to a fair and reasonable working environment and conditions. Reasonable working conditions include the right to personal and physical safety. If you suffer injury at work due to your employer's negligence or unsatisfactory working conditions, you have the right to claim worker's compensation for any injury, discomfort, and loss of earnings you may incur as a result of that injury. Sexual harassment is also considered to be a fundamental denial of the right to a fair and reasonable working environment, and employers have been taken to court because they have allowed offensive or pornographic posters and pictures to be displayed in common staff areas. Most public employers and many larger corporate ones will have a sexual harassment officer on their staff who will provide confidential advice and liaison in the case of complaints.

As an employee, you have the right to a fair dismissal and each trade and industry has its own rules about acceptable practice. It is illegal to breach the contractually stated dismissal procedure and if you believe that you have been treated unfairly, you can contact your workplace authority directly, under the current WorkChoices Act.

WorkChoices

WorkChoices was a controversial John Howard initiative, which came into effect in March 2006, and was the most comprehensive change to industrial relations in Australia for almost a century. The WorkChoice changes were intended to improve national economic performance rates and employment levels. They attempted to achieve this by altering unfair dismissal laws, removing the 'no disadvantage test', and making it possible for workers to submit their certified agreements directly to Workplace Authority rather than going through the Australian Industrial Relations Commission. There were also clauses in WorkChoices that made it harder for workers to strike, made it easier for employers to force their employees onto individual workplace agreements rather than collective agreements and banning clauses from workplace agreements that supported trade unions.

'No disadvantage test': www.workplaceauthority.gov.au

Workplace Authority and Fairness Tests

The Workplace Relations Amendment (A Stronger Safety Net) Act 2007 received Royal assent on 28 June 2007, establishing the Workplace Authority and introducing the Fairness Test. The Workplace Authority Director is responsible for assessing whether agreements lodged on or after 7 May 2007 pass the Fairness Test.

The Fairness Test is applied to Australian workplace agreements and collective agreements to ensure they provide fair compensation for the removal or modification of protected award conditions, such as penalty rates and overtime loadings.

The current Prime Minister, Kevin Rudd, hopes to significantly overhaul the Howard 'WorkChoices' initiatives by the end of 2008, replacing them with a national system.

 Up to date changes on these laws: www.workplaceauthority.gov.au

Useful resources

The Australian Council of Trade Unions (ACTU): Represents 1.9 million workers and provides information on legislated employment rights at www.actu.asn.au.

Commonwealth Department of Education, Science and Training (DEST): www.dest.gov.au

Department of Employment and Workplace Relations: www.dewrsb.gov.au. The Department of Employment and Workplace Relations aims to support an efficient and equitable labour market that links people to jobs and promotes the transition from welfare to work and fair and flexible workplace relations at the enterprise level.

Office of Small Business: Department of Industry, Tourism and Resources, Federal Awards; 02 6121 6000; www.industry.gov.au

Women in work

Australian women are ambitious and hardworking, and are seen as equals both in the home and the workplace (although as you will see below, the pay doesn't always reflect this). Some men now stay at home and play 'househusband' while their wives go to the office and make the income for the family.

Discrimination on the basis of gender is illegal in Australia and equal pay for women has been an accepted basic right for decades. Nonetheless, women in Australia, like their counterparts throughout western industrialised nations, are still slightly behind in the wages stakes and their participation at the highest levels of management and industry is still low. With girls now easily outstripping boys in educational achievement and with the gender balance tipping in favour of women in many university courses (women now outnumber men in medicine, for example), it is likely that this situation will change in coming years. Currently, a number of incentive schemes, such as WISE (Women in Science and Engineering), are in place to encourage women into-male dominated professions and some public employers, particularly in the tertiary sector, operate positive discrimination policies to draw highly qualified women back into the workforce after having children. A greater proportion of female employees work part-time ; 45% of females compared with 14% of men. The retail trades and health and community services are the largest employers of females, employing about 17% of the total female workforce. Women professionals outnumber men and more women than men work in intermediate clerical, sales and service work. 55% of females employed in Australia work on a full-time basis.

Women, in general, seek more flexible employment opportunities and are more likely to be found in part-time or freelance work. They are also likely to seek shorter hours, with statistics showing that single mothers work around 12 hours per week fewer than men with similar family responsibilities. In income terms, men continue to receive higher average earnings than women in the same occupation group. For example, women managers and administrators are likely to receive about 85% of a man's average weekly total earnings employed in the same profession. For tradespeople, women's earnings average out to be around 70% of men's.

◣ WORKING CULTURE AND ETIQUETTE

One might assume that Aussies, being the laid-back nation that they are, are somewhat casual when it comes to their business attire, customs and etiquette. While they aren't as stuffy as their English, European or American counterparts, you will encounter some interesting practices when first joining a company. So to help you adjust, here are a few pointers:

- Always look the person you are meeting in the eye, as Aussies like to feel they can trust you. This goes for business meetings too. A nice firm handshake is seen as a good sign, as is a pat on the upper arm as a welcome. A kiss hello is rarely called for, so offer a hand and if they go for a kiss then reciprocate. Introduce yourself with a smile (Aussies are very smiley people) and repeat their name back to them after they have told you. So after they have said 'Oh hi Anne, I'm Terry', you can respond with 'Nice to meet you, Terry' or 'How are you today Terry?'
- Australians will most likely pity or dislike you, if you introduce yourself by mimicking them, so try and refrain from saying 'G'day mate'.

'I think in some ways UK people are more resourceful and driven than Australians. Some Australians seem quite happy with the status quo and like to be led rather than to take initiative in things. Perhaps this is why recruiters are cautious about hiring anyone without a proven track record. A lot of UK expats I have encountered have done well in Australian companies, reaching higher levels of management because of their can-do attitude and ability to problem-solve.

The most important thing to remember is that salaries do not translate between the UK and Australia and you need to adjust your expectations to local market rates, and try to avoid comparing things to your previous earning status in the UK. You also will need to rebuild your entire industry knowledge and contacts (unless you are very lucky), so when you arrive in Australia, you find yourself in the very strange position of having a certain number of years experience in a career, but having the same level of industry knowledge or contacts as a new starter – quite frustrating!'

- Australians will often refer to you by your first name, 'mate' or surname – or a derivative of all three – as they love to make up nicknames. It's very rare that they will call you Mr, Mrs or Ms unless they are of the older generation.

- Overfamiliarity is also a very Australian trait and they will most likely enquire about your home, back garden, family, past, etc. This is how they form friendships so quickly.

- Always be punctual for interviews.

- The Aussie accent and inflection may make some conversations hard to follow (See page 69 for a sample of some Aussie words) Many of their sentences are cut short, join together or seem to be posed as a question. They won't mind if you say 'pardon?'; the word 'what?' however is seen as abrupt and impolite.

- Working hours can often be made flexible. Australia has a very nice culture of hard work and hard rewards. So finish your work early and you may be able to leave for an afternoon surf. Australian businesses do, however, excel in the world of finance and this doesn't come from slacking off.

- Smoking is banned from all office buildings, toilets and in restaurants and bars.

Working in Australia

- It is perfectly OK to bring your own packed lunch into the office. Having said that, most offices are close to a myriad of shopping malls, which have huge brasseries' inside so there is a choice. If you invite a colleague out for a coffee or a drink it is normal for you to pay for the first round. Aussies will always pay you back when it's their turn for a 'shout'.

- If you are invited over to a colleague's place for a barbeque or for drinks, it is polite – and usually expected – that you will bring a bottle of drink or salad to contribute towards the evening.

- As with all office environments, the mobile phone/blackberry/iPod should remain turned off for the duration of your meeting.

- Men are often required to wear dark suits, but check with your employer beforehand for the dress code. Because most offices are air conditioned, long-sleeved business shirts are the norm once inside, as are ties. Men must be clean-shaven or keep their beard/moustache trimmed and tidy for the office. Women also dress neatly for the office, in dark or grey skirt suits and heels. However, this depends on the type of employment you are in and you might find that your office operates a casual jeans and shirt policy. One tip, however – red is seen as a very aggressive colour and should be avoided in the boardroom. Fridays are often 'mufti' day; which means it's OK to dress in jeans and trainers.

- Heavy smelling perfume is banned in many Australian offices and dentists, hospitals and doctors' surgeries as it gives co-workers headaches.

- Wearing colourful socks under men's business suits is a very British trait and isn't common in Australia.

- Women do not normally wear a full face of makeup to the office. The more natural approach of simple foundation and mascara and lipgloss is more common and is seen as more professional.

- If you are making a coffee or tea, offer those closest to you if they would also like one.

- Australians will consider you to be a 'show off' if you constantly talk about yourself and your past achievements. Don't forget to enquire after your colleagues as well.

- During a serious executive-style meeting it is wise not to cut in while others are talking. Listen and then make your valid points when there is a slight lull in conversation.
- Social networking sites such as MySpace, Facebook and Bebo are banned in many offices as they distract employees. If they are allowed, be conscious of personal material/pictures uploaded on to these sites, as many a worker has been dismissed as a result of this new age phenomenon.
- A verbal promise is as good as a contract with many Aussies, so try and stick to your word.

■ INDUSTRY OVERVIEW

Agriculture and food processing

It is generally acknowledged that Australia got rich 'off the sheep's back', and today agriculture is still the backbone of the Australian economy. The traditional export products of wheat and wool, however, have long since ceded prominence to other sectors, including fisheries and viticulture, and exotic produce such as native bush meats and wildflowers.

The Australian agricultural sector continues to suffer difficulties at present, due to one of the harshest drought periods in Australian history. Challenges to the future of Australian agriculture include developing sustainable water management strategies for a drought prone environment and combating dry land salinity. Domestically, some commodities are facing increased competition from imports. Drought disrupts cropping programs, reduces breeding stock and threatens permanent erosion of the capital and resource base of farming enterprises. Declining productivity affects both rural Australia and the national economy.

The Australian Bureau of Statistics (ABS) notes that the gross value of all crops in 2006–07 decreased by 20% to A$16.0bn, largely as a result of drought conditions. Decreases were reported for all the major cereal crops, except grain sorghum. The value of wheat fell by 51% to A$2.5bn; barley fell by 30% to A$1.0bn; oats for grain fell by 32% to A$174m; and rice fell a jaw dropping 80% to A$51m. The decreased values were mainly due to significantly reduced production, partially offset by increases

in average prices. The value of grain sorghum increased by 2% to A$292m, as production fell by 32% and the average price increased by 49% due to reduced supply.

Decreased production values were also recorded for canola (down 59% to A$202m) and lupins for grain (down 53% to A$125m), again with lower production partially offset by increased average prices. Cotton reported a 46% decrease in value to A$514m as production fell by 50% and the average price increased by 9%. The only increase in production came from the sweeter side of agriculture, as the value of sugar cane cut for crushing, rose by 12% as increased prices more than offset the fall in production. During this period the gross value of hay rapidly increased by 13% to A$1.6bn, despite a 35% fall in production, thanks to the drought. Average prices rose by 73% due to the general shortage of stock feed.

Fruit production also suffered a knock-on effect of severe weather conditions and saw production of apples fall by 2% and average prices increase by 35%.

Year Book Australia 2007 (ABS) found that employment in agriculture and services to agriculture declined in 2006 to just over 330,000, compared with 412,000 in 2002. The biggest fall over that period, 62,000 in 2003, was largely the result of drought.

Automotive

Australia has a strong automotive industry with Ford, Holden, Mitsubishi and Toyota all producing cars in Australian factories. There are also more than 200 component, tooling, design and engineering firms. The industry is based largely in South Australia and Victoria, with a small share of activity in New South Wales. In total, the automotive industry employs more than 239,219 people Australia-wide. The manufacturing side of this industry employed 17,740 in 2007–08. This breaks down as follows:

- GM Holden   6,500
- Toyota   4,700
- Ford Motors   4,700
- Mitsubishi   1,570

Car sales are currently buoyant, reflecting the general economic situation in Australia, and sales of locally produced cars are strong as luxury taxes make imported cars expensive. All automotive manufacturers are investing heavily in robot technology, so that the employment outlook for factory floor workers is poor, while people skilled in computer technology can expect a good outlook. Exports of automotive products (the majority going to the Middle East, New Zealand, the USA, Canada, Mexico and South Korea) have grown consistently.

 For a guide to jobs in this sector: www.automotivepersonnel.com.au

Executive employment

Executive employment prospects are generally good, particularly with smaller companies. After a period of rationalisation, business has stabilised and most firms are experiencing reasonable growth. The Department of Workplace and Employee Relations (DEWR) assesses the employment outlook for generalist managers and administrators as average in both the short and long-term, while those with specialist skills have above average prospects. Marketing personnel, sales reps, accountants, finance professionals and management all have good job prospects in Australia.

Finance and property

Year Book Australia 2007 (ABS) noted that Property and business services employed 1.1 million people in the 2006 period, which accounted for 12% of the total employment market. However this industry has recently encountered difficulties, due to rising interest rates and a decline in residential building projects.

Finance has seen a small decrease in the number of jobs available, although average weekly earnings remain very high in this sector, and are second only to mining. However, the downturn of the financial sector globally (due to the looming recession in the USA) has seen job cuts and cutbacks in banks and financial institutions. There is at present a lack of accountants in most states. Qualified graduates, with degrees in either business or finance, or with experience in a related field are most likely to succeed in finding work in this sector.

Information technology

Information technology (IT) is a major growth sector in the Australian economy and is projected to continue to expand through 2008. Australia has a vigorous, high-tech industry, particularly in the fields of information and medical technologies. Australians are keen to maintain a leading technological edge and are continually updating their technology. Twenty international IT firms have their regional headquarters in Australia and this is, in many ways, due to the sophistication of the Australian IT market. This is also due the fact that Australia has the second highest number of computer owners and one of the largest number of Internet users in the world. Job prospects are strong for well-qualified and experienced professionals, and there is a particular need for people with Powerbuilder, Linux, Unix, and SAP skills among others. The Government is keen to encourage the IT sector, particularly in areas where application of new technology will enhance Australia's competitiveness in the export market.

Medical

Medical practitioners hoping to work in Australia, will need to prove that there are no Australian doctors qualified to do the same job. Overseas-qualified doctors, already granted permission to work in Australia, are required to pass stringent registration examinations, before they are permitted to practice. In 2006–07 there were an extra 1,050 places granted for doctors.

Registered nurses and nurse educators and researchers are in demand throughout Australia, particularly those qualified in specialist fields such as A&E intensive care and psychiatry. You will need to have your qualifications ratified by the Nurses Registration Board in the state in which you live and then register with this Board before you are able to apply for work.

Health therapists, such as physiotherapists, occupational therapists and speech therapists, also need to have their qualifications approved by Australian authorities before practising in Australia. In some cases, further study may be necessary before your registration can be accepted. There is currently an identified shortage of obstetricians and gynaecologists, occupational therapists, ophthalmologists, paediatricians, pathologists, physiotherapist, podiatrist, psychiatrist, radiologist, registered mental health nurses, registered nurses, retail pharmacists, specialist medical practitioners, specialist physician, speech pathologists, sonographers and surgeons.

Petrochemicals

There has been massive investment in oil and gas exploration, particularly in the North-West Shelf Natural Gas Project off the coast of Western Australia, and a record number of oil and gas discoveries have recently been made in Australia. Engineers of all types are in demand in this industry. Almost 90% of the petroleum products consumed in Australia are produced by Australian refineries. As a result, it makes a major contribution to national welfare in terms of output, employment, exports, tax revenue and energy self-sufficiency. There are 12 major players in the oil and gas exploration and production industries in Australia: Apache, BHP Billiton, BP, ChevronTexaco, Exxon Mobil, Magellan, Nexen, OMV, EnCana, Santos, Shell and Woodside.

Retailing

Year Book Australia 2007 (ABS) noted that of the 9.8 million Australians employed across all industries at last count, the retail trade employed the largest number (1.5 million or 15%). The health of the retail industry in Australia has seasonal highs and lows; the Australian Retailers Association noted that on Boxing Day 2007, Australians spent more than A$6billion on their post-Christmas shopping sale items, a 7% increase on 2006 sales. The biggest selling items were household and entertainment products. Employment prospects in both retail sales and management are good. DEWR assesses both the short- and long-term outlook for employment in retail management as sound, and in retail sales as good. This is particularly true in 2008 as Australia experiences its lowest unemployment rate in over 30 years. Inflation is creeping higher, which means people are spending more of their disposable income on retail items.

Steel and non-ferrous metals

Australia is one of the world's largest exporters of iron ore, although its steel-processing sector is much less developed. Mining is a major employment sector and is the highest paid industry in the country, with average weekly earnings in excess of A$1,300 per week. Mining continues to employ large numbers and short and long-term employment prospects are sound in professional, skilled, and semi-skilled occupations. The Australian mining industry is one of the most highly productive in the world and is a significant investor in capital equipment. British equipment suppliers enjoy a large share of the underground black coal mining market. Australia's aluminum industry is one of the major building blocks of Australia's economy and produces nearly 40% of world bauxite, and almost 30% of world alumina, making it the world's largest producer of both. The Stanwell Magnesium Project is the world's largest magnesium plant, employing up to 400 people. Metal production at the Australian Magnesium Corporation plant commenced in October 2004.

Australia is also rich in other natural resources including manganese, uranium, diamonds, zirconite, mineral sands, opals, lead, zinc, copper, gold, silver, alumina and bauxite. These mining industries operate on a large scale across the country and are all significant employers of skilled and unskilled labour.

Teaching

To teach in Australia, you will be required to be four-year-qualified, that is, you must hold either a Bachelor's degree plus a one year Graduate Diploma of Education (equivalent to a postgraduate certificate of education PGCE) or a four-year Bachelor of Education. Teachers in both the state and private education sector who are not qualified at this level are now required to upgrade their qualifications by means of external study and summer schools. Primary school teachers require a specialist degree in primary education while secondary school teachers normally teach in a subject area related to their degree major. Whereas private schools were once prepared to employ non-teacher-trained graduates, this is now extremely rare and teachers arriving from overseas with experience but no qualification are unlikely to find work in either the state or private sector. Teaching, tutoring and lecturing posts in the tertiary sector are oversubscribed and obtaining a position is highly competitive.

Education is the responsibility of each state government and to obtain work as a teacher you will need to apply to the Ministry of Education in your state. Some states require new teachers on the permanent register to work for a period in a remote rural location, before offering a choice of more convenient schools. If you are unable to do this, you may have to undertake work on a temporary or casual basis for some years before being offered permanency. Employment prospects for primary school teachers are expected to remain low and employment has fallen slightly over the past five years. Employment of secondary school teachers has remained steady, while job prospects for music, dance and other extracurricular teachers are average. Employment in this area on the whole has fallen over the last five years. Special education teachers have good prospects of finding employment and the number employed in this sector have risen in the past five years, however, job turnover for special education teachers remains low.

> *i* Jobs in teaching: www.teachers.on.net
> www.australiateachers.com
> www.seek.com.au/education-jobs

◼ MAJOR EMPLOYERS

Major companies inevitably require staff from time to time to maintain their basic operations. Even though it may be more difficult to find companies that are advertising for additional staff, it is worth knowing who the big companies are so that you can approach them before they advertise. It is a good idea to approach their overseas office in your country (if applicable) before you depart.

Retail giant Woolworths is now Australia's biggest employer after staff levels rose to 94,408 (2006), which is a whopping 19% increase. This is mainly due to their many acquisitions, which include the Tavener group and Foodland. However, this figure could be misleading as despite increasing its revenue by 75% since 2001, it has in fact cut its workforce by 27% during the same period.

Some of Australia's biggest growing companies have also had to tighten their belt of late. Out of the top 10 employers on the BRW 1000 list, five have had to cut their workforce down over the past year. One such example is the National Australia Bank, which recently cut 4,584 staff.

Thankfully these job cutbacks are not universal and most Australian industries are eager for staff. Health Scope (one of Australia's leading private healthcare operators, and the second largest private hospital provider) posted the biggest jump in employees, up by 52.8% to 16,549. As with Woolworths, this is due to one of their many acquisitions during the year, mainly the purchase of 14 hospitals from Ramsay Healthcare.

The resource boom has also seen engineering companies increase their workforces. Companies such as Sinclair Knight Merz and WorleyParsons have increased their staff numbers by over 20%.

Australia's Biggest Employers 2007

	Organisation	Number of employees	Change from 2006 (%)
1	Woolworths	94,408	+19.0%
2	Coles Myer	94,000	+0.2%
3	Queensland Health	47,520	+9.2%
4	Telstra	44,452	−3.8%
5	National Australia Bank	38,933	−10.5%
6	Commonwealth Bank Group	36,664	+3.8%
7	Australia Post	34,842	−0.5%
8	Qantas	34,832	−1.9%
9	BHP Billiton	33,184	−3.0%
10	ANZ Banking Group	32,256	+4.1%
11	Rio Tinto	31,854	−1.8%
12	Wesfarmers	30,000	+0.0%
13	Spotless Group	29,200	+0.6%
14	Toll Holdings	28,000	+59.6%
15	Westpac Banking Corporation	27,138	+0.5%
16	Leighton Holdings	25,405	19.4%
17	Amcor	24,538	−9.9%
18	Centrelink	23,315	−3.5%
19	Tempo Services	21,844	−6.0%
20	Australian Taxation Office	21,511	+3.4%
21	Downer EDI	21,219	+20.5%
22	Paul Ramsay Holdings	20,500	No change
23	Ramsay Healthcare	20,377	−33.3%
24	Sydney South-west Area Health Service	19,318	No change
25	South-eastern Sydney and Illawarra Area Health Service	19,111	No change
26	Coca-Cola Amatil	18,872	+12.0%
27	BlueScope Steel	18,000	+2.9%
28	Fonterra Co-op Group	17,400	−6.8%
29	Healthscope	16,549	+52.8%
30	Competitive Foods	15,981	+22.3%

31	Boral	15,802	+4.1%
32	Fletcher Building	15,500	+6.9%
33	Rinker Group	14,358	+8.1%
34	WorleyParsons	14,310	+19.3%
35	Skilled Group	13,480	+11.4%
36	Transfield Services	13,000	+42.3%
37	Queensland Rail	12,961	−2.1%
38	Sydney West Area Health Service	12,763	No change
39	Brambles Industries	12,249	+3.7%
40	Insurance Australia Group	12,093	+5.1%
41	Sonic Healthcare	11,930	+19.9%
42	Ansell	11,317	+2.3%
43	Publishing and Broadcasting Ltd	11,227	+5.3%
44	Orica	10,952	+8.3%
45	RailCorp	10,820	No change
46	United Group	10,678	+35.5%
47	Symbion Health	10,586	−13.5%
48	Tabcorp	10,339	+22.2%
49	Air New Zealand	10,233	−5.5%
50	SingTel Optus	10,124	+8.6%

(Source: IBIS World, 9 November, 2006)(www.ibisworld.com)

■ REGIONAL EMPLOYMENT GUIDE

This section summarises the employment opportunities and economic strengths of each state and territory.

Western Australia

Main city: Perth (population 1,50,790, 2007 census)

Other major cities/towns: Fremantle (population 26,000), Bunbury (population 57,744)

Regions: Coral Coast, Outback, North-west, South-west

Regional newspapers: The West Australian, Western Australian Business News, and Sunday Times

Chamber of Commerce: Chamber of Commerce and Industry, 180 Hay Street, East Perth, WA 6004; 08 9365 7555 advice@cciwa.com.au; www.cciwa.com.au

Major companies: Multiplex, Fortescue metals group, Macmahon holdings group, Griffin Group, Western Australia Meat Exports, West Australian newspapers, MG Kailis Group, Wesfarmers, Alinta and Woodside Petroleum

Employment prospects

It is a great time to seek employment in Western Australia (WA), as it is a major exporter of a wide range of commodities worldwide, and currently

provides a massive 40% of Australia's total exports. This is extraordinary considering that WA only houses 10% of Australia's total population. This commodities boom is largely due to the fact that Perth is the only major city in Australia that can call and email Europe during business hours and is in the same time zone as Hong Kong, Seoul, Beijing, Manila and Singapore. Therefore Perth does a great deal of trading with both the European stock exchanges and those in Asia.

WA now generates more export income than Australia's two most populated states, New South Wales and Victoria, combined. This means that WA can now provide significant financial subsidies to all of the other Australian states. The state boasts high incomes, strong corporate activity, lower unemployment, mineral revenue and a younger population. The Western Australian economy is so strong at present, that they are currently experiencing a major labour deficit. In response the government has launched an appeal for more people to relocate and emigrate at www.gowestnow.com.

It may be worth considering this Western state as a base, as in 2007,the average weekly annual full-time income was A$61,662 compared to the Australian national average of A$57,387. This makes Western Australia the second richest state (income-wise), after the Australian Capital Territory.

The state has a highly educated workforce of 862,000 and mining and property are the state's current fastest growing sectors of industry. The state government has identified and is promoting a group of key strategic industries to reduce dependence on raw materials export. These strategic industries include: building and construction, defence and aerospace, education and training services, health and medical services, information technology and telecommunications, marine industries, mining equipment and services, oil and gas equipment and services, processed foods and wine, and professional services.

Asian markets play a significant role in Western Australian industry as significant refining and manufacturing industries are located in the state and continue to grow strongly with the state's booming economy. These include petrochemicals, fertiliser production and liquefied natural gas production mainly for export to Asia. So strong are their ties with Asia, that in September 2007, the president of China, Hu Jintao, committed to the purchase of A$45bn worth of gas over a lengthy period. As you would assume, this is the largest export contract Australia has ever had.

WA has one of the world's largest and most technologically advanced mining sectors, and mineral and energy production is forecast to experience continued growth. Bulk commodity export is under some pressure, however, as a decreasing international scarcity of non-reproducible natural resources has made the market highly competitive. Reforms have been implemented in the industry to make it more competitive and these have included a decline in traditional award-type employment, which has been

FACT

WA has one of the world's largest and most technologically advanced mining sectors, and mineral and energy production is forecast to experience continued growth.

replaced by staff-only operations. There is likely to be a sharp increase in contracting-out in the mining industry.

Western Australia produces more than 20% of the world's alumina and is also the world's third-largest iron ore producer, producing around 15% of the world's total iron ore output. It is also home to the world's largest zirconia plant. ALCOA, Worsley Alumina, and Dampier Salt are the three major investors in mineral extraction and processing, and between them employ around 4,000 people. Western Australia's goldfields are based inland around Kalgoorlie, 372 miles (600km) east of Perth, and this area is experiencing renewed rapid growth after a period of recession. WA currently extracts up to 75% of Australia's 240 tonnes of gold. Only the diamond industry is expected to experience any decline in the short-term, with implications for the economic strength of the Kimberley region. The oil and gas industry is a major contributor to the state's economy and is centred on the North-West Shelf, which contains one of the world's largest deposits of natural gas. Oil and gas exploration is ongoing in WA, and further major finds are expected. Since 1994, numerous international companies associated with the petroleum industry, including Western Geophysical, Nopec, Drillex, WS Atkins, ESD Simulators and Global Drilling, have all established South-East Asian regional headquarters in Perth. Engineers, metallurgists, and other mineral extraction industry professionals are in demand in WA, and employment prospects in both the short and long-term are good. More than 90% of Australia's oil and gas resources are located off WA. A steady increase has been forecast for the production of gas.

Western Australia has the largest marine industry in Australia. It has an international reputation for building quality ships (this is largely conducted at Austal yards in Henderson, which is south of Fremantle) and infrastructure for offshore oil and gas production and for providing a wide range of marine services. The state supplies about 20% of the world's lightweight high-speed ferries. A marine industry technology park is currently being developed at Lake Coogee. A State Government initiative, it aims to provide land and opportunities for marine-related high-tech industries, such as ship design, maritime training and testing of naval defence systems. Some 400 companies work in the IT and telecommunications industry. These include manufacturing, developing and wholesaling equipment, software and services for information processing, multimedia or communications. Most of these companies are located in Perth.

There are around 3,000 different manufacturers in WA. Food processing, base metal processing, wine production and pharmaceuticals have experienced strong growth, with continued expansion forecast. The Government recognises the importance of the industry to the economy of the state and offers programs designed to assist companies in the food industry. Agriculture is increasingly focused on niche markets, such as emu, kangaroo, ostrich, deer and genetically modified animals (approximately 50% of Australia's live cattle exports come from WA) and on value-added crops, such as specialised noodle wheat. The raw grains market (wheat, oats and barley) has a positive medium-term outlook, (currently amounting to approximately 3% of gross state product (GSP).

In forestry, there has been rapid expansion in eucalypt plantations in the south-west of the state. The fisheries industry is experiencing rapid growth, hampered only by the restrictions of wild harvesting. Mariculture (sea-based) and aquaculture (land-based) fish production is therefore being encouraged and these industries have a strong economic outlook. WA's major success in aquaculture has been the culture of pearl oysters. Based in the Kimberleys, in the far north of the state, the industry represents Australia's largest and most successful aquaculture venture, producing quality pearls worth around A$150m a year. WA is also the world's largest exporter of live animals and a major exporter of skins and hides.

The services sector of the Western Australian economy currently accounts for more than 70% of the state's GDP. The financial sector has expanded rapidly since deregulation in the 1980s and there are now more than 20 banking groups represented in the state. This includes state head offices for all the major banks, such as Commonwealth, National Australia Bank, Westpac and ANZ. It is also home to the Head Office of Woodside Petroleum and has major offices for Rio Tinto, BHP and Western Mining Corporation.

WA exports consultancy services in mining, engineering, forestry, agriculture and conservation and the state's highly regarded medical research and hospital facilities have made Perth a centre for Australia's 'medical tourism' industry. The service sector's biggest growth area is currently tourism, with most visitors coming from the United Kingdom and Ireland, Singapore, Japan and Malaysia.

Strong business investment has lifted WA's economic growth above the national average for each of the past three years. Perth has become a favoured location for international companies choosing a regional base for South-East Asia, especially in industries servicing the oil and gas sectors. Retail trade, property and business services, health and community services, manufacturing and construction employ nearly half of the workforce and employment rates in these industries continue to grow.

Temporary work

Harvest work is available throughout the year, mainly in the south-west of the state. The grain harvest which takes place in the summer months in the wheatbelt and south-west regions is a traditional source of short-term country employment. Casual work in the fishing industry around Carnarvon is available between March and October. General agricultural labouring can usually be found on cattle stations and on sheep stations, particularly at shearing time. The hospitality industry always needs short-term employees, with work available year-round in Perth and during the tourist season in other major centres, for example May to September in Broome and the summer months in other areas. Unskilled mine work is relatively easy to find in the north-west and can be highly paid. In Perth, all the usual temporary employment opportunities, including office work, teaching and nursing are readily available.

Northern Territory

Main city: Darwin (population 106,000)

Other major cities/towns: Alice Springs (population 27,600)

Regions: Top End, East Arnhem, Katherine, Barkly and Central

Regional newspapers: Northern Territory News

Chamber of Commerce: Chamber of Commerce and Industry, Confederation House, 1/2 Shepherd Street, Darwin, NT 0800; 08 8936 3100; www.ntcci.com. au

Major companies: Bechtel

Employment prospects

The Northern Territory has a population of just 215,000, which is about 1% of the Australian total, yet it produces 14% of the nation's exports. The Northern Territory is rich in natural resources, which are being developed by the private sector with the support of the state Government, which has currently undertaken a A$16m geophysical survey of the Territory. This data has been produced mainly for mineral and hydrocarbon exploration companies.

 Geophysical survey results: www.nt.gov.au

Unemployment in the state is currently at an all time low of 2% which equates to over 101,700 'Territorains' in employment. Economic growth is forecast at 6.2% and employment growth at 5%.

The Northern Territory continues to experience economic growth and has benefited from an increase in private capital expenditure in mining, capital investment and tourism. Advertised job vacancies are increasing steadily in the Territory and are generally stronger in the dry season, from May to October.

The mining industry is the Northern Territory's biggest earner and is the state's major employer. It contributes over A$2.5bn to the gross state product (GSP) and employs approximately 4,600 people. There are 14 operating mines, and minerals, including alumina, manganese, gold, bauxite and uranium, dominate the territory's overseas exports. Zinc, lead and silver are mined at Woodcutters mine, McArthur River, and uranium is mined at Alligator River. Gold mines are located in the Adelaide River/ Pine Creek region, the Tanami Desert and at Tennant Creek. Oil and gas production occurs onshore at Mereenie and Palm Valley in the Amadeus

FACT

■ Unemployment in the state is currently at an all time low of 2% which equates to over 101,700 'Territorains' in employment. Economic growth is forecast at 6.2% and employment growth at 5%.

Basin and offshore on the Jabiru and Challis fields in the Timor Sea. Natural gas production for export is being developed on the Petrel and Tern gas fields in the Bonaparte Gulf. Oil and gas account for approximately 35% of the state's exports.

In the East Arnhem region of the Northern Territory, which comprises the eastern half of Arnhem Land and Groote Eylandt in the Gulf of Carpentaria, bauxite and manganese are produced in two of the world's largest mines of their type. Gove Joint Venture mines bauxite on the Gove Peninsula, exporting it as alumina and aluminium hydroxide. The mine, which is managed by Nabalco, employs more than 1,000 people, of whom 260 are independent contractors. The mine is expected to be operational until 2035. Manganese is mined by the BHP subsidiary, Groote Eylandt Mining Company (GEMCO), which produces more than 10% of the world's manganese output. Mining support businesses in the region turnover around A$45m per annum. Apart from the mining industry the East Arnhem region supports mainly small business, in particular retail and property services.

Growth industries in the Northern Territory include building and construction and prawn fishing. More unusually, another growing industry services the need of farming, mining and conservation sectors to harvest the 30,000 head of wild buffalo (feral cattle), which cause massive damage as they rampage across the fragile landscape. The Northern Territory cattle industry is also booming with exports, mainly to the Philippines and Indonesia.

Traditional industries are continuing to show strong growth. The tourism industry has averaged 7% growth over the last seven years and currently employs 8% of Darwin residents. Current tourism-related activity (many tourists are now spending time in Darwin during both the dry and wet seasons) suggests a positive trend and continued growth is projected. It is estimated that 1.38 million people visited the Northern Territory (mainly heading towards the eco tourism of Ultra (Ayres Rock) as well as Kakadu National park) during the period 2005–06. According to the Australian bureau of statistics, they stayed for 9.2 million nights and spent over A$1.5bn.

The Northern Territory Government continues to develop Darwin as a transport hub between the markets of Australia and Asia (currently injecting A$100m into development). The A$1.3bn, 932 mile (1,500km) Darwin to Adelaide rail link is now in full operation and runs from Darwin in the north of Australia to Adelaide in the south.

Oil and gas deposits in the Timor Sea, have led to a shift in the focus of Australia's oil industry to the north and north-west of Australia. This has meant a continuing need for an oil and gas industry infrastructure, and services including engineering, transportation and communications continue to see growth. Timor Sea gas will be brought ashore at Darwin and this will mean the construction of about 310 miles (500km) of submarine pipeline and the establishment of a range of service and support companies to the offshore oil and gas industries in the new East Arm Port industrial complex.

The military population of the Northern Territory has also risen since 2001, due to the continued involvement of the Australian Army in the stabilisation of East Timor.

Temporary work

Most temporary jobs are provided by the tourist industry, especially during the tourist season from May to December although they are found all year round at Alice Springs. Remote resorts have a high staff turnover and are frequently able to offer short-term employment. There is occasional station work available to those with good horse skills.

South Australia

Main city: Adelaide (population 1,139,500)

Other major cities/towns: Mt Gambier (population 23,494), Whyalla (population 19,587), Port Augusta (population 13,897)

Regions: Barossa Valley, Eyre Peninsula, Kangaroo Island, Mid North, Murraylands, Mount Lofty, Outback and Finders Ranges, Riverland, South-East, Upper Spencer Gulf, and Yorke Peninsula

Regional newspapers: *The Advertiser, Sunday Mail*

Chamber of Commerce: Department of Trade and Economic Development, Level 10, Terrace Towers, 178 North Terrace, Adelaide, SA 5000; 08 8303 2400; www.southaustralia. biz

Major companies: BRL Hardy Wine Company, Coopers Brewery, Orlando Wyndham, BHP Billiton, BT Financial Group, Cap Gemini, EDS Australia, Malaysia Airlines, Southcorp and The News Corporation

Employment Prospects

The total number of persons employed in South Australia (SA) in February 2008 was 775,800. This was a 2.9% increase on the number of persons employed in February 2007 (754,200). The ABS reports that in January 2008, South Australia's value of exports (in original terms) peaked at A$657m, an increase of 10.8% from the value of exports in January 2007 (A$593m). The largest reported increases in value of exports over this period were for road vehicles, parts and accessories (up A$58.6m or 502.4%) and petroleum and petroleum products (up A$5.9m or 25.9%). The largest declines in value were reported for the exports of metals and metal manufactures (down A$66.0m or 37. 5%) and wine (down A$6.6m or 6.1%)

The state's information technology development programme aims to make the state an internationally recognised centre in the five specialist areas of software development – multimedia, spatial information, electronic services and education. Motorola, TechSouth, AWA Defence Industries, Telstra and Tandem have already made major investments and South Australia hopes to attract more key investors. The global communications giant, Motorola, has established its Australian Software Development Centre in Adelaide and Technology Park in Adelaide is home to more than 35 technology organisations, including British Aerospace Australia, Computer Science Corporation and Celsiustech. There are a further six research centres, including the Signal Processing Research Institute, which undertakes research in mobile and defence communications. The electronics sector provides employment for over 10,000 scientists, engineers, technicians, production and support personnel.

The motor vehicle sector is South Australia's largest single industry and is the state's largest employer, with Mitsubishi Motors Australia and Holden together employing more than 15,000 people. Of the total production of cars made in Australia in 2007, about 48% were manufactured in South Australia.

The two major overseas markets for cars are the USA and Middle East. Engine components are exported to Asia. The automotive components industry in SA provides more than 20% of the national production, and directly employs a further 6,000 people.

South Australia is at the centre of Australia's defence industry and attracts around 40% of the nation's defence development budget. Facilities include the Defence Science and Technology Organisation (DSTO) complex in Adelaide, the Australian Submarine Corporation (ASC) construction and maintenance site at Osborne for conventionally powered submarines, a dedicated Defence Technology Precinct at Edinburgh Parks, the RAAF Base at Edinburgh and the Woomera Rocket Range test and evaluation facility. There are some 30 defence-related companies located in South Australia and breakthrough research and development is a strong attraction for multi-national companies. BAE Systems, SAAB Systems, Raytheon Systems, and Tenix Defence all have a presence in Adelaide.

South Australia is Australia's largest producer of wine, growing around 30% of the national crop and employs about 4,000 people. However 2008 has seen a minor decrease (6.1%) in wine production from this state, due to the ongoing drought. There are more than 180 small to medium-sized businesses involved in wine production spread throughout the six wine-growing regions. The major producers, Kingston, Orlando Wyndham, Hardy, Petaluma, Peter Lehmann, Southcorp and Beringer-Blass have a national and international presence. For the 2007 vintage there were 385 locations around Australia that crushed 50 tonnes or more of grapes. Over 30% of all locations were in South Australia and they accounted for 43.3% of the national wine grape crush, a fall from the 48.0% recorded in 2006.

SA is also a leading producer of wheat and barley. Aquaculture is thriving and incentives are in place to encourage development in this industry. The value of the state's aquaculture harvest represents 60.5% of total seafood production. Blue fin tuna, abalone, yellowtail kingfish, mussels and Pacific oysters are farmed and exported on a large scale. Agricultural products contribute around A$3.3bn to the South Australian economy each year.

A recent Australian Bureau of Statistics (ABS) study concluded that in 2006–07, the South Australian mining industry contributed A$2,550m in original, chain volume terms, to Gross State Product (GSP). This was an increase of 3.6% from the A$2,462m gross value added in 2005–06. The average annual number of people employed in the mining industry in South Australia has increased steadily from 3,175 in 1999–2000 to 11,175 in 2006–07. It is commonly reported that employment in the mining industry will continue to increase in the coming years due to the proposed expansion of Olympic Dam. Around 3,000 people currently work at Olympic Dam and this number is expected to increase when the mine is expanded to more than double its current production capacity.

In the minerals and energy sector, South Australia has one of the world's largest lead/zinc smelters. It also has one of the largest copper/uranium sites in the world, and its on-shore oil and gas resources are among the most significant in Australia. The state is also developing strengths in niche industries, such as water management and environmental services.

South Australia is renowned for having slow economic growth compared to the rest of the country and has lagged behind the rest of Australia for some time. However, performance seems to be improving (forecast 3.9% for 2007/2008). It took a decade to rebuild the nations credit rating after the fateful State bank collapse of 1992. South Australia's credit rating was recently upgraded to AAA+. South Australia produces about A$48.9bn in, representing approximately 7% of Australia's Gross National Product (GNP). Unemployment in the state is decreasing (currently 4.6% as of Feb 2008) and recently built infrastructures such as the Adelaide to Darwin Railway

FACT

◼ In the minerals and energy sector, South Australia has one of the world's largest lead/zinc smelters. It also has one of the largest copper/uranium sites in the world, and its on-shore oil and gas resources are among the most significant in Australia.

and the Pelican Point Power Station are expected to improve the efficiency of South Australia's key industries and access to export markets.

The South Australia government encourages new business and the workforce is well educated and highly skilled. Government supported research and development in South Australian information industries is worth more than A$80m a year, accounting for one-third of all research and development expenditure in the state. In addition, real estate and office space is cheaper than in some of the other states. High productivity levels and low operational base costs combine to make the capital, Adelaide, more economical and responsive than other cities in Australia, and significantly better than many overseas cities. Business opportunities are to be found in light and heavy industry, agriculture, IT, agribusiness, engineering (especially foundries and tool making), defence and aerospace, food and wine, aquaculture, and traded services, particularly health and tourism. South Australia also has well-developed links with markets in Asia, North America and Europe.

Temporary work

Grape picking is available in the Barossa Valley and Adelaide Hills from February to April, and other harvesting work is available throughout the rest of the year. Hospitality and office temporary work is available in Adelaide all year, particularly during the summer months.

Tasmania

Main city: Hobart (population 200,525)

Other major cities/towns: Launceston (population 99,675), Devonport (population 23,814), Burnie (population 19,030)

Regions: North-west Coast, North and North-East, Tasman Peninsula, Southern Tasmania, West Coast, Central and Midlands

Regional newspapers: *The Mercury, Western Herald*

Chamber of Commerce: Tasmanian Chamber of Commerce and Industry, Industry House, 30 Burnett Street, North Hobart, TAS 7000; 03 6236 3600; admin@tcci.com.au; www.tcci.com.au

Major companies: Gunns Limited, Classic Foods, Comalco, and Alinta

Employment Prospects

Tasmania has always been behind the rest of Australia in terms of economic growth and employment prospects. Many Tasmanians are optimistic, however, despite a current 6% unemployment rate and an economy that continues to lag behind most other Australian states. The ABS notes that during 2006–07, Tasmania had the lowest (Australian overall) employment participation rate (60.3%) and the highest unemployment rate (5.7%).

FACT

■ www.wilderness. org.au reported that on Friday 1 February 2008 the Federal Environment Minister Peter Garrett gave Gunns approval to begin clearing vegetation on the pulp mill site in Northern Tasmania, despite Gunns not having demonstrated it can meet major conditions, including the environmental impact of dumping 64,000 tonnes of toxic effluent into Bass Strait every day.

The Tasmanian Government welcomes investment, but only on Tasmania's terms. Although the state is actively pursuing economic development, Tasmanians have not abandoned their environment-friendly sentiments and all sides have made it clear that investors will have to meet various environmental and quality of life standards before their projects will be given the go ahead in the State. This is why the soon to be developed Gunns pulp mill in the Tamar Valley has completely turned the tables on this green state and caused massive controversy. Residents are furious that the government has seemingly chosen industry over the environment.

On Friday 1 February 2008 www.wilderness.org.au reported that the Federal Environment Minister Peter Garrett gave Gunns approval to begin clearing vegetation on the pulp mill site in Northern Tasmania, despite Gunns not having demonstrated it can meet major conditions, including the environmental impact of dumping 64,000 tonnes of toxic effluent into Bass Strait every day. Peter Garrett's pre-emptive approval could see Gunns clear endangered species' habitat at the pulp mill site any time now. Tragically, clearing can begin before the project even has all the approval it ultimately needs.

The aforementioned Federal Environment Minister, Peter Garrett is the ex-lead singer of Australian rock band 'Midnight Oil' (1973–2002). Prime Minister Kevin Rudd appointed Garrett as Minister for the Environment, Heritage and the Arts after the Labor party won in the 2007 election.

Tasmania is rich in mineral resources, especially iron, copper, lead, zinc, tin and tungsten, and a current geological data survey has revived interest in gold mining in the region. There are seven major mining operations at Henty, Savage River, Beaconsfield, Hellyer, Mount Lyell, Pasminco Roseberry and Renison. After a long period during which the mineral resources industry was starved of investment, the Tasmanian government is now committed to developing the infrastructure and investment conditions necessary to encourage the growth of multiple-stage mineral processing in the state. The government is seeking to combine innovative agricultural and manufacturing techniques with Tasmania's natural beauty and environmental cleanliness.

Tasmania has a highly diversified rural sector, of which the major components are the vegetable, dairy, sheep, and beef cattle industries. Continuing problems in the wool market have meant that the sheep industry, once the mainstay of Tasmanian agriculture, is now the poor relative of vegetable and dairy farming, and currently beef has experienced a similar downturn. Tasmanian agriculture is strongly export-orientated, both to mainland Australia and internationally.

Dairying is considered to have the best medium to long-term prospects and is already the state's largest agricultural industry: in addition to 747 dairy farms, Tasmania has seven fresh milk processing plants, one UHT milk processing plant, seven manufacturing plants, 10 farm cheese producers, and three cheese shredders. The industry employs 2,000 people at farm level and a further 1,600 people at factory and distribution level. Emerging rural industries include emus, poppies, lavender and wine grapes, while apple farmers are experiencing renewed economic growth.

Sea fisheries are a rapidly growing industry; the most valuable sector of the fisheries market is Atlantic salmon, which is mainly grown in the marine farms of the state's south-east. Abalone and rock lobster account for half the total value of Tasmanian marine production, and the marine farming sector as a whole provided more than 40%. Tasmania's wild fisheries have now reached the limits of their sustainable exploitation, although, intensification and expansion is expected in the area of cultured fisheries. Around 2,000 people are employed in marine industries in the state.

The largest sectors of Tasmania's manufacturing industry are food, beverage and tobacco, which together make up 30% of the manufacturing industry. Tasmania is also the base for Incat, one of the world's largest manufacturers of high-speed ferries. Wood and wood products, textiles, clothing and footwear, paper and paper products, chemical and petroleum products, basic metal products, fabricated metal products and transport equipment industries also contribute to the state's economic base; however, there has been a marked decline in employment in these sectors in recent years. Retailing is experiencing slow to moderate growth but there is strong growth in the tourism sector, particularly in eco-tourism. Cheaper air fares, economic growth throughout the rest of Australia and two new

Spirit of Tasmania ferries have seen a marked increase in domestic travel to this state.

Ongoing economic developments include the production of pyrethrum, a plant which produces a natural pesticide; the booming aquaculture industry; continued investment in the natural gas project and the Government's plan to increase its energy supply by building a gas pipeline and an electricity cable to mainland Australia. Tasmania's hydroelectric system produces 60% of Australia's renewable energy and alternative technologies such as wind power are also being explored in Tasmania. There is further expansion in the State's call centre industry, including the employment of 450 people by the Commonwealth Bank in its two call centres. Recently the Government announced a reduction in payroll tax rates so that employers with 50 employees now pay less in taxes than any other Australian state.

In the past small businesses have struggled to stay afloat in Tasmania, yet there have been a few success stories such as the Moorilla Estate, International Catamarans and Tassal.

Temporary work

Hospitality work is available in the Mount Field and Ben Lomond Ski Resorts during the ski season from June to August. Fruit picking is available from December to April in the Huon Valley, Derwent Valley, Tasman Peninsula, and West Tamar. Scallop splitting work can be found in Bicheno in January and February.

Victoria

Main city: Melbourne (population 3.74 million)

Other major cities/towns: Ballarat (population 85,197), Mildura (population 30,016), Warrnambool (population 30,392)

Regions: Great Ocean Road, Grampians, Goldfields, Oasis Country, Murray River, Goulburn Murray Waters, The High Country, Lakes and Wilderness, Gippsland, Yarra Valley and Ranges, Macedon Ranges, The Islands and Bays

Regional newspapers: *Herald Sun, The Age, The Weekly Times, The Border Mail*

Chamber of Commerce: Department of Innovation, Industry and Regional Development, 55 Collins Street, Melbourne, VIC 3000; 03 9651 9999; enquiries@iird.vic.gov.au; www.dsrd.vic.gov.au

Major companies: SAAB, Kodak, Ford, Ericsson, Mercedes Benz, BMW, Toyota, Olivetti, NEC, Oracle, Kraft, Heinz, and Simplot

Employment prospects

Victoria continues to ride the wave of success, built up for the March 2006 Commonwealth Games. This event saw a massive influx of jobs in the construction and tourism arena. Two major redevelopment projects

Art installations in Melbourne's docklands

completed in time were the Southern Cross Station (formerly Spencer Street Station) and the impressive centrepiece of the Commonwealth Games, the redevelopment of the Melbourne Cricket Ground. This world-class stadium was used for the opening and closing ceremonies of the Games and injected A$434m in to the labour market via its construction. Victoria was also very much in the public eye later that year, when in November riots broke out during the hosting of the G20 summit. Victoria has made a name for itself as a world player in global events.

Other redevelopments set to increase employment for the construction and property trade include the multimillion-dollar Docklands project and the 5000-seat Melbourne exhibition and convention centre, which began construction in February 2006. Tourism will also continue to play a part in economic growth for Victoria, as in 2006 it welcomed 19.0 million visitors, an increase of 10.1% from 2005. Employment prospects are looking good in this state.

Many international corporations have their Australian base in Victoria and the Australian headquarters of seven of the top 20 US *Fortune* 500 companies are based in Melbourne. Finance, however, is Victoria's strongpoint and Melbourne was recently rated 34th in the top 50 financial cities, as surveyed by the *MasterCard Worldwide Centres of Commerce Index* (2007), wedged between Barcelona and Geneva.

**Expat Joanne has found it relatively easy
to find employment in Melbourne:**

**Expat Joanne has found it relatively easy
to find employment in Melbourne:**

'I found it easy to get work as a graphic designer, as my skills
are relatively hands-on and practical. I started with a temp
agency and while I wasn't working in the same industry
as in the UK, and was doing a slightly different job, I obtained
valuable corporate experience and learnt a lot in the
year I was in the (temporary) job.'

In the foreseeable future, the city could potentially house the world's fourth largest company if the upcoming merger between the financial giants BHP Billiton and Rio Tinto Group follows through. In the meantime Melbourne is known as Australia's leading centre for superannuation funds, with 40% of the total and 65% of industry super-funds.

The government of Victoria's strong commitment to encouraging international competitiveness in local business has lifted export growth, which is currently strongest in chemicals, the automotive industry, information technology and medical and scientific equipment. Employment prospects are also strongest in these sectors. Over half of Australia's automotive industry production occurs in Victoria, with Ford, General Motors and Toyota all manufacturing in the state, together with more than 500 components producers.

Victoria's food processing industries account for around a third of the state's export earnings; agriculture and food provide more than 35% of the state's export income. 40% of the nation's aluminum production occurs at the primary aluminum smelters at Portland and Point Henry. Victoria is also the centre of Australia's textiles, clothing and footwear industries and continued growth is expected in niche and designer sectors.

Victoria has Australia's largest industrial concentration of information technology scientific and medical facilities, as well as a highly skilled workforce. Melbourne boasts an ICT industry that currently employs one third of Australia's ICT workforce (60,000 people). It has an annual turnover of A$19.8bn and revenues in excess of A$614m. Traded services, such as the health and education sectors, are becoming highly competitive in the export market and are actively seeking new business overseas. The education sector currently generates around A$520m in annual exports and is experiencing continued growth.

As mentioned above, Victoria boasts a significant and prosperous history in the finance and banking sectors. Two of Australia's largest banks, the National Australia Bank and ANZ, have their headquarters in

Melbourne and Melbourne stockbrokers account for more than half of all capital raisings on the Australian Stock Exchange (ASX). Melbourne is one of Australia's leading industrial centres and is Australia's leading centre for biotechnology in the Asia-Pacific region. Melbourne is also home to the A$40bn Federal Government Future fund.

Melbourne has Australia's largest throughput cargo airport and its largest container seaport, the Port of Melbourne, handles 39% of Australia's container trade and handles more than A$75bn worth of trade every year. The two terminal operators at Swanson dock, Patrick and P&O Ports, are committed to developing their facilities to operate at international best practice performance levels and investment in the redevelopment of these terminals over the next 20 years will exceed A$300m.

Geelong is Australia's eleventh largest city and plays a major role in the country's wool production and textile industries. In addition to these traditional industries, the city is now developing its economic base in high-technology industries, education and research. Geelong is home to manufacturers of textiles, clothing, footwear, petroleum and coal products, chemicals, basic metal products and transport equipment and is the centre of the Australian aerospace industry at Avalon Airport, while major assembly and maintenance plants are operated by ASTA and Hawker de Havilland in Melbourne. Ford Motor Company, Shell Oil Company of Australia and the aluminum giant ALCOA are the largest among the many industries that have chosen to expand in the region.

As a result of the Victorian government's approach to financial management, Victoria has very low debt levels and is in a strong economic position. Victoria is also a world leader in innovation, science and technology. There has been a massive funding injection for science, technology, research, education and skills development. The state government is committed to science, technology and innovation. The development of a biotechnology precinct in central Melbourne and the national Synchotron facility will make Victoria a global leader in biotechnology and scientific research, with the aim of developing knowledge-based industries, professional services, design, advanced manufacturing and environmental management. The government has also committed funding for a high-tech film and television studio facility at the Melbourne Docklands.

Victoria contains the largest concentration of research institutions in Australia and accounts for 35% of the country's total business research and development. Employment in rural and regional Victoria accounts for more than a third of the state total.

Temporary work

Harvest work is available around Mildura and Shepperton from January to April, and around Echuca and Lilyfield from September through to February. The Northern Victoria Fruit-growers' Association in Shepperton and the

Victorian Peach and Apricot Growers' Association in Cobram are both able to offer jobs during the harvesting season. Hospitality work is available during the ski season in the Snowy Mountains. Temporary secretarial, office and administration work, as well as hospitality work (including gaming) is widely available in Melbourne.

New South Wales

Main city: Sydney (population 4.3 million)

Other major cities/towns: Gosford (population 301,551), Parramatta (population 148,323), Newcastle (population 288,732), Wollongong (population 263,535)

Regions: The North Coast, Southern Highlands, Illawarra, Southern Tablelands, Shoalhaven, Clyde Coast, Eurobodalla, Snowy Mountains, and Sapphire Coast

Regional newspapers: *Daily Telegraph, Sydney Morning Herald, Australian Financial Review*

Chamber of Commerce: State Chamber of Commerce, Level 12, 83 Clarence Street, Sydney, NSW 2000; 1300 137 153; enquiries@thechamber.com.au; www.thechamber.com.au

Major companies: Goldman Sachs, MasterCard International, Caltex Australia, Macquarie bank, Citibank, Acer, Nokia, BAE Systems, Kellogg, Southcorp, Inghams, Windsor Farm Foods, Qantas, Boeing, and Rio Tinto

Employment prospects

The Australian Bureau of Statistics (ABS) predicts that by the year 2051, Sydney will have a population of 5.6 million. This would make New South Wales the most populated state of Australia. This is a title it currently clings to, as a current ABS study concluded there were 4,000 people jammed into every square kilometre. There is good reason why hordes of interstate residents and overseas migrants head to the east coast of Australia and land in the imposing shadow of the twins (the Opera House and the Harbour Bridge) and it isn't all to do with Bondi Beach and the harbour. The economy prospers here its workforce enjoys the highest median household income (A$46,463) of any major city in Australia and there is an unemployment rate of just 4.3%. Not only that, a current AUBS survey ranks Sydney as 18th in the world in terms of net earnings. One can then easily see how Sydney provides approximately 25% of the country's total GDP.

One downfall, however, is the cost of living in such a prosperous city. The Economist Intelligence Unit's *Worldwide Cost of Living Survey*, found that Sydney is the 16th most expensive city in the world. As of 20 September 2007, Sydney had the highest median house price of any Australian capital city at A$559,000. So, you better read on, if you want to make a sufficient income to live as the Sydneysiders do.

The strength of the New South Wales' economy is due to its diverse range of industries. The state has one of the world's leading service economies, and also has a significant manufacturing and primary industry base. The state's capital, Sydney, is a sophisticated, global city, and is the base for Australia's major financial institutions – the Reserve Bank of Australia, the Australian Stock Exchange and the Sydney Futures Exchange (one of Asia Pacific's largest options exchanges, seeing 64.3 million contracts traded in the year 2005). It is a major financial centre in the Asia–Pacific region. The majority banks, both national and multinational, have their headquarters in Sydney. NSW accounts for almost a third of the total Australian workforce and nearly 45% of all employees in the finance and insurance sectors.

New South Wales is the location of the regional headquarters of a number of multinational companies in Australia and 50% of the top 500 companies in Australia are located in the state. There are a number of industry sectors present in NSW, including: information technology, telecommunications, aerospace, medical equipment, pharmaceuticals, environmental industries, industrial textiles, shipping and railways, construction and mining equipment, metal and minerals processing, processed foods, paper and pulp, banking, tourism, advertising, film and audio products. European and Japanese companies are all represented. NSW is the base for 44.8% of Australia's finance and insurance industry, 40.7% of its property and business services (including IT) industry and 35% of its communications industry.

New South Wales is Australia's premier agribusiness state, accounting for around one-third of the national primary industry output and many leading agribusiness companies have their headquarters in Sydney. The agribusiness industry includes farming, processing, transport, distribution, export and supply. The industry's strengths have traditionally been in bulk commodities and minimally processed products such as wool, grains, meat and sugar; however, current innovation and new product development has made the sector increasingly market focused. Sector growth is focused, in particular on the Asian food market, with heavy demand projected for western foods over the next five years. The processed food industry employs 50,000 people and exports generate around A$3bn.

The state has a well-established chemical industry and is home to the country's largest petrochemical complex. Its mining and mineral processing industries generate an annual output of more than A$12bn, of which coal production accounts for 80%. The major minerals derived from the state's rich mineral resources are black coal, copper, gold, silver, lead, zinc, mineral sands, and gemstones. NSW is also a major minerals processing state with established steel and aluminum production, and new copper smelting capacity currently coming into operation. The government of NSW is spending A$35m to expand the geological database of the state to attract new mineral and petroleum exploration and development. The Lithgow Minerals Processing Park has been located in the central west of the state to encourage development in that area.

Mining is a significant industry in New South Wales generating A$5.2bn in export revenue in 2005–06. It is a low-cost producer of metals and minerals, including coal, gold, copper, silver, lead, zinc and gemstones. Australia currently has 95% of the world's natural opal production and NSW accounts for more than half of the national output. Coal dominates the industry with four major coalfields producing more than A$5bn of black coal annually. Coal generates 92% of the State's electricity.

The electricity sector dominates New South Wales' energy industry and employs more than 4,000 people. The government monopoly has currently been restructured to form three independent power generators, Pacific Power, Delta Electricity, and Macquarie Generation. The New South Wales gas sector is 95% controlled by Australian Gas Limited (AGL), a publicly listed company with 2,100 employees. Environmental management is a growth industry in the state and is currently the largest in Australia.

The state is also a leading information technology and telecommunications centre and the base for almost half of Australia's IT industry. This sector generates A$27.5bn a year and employs 100,000 people, 41% of Australia's IT professionals. The state is a significant producer of digital material content for multimedia and has a strong film and television production sector. Fox Studios in Sydney has become one of the largest film and television studios in the southern hemisphere and offers many opportunities

> **FACT**
>
> ▪ Fox Studios in Sydney has become one of the largest film and television studios in the southern hemisphere and offers many opportunities in the digital post-production industry (Return Superman 2006 was one Hollywood blockbuster that was currently shot here).

in the digital post-production industry *Returns Superman* (2006 was one Hollywood blockbuster that was shot here). Sydney is regarded as the contact centre capital of the Asia Pacific and continued growth in international and domestic centres is forecast.

NSW and Sydney are the major entry points to Australia, with Sydney Airport providing the bulk of airfreight and business air passenger activity. NSW is a major centre for aerospace, electronics and defence industries. These industries are among the fastest growing in the state, with extremely strong investment growth expected over the next five years. The state is the base for more than 30,000 defence personnel and Sydney Harbour is an important naval base and centre for marine repair activity. Airframe and systems support, sensors, processors and defence aerospace training systems are all under development in NSW, as is world-leading C2I technology.

Cultural industries generate an estimated A$4bn in turnover for NSW and education continues to be a growing market, with more than 50,000 international students studying at various educational institutions.

The greatest proportion of international student enrolments in 2006 were in Victoria (28%), followed by New South Wales (27%). This shows a 35% increase from the previous year. A total of 9,100 international students won places at the University of Sydney and a further 8,500 joined the University of NSW. Other smaller NSW Universities also noted enrolment growth during 2006.

Food processing comprises 10% of the state's GDP and retail trade for 15% of the economic output. Both of these sectors are significant employers. The state's largest service sector is tourism, which currently injects A$17bn a year into the economy. In 2005–06 over 8.2 million domestic and 2.7 million international visitors holidayed here. Travel centres, hostels, backpacker bars and backpacker and luxury transport companies have all seen an annual increase in trade.

NSW also accounts for 38.6% of national output in the 'lifestyle' industries – accommodation, retail stores and food outlets and 36.3% of cultural and recreational services. With the increasing commercial role of Sydney's many medical laboratories and research centres, science and research is another strong growth sector

Temporary work

The full range of temporary work opportunities is available in NSW, ranging from harvest and seasonal farm work in almost every region, to hospitality and office work, particularly in Sydney.

Australian Capital Territory

Main city: Canberra (population 339,900)

Regional newspapers: *The Canberra Times, City News*

Chamber of Commerce: ACT and Region Chamber of Commerce, 12a Thesiger Court, Deakin, ACT 2600; 02 6283 5200; chamber@actchamber.com.au; www.actchamber.com.au

Major companies: Biotron and CEA Technologies

Employment prospects

The Australian Capital Territory (ACT) has the highest current employment participation rate at 73.6% and lowest unemployment rate (3.0%) of all the Australian states and territories. Employment opportunities in the ACT are concentrated in Canberra. Most permanent work available is either service-based, reflecting the city's political function, or in the extensive public service which supports the government and federal ministries. The Commonwealth Government is the territory's biggest employer. In current studies, government administration and defence accounted for 26.1% of Gross Territory Product, and employed over 40% of Canberra's workforce. There are more than 13,000 businesses in the ACT. Canberra's workforce is more computer-literate and highly educated than any other workforce in Australia, with 51% possessing university degrees. This reflects the latest figures from the ABS, which note that the unemployment rate in Canberra is currently 2.5%, well below the national unemployment rate of 4.1%, with labour shortages reported in some sectors.

Canberra also has the highest average equivalised (total weekly net income, from all sources of all household members, including dependents) disposable income of any Australian city; this is a result of low unemployment and substantial levels of public sector and commercial employment. Several hundred national associations have their headquarters in Canberra, and the city is home to a number of multinational companies including Hewlett-Packard, NEC, British Aerospace, Fujitsu, Unisys, Oracle and Intec. Companies dealing in advanced technology manufacturing, defence-related services, call centres, information and business services, light manufacturing and assembly and agribusiness can all be found in Canberra. Small business plays an important role in the ACT and there are 20,000 companies representing 96% of all private sector businesses in the Territory. Future opportunity is in the biotechnology sector where the ACT has established capability, primarily research and development focused, in niche markets such as plant science, neuroscience, hypertension, immunology, phenomics, genetics and medical services and devices. In current years, there have been a growing number of independent software vendors-such as Tower Software, The Distillery, RuleBurst and QSP setting up in Canberra, hoping to capitalise on the concentration of government customers. The space sciences industry employs 300 people and is ranked as 21st in the world for its research. Other significant industries are property and business (14% of employment and 14% of GSP), retail trade (13% and 4%), health and community services (9% and 6%) and education (9% and 5%).

Temporary work

Temporary employment in Canberra will be available in the IT and service industries and will include clerical and hospitality work.

Queensland

Main city: Brisbane (population 1.8 million)

Other main cities/towns: Gladstone (population 280,000), Rockhampton (population 69,835), Caloundra (population 89,000), Mount Isa (population 21,421)

Regions: Gold Coast and Hinterland, Sunshine Coast, Toowoomba and South-west Queensland, Rocky and Central Queensland, Mackay and Central Coast, Townsville and North Queensland, Cairns and Far North Queensland

Regional newspapers: *The Courier Mail, Western Echo, The Sunday Mail*

Chamber of Commerce: Commerce Queensland, Industry House, 375 Wickham Terrace, Brisbane, QLD, 4000; 07 38422244; info@commerceqld.com.au; www.commerceqld.com.au

Major companies: QMI Solutions, Hard Metal Industries, Burley Engineering, AJM Environmental Services, Suncorp-Metway Ltd, Orrcon, Credit Union Australia, Mincom Ltd, PIPE Networks, Wotif.com

Employment prospects

Queensland continues to experience strong economic growth. ABS figures from May 2007 show that the state's jobless rate was down to 3.4%. This was the same figure as April 2007, but well below the 4.8 % recorded 12 months prior. These figures bettered the national rate of 4.2% and saw employment rise by 104,300, which in total was 37% of jobs created nationally. Queensland has been below the national unemployment rate for almost three years.The current Queensland premier, Peter Beattie commented (6 June, 2007, *Courier Mail*) that although this was an extraordinary achievement, it brought its own problems, in the form of skills shortages. Therefore, the Government has launched a A$1.1bn Queensland skills plan, which aims to reform the vocational education and training sector, so that it better meets the skills needs of business and industry.

There are three main hubs of economic activity throughout the Sunshine State. Financial and property markets prosper in Brisbane and both the Gold Coast and Northern Queensland enjoy a vibrant tourism industry. The state benefits greatly from rich natural resources and diversified agriculture.

The state government has allocated large sums towards maintaining Queensland's favourable economic position, including a A$1.6bn Infrastructure Rejuvenation Package. A further A$4.8bn is being spent in developing the state's regional road networks, and another A$690m on Queensland Rail. Queensland has Australia's lowest state taxes and debt levels, and welcomes foreign investors

Queensland is Australia's most decentralised state, and has the largest rail network and more deepwater ports, than the whole of the rest of Australia combined. Infrastructure developments to which the Government has made a commitment include the installation of a water management system and weir in the Atherton Tablelands, expansion of the Dalrymple Bay Coal Export Terminal, a 10-year development of the Port of Mackay and a cruise liner port in Brisbane. Brisbane is now the third most important port in Australia for value of goods. The major exports are sugar, coal, grain and container freight. Most of the port facilities are less than 30 years old and some are built on reclaimed land. The Queensland Hospital Project will upgrade all the state's hospital facilities and gas turbine power plants will be built at Yabulu and Mount Stuart. New wharf facilities are being built at Fisherman Islands to handle large container vessels.

Agriculture is the cornerstone of Queensland's economy, with grains, beef and wool dominating rural industry. Tropical and citrus fruits, dairy products, vegetables, cotton and tobacco are also important and the state has the world's highest yielding sugar cane industry. Queensland's fishing industry is second only to Western Australia's, with nearly 5,000 commercial fishing vessels in operation, mainly fishing prawns, crustaceans and fin fish for export to Asia, Europe and the USA. Recently established food processing plants include a high-tech piggery and integrated pork processing facility (DanPork Australia), and an upgraded Golden Circle Canned Fruit and Vegetable Plant. The cattle and calf industry is the state's largest primary industry and accounts for about 30% of the state's gross value. The outlook for the sugar cane industry is favourable due to an expected increase in world sugar prices.

Mount Isa Mine is one of the world's leading producers of lead and silver, and is ranked in the world's top 10 for copper and zinc production. The state's high-grade coal and bauxite reserves are among the largest in the world, and magnesite, phosphate rock and limestone are also mined. Queensland is the largest Australian producer and exporter of black coal. The coal industry has currently benefited from increased industrial production in Asia, particularly China. Large resources of magnesite, oil, shale, uranium, tin, mineral sands, clay and salt remain untapped, and continued development is projected. New mines are being developed at Cannington Base Metals Deposit (BHP), Century Base Metals Project (Century Zinc), Ely Mining Project (Alcan South Pacific), Ensham Coal Mine (Bligh/Idemitsu), and Enterprise Mine (MIM Holdings), among many others. Minerals mined in these projects include

lead, zinc, bauxite, copper, gold, and, predominantly, coal. In addition, a number of minerals processing plants have been brought online, such as the Sun Metals Corp Zinc Refinery in Townsville, Dupont/Ticor Sodium Cyanide Plant and the Boyne Island Aluminium Smelter. Manufacturing industries in Queensland have developed to support the state's mineral processing and agricultural industries. The manufacturing sector is dominated by food, beverage, tobacco processing, fabricated metal products, chemicals, petroleum and coal products. The processed food industry employs around 38,000 people and is Queensland's largest manufacturing sector. The state's service industries include construction, wholesale and retail trades, communications, business and financial services and tourism.

The environmental management industry is a new growth sector in Queensland and is concerned with creating sustainable development through pollution abatement, environmental protection and the monitoring, planning, management and rehabilitation of the environment. It is estimated that the global environment market is worth about A$A100bn a year with the Australian market worth at least 10% of that figure. The potential for growth and technological innovation in this sector is significant. At least 125 Queensland firms are already delivering environmental expertise and services overseas.

Queensland has Australia's most successful tourism market and this sector employs a significant proportion of the state's workforce. Four major tourist resorts have been developed at Coomera Waters, Cowan Cove, Port Hinchinbrook and East Hill, an integrated urban/resort project, covering 605 acres (245 ha).

Japan is the major destination for Queensland merchandise exports. Major export earners for the state include coal, meat, non-ferrous metals and crude minerals. Business and investment opportunities occur in the traditional industries and there has been recent growth in communications services, biotechnology, IT and leisure industries. The area surrounding Surfers Paradise on the Gold Coast has become Australia's third largest city and is the fastest-growing area of Australia.

Brisbane houses the third largest major business district in Australia. Many major Australian companies, as well as numerous international companies, have contact offices in Brisbane (both blue and white collar industries). DHL Global's Oceanic distribution warehouse is located in Brisbane, as is Asia Pacific Aerospace's headquarters.

Temporary work

Fruit and vegetable picking is available throughout the state, particularly at Stanthorpe, Bowen and Warwick. Employment in the hospitality sector is widely available at resorts during the tourist season, especially on the Gold Coast and also at amusement parks-Movie world, Dreamworld, Wet and Wild Work on prawn trawlers can be found in Cairns and Karumba. Mining and cattle station work is available in the Mount Isa region.

Key online employment sources

Australian Government Information: www.nla.gov.au/oz/gov. Entry point to all Australian government websites.

Australian Taxation Office: www.ato.gov.au. Information on Australian tax laws.

Department of Employment and Workplace Relations: www.dewrsb. gov.au. Workplace relations in Australia, maritime transport, policy and legislation, government employment, and related sites.

Office of Small Business: Department of Industry, Tourism and Resources www.industry.gov.au. The small business sector has accounted for 70% of jobs growth over the past decade.

Melbourne City Council: www.melbourne.vic.gov.au. Includes information on products and services of Melbourne City Council as well as details of forthcoming events, maps and guides.

NSW Department of State and Regional Development: www.srd.nsw. gov.au. Information for potential investors and business migrants to Sydney and New South Wales.

New South Wales Government: www.nsw.gov.au. Includes information on doing business with the NSW government, rural information, reports and papers and related links.

Queensland Government Online: www.qld.gov.au. Includes information on business in Queensland, and government departments and agencies.

Tasmania Online: www.tas.gov.au. Includes information on investing in Tasmania and migrating to Tasmania.

Government of Victoria: www.vic.gov.au. Includes information on state projects, arts, business and education.

Australia White Pages: www.whitepages.com.au. Online access to eight million residential, business and government listings.

The Australian Yellow Pages Telephone Directory: www.yellowpages. com.au. National searchable database.

Starting a Business

Australia used to be considered the 'Lucky Country' or the 'Land of Opportunity' and businesses of all shapes and sizes blossomed across the country. Aspiring entrepreneurs have always been a part of the Australian social landscape and small businesses such as plumbers, caterers, painters and decorators, landscapers, hairdressers, beauticians and potters have not only found space for themselves in the Australian market, but remained solvent and generated good incomes.

With the recession of the 1980s, however, came a much more depressed business climate and large and small businesses collapsed in dramatic profusion. Although the Australian economy has recovered well it has, in general, become far more difficult for new businesses to survive their first year.

Business growth is now being encouraged and protected by legislation, government assistance and an extensive network of government small business offices and advisers, to ensure that once off the ground new enterprises stay airborne. Tax incentives are at offered now in the recognition that the earlier tangle of red-tape and taxation was enough in itself to discourage new business.

The small business sector employs almost 3.5 million people and has accounted for 70% of jobs growth over the past decade, as well as around 15% of the gross domestic product (GDP). Of the 1.2 million small businesses, 39% operate in regional Australia. Small businesses produce some of Australia's best innovations and are predominant in the property, business services, construction and retail trade sectors.

The retail, construction and services industries are the most successful sectors of the market. The need to become more competitive internationally has forced small businesses to provide higher quality products and services at costs that can challenge international businesses. Economic analysts believe that this trend is likely to continue for some time and the Government is particularly keen to encourage an export-based economy, offering many incentives to businesses to export both products and services.

The Australian Government is committed to selecting high quality business migrants and both top-flight executives and well-heeled investors continue to head south to take advantage of the relatively stable economic conditions, highly qualified labour market and the various incentive programmes available to help build new enterprises. Business migrants to Australia take with them a knowledge of overseas markets, business networks, cultural practices and languages other than English, as well as their specific business skills and experience. Recent figures show that the top 10 source countries for business migrant visa grants were China, the UK, South Africa, Singapore, Taiwan, Zimbabwe, South Korea, Hong Kong, Malaysia and Indonesia. A two-year survey of Business Skills migrants showed that 38% had settled in New South Wales, 20% in Western Australia, 16% in Queensland, 16% in Victoria, 1% in South Australia and less than

FACT

■ The World Bank report Doing Business 2008, shows that Australia is the ninth easiest country in which to start up a business.

1% in Tasmania, Northern Territory and Australian Capital Territory. During 2006–07 business migration visas decreased somewhat to 5,400 places for business people and their families. This compares to 5,670 visas granted in 2003–04, 7,364 issued in 2000–01 and 6,260 in 1999–2000.

This chapter aims to give practical advice about starting a new business as well as suggestions as to those businesses which are likely to succeed in Australia. Careful research and preparation will help prevent your business from becoming one of the failures. It also provides preliminary information about the taxation rules and regulations relevant to creating a new business as well as the procedures for buying an existing business. The *Useful Resources* section at the end of the chapter (page 359) may be particularly helpful in providing the contact names and addresses of advisers and authorities to help you get your new business venture off the ground.

■ ESTABLISHING A NEW BUSINESS

If you have an idea for a new venture, you will need to do some careful market research and ask yourself some searching personal questions. Do you have the right background or qualifications to set up the sort of enterprise you are considering? Are you prepared to risk almost everything to achieve your goals? You will need to be completely familiar with your product or service and have detailed technical knowledge of it. You must also ensure that there is a market for this product and you should identify the size, geographical and socio-economic distribution of that market. Research is the key to success and you would be well advised to find out as much as possible about both your target population and your competition. This kind of information can be gained from government statistics (the Australian Bureau of Statistics, www.abs.gov.au, is particularly helpful), universities and institutes of technology, small business agencies, advertisements and telephone directories (both the yellow pages and the business directory). In addition, you should find out whether there is a trade association that deals with the product or service you are offering, as this is likely to be a good source of information, advice and assistance. The Australia and New Zealand Chamber of Commerce UK (www.anzcc.org.uk) is a primary source of information (for other contact details see *Useful resources* on page 359) and has an invaluable database, updated daily, of more than 6,000 Australian and New Zealand businesses – a valuable research tool for anyone considering setting up a business in the region. This organisation also offers regular investment and business seminars, as well as a library of information on Australian and New Zealand business taxation, and government regulations.

The Australia and New Zealand Chamber of Commerce UK:
www.anzcc.org.uk
Yellow Pages Australia: www.yellowpages.com.au
Information and advice on starting a business in Australia:
www.business.gov.au
Find your local Business Enterprise Centre: www.beca.org.au

Protecting your intellectual property

Legally protecting your business image and the products you have developed can be vital in maintaining your competitive advantage. Businesses built on innovation and design need to protect their intellectual property rights, which in commercial terms means your proprietary knowledge. There are several different types of intellectual property, and various methods of protecting them:

- **Circuit layout rights** are granted for three-dimensional configuration of electronic circuits or layout designs.
- **Copyright** is granted for original material in literary, artistic, dramatic or musical works, films, broadcasts, multimedia and computer programmes.
- **Designs** refers to the features of shape, configuration pattern or ornamentation that can be judged by eye in finished articles. A new or original design may be registered for up to 16 years. Registration gives the owner the exclusive rights to make, use and sell articles incorporating the registered design.

Life coach Rebecca Wells tells us how she felt starting up a business in Australia in 2008:

'Starting up a business in Sydney was really straightforward. You need to work out first what your business structure will be, i.e. will you operate as a 'company' or 'business' and then applying for the correct registration. My local Office of Fair Trading was extremely helpful and registration was done in minutes. I also arranged to see a consultant at my local BEC (Business Enterprise Centre) who gave me lots of information about the resources available to me, and some advice on tax registration. Incidentally, BECs run various workshops for owners of business start-ups with everything from 'how to write a business plan' to 'networking effectively' on offer. Meeting other business owners at BEC events is also really useful because you can develop your professional referral network more quickly. Overall, setting up was straightforward and fairly painless!'

- **Patents** are for inventions that are recognised as new, novel, non-obvious and useful. Inventions that serve an illegal purpose or which are unrelated to manufacturing processes are not patentable. A patent lasts for up to 20 years and gives its owner exclusive rights to exploit the invention or to authorise others to exploit it.
- **Plant breeder's rights** are also available and are granted for new varieties of plants. These are administered by the Plant Breeder's Rights Office, under the Department of Agriculture, Fisheries and Forestry-Australia (www.affa.gov.au).
- **Trade marks** are granted to protect words, symbols, pictures, sounds and smells, or a combination of these, distinguishing the goods and services of one trader from those of another. Initial registration of a trademark lasts for 10 years.
- **Trade secrets** protection covers 'know-how' and other confidential information.

Intellectual property rights (patents, trade marks, designs, and plant breeder's rights) are administered in Australia by the federal Government agency IP Australia, which is a division of the Department of Industry, Tourism and Resources. Formerly known as the APIO, IP Australia provides valid IP rights, monitors the Australian IP system, and partakes in the harmonisation efforts in relation to IP laws throughout the world. The agency also administers the Olympic Insignia Protection Amendment Act 2001.

 IP Australia: 02 6283 2999; assist@ipaustralia.gov.au; www.ipaustralia.gov.au

The Patent Co-operation Treaty (PCT) allows companies to file an international patent application, protecting the product in all participating PCT countries. There are 77 countries participating in the PCT, including the USA, Canada, Japan, the UK, Austria, Belgium, Switzerland, Germany, Denmark, Spain, France, Greece, Ireland, Italy, the Netherlands, Norway and Sweden. There are also many other participating countries from Eastern Europe, Africa and the Asian–Pacific region. The patent application consists of several forms and a detailed set of drawings, and the cost of submitting an application is dependent upon the complexity of the drawings. A schedule of fees is available from IP Australia and applications are submitted to that office. There are Patent Offices in every PCT country.

If your product is competing with others of a similar type, it may be advantageous to register a trademark. A trademark can be registered with IP Australia and once registered will be protected indefinitely provided that renewal fees are paid 10 years after the initial registration. Processing time for trademark applications is around six months and this time lag should be incorporated into your business plan. On acceptance, your trademark will be published in the *Official Journal of Trade Marks*, after which objections may be filed in three months. If there is no opposition, or if opposition is unsuccessful, your trademark will be registered when you pay the registration fee (to be paid no later than six months from the date the acceptance was advertised). Your new trademark is then registered from the date you filed your application, recorded in the *Register of Trade Marks* and you will be sent a Certificate of Registration.

New products can also be assessed by SAI Global, formerly Standards Australia International, which is the most widely established supplier of independent conformity assessment, certification and training services in the Asia Pacific region. If your product meets the strict standards of this organisation, you will be able to use the product certification mark and benefit from the associated product credibility.

 SAI Global www.sai-global.com

Registering a business

Establishing a new business means you must comply with numerous licensing laws and other regulations. You must register your business with the Australian Taxation Office and obtain a tax file number (TFN) and an Australian Business number (ABN). Depending on your business structure, you may also need to register with the Australian Securities and Investments Commission (ASIC) to obtain an Australian Company Number (ACN). Business registration with the Australian Taxation Office and with the ASIC can now be completed electronically via the Australian Government Business Entry Point website and this site also provides electronic links to the Business Names Registration offices in each state and territory. Before you start a business, or if you are not sure which licences, permits or approvals your business needs, you should contact your local Business Licence Information Service (www.bli.net.au or via the Australian Government Business Entry Point website), which will provide you with all the necessary application forms.

 Australian Securities and Investments Commission: 03 5177 3777;
www.asic.gov.au
Business Registration: www.business.gov.au
Registering a business in NSW: www.fairtrading.nsw.gov.au

Forming a company

Any new company may be registered either as a proprietary company or a public company. When a company is registered under the Corporations Law it is automatically registered as an Australian company and thus may conduct business as a company throughout Australia without needing to register in each individual state or territory jurisdiction. Most companies in Australia are registered as proprietary companies under the Corporations

Law. Proprietary companies are generally cheaper and easier to register than public companies, as with the setting up of a public company in any other country, the bureaucracy, legal costs and legislative controls are necessarily more restrictive. A private company only needs to have a nominal share capital to commence operating. Directors and a company secretary must be appointed and as soon as is practically possible after incorporation, a public officer has to be appointed for taxation purposes. For proprietary companies, there must be at least two directors, one of whom must be an Australian resident. Public companies must have at least three directors, two of whom must be residents of Australia. There are several steps in the process of registering a company:

Choosing a name

First, you must select a name, which may either be one of your choice or the company's ACN (Australian Company Number). Before you decide on a name, you should consult the alphabetical listing of company and business names available by checking the National Name Index at the ASIC internet site. The ASIC will reject your name if it is identical or similar to any other company name. A company name must indicate the company's legal status, with a proprietary company including the word 'proprietary' or its abbreviation 'Pty' in the name. The liability of a company's members must also be indicated, so that where liability is limited, the name must end with the word 'limited' or its abbreviation. The British form, PLC, is not used in Australia, is usually Pty Ltd.

Registering a company

Next, you will need to obtain the consent of proposed directors and a company secretary and formally appoint them via the application process. After your application has been received and successfully processed by the ASIC, a certificate of registration will be posted to the registered office of your company, and only once you have received this can the directors officially commence operating as a company. Such operations include opening bank accounts, which cannot be done before the completion of registration. The law requires that the company's name be clearly displayed at the registered office and at each business address. The Australian Company Number (ACN) must appear on the common seal, every public document issued, all documents required to be lodged with the ASIC under Corporations Law and on every eligible negotiable instrument issued.

Off-the-shelf companies

The formation of a company from scratch takes between one to two weeks from application and will cost around A$1,200, not including professional fees (which are likely to be high). If you need to establish the company very quickly, agents and solicitors can also offer ready-made 'off-the-shelf' companies, which can be purchased more cheaply as legal expenses are then kept to a minimum. Shelf companies are incorporated with names (which in most cases will be unsuitable) and amendments will need to be made to the company's Memorandum and Articles of Association. A change of name usually takes approximately four weeks to be processed and approved and the ASIC must issue a Certificate of Incorporation on Change of Name. The additional cost of changing the name of the company and the Memorandum and Articles is around A$350.

If you do choose to buy a shelf company, you should consult with your advisers to consider whether the Articles of Association need to be amended. You need to consider whether the existing constitution allows for: the rights of directors to decline to register a future share transfer; the requirements if a shareholder ceases to be a director or employee or dies; the chairperson's casting vote; the shareholder/director's voting rights; who controls the company, as different levels of shareholding confer different rights and there may also be different classes of shares conferring different rights.

When you purchase a shelf company, you should receive a complete set of first board minutes and statutory books. If you do not receive these, it would be advisable to check with the previous owners as they can often contain important information and you are expected to hold them.

Partnership/sole trader legalities

If you are starting the business as a partnership or sole trader (see *Business Structures,* page 351), there are no legal formalities involved other than the notifications required for tax purposes. In the absence of a partnership agreement, the partnership will be governed by the Partnership Act of the relevant state or territory, which will specify how a partnership should administer its affairs. Most partnerships, however, prefer to draw up a tailor-made agreement to meet their own particular needs. Partnership agreements are usually drawn up by a solicitor and should include details of the arrangements for partners' capital, banking accounts, profit sharing, salaries (if relevant), drawings, change or termination of partnership and voting rights. This agreement is particularly important if a dispute between partners arises, but business experts claim that the more important course of action is to avoid such potential disputes by choosing the right partner(s) in the first place.

If you are planning on setting up a company, please note that this information is intended only as a guide. It is *essential* that you seek professional advice in the process of forming a company and that you are fully aware of your obligations and commitments when registering a company.

Choosing an area

If you choose to buy an existing business your area will generally be predetermined, but if you are starting your business from scratch the decision of where to locate your business, including the type of premises you require, can be vitally important to its future. The needs of your business should determine its location. Various factors, such as whether you expect frequent deliveries from suppliers or visits from customers and whether you need to attract passing trade, can influence your decision as to the best location. You will also need to consider the likely needs of your staff, especially in terms of public transport and parking.

Renting business premises

The rental rates of commercial properties vary greatly across Australia. Melbourne and Canberra offer lower rents (calculated in dollars per square metre) compared with similar properties in Sydney or Perth. The rates of leasing commercial property in Darwin, Adelaide and Hobart are markedly lower than that of comparable properties in the central business districts of Sydney or Brisbane.

Whether leasing or purchasing, you need to make sure that the premises have adequate facilities such as security, access, essential services (including electricity, water, waste collection, energy efficiency, sound and thermal insulation), flexibility of design should you wish to expand at a later date and that the dimensions in terms of height and floor space are sufficient. You also need to ask your solicitor to check that your type of business will not breach any environmental laws if you conduct that business in those particular premises. The buildings must comply with fire and safety regulations, town planning and other regulations, the Health Act and the Shops and Factories Act (obtainable from the Government Printer or various technical publishers) applicable in your state or territory.

If you choose to lease premises, ensure that the lease is checked by a solicitor and, if possible, by an accountant. The terms of the lease are always negotiable and your solicitor or accountant will advise you on the negotiation of terms and conditions. You should attempt to negotiate a rent-free period, a lower initial rental, reduced annual escalations, payment by the landlord for any improvements or refurbishments to the property and payment by the landlord of any outgoings associated with the property. You should identify who is responsible for insurance, property taxes and maintenance, what your rights are to make alterations or renovations and whether the lease permits subletting of the premises. Your negotiating power will always depend on the state of the property market at the time. At present, this tends to be favourable to lessees.

The term of the lease can be important, as a long lease may reduce flexibility. A shorter lease with the option to renew can be preferable, depending on the current economic conditions and your choice of premises. When considering a lease, it is helpful to ask for a plan that clearly states the extent of the premises being let and to make sure that the proposed use of your building does not breach any terms of the lease. Before you sign, you should also compare the rent, rates and service charges (usually given on a dollar per square metre basis), annual escalations and rent review clauses with those of other premises. You should also be aware that a verbal lease, which is binding on both parties, is recognised by law but should be avoided as such agreements are fraught with difficulties.

Your choice of premises will also have tax implications as payments for the rent of business premises are tax deductible, but the rate of such deductions will vary according to the age of the building. Moveable furnishings and equipment in the buildings are subject to higher rates of depreciation for taxation purposes.

Raising finance

You can have the best ideas, products and service in the world, but if you cannot manage to raise the finance to put your plans into practice, your dreams (not to mention potential profits) will remain unrealised. Before you approach any potential source of finance, you will need to be fully prepared to explain your business concept and to answer any questions about your proposal. A thorough and careful business plan is the first key to success.

Business plan

A completed business plan is a summary and evaluation of your business idea. It is the written result of the planning process and a blueprint for your business operations. Your ability to make it work depends on checking your progress against the plan and reviewing that plan as your business evolves. In the early stages of development, when you are seeking finance, your business plan may well be the only tangible aspect of your intentions. The business plan, which you present to a bank or other moneylender, should contain a fully considered financial plan, including a budget for at least the first 18 months. You should make sure that you include an allowance for unexpected and intangible expenses, in particular taxes such as provisional tax (tax paid against estimated future earnings), as one of the most common reasons for business failure is the lack of planning for such contingencies.

There are many publications available which will help in preparing your business plan, and assistance is also available from your nearest Small Business Development Corporation, industry associations, chambers of commerce and from business advisers and accountants. The Commonwealth Bank of Australia offers a guide in its *BetterBusiness Planner,* available either as a software package or in hardcopy form. The software package includes a sample business plan, financial templates which automatically calculate budgets and cash flows, and follow-up software to keep track of your business plan's progress.

BetterBusiness Planner: 1800 657 151 ; www.commbank.com.au
Home Business Manual: www.homebusinessmanual.com.au
Australian Securities and Investments Commission: Financial tips and safety checks at www.fido.asic.gov.au

■ FINANCING A BUSINESS

One of your first steps in drawing up a business plan is to consider the different sources of finance available to you. The Commonwealth Bank of Australia strongly recommends that business owners should look much more carefully at maximising the business's ability to generate internal funds, so as to avoid relying too much on external sources for the funding of its operations. Although for the first three years a new business is hardly likely to be in the position to generate enough internal funds to become self-sufficient, you should think very carefully about trying to borrow as little as possible from outside sources in the long term, and incorporate self-sufficiency into your long-term business proposal. Once you have done this, you need to look very carefully at all the different financial institutions and the options available to you to choose one or a combination that is most appropriate to the needs and goals of your company, and your repayment capacity. Lenders will also expect a significant level of personal capital investment in your business. One of the most common reasons for finance refusal is that applicants have not allowed for sufficient personal contribution; this is seen, at best, as a demonstration of lack of commitment.

As discussed in the *Daily Life* chapter, there are many different financial institutions in Australia. Deregulation of banking has led to increased competition and, as a consequence, more innovative and sophisticated banking techniques have been introduced. In addition, opportunities to obtain loan funds have greatly increased and there are now many more options available in terms of structuring loan agreements. In an effort to encourage the growth and development of Australian industry and resources, a number of industrial banks have been established which provide development finance, equity funding and financial advisory services. Other methods of raising finance can include accessing venture capital, which may provide funding for high-risk projects, or floating a company on the stock exchange.

Types of finance

Equity, long-term loan finance and working capital finance are the three principal types of finance available for starting a new business in Australia. Equity is usually contributed by the owners of the business and businesses with significant equity will find it easier to attract financial backing from other sources. If you are seeking finance for a major project, such as investment in plant and machinery for your business, long-term loan finance is likely to be the most appropriate option. In many cases the loan will be secured against the business or the equipment purchased. In addition, the financial institution will generally require personal guarantees from the business owners. There is usually a substantial difference between the amount of the loan and the value of the asset to allow for risk and for the costs involved should the business fail.

There are a variety of options available in obtaining long-term business finance. Firstly, it is important to calculate how much of your own personal contribution can be used as share capital and how much can be used as loan capital – this proportioning of capital can affect your taxation (see *Taxation,* page 356). Cash subscription from your family and friends can also be used as long term finance, as can cash received from any other sponsor or from venture capital. Most often, however, long-term business capital is raised through a bank or finance company loan or through leasing or hire purchase finance. It must be noted, however, that leasing or hire purchase finance generally have interest rates which are significantly higher than other sources.

In the very competitive finance market, banks and other lenders are increasingly offering tailored loan packages and the variety of types of finance is growing exponentially. Options are also changing almost every month, and the best advice is to start by approaching the major banks to discuss the available financing methods. Most larger bank branches now have specialist business advisers who will be only too happy to guide you – remember they are selling a product too.

Government-backed finance

The Australian Government, at both federal and state levels, is very keen to promote new business and to ensure that such businesses are successful. Government agencies exist in every state to provide various kinds of assistance, technical as well as financial. Financial assistance can include direct cash grants, subsidies and tax concessions, while technical assistance will include both professional and technical advice and research and development seminars. There are many opportunities for small businesses to benefit from government-backed schemes, with substantial incentives available to all kinds of enterprises. There are a number of different financial assistance schemes run by the state and federal governments and by various industry agencies. AusIndustry is the best starting point for obtaining information on these schemes. Their database contains information on all federal, state and territory government support programmes, as well as programmes offered by industry associations and chambers of commerce around Australia. The AusIndustry Hotline can also put you in touch with sources of information in research and development, networking, management, strategic planning, benchmarking, diagnostic reviews, environmental management, marketing, export planning and business licensing.

 AusIndustry: 0132 846; www.ausindustry.gov.au

Rebates and subsidies are also offered to employers as an incentive to provide employment and to encourage them to provide training for their employees, or to allow employees to attend trade or development courses. Such schemes, which are usually aimed either at the youth or long-term unemployed workforce, are administered by the Australian Job Network (AJN), which can provide further information. Employment incentive schemes are a favourite vote-winner for governments and tend to be restructured with each budget and change of government.

Most states and territories also provide financial assistance in the forms of loan funds or guarantees to businesses. However, this assistance is generally only provided as a final resort. Other assistance can include transportation and freight subsidies, or advice services in areas such as effective business operations, production processes, technological development and export market opportunities. State government assistance is generally given to encourage the establishment of new businesses or the expansion of existing industries in the state or territory. To receive such assistance businesses must demonstrate that they are viable, both in the short- and long-term, and that they can provide assessable benefits to the state. The Government will be likely to favour business that will create new permanent jobs, provide new skills, increase the state's technology or production capacity, tap new markets outside the state, or offer diversification of the state's industrial base or range of products. For further details about state government assistance, contact your state's Small Business Development Corporation or similar body, the Australian Job Network, or AusIndustry (see *Useful resources*, page 359).

Importing/exporting

Australia has a policy of gradually and systematically removing trade tariffs on imported products. However, in those industries still subject to protection, bounties are sometimes offered, which are direct cash payments to Australian manufacturers (operating in Australia) in lieu of, or supplementary to, assistance provided by means of tariff or customs duty. Bounties can assist manufacturers to compete more effectively with imported products. Many imported goods will also be liable to the Goods and Services Tax.

 Australian Customs Information Centre: 1300 00 363 263 ; www.customs.gov.au

If your business is involved in exporting goods from Australia, Austrade (The Australian Trade Commission) will be able to provide marketing advice and assistance. Additionally, the R&D (research and development) Start Program, available to non-tax-exempt Australian companies, is a merit-based program designed to assist the commercialisation of Australian industry and to undertake research and development through a range of grants and loans. The Federal Government also offers a range of tax incentives.

 Austrade: 132 878 (local); www.austrade.gov.au

Summary of financing

Although a potential financier will want a thorough plan, they will not want a long report, so you should try to keep your proposal down to between 10 and 12 pages. You must ensure that you describe your product, the premises from which you intend to operate, relevant information about each member of the management team, your marketing strategy, your competition, past performance (if any), financial projections and assumptions relating to them, the financial resources required and what changes will be necessary if your assumptions prove to be either pessimistic or optimistic, and your assessment of the risks involved in the project. A professional-looking presentation is important, as this is the document that will 'sell' your business to lenders. It is vitally important to obtain impartial professional advice when preparing a business plan, but you must also be fully involved; when you come face-to-face with the bank manager, you are the one who will have to answer all the questions.

Accountants

A good accountant is essential to the success of your business. You will find that the process of creating a new business or buying an existing one is so complex and involved that you will not be able to complete it without expert assistance. Your accountant should be registered with one of the industry associations and it is essential that you confirm this. You should also shop around and obtain quotes in respect of hourly rates and estimated annual expenses. Your accountant will act as your financial and, on many occasions, as your legal adviser and will often undertake duties that could also be done by a solicitor. If the advice you receive is false or misguided it could mean the failure of your business and possibly even fines and legal costs. For this reason, you will want to make sure that the accountant you decide to use is reliable and reputable.

Large accountancy firms are likely to be considerably more expensive, but may be more reliable and offer backup guidance. Your accountant is really another business investment you will have to make, so you will want to reduce the element of risk. It is advisable to consult your accountant on every initial business decision you make, as a good accountant will always give you more impartial advice than you may receive from a real estate agent, bank business adviser or business broker.

Useful resources – Starting a Business
AusIndustry: 132 846; www.ausindustry.gov.au
Austrade: (London) 020 7887 5226; (Atlanta) 404 760 3400; www.austrade.gov.au
Australia and New Zealand Chamber of Commerce: (UK) 0870 890 0720; enquiries@anzcc.org.uk; www.anzcc.org.uk
Australian Copyright Council: 02 9318 1788; info@copyright.org.au; www.copyright.org.au
Department of Industry, Tourism and Resources: 06 213 6000; inquiries@industry.gov.au; www.industry.gov.au. ITR is based in Canberra

with offices in all Australian state capitals, and representatives in North America, Europe and Asia.

Inventors' Association of Australia: (Adelaide) www.inventors.asn.au. Has chapters in several other states.

Institute of Patent and Trade Mark Attorneys of Australia: 03 9857 0311; www.ipta.com.au

SAI Global: 02 8206 6186

United Kingdom Patent Office: (Newport) 01633 813930; enquiries@patent.gov.uk; www.patent.gov.uk

Small business agencies

These provide advice and referral services for intending, starting and existing businesses in each state:

ACT: ACT and Region Chamber of Commerce and Industry: 02 6283 5200; chamber@actchamber.com.au; www.actchamber.com.au

NSW: NSW State and Regional Development: 1300 134 359; www.smallbiz.nsw.gov.au

NT: Business Services, Department of Business, Industry and Resource Development: 08 8924 4280; www.dbird.nt.gov.au

QLD: State Development and Innovation: 07 3001 6359; www.sd.qld.gov.au

SA: Department of Trade and Economic Development: 08 8463 3800; www.cibm.sa.gov.au

TAS: Department of Economic Development: 03 6233 5888; www.development. tas.gov.au

VIC: Business in Victoria: 132 215 (local); www.business.vic.gov.au

WA: Small Business Development Corporation: 08 9220 0222; info@sbdc.com.au; www.sbdc.com.au

Accountants

Most accountants advertise in the Yellow Pages of their state telephone directory. The Institute of Chartered Accountants, the Australian Society of Accountants in your capital city, or the National Institute of Accountants can also provide lists of professionals associated with their organisation. A brief list of other contacts is given below:

Australian Accounting Group: 56 Neridah Road, Chatswood, NSW 2067; 02 9411 4866.

Collett & Co: 03 9686 5580 (Melbourne); 08 9261 7762 (Perth); 02380 488786 (UK); info@collettandco.com; www.colletandco.com. Provides tax and financial planning advice to businesses and individuals heading for Australia.

Deloitte Touche Tohmatsu: 02 9322 7000; www.deloitte.com.au

Ernst & Young: 02 9248 5555; www.ey.com/au

Institute of Chartered Accountants in Australia: 02 9290 1344; www.icaa.org.au

KPMG Australia: www.kpmg.com.au

PricewaterhouseCoopers: 02 8266 0000; www.pwcglobal.com/au

Trading banks
Australia and New Zealand Bank (ANZ): 1800 00 801 485 (small business hotline); www.anz.com.au
Commonwealth Bank of Australia: 0061 131 998; www.commbank.com.au
National Australia Bank Ltd: 03 9641 3500; www.national.com.au
Westpac Banking Corporation: 02 9226 3311; www.westpac.com.au
(See also the banking section of Chapter Four, *Daily Life,* page 167 for the British branches of these banks.)

Merchant banks
BNP Paribas Australia: 02 9216 8633; www.bnp.com.au. The third largest foreign bank in Australia, in terms of assets, and the 12th largest bank in Australia overall.
BT (Bankers Trust) Financial Group: 02 9034 4900; customer. relations@btfinancialgroup.com; www.btonline.com.au
Deutsche Bank AG: 02 9258 3666; www.aus.deuba.com
JPMorgan: 02 9220 1333; www.jpmorgan.com.au
Macquarie Bank Ltd: 02 9237 3333; www.macquarie.com.au.

Finance companies
GE Commercial Finance (GE): 02 8234 4455; www.gecommercial.com.au
Esanda Finance Corporation Ltd: 132 373 (local); 03 9666 9100 (international); www.esanda.com.au. Australia's largest asset-based finance company.

Real estate
There are countless real estate agencies in every area of Australia. To locate those in the area of Australia to which you are moving, try searching Telstra's online database at www.telstra.com.

Books and information packs
Starting a Business in Australia: Vacation Work Publications (www. vacationwork.co.uk), published January 2006.
Other books in Crimson's *Live and Work* series may be useful if you are considering setting up an export business; each book in the series contains a 'Starting a Business' section relevant to the particular country or area covered.
Australian Bureau of Statistics (ABS): 1300 135 070 (local); 02 9268 4909 (international); www.abs.gov.au. The Australian Bureau of Statistics has offices in every Australian state/territory and publishes yearbooks containing the results of every recent survey and research project, which are useful when undertaking initial market research.
Doing Business in Australia: Published by Ernst & Young as part of their *International Business* series. Copies available from their Australian office (listed above) are under *Accountants* and also online from www.ey.com. Copies are also held by their international branches, and you should

consult the telephone directory in your country's capital city for further information.

Periodicals

Australian Business for Sale News: 02 9281 4599; www.businessforsale. com.au. A magazine produced every three months, which gives information and details about franchising, business opportunities, distributorships and licenses, plus information on how to buy or sell a business. Available in the UK from the Subscription Department, Consyl Publishing, 3 Buckhurst Road, Bexhill-on-Sea, East Sussex, TN40 1QF; ?01424 223111; www.consylpublishing.co.uk.

The Australian Financial Review: 09 282 2833; www.afr.com.au
Dynamic Small Business Magazine: 02 9955 6311; www.dsbmag.com.au. A bi-monthly magazine regarded as essential reading for Australian small business.

Economic Outlook: 108 8231 0941; eo@econ-outlook.com.au; www.econ-outlook.com.au

Franchising

Franchising and Own Your Own Business Magazine: Bimonthly magazine which gives the latest national and international news, discussion of key industry issues and information from the Franchising Council of Australia. The magazine also includes information on how to choose the right franchise and how to franchise your existing business. It is available from Niche Media, PO Box 2135, St Kilda, VIC 3182; 03 9525 5566; www.franchise.net.au

Franchisenet: A very useful website with industry information, a links page and a franchise directory at www.franchise.net.au

The Franchising Council of Australia: 1300 669 030; www.franchise.org.au

▌ RELOCATION AGENCIES AND BUSINESS SERVICES

In addition to assisting with housing, education and employment arrangements many of the relocation companies also specialise in finding appropriate business premises and in relocating complete companies, including plant and machinery. These services tend to be very expensive and are best suited to large, international companies. Most large relocators have offices overseas or have reciprocal arrangements with some firms in Australia. However, many relocators in the UK are established to provide services for those relocating to the UK from other countries. If you require the services of a business relocator it may be most appropriate to engage the assistance of a specialist Australian firm, of which some are listed below.

Relocators

The following relocators specialise in the relocation of executives, company personnel and their families.

Allied Pickfords: offices Australia-wide. 02 9636 6333; call 132 554 to find nearest office location, or www.allpick.com.au.

Australiawide Relocations Pty Ltd: 02 9488 9444; www.relocations.aust.com

Expat International: 03 9670 7555; info@expat.com.au; www.expat.com.au

Grace Removals: Executive and Commercial Relocations; 02 9838 5600; info@grace.com.au; www.grace.com.au. Grace is Australia's largest mover of business and household goods internationally, both from and to Australia.

Relocations in Melbourne: 03 9533 6831; www.relocations-melb.com.au

■ IDEAS FOR NEW BUSINESSES

The various state governments have all identified strategic industries in which the greatest opportunities for investment lie, these are outlined in the Regional Employment Guide on pages 300–325. Most state governments can offer incentive packages to investors. In overview, Australia is a leading exporter of commodities such as coal, iron ore, wheat, beef and veal, petroleum and gas and cotton. However, the export market in unprocessed foods, fuels, minerals and other primary products is declining.

Service industries now make up 64% of the economy and Australia is becoming an information-based economy. Australia is developing a new competitive edge in high-tech exports, such as scientific and medical equipment, telecommunications, software and aerospace products. Knowledge-based industries now contribute almost half of Australia's GDP and the information and communications technologies are Australia's fastest-growing sectors. The manufacture of components for mechanical and electronic equipment and cars has also recorded strong growth in the last decade. The shift from an economy based on manufacturing to services has been rapid; the growth rate of non-service industries has dropped, while service industries continue to grow. About 36.5% of Australians now work in professional, technical, managerial or administrative jobs and the service industries are Australia's biggest employers. In the past decade, according to the OECD (Organisation for Economic Co-operation and Development), the service industry employees accounted for almost 77% of total employment in Australia.

New businesses that either compete directly in these sectors or which provide related services, are the most likely to succeed. Import businesses are prospering due to the strong Australian dollar, compared to the weakening US dollar. Both federal and state governments are, however, strongly export-oriented and any business that exports Australian goods and services is likely to be eligible for a variety of export subsidies and incentive schemes.

■ WOMEN IN BUSINESS

According to figures from Women's Network Australia, while nine out of 10 businesses in Australia are small businesses, women are opening small businesses at twice the rate of men. Currently, 38% of all small businesses across Australia are owned and operated by women and every year up to 40% of women leave salaried employment to open their own small business venture. Australian women are opening businesses at nearly twice the rate of men and their businesses have a higher success rate, particularly in the first five years. Women are considered to be more successful in business because they are willing to acquire formal business skills and to develop non-formal management skills such as networking and flexibility, which may give them a competitive advantage over men.

In many states today, women-centred business networks have been developed and women entrepreneurs generally view these as valuable resources. A survey by Yellow Pages Australia found that both men and women believe that women business owners are more persuasive, more prepared to ask for advice, are better at dealing with customers, learn faster, are more hard-working and are more pleasant to deal with. The trend in business ownership and operation by women leans towards a far greater involvement in the services sector of the economy, with around 83% of businesses operating in this sector owned by women. Most states have specific programmes to encourage the development of women in business and details of schemes can be found on the Women's Network website. The Australian Businesswomen's Network is an organisation seeking to help women in business by raising their profile and providing exposure to a range of business success models.

> **Women's Network Australia:** 07 3272 8222; www.womensnetwork.com.au
> **Australian Businesswomen's Network:** 1300 720 120; www.abn.org.au
> **Yellow Pages Australia:** www.yellowpages.com.au

■ BUYING AN EXISTING BUSINESS

One of the options you may have when starting in business is to purchase an existing operation. Getting into business in this way can be much less risky and can be profitable more quickly than starting your own business from scratch; but it is not entirely risk free and your success will depend heavily on how wisely you evaluate and choose the business you buy.

Buying a business will include the purchase of plant and equipment, stock in trade and, usually, a goodwill component. Goodwill is represented in part by location, existing customers and reputation, but also by other factors that can influence the profitability of the business or its income-producing capacity. The correct assessment and identification of the value of a business is crucial in the process of buying a going concern, and it is highly recommended that you obtain professional assistance in making this assessment. When you investigate a prospective business purchase you should make sure that you examine the following:

- financial statements
- payables and receivables
- employees
- customers
- location
- facilities
- competitors
- registration
- zoning
- image

Financial figures should be accompanied by an audit letter from a CPA (certified practising accountancy) firm, and you should make sure that business licences and other legal documents can be easily transferred; you should also determine the costs involved in doing so. Customers are your most important asset, however, and you should make sure that they are as solid as the other tangible assets that you will be acquiring. Check if the current clientele has a special relationship with the present owner, are they long-time friends, neighbours and relatives? How long have these accounts been with the business, and what percentage of income do they represent? Will they leave when the business passes to new hands? Make sure, too, when you are buying a business that you understand the competitive environment in which it operates. Check whether local price wars are common, or whether any competitors have gone out of business recently. You can track down this information by contacting an industry association or by reading trade publications. Finally, look at how a business is perceived locally and in general. This 'goodwill' factor cannot necessarily be established from a balance sheet and you will need to evaluate everything from the way a company services customers to how employees answer the phone. To learn more about a firm's reputation talk to suppliers, competitors, customers, banks and owners of other businesses

The popularity of cafés and bars means a food and drink business could be a popular enterprise

in the area, and remember that it can be very difficult to change a negative perception.

Transferring ownership

Transferring the ownership of a business from one owner to the next requires a management plan to ensure a smooth transition of the business and its assets, including goodwill and the customer base. You will need to notify the Australian Taxation Office of the transfer and, in the case of an incorporated business, the Australian Securities and Investments Commission and supply details of new directors and the transfer of trading name. You may also have to transfer ownership of any licences that are required to operate the business, for which you should contact your local Business Licence Information Service.

Business Licence Information Service: 08 9220 0234 ; www.licence.sbdc. com.au

Franchising

Australia is the most franchised nation per head of population in the world and has at least three times as many franchise systems per head of population than the United States. Because many new business owners are attracted to the ready-made brand awareness and back up available to franchisees, each year franchising contributes over A$77bn to the Australian economy. There are more than 747 different types of franchise available in Australia. One such franchise that continues to grow in popularity is the landscaping business Jim's Mowing.

The Franchising Council of Australia (FCA) should be your first port of call if you are considering this type of business option. The FCA has a strict code of conduct that protects members from unscrupulous operators and can also direct potential franchisees to accountants and lawyers who are members of the FCA and who understand the specialist field of franchising practice. The FCA publishes *The Franchisee's Guide: Everything you need to know as a Franchisee* for intending franchisees, available from the FCA Franchise Library.

> **Franchising Council of Australia:** www.franchise.org.au, lists over 1,600 different franchise businesses.

The position of the franchise in the market in which it trades should be carefully assessed. You should not only look at the particular franchised business in relation to its own activities, but also make an assessment of the prospects for the industry overall. The franchise will either be dealing in goods, products or services and you should consider whether these are new or have distinct advantages over their competitors. Check that the franchised business has been thoroughly proven in practice, or whether it is exploiting a fad or current fashion that may be transient or short-lived. If the product is strongly associated with a celebrity name, remember that a person's fame can fade as quickly as it rose, and that your business, built on a name, may fade with it.

The basis of any franchise operation is the franchise agreement. This must be considered very carefully and it is advisable to consult your accountant/solicitor before signing anything. Before you enter into any franchise agreement, you need to consider whether you are technically able to deal with the product or service, as well as the extent of the competition. If the franchise involves evolving technology you will also need to assess whether the franchiser also has the expertise and resources to be able to compete successfully in the market. If your product is manufactured overseas, or is composed of parts made elsewhere, you must identify delivery times and calculate the risk of delays and the potential for foreign currency losses. In addition, you will have to ascertain whether there are any import duties or regulations that have an impact on

FACT

■ Australia is the most franchised nation per head of population in the world and has at least three times as many franchise systems per head of population than the United States.

the price of the product. You should also be clear on how much assistance is given, and control exercised, by the franchiser and you would be well advised to investigate the franchiser's financial credibility and stability. It can be beneficial to talk to other franchisees about the business and the franchiser's methods of operation. It is imperative that you understand what the duration of the franchise is, what costs and fees are involved, whether you have to pay a royalty to the franchiser (and if so, how much), and what the arrangements are for termination.

Franchising offers significant benefits to business owners and can be considered as going into business with an experienced partner. A good franchiser will offer training and continuing assistance; while the franchisee will benefit from established brand recognition and a customer base. The franchisee will usually need less capital than they would if setting up business independently. Although business risk is significantly reduced because you are under the umbrella of a franchise, setting up your own business is still a risk.

Other businesses

Most businesses for sale are advertised with real estate agents, business brokers, trading associations and in the national and local newspapers. A successful acquisition depends on a thorough study of the business or

Rack of t-shirts in a surf shop on the Gold Coast

company from many different angles. Your accountant should check out the value of stock and the cash flow of the business. Profit should be calculated after the fair working salaries of proprietors or partners have been deducted. Your accountant should also advise you on the stamp duty and tax implications of the purchase of a particular business. The last three years' accounts of the company (audited if possible) should be examined, together with current management accounts and projections (if available), particularly in terms of the valuation of assets, contingent liabilities and the company's tax position. Finally, you need to ensure that you will be able to raise the finance required before committing yourself to the purchase; this applies to the purchase of either a business or a company. Further details are given in *Raising finance, page 336.*

◼ BUSINESS STRUCTURES

Companies

Most small businesses in Australia are embodied in some kind of legally recognised entity. Australian company law is mainly governed by the Corporations Law of individual states, which is basically the Commonwealth legislation for the Australian Capital Territory with minor variations pertinent to that particular state. The Corporations Law contains the rules, procedures, accounting and reporting requirements for companies. This is administered by the Australian Securities and Investments Commission (ASIC) and detailed information about Corporations Law can be obtained upon request (see address below).

Public and proprietary companies

A company is a legal body distinct from its individual members. Generally, investors combine their capital to form a company and share its profits. Usually, this is without the risk of loss beyond their original investment or guarantee amount. Companies can buy, sell and hold property, sue and be sued, and enter into contracts. They have what is known as 'perpetual existence', which means that unless there are exceptional circumstances (such as in the case of default on payments to their creditors), they cannot be involuntarily terminated. Of the various types of companies that operate in Australia, two types of corporations have limited liability, public and proprietary/private, and there are also no-liability companies and foreign companies. Public companies can invite public subscription of their shares and be listed on the stock exchange, whereas proprietary companies cannot. A proprietary company must have at least two, but no more than 50, members. It is not allowed to invite public subscription of its shares. A no-liability company is usually only used by specific mining companies and oil and gas ventures. A foreign company is considered to be one which originated overseas but conducts business in Australia.

The advantages and disadvantages of a limited (registered) company

Advantages

- The liabilities of the company are the responsibility of the company so that shareholders are liable to lose only the share capital they subscribed. Directors may be personally liable for any debts incurred when the company is unable to pay its debts.
- After tax, profits of the business can be retained in the company to provide funds for future expansion.
- In some cases greater superannuation benefits can be secured; tax on company profits is currently 30% compared to the current maximum personal tax of 45% (excluding the Medicare levy).
- It is easier to spread ownership of the company.
- The company has an ongoing existence and does not need to be disbanded in the event of death or permanent disability of any of the directors or shareholders.

Disadvantages

- Financial and other information must be filed on public records, although in the case of a proprietary company accounts need not be lodged and only certain declarations and statements are required to be made.
- Loans can be made to directors of proprietary companies. However, in the case of other companies, the shareholders in the general meeting have to approve such loans as part of a scheme for making loans to full-time employees and disclosure of such loans must be made in the company's accounts.
- There may be tax consequences of making loans to shareholders and/or directors.
- Compliance with the extensive requirements of the Corporations Law can be time consuming and costly.
- Lenders often seek personal guarantees from directors, which tend to significantly reduce the value of limited liability.
- Tax is payable when accumulated profits are withdrawn from the company as dividends or extra remuneration.
- Auditors must be appointed unless all shareholders agree that this is not necessary. Losses in a company are not distributable to the shareholders and therefore cannot be offset against other income of the owners.

Partnership

As an alternative to the company structure, many small businesses choose to structure themselves as a partnership. A partnership is usually formed by two or more people (individuals or companies) to conduct business for profit as co-owners. It is governed by the Partnership Act of the relevant state and the terms of the partnership agreement, which should be in writing. This partnership agreement means that each partner has the same rights, liabilities and powers as any other partner, unless the agreement specifically states otherwise. As a member of a partnership each partner is jointly responsible for partnership debts. In Western Australia, Tasmania and Queensland, limited liability partnerships can be used. A limited liability partnership allows some partners who are not as involved in the management of the partnership to have a limited liability. The Australian Taxation Office requires that partnerships maintain 'appropriate' accounting records, but they are not legally required to be audited. Unlike a company, a partnership is not usually considered as a separate legal body from its partners. This means that the partnership's profits are taxable to the individual partners, regardless of the distribution of those profits. Even so, partnerships must also file an annual tax return separate from, and in addition to, that of each partner.

Joint venture

Another form of business structure is the unincorporated joint venture. This occurs when an Australian entity joins with either an Australian or foreign entity to create a venture for their mutual benefit. Examples of such joint ventures are most often found in various mining and exploration projects. A contractual relationship exists between the joint venture participants, meaning this form of business entity has become increasingly popular. Unincorporated joint ventures are often considered to be partnerships for tax purposes if the income is jointly derived, which means that each 'partner' is required to file partnership tax returns. It is possible, however, to set up an unincorporated joint venture so that participants share in the production rather than the income. This kind of joint venture is not considered to be a partnership by Australian law, so each venturer is required to state its share of the income and expenditure from the joint venture project in the venturer's tax return. Incorporated joint ventures are considered to be the same as ordinary companies and are treated and taxed accordingly.

Sole trader

It is possible to be a sole proprietor if you individually own an unincorporated business, if you receive all the business profits and incur all of its liabilities. On the whole, if you are the sole proprietor, you will be actively involved in the management and conduct of the business. You can form sole proprietorship without official approval and you need not have your financial statements audited. You do, however, need to supply the tax authorities with proper accounting records.

Advantages and disadvantages of sole trader partnership

Advantages
- Confidentiality is maintained since the public has no access to financial accounts.
- PAYG (income tax) and Medicare levy contributions do not need to be paid when proprietors or partners draw cash but is paid on a partner's share of the profits.
- Losses from the business can be offset against other income.
- It is relatively easy to transfer the business to another legal structure (eg. a limited company) at a later stage.

Continued

Disadvantages

- The owner is personally liable for the business, which means that if one partner fails to meet his share of the partnership debts, other partners will have to settle them.
- There is less flexibility in transferring ownership (for example to other family members).
- In the event of death, permanent disablement or retirement of the sole trader/partner there may be difficulties in maintaining the business structure.

Trusts

Trusts are not normally used for a sizeable partnership or joint venture with Australian residents, but more for wholly owned projects or ventures. This is largely due to the fact that a trust is not considered to be a separate legal body to the beneficiary's property, and so it may not enter into contracts in its own right. As a result, creditors and bankers will not grant credit to the trust or allow it to open and use a bank account unless personal guarantees are obtained from the trust or beneficiaries.

Advantages and disadvantages of a trading trust

Advantages

- Confidentiality is maintained since the public has no access to the trust's accounts, although some information is disclosed in the trustee's accounts.
- Income is distributed to beneficiaries who pay tax on their allocation of profits at their respective personal tax rates.
- Trusts are not subject to income tax on their profits provided they are fully distributed to beneficiaries.
- A discretionary trust is usually preferred because it provides flexibility to the trustee to allocate income among various classes of beneficiaries under the trust.
- To some extent, limited liability can be achieved through the establishment of a trust with a company acting as a trustee.

Disadvantages

- Generally banks and financiers require assurances from solicitors that the trust has been properly constituted.
- In the case of corporate trustees, there is a necessity for compliance with the extensive requirements of the Corporations Law.
- Losses derived in a trust are not distributable and therefore cannot be offset against other income of a beneficiary (owner) of the trust.

There are also subsidiary businesses, branches and representative offices, but these are usually owned by existing foreign companies that wish to operate in Australia.

Duties of directors and company office-bearers

Every company, whether public or private, must appoint directors and a company secretary. These company officials have clearly defined duties under law. The directors of a company are not necessarily actively involved in the daily management of the business, but they are responsible for the actions of the management of the business. In accordance with the Corporations Law, a director must act with the utmost good faith towards the company and its members, and must not obtain any benefit for him/herself from the activities of the company, other than remuneration. A director is expected to exercise skills that reflect his or her qualifications and experience. Although a director is responsible for the keeping of the statutory records and the books of account, this duty is usually delegated to an appropriate professional, such as an accountant.

The Corporations Law clearly specifies the kinds of books and records, which must be kept and it is important that you seek professional advice in these matters. A director may accept a loan from the company providing the shareholders have approved that loan. It should be noted that such loans must be shown in the accounts in accordance with statutory requirements. A director has the power to appoint an alternative director who has the full powers and duties of a director. If the business becomes insolvent, the directors become personally liable for any debts contracted by the company during the period of insolvency.

In one month of the first and every annual general meeting, companies must provide the ASIC with their directors' names, ages, addresses, company share holding and details of other public company directorships. The appointment of additional or new directors, the company secretary, and an auditor (if required) should also be made at this time. Banking arrangements and the end of the company's financial year (normally 30 June) should also be determined. Shares should be allotted and transfers of subscribers' shares should be approved. Arrangements should also be made for keeping statutory books such as the Register of Members, Register of Directors and a Minute Book and the company's registered office must be specified. A Public Officer must also be appointed for income tax purposes.

The company secretary is responsible for statutory duties and must be a resident of Australia. Public companies must have at least five members, while proprietary companies need only have two. Wholly owned subsidiaries, public or proprietary, have no minimum requirement. A proprietary company must have between two and 50 shareholders, whereas public companies must have a minimum of five shareholders and have no maximum limit. Shares may be sold for cash or otherwise issued, but details must be reported to the ASIC. For both public and proprietary companies, the minimum capital derived from shares is one share per subscriber. The minimum time required to establish a company is three to four days and ASIC fees must be paid during the process of registration.

■ RUNNING YOUR BUSINESS

Once you have had your business plans approved, secured financial backing, established the business as a legal entity, chosen and registered its name and have obtained premises from which to operate your business, then it is time to consider the daily operations of your new livelihood. The critical factors are staff and taxes. If you manage to get both of these areas right, it is likely that your business will run smoothly and be a success.

Taxation

Australian business taxation law is extremely complex and if you are starting a new business there are some things you will have to do and decisions you will have to make. Taxation issues are made even more complex if you have been employed in Australia before setting up your business. The structure you choose for your business may have significant tax consequences, so it is important to investigate taxation thoroughly when planning its structure. There is simply no avoiding the tax maze and it is vital that you get professional advice from the outset. Doing so is likely to mean considerable expense, but will save you costly mistakes in the long term.

Sole traders and partnerships are subject to very different taxes to either companies or trusts. Essentially, for a sole trader or partnership, any profit earned from the business is added to any other income that you have and you are taxed on the total. Your level of taxable income is determined by the financial statements you produce for the Tax Office, although there are some adjustments that are made to the income shown on the statements to arrive at a taxable income. You may, for example, be allowed to claim special deductions such as those available for research and development costs. Tax concessions and grants are available to cover research and development costs and for businesses seeking to develop new export markets. Some of the income you receive may not be subject to tax such as the rebates paid to you under special youth employment schemes. Depreciation can be claimed on all of your plant equipment and other business fixed assets, and some items valued under the current threshold (A$300–A$400) or with an effective life of less than three years can be written off in the year of acquisition.

Companies are taxed differently because they are considered to be separate legal entities from their owners. A company is subject to income tax on its taxable income, whereas the partners in a partnership are taxed on their share of partnership taxable income even though a tax return must be lodged for the partnership. An important difference to note is that there is no variation according to income of the tax rate for companies as there is for individuals. Both resident and non-resident companies are subject to corporate income tax of 30%.

The calculation of a company's or family trust's taxable income is roughly the same as that used to assess a partnership or sole trader, with some significant differences. Firstly, providing that it is at a reasonable level, the remuneration of the company's directors (or owners in the case of a family company) is a deductible expense in determining the company's taxable income. Secondly, there is a complicated system known as 'Dividend Imputation', which refers to the distribution of a company's dividend income. Dividend imputations distributed by Australian resident companies have a tax advantage attached to them, if the dividends are paid from profits which have been taxed in the company's hands at the company rate. Basically, this means that the system allows shareholders a tax rebate to the extent of the difference between personal and corporate income tax rates.

Any excess rebate may be offset against any other income tax of the shareholder, including capital gains, and these dividends, which have been relieved of tax, are known as 'franked'. If the company holds on to its dividend, it will generally be subject to credit under the 'Dividend Imputation' system. Your taxation adviser will be able to explain the system of tax payment, as companies must pay installments of tax by certain dates.

If you decide to take over an existing company, you should ask your accountant to help you draft taxation warranties and indemnities which should appear in the purchase agreement, as these will protect you from any unexpected tax liabilities that may arise as a result of the acquisition. The capital gains tax-exempt status of assets owned by a company may be lost when ownership of the company is changed.

As the owner of a business, whether new or already in existence, you will be expected to pay Goods and Services Tax, Fringe Benefits Tax and PAYG deductions. If you employ staff, you are responsible for deducting taxation instalments (PAYG) from your employees' wages and paying it to the Commissioner of Taxation. To do this, you must register as a group employer with the Commissioner of Taxation and each employee must submit their personal particulars to you, including a tax file number (TFN), on an income tax instalment declaration form. PAYG must be deducted from wages, overtime pay, commissions, fees, bonuses, gratuities, lump sum payments and any other allowances.

The Australian tax year ends on 30 June and for companies that also end their financial year on this date, tax returns must be filed by the following 15 March or, sometimes, 15 December of the end of the following tax year. If an alternative financial period has been adopted by the company, its tax returns must be filed at the earliest by the 15th day of the sixth month following the year-end, with a maximum extension to the 15th day of the ninth month or 15 June following the end of the alternative financial year. Tax returns of individuals, partnerships and trusts must generally be filed by 31 October each year and an extension may be granted if the return is

Australian wheat field a month from harvest

to be filed by a registered tax agent. It is important to note that penalties of up to 200% of tax underpayment may be imposed for filing an incorrect return, together with interest charges and penalties for the late filing of returns or payment of tax. These penalties are strictly enforced, and the sophisticated data-matching processes employed by the ATO make tax evasion nearly impossible and certainly foolish.

 Australian Taxation Office (ATO): assistance to small business owners, including a wide range of electronic pamphlets to download: www.ato.gov.au

Many Technical and Further Education (TAFE) colleges also now offer short courses and evening courses in managing your taxation affairs as a small business owner.

Employing staff

Equal opportunity or anti-discrimination legislation is operative in all states and territories in Australia and the Human Rights and Equal Opportunity Commission investigates discrimination on the grounds of race, colour or ethnic origin, racial vilification, sex, sexual harassment, marital status, pregnancy or disability. Employers should understand their rights and responsibilities and those of their employees under the human rights and anti-discrimination law. Other legal responsibilities in relation to

employees include; wages and conditions of employment, employees'
awards, workplace safety and dismissal.

Business Entry Point: www.business.gov.au – further information about your
obligations as an employer.

Fair trading

Fair trading concerns the ethical environment in which you interact with
other business and customers. The Federal Government announced a fair
trading reform package for small business in 1997, which strengthened the
Trade Practices Act. The new package protects small businesses against
unconscionable conduct and imposes a mandatory Code of Conduct for
franchisers, to protect franchisees. It also offers support for alternative
dispute resolution to provide businesses with quicker, less costly and more
efficient remedies. It has also extended the Banking Industry Ombudsman
to small businesses. The Australian Competition and Consumer Commission
(ACCC) and the Department of Employment and Workplace Relations can
provide information on both your obligations as a trader and the laws that
are designed to protect your business.

Australian Competition and Consumer Commission (ACCC): 02 9230 9133;
www.accc.gov.au
Department of Employment and Workplace Relations: www.dewrsb.gov.au
Fairtrading: www.fairtrading.nsw.gov.au

Useful resources

General
Australian British Chamber of Commerce: 02 9247 6271;
www.britishchamber.com
Australian Bureau of Statistics: 1300 135 070 (local), 02 9268 4909;
www.abs.gov.au
Australian Business Economists: 02 9299 2610; www.abe.org.au
Australian Business Research Pty Ltd: 07 3837 1333; www.abr.com.au.
Credit and business information services.
Australian Customs Service: 1300 363 263 (local); 02 6275 6666;
information@customs.gov.au; www.customs.gov.au
Australian Industry Group: 03 9867 0111; www.aigroup.asn.au
Australian Securities and Investment Commission (ASIC): 02 9911
2500 for general enquiries, document lodgement and searches;
www.asic.gov.au
Australian Stock Exchange Ltd: 02 9227 9338; www.asx.com.au
Austrade: 132 878; info@austrade.gov.au; www.austrade.gov.au. The
Australian Trade Commission has offices throughout Australia and the

world. In London, Austrade can be contacted at Australia House, Strand, London WC2B 4LA; 020 7887 5226

Department of Employment and Workplace Relations: 02 6121 6000; www.dewrsb.gov.au

Department of Immigration, Multicultural and Indigenous Affairs: 02 6264 1111; www.immi.gov.au

Department of Industry, Tourism and Resources: 02 6213 6000; inquiries@industry.gov.au; www.industry.gov.au

Foreign Investment Review Board: 02 6263 3795; www.firb.gov.au

IP Australia (Patent, Trade Marks and Designs Office): 02 6283 2999; www.ipaustralia.gov.au. Trade marks helpline, 02 6283 2999

Reserve Bank of Australia: 02 9551 8111; www.rba.gov.au

SAI Global: 02 8206 6186; www.sai-global.com

Export

The Australian Institute of Export: 02 9350 8170; www.aiex.com.au

Business Brokers

Century 21 Real Estate: 02 8295 0600; www.century21.com.au

Chris Couper & Associates: 07 5592 0687; www.chriscouper.com.au

Resort Brokers: 07 3878 3999; www.resortbrokers.com.au. Licensed real estate agents.

Wilsons Business Brokers Pty Ltd: 02 4962 3388; www.wilsons.com.au

Taxation

Australian Investment and Taxation Services: 02 9399 8333; www.aitx.com.au

Australian Sales Tax Consultants Pty Ltd: 02 9267 9344

Australian Taxation Office: 132 861; www.ato.gov.au

Australian Tax Planning Consultants: 02 9707 1833

Blake, Dawson Waldron: 03 9679 3000; www.bdw.com

Institute of Chartered Accountants in Australia: 02 9290 1344; www.icaa.org.au

Employment

Employers First: 02 9264 2000; www.employersfirst.org.au

Australian Industrial Relations Commission: 03 8661 7777; www.airc.gov.au

Retiring in
Australia

Australia has traditionally been the destination of young people and most new arrivals have generally been either backpackers travelling on Working Holiday visas or young immigrant families. Indeed, it is well known that applicants under 35 are far more likely to be granted residency in Australia, and the Points System of visa eligibility actively discriminates in favour of youth by docking points as the age of the applicant increases. In the past, the average age of the Australian population was relatively low in comparison with that of other developed countries. However, these days, in keeping with most industrialised nations, Australia is experiencing the 'greying' of its population. On the other hand, the elderly are perhaps not as noticeable in Australia as in Europe, as the climate allows and encourages them to remain healthy and active for much longer.

As Australia has become more accessible in terms of cost and ease of travel, there has been a marked increase in the number of older people both visiting Australia and choosing to retire there. The Australian Government has introduced a visa and residence classification specifically for parents of new migrant settlers, which allows any child who has gained

Retirement is a time to relax – and what better place to do this than in the Australian sun?

permanent residency to sponsor their parents to enter the country on a long-term basis. The warmer weather, cheaper housing and yearning for contact with children and grandchildren are all powerful factors influencing the decision to leave a lifetime's history behind to start a new life on the other side of the world.

Many older people moving to Australia feel that the journey itself is one of the most daunting considerations, as it is both expensive and physically gruelling. Travel agents, however, can recommend ways of breaking your journey, without adding too much to the expense, which enable you to recoup in stages and minimise jet lag. Alternatively, if you buy a cheap ticket, you are likely to find that it is cheap precisely because it is not a direct flight and will stop two or three times for up to four hours during the course of the journey. Many passengers take advantage of these stops to wander around the airports, helping to avoid stiffness, cramping and swollen ankles. Airlines can provide wheelchairs and support staff (who will, for example, help you collect your luggage) providing prior notice is given. You should also tell your travel agent or airline of any special medical conditions or dietary requirements at the time of booking your ticket.

In addition to practical tips and advice, this chapter provides information specifically for those wishing to retire to Australia, including the names and addresses of government support agencies.

◼ DECIDING TO EMIGRATE

Many retired people will experience the 'empty-nest syndrome' most keenly if their offspring have moved not just away from home, but thousands of miles away to Australia. Although the warmer weather, hours of sunshine and lower cost of living are appealing factors in their own right, the deciding factor is likely to be the pull of the heart strings. The fact that many retirees who move to Australia have never previously visited the country suggests that it is the people, rather than the place, that provide the main reason. Although it takes enormous energy and motivation to move abroad when retired, it requires a significant extra input to pack up and transport yourself to the other side of the world. The images most Europeans have of Australia have been carefully packaged by marketing experts to encourage tourism, and as a consequence, they are generally aimed at the young and more mobile independent traveller.

To make sure that Australia really is the place in which you wish to spend the rest of your days, it is highly advisable to take an extended holiday of up to six months to gain a more accurate impression of what life in Australia as a retiree might be like. A long stay in Australia to allow you to familiarise yourself with its people and way of life may help prevent you from eventually suffering too intensely from the inevitable homesickness.

TIP

It is useful to know that if you order special meals for your flight, you are likely to be served first which, in a plane carrying around 300 passengers, can make a big difference to your personal comfort.

There are distinct advantages to be gained by retiring to Australia:

■ You will not need to master a foreign language

■ The weather in most inhabited parts of Australia is superb, with warm temperatures and glorious sunshine. The coastal location of most Australian cities means that residents enjoy the benefits of fresh sea air

■ Senior Citizens are well looked after and receive many special benefits and discounts for various facilities and services including public transport, holidays, utility bills, restaurants and hairdressing

■ The favourable Australian dollar exchange rate, combined with the lower costs of living and property in the country, mean that moving to Australia from most European countries after retirement, particularly to join children who have already migrated, can also be very financially advantageous

People over the age of 60 in Australia are known as 'Seniors'. The rather derogatory terms 'old age pensioner', 'OAP', and 'pensioner' were removed from the official vocabulary years ago. Seniors are generally accorded a level of respect commensurate with their lifetime of experience.

FACT

■ Australia seems to have got tough on pensioners wishing to spend their twilight years, basking in the sun. The 'Investor Retirement' visa is now the only option for retirees and this is only granted in some postcodes. The ACT and Sydney, for example, have politely – yet firmly – closed the gate on new submissions, while in Perth, Queensland and Melbourne it all depends on your future residential address.

■ ENTRY REGULATIONS AND VISAS

Retiring to Australia is a dream many people harbour, particularly those with family connections there. In the past you could apply for the Temporary Residence Retirement visa (subclass 410). If approved, it initially granted applicants a period of four years, which may then be extended in two-year increments while in Australia.

All this has changed however, and on 1 July 2005, the Retirement visa (subclass 410) closed to all new applicants. This visa class remains open to current subclass 410 Retirement visa holders (and their spouses), who will be able to continue to apply to rollover their subclass 410 Retirement visa when they expire.

Some former subclass 410 Retirement visa holders (and their spouses) may also be able to apply to rollover their previous Retirement visa. To be eligible, former subclass 410 Retirement visa holders must not have held another substantive visa since their Retirement visa ceased.

Retirement visa holders who successfully rollover their Retirement visa after 1 December 2005 will be granted four-year stays in Australia; doubling the previous rollover period of two years.

What does this mean for those who do not hold a subclass 410 visa? Australia seems to have got tough on pensioners wishing to spend their twilight years, basking in the sun. The 'Investor Retirement' visa is now the only option for retirees and this is only granted in some postcodes. The ACT and Sydney, for example, have politely – yet firmly – closed the gate on new submissions, while in Perth, Queensland and Melbourne it all depends on your future residential address.

Investor Retirement visa (subclass 405)

This gateway may suit you whether you have family already living in Australia or not, and can be used in tandem with other visa options. In this strategy you must be aged 55, or if you have a partner it only needs one of you to pass this qualification for both of you to be eligible. However, you would need to have no dependants other than your partner. You are also allowed to work a maximum of 20 hours a week on this visa. So, you may be able to enter Australia to retire, providing you meet financial, health and character requirements.

A prerequisite of the Australian Government issuing 405 visas is that those who hold this visa can support themselves by proving they have the financial means to make an Australian investment. In other words, you will be required to contribute to, and not drain, Australian resources. Some of the key financial requirements are featured below. You will also be expected to have your own medical insurance, as well as paying a visa charge every four years. It must be stressed that this visa does not guarantee indefinite leave to remain and initially you are only granted a four-year validity period. Once this expires, you may re-apply for a further four years. This visa will never lead to Australian citizenship.

Criteria for an Investment Retirement visa

To qualify for subclass 405, you must:

- Be 55 years and over – however, this does not apply to the spouse of the visa holder
- Have no dependants, other than your spouse
- Have state or territory government sponsorship. However, this is not an option in the ACT and NSW. Perth, Brisbane, Melbourne and their outer limit postcodes will require you to show net worth of A$1,500,000 and annual income of A$65,000 per application (not per applicant). The rest of Australia requires lower targets of A$1,000,000 and A$50,000 annual income
- Pass health and character tests. These include thorough medical examinations and X-rays, undertaken by Australian health authorities. You must also produce up to date police certificates for all countries you have resided in, for more than a decade before moving to Australia
- Have sufficient assets – see *Residence and Entry Regulations*
- Have held all of the assets for two years before applying, unless the assets relate to inheritance, superannuation, or pension rights
- Maintain independent private health insurance for the duration of the visa

Processing times

The current processing time for migration under the Australia Investor Retirement visa is four to six months from the start of the process. If in doubt, there are many professional companies who can advise and help with the process.

 The Emigration Group: 0845 230 4374 ; www.emigrationgroup.co.uk

Parent visa

If you do have family in Australia, you may additionally be eligible to enter under the Family Stream migration programme, which enables parents (pre or post-retirement) to join children already living in Australia.

Parent visa applicants are dealt with in order of their lodgement and each application is given a 'queue date' in order of its receipt by the Australian authorities. The queue date is the day the application is judged as meeting the initial qualifying criteria. Then, as time passes, visas are processed. For the Australian business year 2007–08, known as 'the programme year', there were 700 visa places for offshore applicants and 300 for onshore applicants. There are many thousands of people in this queue and to alleviate the pressure on the demand for these visas, Australia launched a Contributory Parent visa category. This visa had 3,500 spaces available and these were issued on an 'as-you-qualify' basis. Already by January 2008 the quotas were filled, with another batch issued on 1 July 2008. It's called Contributory because you are expected to pay a sizeable sum of money – part is refundable after 10 years of residency and the larger part is retained by Australia. There is a cost for jumping the queue!

The differences between the two categories can therefore be summarised thus:

- The Contributory Parent category has more visa places available each migration programme year
- Applicants for a Contributory Parent visa pay a substantially higher second visa application charge and a larger Assurance of Support (AoS) bond (with a longer AoS period)

To apply for a visa in the Parent or Contributory Parent category, an applicant must be the parent of a child who is a settled Australian citizen, Australian permanent resident or eligible New Zealand citizen. 'Settled' means a person must have been resident in Australia for a reasonable period, usually two years.

Family Stream migration entitles the parent of any child, who must have been a permanent resident of Australia for a minimum of two years, to be granted residency in their own right.

The potentially prohibitive financial requirements applying to non-Family Stream retirees do not apply in this case. However, your child must guarantee to sponsor you financially for two years after your arrival in the country. Like all migrants, Family Stream applicants are assessed on an individual basis and against Australia's health and character requirements.

You should note that Australia takes a very strict line on visas and immigration, and the authorities will not hesitate to deport people who do not comply with regulations, regardless of considerations of age or compassionate circumstances. A cautionary tale is told of a British couple who were deported after staying on illegally for 16 years. The couple, who had worked and paid taxes in Australia during this period, were given no leeway and were required to leave the country immediately and permanently. They were discovered after making a pension claim.

Another story is about a man who went to join his wife and three children only to be told that she had decided the marriage was over. He overstayed his visa trying to sort out his family affairs and was not allowed back into the country for three years.

■ PENSIONS

This section refers specifically to immigrants from the UK. For information on other countries contact the Australian Taxation Office and the taxation department in your home country.

The pension rights of immigrants from the UK

In March 2001, the Australian Government terminated the social security agreement that existed between Britain and Australia. Until that time, UK citizens emigrating to Australia were able to use their UK pension contributions to help qualify for an Australian pension. Prospective migrants should be aware that now that the Agreement has terminated, there will be no early access to Australia's Age Pension system for migrants from the UK. For those wishing to draw the Australian Age pension, they will now have to accrue 10 years' qualifying residence before being eligible to claim Australian Age Pension. However, this qualifying rule does not apply for widows or those incapacitated through health or accident. In Australia your pension is earned because of your visa class and not because of payment of National Insurance contributions – wherever you are exiting from, your government pension will be different to Australia's.

This means that if you are coming from the UK, although you are fully entitled to and will receive your British pension if you live in Australia, the level of pension payments will be frozen from the date you leave Britain. Also, you will receive cost of living adjustments running up to the date of payment eligibility, but you will not receive any cost of living increases once pension payments made after this date come into payment. Australia will means-test your Australian pension entitlement; today some 30% of the population do not qualify for a pension as their means are greater than the qualifying limits. Once again it pays to take advice before entering the system.

In Britain, pensions are indexed to the cost of living and are adjusted annually, but when you become resident of some countries (but not others) you forfeit this adjustment. Although this may seem a nominal sum to forfeit, over the years it may become a significant amount of money and your pension may cease to be adequate. This must be weighed up against the lower cost of living in Australia and the fact that there is no council tax or VAT on electricity and gas.

Frozen UK Pensions

The frozen pension issue affects the vast majority of British pensioners who live in 48 of the 54 Commonwealth countries. In September 1994 British expatriates in five of the largest Commonwealth countries including Australia, formed an organisation, the World Alliance of British Expatriate Pensioners (http://wabep0.tripod.com), as part of a continuing battle to improve the financial position of those pensioners residing in the countries where British state pensions are frozen.

Their site states: 'The World Alliance of British Expatriate Pensioners is a world-wide alliance of autonomous pensioner organisations dedicated to end discrimination by the British Government against its pensioners living in certain countries outside Britain, and thereby achieve contribution-related British State pensions worldwide. Pensions are upgraded in 30 countries but not in 189.'

Australia is by far home to the largest number of British pensioners. There are, as of January 2007, 242,000 residing in various states in this vast country. These represent about 46% of the 520,000 UK pensioners worldwide who do not receive regular inflation uprating to their UK pension.

In spite of this some do qualify for an Australian pension. In these cases, the Australian Government pays the difference between the UK frozen rate pension and the Australian pension. You will be means tested again to see if you qualify.

FACT

Australia pensioners is home to the largest number of British by far. There are, as of January 2007, 242,000 residing in various states in this vast country. These represent about 46% of the 520,000 UK pensioners worldwide who do not receive regular inflation uprating to their UK pension.

Paying the UK State Pension to Australia

If you intend to become a permanent resident of Australia, the process of transferring your pension payments is surprisingly simple. All you need to do is go to your local social security office and inform them that you are leaving the country. They will then make arrangements on your instructions to have your pension paid to you in Australia, or into a bank account in your home country if you prefer. They can also send a cheque (in sterling) at the end of every four or 13 weeks straight to you in Australia, to your overseas bank or to someone else outside the UK chosen by you. If you are away for less than two years, they can pay your benefit as a lump sum when you return to the UK.

 Pensions Info-Line: 0845 731 3233
Pensions Service, Department for Works and Pensions:
www.thepensionservice.gov.uk
Centrelink International Services: 03 6222 3455 ; www.centrelink.gov.au

■ TAXATION FOR BRITISH IMMIGRANTS

This section refers specifically to immigrants from the UK. For information on other countries, contact the Australian Taxation Office and the taxation department in your home country.

It is not often that one receives good news from the tax office, and therefore it perhaps comes as something of a pleasant surprise to learn that if you leave Britain and you are currently paid a pension, you will not have to pay any British tax on that pension when you leave the country. However, individuals on the 405 visa will still be assessed for tax in the UK, on their UK pensions payment.

If you are not currently retired and therefore are not receiving a pension, it is advisable to have a Retirement Pension Forecast made by the Benefits Agency. This is a simple process that involves going to your local social security office and picking up a BR19 form. On its completion and return, the social security will be able to give you some idea of what kind of pension you can expect to receive when you retire and whether you will be paying any tax on it. This kind of information may be extremely helpful to if you are considering the financial implications of moving to Australia, and may also help you with your taxation returns in Australia.

 Pensions and Overseas Benefits Directorate: 0191 218 7777. Request a pensions forecast.

Tax on pension funds

Although you will not pay tax on income currently received from a state pension in the UK, British residents who settle in Australia can face taxes of up to 45% on any growth in their pension fund since leaving the UK. This developed from a series of rulings brought in by the Australian Taxation Office between 1993 and 1994, which seeks to prevent tax avoidance through offshore funds.

When holders of non-government and non-Australian retirement schemes hold permanent visas and are living in Australia, they receive an actual or perceived benefit from their pension funds. Any growth since the date they arrived in Australia could be taxed as income – at the highest marginal rate of 45% plus Medicare levy. Careful planning will ensure that the liability is negated or seriously reduced.

This rule applies to some money-purchase pensions only and not to final salary or employer-sponsored schemes. This is known as the FIF legislation (Foreign Investment Fund), and there are exemptions. The golden rules are: never presume, never assume and never ignore – always take specialist advice, it pays dividends and could even create tax advantages.

Those moving to Australia should also be aware that even if money is left in a UK fund, the Australian Taxation Office could still regard growth in fund value as income.

Readers should be aware that a transfer of a pension fund does not take place overnight and can take several months – today's astute migrant will hedge the funds that should be transferred against falling rates of exchange. You will need to decide whether to move your funds if exchange rates are unfavourable.

You should also be aware that life policies, unit trusts, UK personal equity plans and UK individual savings accounts and their foreign equivalent do not necessarily carry the same tax advantages in Australia as in their country of origin, and that there may be tax implications depending on the product in which you have invested.

Anyone in Australia in receipt of foreign source income is required by law to maintain comprehensive records of their overseas investment holdings and penalties are in place for those failing to do so.

Geraint Davies of Montfort International (01483 202072; info@miplc. co.uk) is an acknowledged expert in this field, with experience of both UK and Australian tax laws, and can advise prospective emigrants of their potential tax liabilities and suggest ways of minimising them. Among many services, Montfort offer to analyse how migrants' current financial planning may be affected by a move to Australia. Migrants should be aware that your visa type will impact on your tax position. Sometimes the costs of moving to Australia – house selling and purchase, airfares, sustenance and removals – can be claimed against the taxman. However, in such situations careful tax planning is always essential.

Australian pensions and health insurance

If you meet the requirements for an Investor Retirement visa and are granted entry into Australia, you will not be covered by Medicare (because you will not have contributed towards its costs through the Medicare levy, paid via income taxes), and you will have to make arrangements in your country of origin or take out private health insurance in Australia as a condition of visa grant.

If you enter the country as a Class 103 migrant, your permanent residency entitles you to immediate Medicare provision. It is important to check with Medicare and/or your private health insurer which conditions are attached.

The Disability, Widows and Age Pensions in Australia are administered by Centrelink. Eligibility for pension is subject to a number of statutory requirements including residence requirements. Most claimants, unless covered by one of Australia's Social Security Agreements, must be resident in Australia for 10 years before being eligible for a pension. The full rate of the basic pension for a couple is currently around A$23,500 per annum and for a single person about A$14,000 per annum.

Further benefits can accrue to most pensioners in the form of concessions. You may also be eligible for extra pension payments if you care for dependent children or students. If you rent privately, you may also be able to claim rent assistance. Rates of payment are reviewed regularly.

The Income Test

A full pension can be paid if gross income is no more than A$132 per fortnight for singles or A$232 per fortnight per couple (combined).

For every dollar of income over these set limits, the single pension is reduced by 40 cents and the pension of a couple (combined) is reduced by 20 cents each.

When incomes exceed about A$39,000 for a single person or A$65,000 for a couple, the pension ceases to exist and one is now termed a Self Funding Retiree.

The Assets Test

This test takes into account assets, excluding the family home. The full pension will be paid if the total net market value of your assessable assets is no more than A$166,750 (for a single home-owner), A$287,750 (for a single, non home-owner), A$236,500 (for a home-owner couple, combined) and A$357,500 (for a non home-owning couple combined). If your assets exceed these limits, your rate of pension will be reduced by A$1.50 per fortnight for every A$1,000(single or couple combined) of assessable assets over the limit. If you are eligible for the pension but your spouse is ineligible, you will be paid half the combined married rate.

Senior Australian Tax Offset

This tax offset means many seniors can reduce the amount of tax and Medicare levy they pay. In some cases people may not have to lodge a tax return.

The Age Pension is taxable in Australia. The good news is that as a result of the Senior Australians Tax Offset (SATO), you are unlikely to pay income tax if you receive only the age pension. From 1 July 2000 the Senior Australians tax offset took the place of the pensioner tax offset, for people of pension age or Veterans' Affairs pension age and the low income aged persons tax offset. To qualify you must meet some conditions, such as covering age, eligibility for Commonwealth pensions or similar payments, criminal record and income. A person must meet not one but all of the conditions to be eligible for the tax offset. It does not matter what the source of the income, a person's taxable income does not affect eligibility for the tax offset.

The tax offset provides that aged pensioners will pay no Australian tax should their taxable income and this includes all pension and non-pension income less than the income test free threshold.

Tax rebates

Pensioners receive a tax rebate of A$2,230 for singles and A$1,602 for each member of a couple. The rebate reduces to zero when taxable income is over A$20,000 for singles and A$16,306 for each member of a couple.

 Centrelink: www.centrelink.gov.au

◾ SENIORS' BENEFITS

Most of the benefits to which pensioners are entitled in Australia are claimed by presenting various cards issued by Centrelink and other agencies. These cards give concessions to low-income earners as well as to pensioners for a number of different services. A Pensioner Concession Card is issued to pensioners who qualify for fringe benefits. This card entitles you to some transport and medical services as well as other concessions provided by Government and some private organisations. Some concessions, however, do not depend on a particular Centrelink or other authorised card, but only on age, so if you are able to produce any identification documents that state your date of birth, you may also be able to claim some concessions. It is always worth checking before you pay for anything as to whether you are eligible for a concession on the basis of age. It is estimated that seniors who take advantage of all the concessions on offer will save around A$2,300 per year. The most common cards and transport, amenities and health concessions are listed below.

- **Seniors Card:** A Seniors Card is available to permanent residents of Australia aged 60 and over who are not working full time. The cards are issued free and enable holders to get a wide range of discounts on public and commercial activities. Businesses in one state will usually recognise cards from another and such business will display a 'Seniors Card Welcome' sticker. Seniors Card Schemes are the responsibility of each State and Territory Government, not the Commonwealth Government and the eligibility criteria and the range of benefits vary.
- **The Commonwealth Seniors Health Card:** The Commonwealth Seniors Health Card gives older Australians, access to concessions on prescription medicines through the PBS (Pharmaceutical Benefits Scheme) as well

as payment of a telephone allowance. Many self-funded retirees will be eligible for the Commonwealth Seniors Health Card. To be eligible, you must be an Australian resident, not subject to a newly arrived 'residents waiting period'; you must have reached pension age, but do not qualify for age pension or do not receive any other social security pensions or benefits and have an annual adjusted income of less than A$50,000 (singles), A$80,000 (couples combined), or A$100,000 (couples combined who are separated due to ill health). If you have dependents in your care, the limit is increased by A$639.60 for each child.

- **The Healthcare Card:** The Healthcare Card gives concessions on prescription medicines. Additional concessions may be offered to Healthcare Card holders including health, household, educational, recreational and some transport concessions. These additional concessions vary widely in each state and territory.

- **The Pensioner Concession Card:** The Pensioner Concession Card gives access to concessions on prescription medicines, hearing services and, in conjunction with a Medicare card, basic hospital and medical treatment. Another benefit for cardholders is an A$18 quarterly telephone allowance. The card also entitles holders to some concessions from state and local governments (such as reduction in council rates, water and electricity bills) and from some private organisations and businesses. Concessions vary from state to state. This card should not be confused with the Seniors Card, which is available to everyone over aged 60 who is in paid employment of 20 hours or less per week.

 Pensioner Concession Card: For free information, call: 1800 550 452

▪ **Transport concessions:** All states and territories offer concession travel to people over 60 years of age regardless of whether or not they are in receipt of a pension. Concessions include reduced fares on public transport, reductions on motor vehicle registration and one or more free rail journeys in the state each year. Concessions differ from state to state and though you may be able to get discounts on some products and services while travelling interstate, others may be denied.

▪ **Amenities:** Seniors are generally also able to claim a reduction (the amount varies from state to state) for council rates, as well as some other services. Enquiries should be made at your local council. A rebate on water and sewage rates is also usually offered to qualifying pensioners, and your nearest water authority office will give you further information. If you are eligible for fringe benefits, you should contact your state or territory electricity and gas authorities for any concessions that may be applicable on your electricity and gas bills. You may also be eligible to take advantage of a free mail redirecting service from your local post office if you move house in Australia. Further details are available from Centrelink offices (1800 050 004). The Pensioner Concession Card brochures, available from Centrelink, outline the range of pensioner concessions offered by each state or territory. The brochures include information about concession eligibility and provide a useful contact. Most local councils also offer a rebate on the registration of seniors' dogs. The National Seniors Association (NSA) offers the over-50s discounts on literally thousands of products. You can join this Association for A$29 (A$39 for couples), and have access to guided tours and discounts on travel and insurance, a directory of benefits and services and a subscription to the bimonthly *50 Something* magazine. Under the NSA scheme, thousands of national traders offer discounts on nearly everything, from electrical products, security systems, car tyres, cinema tickets, motel accommodation, through to funeral services.

National Seniors Association: Offices in Brisbane, Sydney, Melbourne, Adelaide, and Perth. 07 3233 9123; www.nationalseniors.com.au
About Seniors: www.aboutseniors.com.au

▪ **Health benefits:** The Pensioner Concession Card and the Common-wealth Seniors Health Card can help with doctors' bills, cut-price pharmaceuticals and ambulance services. You will never have to pay more than A$5.20 for a prescription and if you pay more than A$239.20

in a year for any drugs, all further prescriptions are free. As a pensioner, you are fully entitled to Medicare benefits, but there are many different health services that are offered at reduced rates to holders of such cards. In addition, free dental treatment is offered at some hospitals and dental clinics to holders of a Pensioner Concession Card or a Healthcare Card. It is worth contacting your local hospital to obtain information on the free treatment to which you are entitled and those treatments for which you would only have to pay a concessionary rate.

- Assistance may also be given for the cost of spectacles from some state government health or community service departments. You should contact your local department for details but should also be aware that this assistance is determined by a strict means test.

- Government-subsidised hearing aids, maintenance, repairs and batteries are also available from of Australian Hearing Centres if you hold a Pensioner Health Benefits Card or a Sickness Benefits Card. For assistance, you should contact your nearest Australian Hearing Centre, listed under the Commonwealth Government departments section at the front of the White Pages telephone directory.

- A number of associations have been established to address those health problems that particularly affect older people. These organisations offer information, advice and assistance, and have branches in every state and territory, the addresses of which can be obtained from the national bodies listed below.

Health support groups
Arthritis Foundation of Australia: 02 9552 6085; info@arthritisaustralia.com.au; www.arthritisfoundation.com.au
Australian Hearing: 0131 797; www.hearing.com.au, has more than 70 permanent centres operating five days a week.
Diabetes Australia: 02 6232 3800; www.diabetesaustralia.com.au
National Continence Helpline: 1800 330 066; Open 8:00am–8:00pm, seven days a week.
Stroke Recovery Association: 02 9550 0594; info@strokensw.org.au; www.strokensw.org.au

If you move to Australia as a Class 103 migrant, there is a possibility that at some time your sponsoring child will have either to care or obtain care for you as you get older. Carers associations in each state and territory in Australia operate Commonwealth carer resource centres. Services include providing carers with referrals to community and government services, practical written information to support carers in their caring role, emotional support, educational and training opportunities for carers and service providers, and a counselling service. In addition, respite care can be organised through the Commonwealth Carer Resource Centre (1800 242 636) or the Commonwealth Carer Respite Centre (1800 059 059).

Carers Australia: 02 6122 9900; caa@carersaustralia.com.au;
www.carersaustralia.com.au

■ CHOOSING WHERE TO LIVE

Almost every major city in Australia offers ideal retirement conditions, in terms of beautiful weather and reasonable housing costs. However, Darwin, Alice Springs and other cities and towns in Australia's interior or northern regions, often experience insufferably hot weather in summer, which many people (both old and young) find difficult to tolerate. The southern coastal regions have quite cool winters, but nowhere will have conditions as severe as a typical northern European winter. Many older people love the Mediterranean weather of Perth, Adelaide and Sydney, while others prefer the cooler temperatures of Tasmania, or the unpredictable and varied Melbourne weather. A large number of Australians like to retire to Queensland, particularly favouring Cairns and the Gold Coast, with its abundant tropical sunshine and cheap housing, others find the humidity oppressive and prefer a more temperate climate. In NSW, the Central Coast, particularly around Gosford, is a major retirement area, with many facilities for the elderly. In WA, the regional towns of Safety Bay, Mandurah and Dunsborough have a special appeal for retirees.

Retirement villages

All cities and major regional towns have special accommodation, known as retirement villages, available for seniors. The decision to enter a retirement village usually means a major financial commitment as well as a lifestyle change and should be regarded as an investment in a lifestyle rather than a financial arrangement. Usually, any amount payable on refund will be considerably less than that originally contributed. By law, villages must consist of units for completely independent residents, units with assistance, including some nursing care and meals for less independent residents, and rooms with 24-hour nursing care available for the fully dependent residents. There are both government and privately-owned and managed retirement villages and many are run by church groups of different denominations.

Buying into a retirement village can be complex and will involve a contract. Such contracts are usually lengthy and replete with legalese, so it is wise to obtain the advice of a solicitor or accountant with experience in this area. Not all legal professionals will be aware of important issues for ageing people, such as contracting incomes and advocacy organisations such as the Council on the Ageing (addresses for each state are given below) can provide expert advice.

Questions to ask before signing a retirement village contract:

- Are there any conditions attached to changes of ownership?
- What are the annual charges?
- What are the ongoing costs? (Look especially for items such as water levies, swimming pool maintenance, audit fees and management.)
- Who has decision-making powers? Are there resident panels or elected representatives?
- Are there deferred management fees?
- Is there an arbitration process available in case of disputes?

You should also note that it is not necessarily automatic that you will be moved from one tier of care to another as your circumstances change. Instead, you may be required to terminate the original agreement and buy in again. Buying a home in a retirement village is not an investment, and there is no guarantee of security: if the development has problems, there may be no protection for the money you have put in. Before you sign a contract to live in a retirement village, the retirement village administrators are required by law to provide you with the *Code of Fair Practice for Retirement Villages*. This ensures that prospective residents are given clear information about the facilities and charges and terms and conditions of residence. The Code sets out the rights and responsibilities of both residents and the administering bodies of retirement villages.

Additionally, a prospective resident is entitled to a copy of every contract they need to enter to reside in the retirement village and details of any costs associated with entering into such contracts. Using such information provided by the retirement village administrators will help you to compare villages and work out the likely costs of your preferred choice. The information should also help you decide if a village would really suit your lifestyle.

If you plan eventually to enter a retirement village, you should shop around before placing your name on a waiting list. Villages are generally modern, well equipped and are professionally managed with a high quality of care. They are often built close to shopping centres, public transport and police stations, and have contact with the community through local schools and churches. In general, the Australian attitude to seniors is to keep them active and independent as long as possible and the retirement villages, purpose-built according to strict legal guidelines, reflect this. Further information about retirement villages and other types of seniors' accommodation is available from the organisations listed under *Useful resources* below.

TIP

- Note that if you enter the country on the Retirement visa and you wish to buy a house in Australia, you will need to write to the Foreign Investment Review Board at. The Executive Member, The Foreign Investment Review Board, Department of the Treasury, Langton Crescent, Canberra, ACT 2600. Telephone Inquiries +61 2 6263 3795 (9:00 am–12:30 pm and 1:30pm–5pm AEST, Monday to Friday, excluding public holidays and the period between 25 December and 2 January).

- Foreign Investment Review Board: firb@treasury.gov.au; www.firb.gov.au

As you will never be considered a permanent resident, you will not be eligible for a place in a government retirement village, and you may also find it more difficult to find a place in a private one.

Retirement village terminology	
Accommodation unit	The part of the retirement village in which a resident has exclusive right to reside. This can be an independent living unit, a service apartment or a hostel bed.
Body corporate manager	The manager of the body corporate (legally-constituted owners' association) of a freehold retirement village. The role of the retirement village manager is usually greater than that of the body corporate manager, especially where a range of services are provided.
Deferred management fee	A fee paid to the operators for their part in the operation of the scheme over the time a resident stays in the village. It is usually expressed as a percentage of the price of the unit and increases over the years as a person stays in the village.
Ingoing contribution	The price for the right to reside in a unit in a retirement village.
Nursing homes	Most nursing homes are regulated by the Commonwealth Government under the Aged Care Act 1997.
Sinking fund	A fund established to provide for irregular expenditure (for example, external painting or roof maintenance). Residents usually contribute to the sinking fund through service charges.
Statutory charge	A means of protecting residents' ingoing contributions by registering a security similar to a mortgage on the title to the retirement village land.
Types of ownership	Generally these are either leasehold (usually 99 years), freehold or strata title. Strata title gives you ownership of the living area and a share of any property held in common.

◼ WILLS AND LEGAL CONSIDERATIONS

If you move to Australia, you should really make another will, as there are variations in the law that may significantly and adversely affect your estate. If you wish to have a will drawn up for you in Australia, it is relatively easy to find assistance, as solicitors advertise in telephone directories and also on television and the printed media. The Public Trustee Office of each state specialises in the drawing and storing of wills and it is reassuring to know that their funds are protected by an Act of Parliament. The Trustee's funds are guaranteed by the government and so the office of the Public Trustee can never die, go bankrupt or leave the state, ensuring the efficient and legal execution of the affairs of your estate. Some state Public Trustee Office's have a free will-drafting service and you should contact your state government office or website to find more details on this service. The free and independent financial information service of Centrelink can also advise on wills and estate planning.

 Centrelink Retirement Services: 132 300; www.centrelink.gov.au

If you intend to pass on substantial assets in your will, you may wish to consider establishing a Testamentary Trust. For pensioners, this means that when assets pass to the surviving spouse, those that are included in the Trust will not count against the assets test, ensuring that any pension is protected. Where child beneficiaries are involved, a testamentary trust will significantly reduce tax liability. However, since 1 January 2002, a source and control test operates for existing social security recipients and prospective recipients who have an interest in a family trust. This means that assets that in the past could be 'hidden' from assessment will now be counted if you are either the trustee or appointee of a Testamentary Trust or can influence the distribution of income or assets of the Trust. This is a highly technical area, however, and professional legal and financial planning advice is essential.

Prepaid funerals

Although a subject most prefer not to think about, any discussion of wills and estates should include mention of funeral arrangements. Many seniors want to give their family the comfort of knowing that their funeral arrangements have already been made and paid for in advance. To serve this need, funeral directors now offer pre-paid funeral packages that involve making contributions to offset future costs. If you enter into such an arrangement, you should ensure that the contract is covered under the Funerals (Pre-paid Money) Act, so that your contributions are paid into a trust fund. A contract should specify the amounts to be contributed, whether the amount will cover the full cost of the funeral, and any management, entry or surrender fees.

Funeral Bonds offer another alternative and are a type of friendly society bond attracting tax and social security exemptions. The proceeds of funeral bonds must go towards the funeral expenses of the holder, but bonuses paid during the lifetime of the holder are tax-free. The capital value of any funeral bond is exempt from the Centrelink Income and Assets Tests, for up to A$5,000.

■ HOBBIES AND INTERESTS

Being active and maintaining better health go hand in hand as we get older. In 1987 a report commissioned by the New South Wales Department of Health revealed that more than half of all physical decline in any age group aged over 65 can be attributed to boredom, inactivity and a fear that infirmity is inevitable. Since that report, there has been a widespread effort to promote continuing physical and social activities among seniors in the community. A 1999 report from the same source states that between 40% and 60% of older people live a regularly active lifestyle, and that compared to sedentary adults, those older adults who maintain an active lifestyle have a daily functioning comparable to people aged 15 years their junior.

Sporting activities

In Australia, the favourable weather means that popular pursuits differ somewhat from those in the UK and Europe. Bingo, for example, is very much less popular in general and many more seniors engage in outdoor activities. Bowls is especially popular, and in every suburb, seniors can be seen clad in white playing both competitive and friendly lawn bowls in the summer sun. You should contact your local shire or community centre for information on how to get involved in your local lawn bowls club. Golf and tennis are also widely played, and are not restricted to wealthy club members. Most districts will have well-maintained public golf courses and tennis courts which can be used for a small daily fee. Most public swimming pools will have seniors' sessions (such as the Icebergs club in Bondi, Sydney where a group of vibrant 60-somethings, take a dip; rain, hail or shine), as well as hydrotherapy classes and seniors aquarobics. The very hardy among the senior community can also usually be seen at dawn, enjoying a communal early morning swim or a brisk power walk at their local beach; many veterans swear by this method of keeping fit, and enjoy it winter and summer. There are also a variety of associations and clubs that cater for older as well as younger members, some of which are listed below:

State cycling organisations

These provide organised rides and advice on what kind of bike to buy and how to look after it.

Bicycle Federation of Australia: 02 6249 6761; execdirector@bfa.asn.au; www.bfa.asn.au

Bicycle NSW: 02 9281 4099; info@bicyclensw.org.au; www.bicyclensw.org.au

Bicycle Queensland Inc: 07 3844 1144; www.bq.org.au

Bicycle Tasmania: 03 6266 4582; info@biketas.org.au; www.biketas.org.au.

Bicycle Victoria: 03 8636 8888; bicyclevic@bv.com.au; www.bv.com.au

■ **Walking for Pleasure** is an organisation that specialises in hiking and camping and is a programme developed by the Department of Tourism

Sport and Recreation in New South Wales. Walks are graded as Very Easy (which means it is suitable for wheelchairs and prams), Easy, Medium, Medium/Hard and Hard. The benefit of this programme is that you actually get to meet and talk to other people from every sector of society and every age group while you are exercising. Seniors are also enjoying multicultural pursuits such as Tae Kwon Do and Weng Chung.

> *Walking for Pleasure:* 131 302; info@dsr.nsw.gov.au; www.dsr.nsw.gov.au
> *Federation of Victorian Walking Clubs:* 03 9455 1876; vicwalk@ vicnet.net.au
> *Tae Kwon Do Australia:* www.taekwondoaustralia.org.au

■ **Cultural activities:** If you prefer to be challenged cerebrally rather than physically, most universities and colleges offer part-time courses for mature age students, and you should contact the relevant institution for details. The University of the Third Age runs short courses, for self-study or study in small groups, throughout Australia and its website provides details covering a wide range of recreational interests. Local libraries are usually the best source of information on academic, cultural and social activities for all age levels of the community.

> University of the Third Age: www.u3aonline.org

If your study days are behind you – enquire at your local pub, as Aussies love a good pub quiz, and this is a fantastic opportunity to meet new friends, while using your grey matter and having a beer! A win–win all round, really!

■ **Senior citizens' clubs and National Clubs:** Senior citizens' clubs (SCC) are very active throughout Australia and welcome new members. Most suburbs or districts will have an SCC, which will usually be affiliated with the National Seniors Association. These clubs organise a wide range of activities for their members, including talks and visits to places of interests as well as indoor activities such as regular bingo and chess afternoons, film screenings and community exchanges. Interaction between Seniors Clubs and local primary schools is especially popular, with schools in particular valuing the input from older members of the community. Seniors with special expertise or knowledge of local history may be asked to talk to junior classes during the course of their studies in relevant fields.

The Older Women's Network (OWN) was established in 1991 to counteract the marginalisation of older women and is committed to speaking out against ageist and sexist stereotyping. This group (which has an excellent website at www.own.org.au) publishes a newsletter and has its own theatre group, aboriginal studies group and health group. It also runs a consumer advocacy service.

If you would like to meet and socialise with other settlers from your country of origin, you should check your local telephone directory, internet or with the Department of Immigration and Multicultural and Indigenous Affairs for information on national clubs such as the Italian Club or the Chung Wah Association. There are also Irish, Scottish, English and Welsh Clubs in most capital cities throughout Australia (check your White Pages telephone directory), as well as a United Kingdom Settlers' Association in Victoria.

■ **Religious associations:** Many churches and other religious groups also provide activities and coffee mornings during the week, as well as a welcoming service for people who are new to the area. Most churches advertise in their local newspaper, so you should check your local freesheet or the telephone directory for further details. In addition, members of the Anglican Church will find a very useful website at www. anglicansonline.org which has link to Anglican Dioceses and Parishes worldwide.

■ **Seniors' travel:** You've made the leap and travelled to your dream destination! Why not make the most of it, and experience the country first hand? There are travel options specially designed for this category of traveller. As mentioned in *Seniors benefits*, on page 374, state

governments provide subsidised coach and rail travel. Airlines frequently offer discounts, usually as part of a special promotion, and before you book it is worth asking whether there are any new schemes or offers being launched in the near future.

Seniors Home Exchange charges USA$79 for a three-year listing of your property on their listings service. As a member of the exchange scheme you will be able to take advantage of some 900 properties listed worldwide, cutting down considerably on the cost of holidays.

 Seniors Home Exchange: www.seniorshomeexchange.com

Unfortunately a senior homestay service called 'Senior Citizens Stopovers Australia' which provides an economical accommodation option for travellers, has gone all VIP! Sadly, it is now only available to those referred to the service by existing members. Under the scheme, seniors with a spare room in their home, or even a driveway suitable for a caravan, pay a small once-only membership fee, after which they are placed on a contact list. The list is circulated to all members, who must be available to host overnight visitors, as well as enjoying the opportunity to stay with other members on their travels. It's the seniors version of the popular www.couchsurfing.com, which is a similar concept and has seen over 425,281 people sleep their way around the world; on other people's couches?

Useful resources

Clubs

Australian American Association: 03 9622 8260;
www.australian-american.asn.au
Australia Britain Society 02 6273 2369; www.aust-britsociety.org.au
Australian Irish Society: 02 9440 0695
Older Women's Network, 02 9247 7046; office@own.org.au;
www.own.org.au
The United Kingdom Settlers' Association: 03 9787 3112

Councils on the Ageing (COTA)

Australian Council on the Ageing is a national non-profit organisation designed to provide assistance and independent advice to seniors on issues such as accommodation, financial management or health. COTA is also a major lobby group for older Australians. It has a national branch and branches in each state, many of which have a freecall number for enquiries.

COTA National Seniors: (03 9820 2655; cota@cota.org.au; www.cota.org.au
Council on the Ageing (ACT): 02 6282 3777; cotact@cota-act.org.au;
www.cota-act.org.au
Council on the Ageing (NSW): 02 9286 3860; freecall 1800 449 102;
www.cotansw.com.au

Council on the Ageing (NT): 08 8941 1004; ntsenior@bigpond.net.au

Council on the Ageing Queensland Inc: 07 3221 6822; cotaq@cotaq.org.au; www.cotaq.org.au

Council on the Ageing (SA): 08 8232 0422; free call 1800 182 324; cotasa@cotasa.org.au; www.cotasa.org.au

Council on the Ageing (Tasmania) Inc: 03 6228 1897; www.tased.edu.au/tasonline/cotatas

Council on the Ageing (Victoria) Inc: 03 9654 4443; Seniors Info Service 1300 135 090; cotavic@cotavic.org.au; www.cotavic.org.au

Council on the Ageing (WA) Inc: 08 9321 2133; exec@cotawa.asn.au; www.cotawa. asn.au

▪ **Independent living centres** provide information for those with disabilities or limited mobility who live independently. They also demonstrate and develop products designed to help such people live more easily and retain their independence. Products include bathroom and toilet aids, as well as aids to help with communication, eating, drinking, walking and sitting. Transport and lifting equipment is also available. Information on where to hire such products, as well as their cost and availability, is available from these centres.

Independent Living Centres (www.ilc.asn.au) also produce a number of brochures providing information and updates. Visits to Independent Living Centres are by appointment only.

ACT: 02 6205 1900; ilcact@act.gov.au

NSW: 02 9808 2233; ilcnsw@bigpond.com; www.ilcnsw.asn.au

QLD: 07 3397 1224; enquiries@ilcqld.org.au; www.ilcqld.org.au

SA: 08 8266 5260; ilcsa@ilc. asn.au; www.ilc.asn.au

TAS: 46 03 6334 5899; ilc@ilctas.asn.au; www.ilctas.asn.au

VIC: Equipment Services, 03 9362 6111; ilc@yooralla.com.au; http://deis.vic.gov.au

WA: 08 9381 0608; enquiries@ilc.com.au; www.ilc.com.au

Time Off

■ TOP PLACES TO VISIT

Now that you've settled in Australia, the thought of holidaying abroad may seem too expensive. Fear not, there are an abundance of local activities for you to do in every state of Australia, including four places listed on the World Heritage list – Uluru, Kakadu, Fraser Island and the Great Barrier Reef.

This chapter will focus on those glorious days off from work – your much needed and well deserved time off. Consider yourself lucky, most people only have a few weeks to explore Australia while on holiday. Now that you are based in Oz, the country is your oyster!

Although there are great distances between the states and territories, there are now brilliant transport links throughout Australia that will get you from one plan to the next. Whether it is by coach, train, plane or hire car/van, the journey is part of the adventure, (see Daily Life, Public transport).

The best bits of sightseeing in Australia can be summed up below; some are accessible as a day trip and others are for longer breaks.

Outback experiences

Ayres Rock (Uluru-Kata Tjuta National park)

The spiritual centre of Australia. Uluru-Kata Tjuta National Park is situated in the Red Centre and is where the much photographed red monolith Uluru (Ayers Rock) and Kata Tjuta is to be found. There are many options for tours here and you can usually camp quite close by, so you are ready first thing in the morning to beat the harsh climate conditions. It's best to visit between April and October when the temperature is slightly more bearable – summer temperatures can reach up to the sweaty mid-40° C!

For around A$500 you can do a three-day tour of Alice Springs, Uluru and Kings Canyon. There are many tour companies operating this route.

 Northern Territory tourism: www.tourismnt.com.au or www.atn.com.au/nt/south/uluru.htm

Devils Marbles (Karlukarlu)

The Devils Marbles are an impressive collection of huge, round, red-coloured boulders found in the Tennant Creek region of Australia's Northern Territory. The Devils Marbles are actually seven metre high granite rocks of volcanic origin, which have eroded over time into the shape and formation they are today. This trip is only to be taken if you are heading to the Red centre anyway, as it's a massive distance from Darwin. If going by air, fly to Alice Springs, then rent a car or join a tour. There are many daytrips available from Tennant Creek.

Devils Marbles: www.tourismnt.com.au
www.travelnt.com
www.nt.gov.au/nreta/parks/find/devilsmarbles

Kakadu National Park

In 1992 Kakadu was internationally recognised as a park of cultural, natural and historical significance, when it was placed on the UNESCO World Heritage list. It can be found 172km east of Darwin and is located in the Alligator Rivers Region of the Northern Territory of Australia. It extends almost 200km from North to South and is as big as Israel.

Tip: Many tours of Kakadu are available. A typical tour could include: visiting Ubirr Rock where you will see ancient Aboriginal rock art, a private wildlife croc cruise on the Mary River wetlands, a visit to Twin Falls and lastly enjoying a cooling swim in the Jim Jim falls natural waterhole. You could opt for a tour with accommodation either on a swag under the stars or in a tent. Most tours last for 2–3 days and will cost around A$400.

Kakadu tourism: www.environment.gov.au/parks/kakadu
www.kakadudreams.com.au
www.wildernessadventures.com.au
www.kakadutour.com.au

Ocean highlights

The Great Barrier Reef

The reef is 1,400 miles in length (bigger than Italy, Kansas, the United Kingdom or the entire West Coast of the United States) and one of the only living things to be seen from outer space. It contains 400 different types of coral, 15,000 different species of fish and over 4,000 mollusc varieties. It houses over 3,000 separate reefs and some 600 islands. Australia's famed diving mecca consists of 2,000 islands set in an indigo blue sea, which is populated with darting fish and beautiful iridescent coral. For diving and snorkelling enthusiasts, it's known as the best place in the world. If you are a land lover and prefer to stay dry, there are trips out on glass-bottomed boats that travel between islands and the mainland.

Great Barrier Reef tourism bureau: www.great-barrier-reef.com

The Great Ocean Road

One of the world's most scenic roads, the Great Ocean Road covers an extended area that includes the world-famous Twelve Apostles, the Otway rainforest, Bells Beach on the Surf Coast, and the Great Ocean Road itself.

You will also drive through resort towns like Torquay, Lorne and Apollo Bay, the coastal cities of Geelong and Warrnambool and the historic villages of Queenscliff, Port Campbell, Port Fairy and Portland.

 Great Ocean road tourism: www.greatoceanrd.org.au

Stonehenge unearthed down under!

The Margaret River will now not only be known for its fantastic vineyards, but for its newest tourist attraction – Stonehenge. Local brewer Ross Smith has plans to recreate Stonehenge on his property, by using 2500 tonnes of granite from a quarry on WA's south coast. It will span 33 metres on two hectares of land and Smith hopes that it will attract up to 300,000 visits per year. It will be open to the public and, unlike the authentic version in the UK, you will be able to go up to the rocks and hug them if you wish. When asked why he was doing it, Smith replied 'I'm doing it because I can'. The local council has backed his plan, but Mr Smith is still awaiting final approval.

Urban adventures

Sydney walking tour

Step back in history by beginning your day in Circular Quay and the old Rocks area (which is where the first settlers lived), with its historical seafaring landmarks; the Opera House and Harbour bridge included - you can now also walk over the top of the bridge. Next stop is a walk up George Street towards the heart of the city, where you will pass the lush Botanical Gardens (which is an oasis in the hustle and bustle of the Central Business District (CBD) and has a killer view of the harbour from Lady Macquarie's chair). Pop out at Woolloomooloo for a Harry's Café de Wheels pie and walk up the steep stairs to the Kings Cross area for a peek at the trendy red light district. Along the way you will pass the Natural History museum and the impressive art gallery, not to mention all of the varied sites and landmarks on the street.

 For the history of Sydney's streets and other historical walking tour ideas go to:
Sydney history: www.cityofsydney.nsw.gov.au/aboutsydney/
Guided tours: www.bouncetours.com
www.goaustralia.about.com/od/sydneyaustralia/ss/sydneywalk2

A tram ride through Melbourne

Jump on one of the many trams in the city of Melbourne and you will be transported to an oasis of trendy cafés, mouth watering Italian restaurants and fashionable shopping districts.

Tip: Don't forget that if you buy your ticket on the tram you will need to have some coins ready-as the ticket machine will not accept notes. You may want to think ahead and pre purchase your tickets at one of the many local shops.

Big Things

If you are taking a road trip throughout Australia, you are likely to encounter the strange Aussie phenomenon of 'Big Things'. It all started with the Big Banana in Coffs Harbour – which is basically a massive man-made banana built next to a plantation. It was made in the hope of attracting road-weary tourists. The plan worked and over the years hundreds of other 'big' landmarks have sprung up over the country attracting snap-happy motorists. They are usually found in service stations in the middle of nowhere and offer a welcome respite from the endless motorways and games of eye–spy.

Big Thing	Location
Big Axe	Kew, NSW
Big Barramundi	Daintree, Queensland
Big Bull	Wauchope, NSW
Big Boxing Croc	Humpty Doo, NT
Big Coffee Pot	Deloraine, Tas mania
Big Easel	Emerald; Queensland
Big Golden Guitar	Tamworth, NSW
Big Galah	Kimba, SA
Big Gold Panner	Bathurst, NSW
Big Lobster	Kingston, SA
Big Kangaroo	Border Village, SA
Big match sticks	Sydney, NSW
Big Prawn	Ballina, NSW
Big Penguin	Tasmania
Big Potato	Robertson, NSW
Big Wine Cask	Wentworth, NSW

Big Things: full list, pictures and locations: www.travelmate.com.au/BigThings/ BigThings.asp

Wilderness

Fraser Island can be found on the southern coast of Queensland, Australia, approximately 300km north of Brisbane. Fraser Island is renowned for its sandy, white beaches, flanked by eye catching, multicoloured sand cliffs, over 100 freshwater lakes and cunning families of dingoes. There are quite a few eco-resorts here as well.

Daintree Forest and Cape Tribulation

The Daintree Cape Tribulation coast is where the Great Barrier Reef and the Daintree rainforest meet, the only place on earth where two World Heritage areas exist side by side. The Daintree National Park excels in ecotourism and there are many eco-hotels to choose from. The Daintree tropical rainforest is over 135 million years old and can lay claim to being the oldest in the world. It is located near Daintree, Queensland, on the coast, north of Cairns in the tropical far north of Australia. It was added to the World Heritage list in 1988.

 Daintree Coast: www.daintreecoast.com

 Guided walks: www.responsibletravel.com/trip
www.ccwild.com/
www.city-discovery.com/cairns/tour

Flinders Ranges

The Flinders Ranges is South Australia's largest mountain range and begins 200km north of Adelaide. The area offers great hiking trails and several national parks, which are inhabited by protected species of the area!

 Flinders Ranges: www.flindersoutback.com
www.southaustralia.com/flindersrangesoutback

Blue Mountains

Located a mere 65km from the CBD of Sydney, the Blue Mountains offers a jaw-dropping and remarkable wilderness experience with great walks, breathtaking views and endless eucalyptus forests. Don't miss the Norman Lindsay Gallery in Faulconbridge, the Three Sisters in Katoomba and the 400-million-year-old Jenolan Caves. Remember to bring your walking boots!

 Blue Mountains Visitor Information Centre, Katoomba: Freecall (in Australia only): 1300 653 408 www.visitbluemountains.com.au. Open daily; 9am–5pm. Closed Christmas Day.

The Blue Mountains reach a height of 1,100m, and have been given their name due to the blue haze that hovers above the mountains, which is produced by the oil from the plentiful Eucalyptus trees. On a hazy day it will seem like your head is encased in a blue cloud.

Hiking around Tasmania

Tasmania is well known for its natural diversity, which ranges from gentle rolling pastures to rocky gorges. There are also amazing walks through the many National Park areas, including the popular Overland Track from Cradle Mountain to Lake Saint Clair. Over 20% of the island has been declared a World Heritage Site and is the home of the wild, carnivorous Tasmanian devil.

 Tasmania's National parks: www.parks.tas.gov.au
General tourism information: www.discovertasmania.com

Fun for kids and big kids

Luna Park in either Sydney or Melbourne

These two amusement parks can be found in the most picturesque places of both cities. In Sydney Luna Park lives under the Harbour Bridge, gaping its mouth at the Sydney Harbour and in Melbourne it is on the foreshore of Port Phillip Bay.

 Luna Park Sydney: www.lunaparksydney.com
Luna Park Melbourne: www.lunapark.com.au

Ferry ride from Manly to Circular Quay

For many this is a daily commute to the office. The Sydney ferry departs frequently from both sides of the harbour and provides an inexpensive bird's eye view of both the Harbour Bridge and the Opera House.

 Sydney ferries timetable and ticket information:
www.sydneyferries. info/timetables/manly-ferry

Wine tasting

Barossa Valley wine tasting

60km north-east of Adelaide, the Barossa Valley is one of the main regions for wine producing in Australia and the surrounding region is a tourist haven for relaxed wine tasting weekends and winery tours. Other great wine regions that encourage cellar door visits include the Hunter Valley in NSW, Margaret River in WA and the Yarra Valley in Victoria. See *Wine*, page 183.

Wine regions

Barossa Valley: www.barossa.com
Hunter Valley: www.winecountry.com.au
Margaret River: www.margaretriver.com

Yarra Valley: www.visityarravalley.com.au
Hunter Valley: www.winediva.com.au/tours/hunter-valley
Margaret River: www.margaretrivertours.com
Yarra Valley: www.austwinetourco.com.au

Australia's best beaches

- **Surfers Paradise:** This tourist haven is on the Gold Coast of Queensland. There are plenty of things to do in Surfers Paradise, such as world-class shopping, casinos, restaurants, bars, clubs (which cater mostly for 18–30s) and the miles of golden sand and quality waves for surfing (Burleigh beach is best for surfing) or swimming. Amusement parks such as Wet 'n Wild, Dream World and Movie World are a short drive away. During the school holidays this area will be extremely busy and for most of the year it will be packed full of tourists (locals have been known to call it 'Sufferers Paradise'). It caters heavily for the Japanese market (in particular) and over the years has changed drastically to suit the swathes of tourists from all around the world.

Surfers Paradise: www.surfersparadise.com

- **Bondi Beach:** Sydney's most iconic beach is a magnet for surfers and backpackers alike. The best things to do at Bondi include having a drink at the Icebergs RSL club, which is situated in the far right corner (above the spectacular public swimming pool, which has waves crashing into it). Then afterwards, take a leisurely stroll along the coast, to Tamarama beach which has amazing views on the cliff tops. There is also a vibrant promenade, which is full of trendy cafés and restaurants.

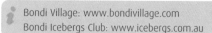

Bondi Village: www.bondivillage.com
Bondi Icebergs Club: www.icebergs.com.au

- **Monkey Mia, Shark Bay World Heritage and Marine Park:** If you have ever dreamt of stroking or feeding your very own Flipper on a small beach, head to the north-east of Denham, Western Australia. These dolphins have been visiting the bay on a regular basis for the past 40 years. The best time to experience this is during the colder winter months in the morning as the visits are more regular at that time of year.
- **Cable Beach in Broome:** Located in Kimberley and this is rated as one of the world's top five beaches. It is truly a magnificent sight as the red earth literally runs down to the white sand. One of the great things about this beach is that you are able to drive your car onto the hard sand.

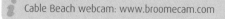

Cable Beach webcam: www.broomecam.com

- **Palm Beach** (Sydney): This beach is largely used by the locals and isn't as busy as some of Australia's other hot spots. It has an impressive long stretch of white sand and is known as a great surfing spot. It is also home of 'Home and Away'; yes, Summer Bay really does exist! There is also an impressive golf club here.

- **Hyams Beach** (Jervis Bay, NSW). This beach is also known as Squeaky Beach as the sand squeaks as you walk across it. It is also holds the title as the whitest beach in the world. You are strongly advised to wear sun block when you venture down to its shores as the reflection of the sand can cause extreme sunburn.
- **Four Mile Beach** (Port Douglas, QLD): The sea is a brilliant turquoise, and the beach really does run for four miles as its name suggests. Only thing to keep an eye out for are the potentially deadly marine stingers. If swimming from September to June, stay in the stinger net.
- **Mission Beach** (QLD): Mission Beach is equidistant from Townsville and Cairns. This beach is for those wanting uninterrupted views of distant islands and crystal clear, azure blue water. It is normally pretty quiet and untouristy. You can plan a day trip from either Cairns or Port Douglas; it takes just under two hours from Cairns to Mission Beach.

- **Whitehaven Beach** (Whitsunday Island, QLD): This beach is a favourite stop-off point for those sailing around the majestic Whitsunday islands. It stretches for 6km and the sand is a vibrant white.
- **Cottesloe Beach** (Perth, WA): This beach is Perth's finest, with crystal clear waters and reefs suitable for snorkelling. It was a favourite surf spot of the late film actor Heath Ledger, his wake was held here in 2008. It can be found a mere 15-minute drive from the centre of Perth. Free parking is available but it can get quite busy, especially on Sundays. Regular Transperth bus services run to Cottesloe or it's about

FACT

■ Vinegar is the
best way to treat a
mild marine sting.
Most beaches have
containers of vinegar
available for use if
a sting occurs; just
ask the resident
lifesaver. Symptoms
of a severe sting are
known to include
nausea, breathing
difficulties and
severe abdominal
pain. In these cases
you must go straight
to the hospital. You
need to get tangled
up in at least 10
feet of tentacle in
order to experience
its ultimate effect
- death. There is
however an anti-
venom available at
hospitals for those
quick enough to
make it there.

a 600-metre walk from the Cottesloe Train Station on the Perth to
Fremantle line.

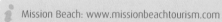

Mission Beach: www.missionbeachtourism.com

Cottesloe Beach webcam: www.dpi.wa.gov.au/imarine/coastaldata/1735.asp

Wildlife watching

■ **Pebbly Beach** (NSW): Eastern grey kangaroo spotting.

www.visitnsw.com/pebbly_beach
www.southcoast.com.au/durras/index.html

■ **Montague Island** (Narooma, NSW): This is the place to see dolphins,
fairy penguins, and Southern right and humpback whales during whale
watching season.

Montague Island: www.montagueisland.com.au

■ **Daintree Rainforest** (QLD): This unique area north of Cairns is home to
the greatest concentration of animal species that are rare or threatened
with extinction, anywhere in the world. The Daintree contains 30%
of total frog, marsupial and reptile species in Australia, and 65% of
Australia's bat and butterfly species. 20% of bird species in the country
can also be found in this area. However, one of the most well-known

and dangerous animals living in the Daintree Rainforest area is the Estuarine Crocodile.

 Daintree Rainforest: www.daintreerainforest.com

- **Jervis Bay** (NSW): Possums, dolphins and hundreds of native bird species (including the rare black cockatoo) all reside in this picturesque NSW coastal area. This is also known as the closest place to Sydney for setting your sights on kangaroos in their natural habitat; you can often get close enough to pet them as well, as they are normally quite tame. Be careful however, as some of the larger kangaroos are extremely strong and can box you down with their powerful fists.

 Jervis Bay tourism: www.jervisbaytourism.com.au

- **Lone Pine Koala Sanctuary** (Brisbane, QLD): Cuddle a koala (and have your picture taken while you're at it) at the world's first and largest koala sanctuary. Located in Brisbane, approximately 50 minutes' drive from the Gold Coast. Apart from some 130 koalas, lots of other Aussie wildlife – including wombats, Tasmanian devils, kangaroos (which you can hand-feed) and colourful parakeets, are on show.

 Lone Pine Koala Sanctuary: www.koala.net

- **Hervey Bay** (QLD): This is the perfect location for humpback whale watching and each year between July and early November, you may be lucky enough to witness a whale giving birth. These gentle giants

Kathy Marks, writing in The Independent on Sunday, 6 April 2008:

'The future of the koala, perhaps Australia's best-loved animal, is under threat because greenhouse gas emissions are making eucalyptus leaves – their sole food source – inedible. Scientists warned yesterday that increased levels of carbon dioxide in the atmosphere were reducing nutrient levels in the leaves, and also boosting their toxic tannin content. That has serious implications for koalas and other marsupials that eat only, or mainly, the leaves of gum trees. These include a number of possum and wallaby species. "What we're seeing, essentially, is that the staple diet of these animals is being turned to leather," said Bill Foley, a science professor at the Australian National University (ANU) in Canberra.'

of the sea migrate between their feeding grounds in Antarctica and the Great Barrier Reef, where they mate and breed. The natural warm waters surrounding Platypus and Hervey Bay encourage the whales each season.

 Whale watching cruises, Hervey Bay: www.hervey.com.au/WhaleSong/default.htm

 Port Phillip penguins (VIC): Watch penguins frolic alongside this picturesque coastline. A colony of approximately 20,000 penguins resides in the sand hills of Phillip Island. They have been known to travel the 120km to Port Phillip Bay on feeding trips. It is thought that on one such foraging trip, some Phillip Island penguins found the St Kilda breakwater and stayed.

Night penguin tours: www.stkildapenguins.com.au

Australian Butterfly Sanctuary (Kuranda, near Cairns, QLD): Walk through the biggest butterfly 'aviary' in Australia. You can see some of Australia's most gorgeous butterflies, including the electric-blue Ulysses. It is 3,666 cubic metres in total and home to over 1,500 tropical butterflies which are hand reared on the premises. If you opt to wear pink, red, or white butterflies might even land on you for a picture opportunity. The aviary was opened in 1987 and has been visited by over a million people since.

 Australian Butterfly Sanctuary: www.australianbutterflies.com

Wait-a-While Rainforest Tours (QLD): Tours for spotting possums, lizards, pythons, platypus, and occasionally the rare and bizarre-looking Lumholtz's tree kangaroo.

 Wait-a-While Rainforest Tours: www.waitawhile.com.au

Heron Island (off Gladstone, QLD): Giant green loggerhead and hawksbill turtles come ashore to lay their eggs between November and January. From late January to March, the hatchlings emerge and head for the water. You can see it all by strolling down to the beach. Also home to around 900 species of fish, Noddy terns, mutton birds and 72% of the coral species found in the Great Barrier Reef.

 Heron Island: www.heronisland.com
www.heronislandaustralia.com

■ **Currumbin Wildlife Sanctuary** (Gold Coast, QLD): This sanctuary is all about the rainbow coloured lorikeet. There is an impressive show, which involves holding a handful of seeds and being literally inundated with flapping birds from head to toe. There are also over 1,400 native Australian animals on display in natural bush land and rainforest settings,

Currumbin Wildlife Sanctuary: www.currumbin-sanctuary.org.au

■ **Kakadu National Park** (NT): One-third of Australia's bird species live in Kakadu; so do lots of saltwater crocs. Two main species of crocodiles live in Kakadu; the Freshwater crocodile (*Crocodylus johnstonii*) and the Estuarine, or Saltwater Crocodile (*C. porosus*). The maximum size of a freshwater croc is three metres, while a saltwater can be a terrifying six metres. There are also over 25 different frog species croaking their way around Kakadu's expansive parkland. Two such varieties are the Northern bullfrog and the Marbled frog.

Kakadu: www.environment.gov.au/parks/kakadu
www.kakadunationalpark.com

■ **The North-West Cape (WA):** If your idea of a good time is swimming/snorkelling beside a 6 ft cousin of Jaws, then head to the North-West cape, Western Australia between March and early June.

■ **Tangalooma (QLD), Bunbury (WA) and Monkey Mia (WA):** Tangalooma wild dolphin resort on Moreton Island (near Brisbane) is a haven for dolphin lovers, as you can watch and feed them. If you would prefer to spot them el natural then head to Bunbury, which is located to the south of Perth, where you can join sight seeing cruises and often swim with them. Another great location for close and personal relations with dolphins is Monkey Mia on the coast of WA. Try a cruise on the Shotover catamaran for sightings of turtles, dolphins and sea snakes.

■ **Kangaroo Island/Galapagos Islands (SA):** This island, which is home to over 21 National parks and wilderness protection areas, is full to capacity of native Australian wildlife. These include sea lions, seals, koalas, goannas, wallabies, kangaroos and hundreds of kinds of bird. To get to Kangaroo Island take either the multiple daily ferry or air departures from Adelaide and the Fleurieu Peninsula. Bookings are necessary. Travelling time is a comfortable 45 minutes.

 Ferry to Kangaroo Island: 13 13 01, www.sealink.com.au
Galapagos Islands and surrounding wildlife: www.galapagos.com

◼ PUBLIC HOLIDAYS

The long weekend has become an Australian institution and is taken very seriously as an opportunity to get in some quality leisure time. On Friday afternoons at the start of a long weekend there is inevitably heavy traffic as people head out of the city to various beach and bush locations, something to be repeated on the following Monday evening as the traffic streams back. Every state legislates its own public holidays, however, there are also a number of country-wide holidays, which are usually occasions of national or religious significance.

Public holidays throughout Australia

- **New Year's Day**   1 January
- **Australia Day**   26 January

   This is the day Australians celebrate the anniversary of the landing of the first fleet at Port Jackson in NSW, a date popularly considered to be Australia's birthday. All around the nation, local councils and authorities mount concerts and firework displays to help the celebrations get under way with a bang. Fireworks are considered a centrepiece of the occasion (especially as Guy Fawkes' Day is not commemorated and, everyone needs an excuse to let off some rocket!).

- **Good Friday**   March/April
- **Easter Monday**   March/April
- **ANZAC Day**   25 April

   This national holiday commemorates the sacrifices of Australia's war heroes. Originally designed to recognise the soldiers of the Australian and New Zealand Army Corps who died at Gallipoli during WWI in a defining moment in Australian history, it now includes all Australian military personnel and commemorates their participation in campaigns in both world wars, Vietnam and Korea. Every major city and town hosts marches by old soldiers and, these days, their descendants, wearing uniforms and medals. There are dawn ceremonies at war memorials around the country, and the day is considered to be a solemn one. Many citizens line the streets to watch the marches.

Public holidays are times to chill out with family – in a hot tub if you are lucky enough!

Queen's Official Birthday

This is a movable holiday, which always falls on the second Monday in June (except in WA where it falls on the last Monday of September)

Christmas Day   25 December

Boxing Day   26 December

Regional holidays

Holiday	Date	Region
Labour Day	7 March	(WA/TAS)
Labour Day	14 March	(VIC)
Canberra Day	21 March	(ACT)
Bank Holiday	5 April	(TAS)
Labour/May Day	2 May	(QLD/NT)
Adelaide Cup Day	16 May	(SA)

Continued

Foundation Day	6 June	(WA)
Alice Springs Show Day	1 July	(NT)
Darwin Show Day	22 July	(NT)
Bank Holiday	1 August	(NSW/ACT)
Picnic Day	1 August	(NT)
Labour Day	3 October	(NSW/ACT)
Queen's Birthday	26 September	(WA)
Labour Day	11 October	(SA)
Recreation Day	7 November	(TAS)
Melbourne Cup Day	1 November	(Melbourne Metro only)

The dates of some of these holidays may be variable.

■ FESTIVALS

Each city has its fair share of cultural and historical festivals throughout the year. Here is a list of the top ones.

Melbourne International Comedy Festival

The Comedy Festival is one of the three largest comedy festivals in the world, alongside Edinburgh Festival Fringe and Montreal's Just for Laughs Festival.

An annual event, the Melbourne International Comedy Festival literally takes over Melbourne every March and April, with an enormous programme of stand-up comedy, cabaret, theatre, street performance, film, television, radio and visual arts.

The Festival was launched in 1987 by Barry Humphries (Dame Edna Everage) and Peter Cook. 22 Festivals later, with attendances of over 400,000, it has grown to be Australia's largest cultural event. With an average ticket price of just A$22, the Comedy Festival is both a hugely popular and extremely accessible event.

 For more information: Melbourne Comedy Festival: www.comedyfestival. com.au

Melbourne International Film Festival

This is the largest film festival (July/August). It is in the Southern Hemisphere featuring shorts, documentaries, animation, experimental films, multimedia, etc.

www.melbournefilmfestival.com.au

Melbourne Cup

This is Australia's most famous Tuesday. At 3.00pm Melbourne time, on the first Tuesday in November, Australians everywhere stop for one of the world's most famous horse races. Since 1877, Cup Day has been a public holiday for Melbourne and crowds have flocked to the track. People from all over Australian states usually take the time to stop what they are doing and watch the race to see if their 'flutter' has paid off. This includes many schools, which wheel televisions in to the assembly hall for the children to watch.

 Melbourne Cup: www.melbournecup.com

New South Wales

New South Wales has many special events during the calendar year. The Festival of Sydney usually takes place in January, as does the New South Wales Tennis Open and the Country Music Festival. The Sydney Royal Easter Show usually occurs between March and April and the Sydney Film Festival takes place in June, as does the Darling Harbour Jazz Festival. The Rugby League Grand Final is held in Sydney in September. Other major state sporting events include the Toohey's 1000 Bathurst Touring Car Race at Bathurst in October, and the Sydney to Hobart yacht race, which commences on Boxing Day every year.

Sydney Gay and Lesbian Mardi Gras

Sydney has been celebrating this annual event every February for the past 30 years. Think Rio mixed with Notting Hill Carnival, flaunting a mixture of men and women wearing glitter, feather boas and not a great deal more. The streets of Oxford Street and Kings Cross are closed during the parade and tens of thousands of spectators line the streets to cheer them on. There are also after-parties such as the notorious 'Sleaze ball'.

 Mardi Gras: www.mardigras.org.au

Tropfest

This short film festival, which began in Sydney some 15 years ago, has entrants from all over Australia. There are venues in Sydney, Melbourne, Brisbane, Perth, Canberra and Hobart. Over 150,000 people will come together in February to view the 16 finalist films selected from over 700 entries. Each year all entrants (which are open to all ages, backgrounds and experience levels) are given a common theme to work around.

 Tropfest: www.tropfest.com

Sydney Festival

For three weeks every January, the Sydney Festival takes over the centre of Sydney. It offers a rich program of around 80 events, involving over 500 artists from Australia and abroad covering dance, theatre, music, visual arts, cross media and forums. In any given year, it makes use of most of the main theatres across the city including Sydney Theatre, Carriage Works, City Recital Hall and venues at the Sydney Opera House.

Sydney Festival also presents a number of quality, free outdoor events such as the long-running Domain Concerts, which attract up to 100,000 people a time. In 2008 the Festival took to the streets with a new free event entitled Festival First Night, a large-scale celebration of music and performance which drew up to 200,000 people into in the heart of the city.

 Sydney Festival: www.sydneyfestival.org.au

Big Day Out

This is the Australian equivalent of Glastonbury. It's an annual January–February music festival which travels around each state and showcases American, UK and local bands. Past acts have included The Killers, Lily Allen, Tool, Muse, Violent Femmes, Carl Cox, The Streets and Silver Chair.

 Big Day Out: www.bigdayout.com

Brisbane

Brisbane has festivals year-round, from St Patrick's Day parades to its wine and cheese festival or its literary festival.

 Brisbane festivals: www.totaltravel.com.au/travel/qld/brisbanearea/innerbrisbane/directory/festivals

Perth

Perth holds an annual International arts festival from 8 February till early March. This is a showcase for the diverse culture in Western Australia; from opera to pop and jazz concerts to theatre, food and wine events.

Perth Festival: www.perthfestival.com.au

Canberra

The Celebrate Canberra festival is an annual 10-day festival celebrating the city, its culture and people. The event is built around Canberra's birthday (10 March) and encourages Canberrans to join in the celebrations.

 Celebrate Canberra: www.australianexplorer.com/canberra_events.htm#

Adelaide Fringe

The Adelaide Fringe began in 1960 as an alternative to the Adelaide Festival they then ran side by side, every second year for over 30 years until 2007. Now the Fringe stands alone as an annual arts event of its own accord.

Adelaide Fringe is renowned for fresh ideas, risk, imagination, spontaneity and fun. It is the largest arts event in Australia and has artists from across the globe participating alongside homegrown talent, in all art forms.

 Adelaide Fringe: www.adelaidefringe.com.au

Tasmania

Tasmania has a range of annual festivals including: Antarctic Tasmania (Mid Winter Festival), Cygnet Folk Festival (Tasmania's folk, world and roots music event), The Longest Night Film Festival, Tasmanian Symphony Orchestra, Sydney to Hobart Yacht Race, Tamar Valley Festival of the Senses (Launceston), Hobart's Summer Festival, Hobart Comedy Festival (each January) and the Tasmanian Falls Festival.

 Tasmanian festivals: www.bcl.com.au/hobart/wotson/confest.htm

MEDIA

The Australian media provide much the same type of services as in the UK, Europe and the USA. Its film, television and radio output is highly regarded internationally and much of it is distributed overseas (including children's television and art films, along with *Neighbours*, *Home and Away* and films such as *Priscilla Queen of the Desert*, *Strictly Ballroom* and *Chopper*). Each state has a range of local and regional newspapers, as well as access to the national press. Editorial content is considered to be mostly fair and unbiased, although media monopolies are under constant surveillance to maintain standards and to prevent the exercise of undue political influence. Australians are news-hungry, and newspaper and magazine readership per capita is one of the highest in the world. Most news providers offer both domestic and international news, although some say local news dominates the press. In the communications sector, the monopoly of the state-owned Australian Telecom has now given way to a more open market with several providers competing to supply both domestic and business users.

The Government agency, Australia Post, provides mail and ancillary services to the whole country. Australia has one of the highest proportions of personal computer and mobile telephone ownership in the world and the internet take-up rate is second only to the USA (consider: population of the USA 290.6 million people; population of Australia 21 million people). As a result, Australian communications are heavily geared to the electronic environment – noticeably more so than in Europe – and most government agencies, schools, television channels, newspapers and community services have websites on which they post constantly updated information. Even the telephone directories are online and at the touch of a button you can access and search Telstra's telephone databases for both business and residential numbers.

Newspapers

Australian newspapers are largely state, or indeed, capital city-based. There is one national daily newspaper, *The Australian*, owned by Rupert Murdoch's News Corp, and sometimes referred to as 'Murdoch's Australian charity'. This broadsheet newspaper is of a calibre equivalent to *The Times* or *The Guardian* in Britain, but like most broadsheet newspapers, it fights a continuing battle for profitability. *The Australian*'s weekend sister publication, *The Weekend Australian*, is similar in style and, as with most broadsheet weekend papers, comes groaning with additional arts, lifestyle, sports and business sections. Apart from the omnipresent Rupert Murdoch, the other big player in Australia's newspaper industry is Fairfax Holdings. This group publishes respected major titles including *The Sydney Morning Herald*, *The Age* (both broadsheets, from Sydney and Melbourne respectively), *The Sun-Herald*, *Business Review Weekly* and *The Australian Financial Review*, the Australian equivalent of *The Financial Times*.

Sydney, Melbourne and Brisbane all have at least three major daily newspapers and other capitals and major regional centres have at least two. In addition, almost every area has a local community newspaper; usually weekly and often of very high quality. One thing you will be hard pressed to find in the Australia press is 'red top' tabloid newspapers such as UK's *The Sun* and *News of the World*. The major papers do not normally have 'Page Three' girls or exposés on celebrity lifestyles.

FACT

■ Sydney, Melbourne and Brisbane all have at least three major daily newspapers and other capitals and major regional centres have at least two. In addition, almost every area has a local community newspaper; usually weekly and often of very high quality.

Expats can keep up with news from home by subscribing to weekly news digests from home or by logging on to home newspaper websites. *The International Express*, sold throughout Australia and New Zealand, is the international sister paper of the *Express* and *Express on Sunday* and has the same tabloid format and human-interest focus. It is printed in Sydney, Melbourne and Perth, and is available in Australia from local newsagents. A one year subscription costs A$62 and is available by writing to: International Publishing Group, PO Box 107, Sydney, NSW 2001; subscriptions@theinternationalexpress.com; www.theinternationalexpress.com.The *Guardian Weekly* is also widely available and offers a selection of higher-brow articles and features in English derived from the previous week's *Guardian*, *Washington Post* and *Le Monde*. Subscriptions are available from *Guardian Weekly*, 164 Deansgate, Manchester M3 3GG; 0870 066 0510; gwsubs@guardian.co.uk; www.guardianweekly.com; or PO Box 2515, Champlain, New York 12919 2515; 1 888 834 1106 (toll free); gwsubs@guardianweekly.com. In Australia subscriptions to the *Guardian Weekly* can be taken out by writing to PO Box 70, Sydney, NSW 2001; 02 9543 7616; australia@guardianweekly.com.

Major Australian newspapers
NSW: *Sydney Morning Herald:* 02 9282 2833; www.smh.com.au
NSW: *The Australian:* www.theaustralian.news.com.au
NSW: *The Australian Financial Review:* www.afr.com.au
NSW: *The Daily Telegraph:* www.dailytelegraph.news.com.au
QLD: *The Courier Mail:* www.couriermail.news.com.au
VIC: *The Age*; www.theage.com.au
VIC: *Herald Sun:* 03 9292 2000; www.heraldsun.news.com.au
VIC: *The Weekly Times:* 03 9292 2000; www.theweeklytimes.com.au
WA: *Sunday Times:* www.sundaytimes.news.com.au
WA: *The West Australian*: www.thewest.com.au

Magazines

Australian editions of *Woman's Day*, *New Idea*, *Vogue*, *Cosmopolitan* and *Marie Claire* are available in all newsagents and most supermarkets, and there are innumerable special interest publications, such as *Australian Gourmet Traveller* and *House and Garden*, which are also of very high quality.

The Australian Woman's Weekly is the most popular Australian women's magazine. Don't be misled by the name; this is a **monthly** magazine. When this long-standing publication underwent a makeover, including name change, a couple of decades ago, they decided against 'The Australian Woman's Monthly' as a title – for obvious reasons! The quality of this magazine is unmatched and its readership and circulation make it the most widely read magazine in the history of Australian publishing. It is particularly famous for its outstanding cooking sections and Australian Consolidated Press publish a continually updated range of cookbooks developed by the magazine staff. It is said that you can never go wrong with a *Woman's Weekly* recipe. The cover price of the *Woman's Weekly* is A$6.40.

If it's celebrity spotting you are after, then opt for Australia's *Who* weekly magazine. It is a cross between Britain's *Grazia* and *Now* and America's *People* magazines. It has local celebrity gossip mixed with the goings on of American and British celebrities.

 Who: http://au.lifestyle.yahoo.com/who

The *Business Review Weekly* is probably the most important financial magazine, roughly equivalent to the *Economist* (which is available in good newsagents). The main domestic current affairs magazine is *The Bulletin*, which incorporates the American publication, *Newsweek*. *The Bulletin* is an old and prestigious publication, particularly well regarded for its efforts to foster new writing, especially poetry. Most international magazines with any significant level of circulation, such as *Time* and *National Geographic* are widely available, although their cover price may reflect import costs where special Australian editions are not printed.

Books and bookshops

Books in Australia used to be expensive but are now pretty much equivalent in price to those in Britain and the USA. All major publishers distribute in Australia, although if you are looking for something unusual you may have to order. Scholarly publications and new hardcover releases tend, however, to be expensive in Australia. There is also a significant Australian publishing industry and much highly regarded fiction is written there, which is meeting with international success. Peter Carey, for instance, has won the Booker Prize twice for *Oscar and Lucinda* (1988) and *True History of the Kelly Gang* (2001) and Thomas Keneally won the Booker Prize in 1982 for *Schindler's Ark*, which was later filmed as *Schindler's List*. Large bookshops are found in all Australian cities, including a number of chains, such as Dymocks and Angus & Robertson; there are also many smaller independent booksellers. The 'book café' has recently arrived in Australia and proved a popular innovation. Book cafés, as the name suggests, incorporate a small, high quality café in among the books, where people can meet for coffee, or just enjoy a break while they browse.

Book clubs and reading groups are hugely popular, and most cities will have hundreds of these small, informal groups which meet monthly for friendship and literary discussion: book cafés provide both a venue for meetings, as well as a selection of new texts for the next get-together.

Specialist bookstores

All Arts Bookshop: 43 Queen Street, Woollahra, NSW 2025; 02 9328 6744; books@allarts.com.au; www.allarts.com.au. Collectors' reference books on antiques, Australian, Asian and tribal art. Phone and mail order.

Angus & Robertson Bookworld: 195 Murray Street, Perth, WA 6000; 08 9325 5622; www.angusrobertson.com.au. Stores Australia-wide.

Boffins Bookshop: 806 Hay Street, Perth, WA 6000; 08 9321 5755; www.boffinsbookshop.com.au. Range of technical, practical and specialist books. Local and overseas special orders.

Dymocks Booksellers: 424 George Street, Sydney, NSW 2000; 02 9235 0155; or 705–707 Hay Street Mall, Perth, WA 6000; 08 9321 3969; www.dymocks.com.au. Stores Australia-wide with comprehensive range of general, technical and education books. Computer access to more than 100,000 titles. Will obtain any book in print.

Television

Many television watchers are probably as familiar with Australian television productions as Australians themselves. Series such as *Neighbours, Home and Away* and *Kath and Kim* are all regularly broadcast in the UK. Indeed, the popular soaps *Neighbours* and *Home and Away* have a much higher profile in Britain than in their country of origin, so much so that Australians visiting the UK are often bemused by fervent requests for updates on the latest from down under. Other famous TV exports include Clive James and Dame Edna Everage and most children will tell you about *Bananas in Pyjamas*, the *Ferals* or *The Fairies.*

There are four main channels broadcasting nationwide. The Australian Broadcasting Commission (ABC) operates Channel Two, and is equivalent to the BBC. The ABC is funded by the Federal Government and provides commercial-free television and radio throughout the country. Advertisements for forthcoming features are screened only at the end of programmes. The three other channels, Seven, Nine and Ten, are commercially owned and operated networks which broadcast around Australia and, like commercial television elsewhere in the world, they are funded by advertising, the airing of which tends to be fairly frequent.

Although the channels are operated by national networks, both advertising and news output tends to be state-specific. In very remote areas, it may only be possible to receive Channel Two and perhaps one other commercial channel specifically aimed at country viewers such as, for example, in Western Australia, GWN (Golden West Network).

The Special Broadcasting Service (SBS) provides multilingual and multicultural broadcasting (both television and radio) across the country. It is specifically designed for viewers of ethnic origins and regularly broadcasts foreign language films. SBS is an optional channel for which you will require a special receiver or antennae. The SBS antennae can usually be installed cheaply enough but these days most houses will already have one fitted. Many people consider that the SBS news is the best available on Australian television, with a high international news content and in-depth analysis. SBS also broadcasts minority and international domestic sports coverage, and is a good way to keep up with your favourite teams back home. Weather forecasts on Australian television in general are more detailed and meteorologically sophisticated than those in the UK.

The best British and American television productions all come to Australian television and you will not have to miss out on *24, Lost, The Sopranos, The Office, Desperate Housewives, Sex and the City, Nip/Tuck, Ugly Betty* or any other favourites. Australian television is ratings-dominated and during ratings periods the television programming is outstanding, with the best films and series from around the world competing for your attention and the advertising dollar. At other less crucial times, programming may be more mundane but sports coverage tends, in general, to be very good. The Government requires a percentage of Australian-produced output (which must *not* be cheap-to-make games shows and the like), so that there is always a good flow of new and interesting local productions. Films are generally broadcast at 8.30pm every night, with a double bill on Sundays.

Cable and satellite television are available in Australia, with cable far more widespread than satellite. The channels available are exactly the same as in the UK or the USA: Nickelodeon, the Disney Channel, MTV, CNN, UK Gold, the Movie Channel, and so on. Cable networks are operated by Foxtel (another Murdoch venture) and Optus Vision. Subscription rates are around A$40–A$50 (basic) to A$80–A$100 (platinum) per month (competition is fierce, so be sure to shop around for the best deal). There are also satellite stations available by subscription, which once again broadcast much the same international fare as the cable channels. Many Australians have subscribed to pay channels and their popularity is growing continually. Most also own a DVD player and DVD rental shops are found in every high street. Videos (what remains of them) and DVDs are cheap to hire and many stores offer special rental deals. A new release DVD will cost approximately A$7 to hire for 24 hours and older movies can be rented for up to a week from as little as A$3.

Television programmes are advertised daily in local newspapers and a weekly lift-out programme guide, usually in magazine format, is available in the weekend papers. There is a TV listings guide, *TV Week*, which is produced in different editions for the different states' time zones.

Probably the most important difference between Australian and British television is that there is no television licensing system. Naturally, you must pay for your own television sets and antennae, but you may have as many televisions in your home or business as you like and you do not have to pay for the privilege of watching them. The Australian Broadcasting Commission is funded from taxation revenue and no further charge is made for broadcasting services.

Radio

The Australian Broadcasting Commission owns and runs five national radio networks (which can be received Australia-wide) and one international radio service. They are renowned for their excellent news coverage. Radio National is the ABC's general current affairs and talk station and is middle to highbrow in its orientation. It produces programmes such as *The Science Show*, *The Law Report* and *The Book Programme*, as well as daily drama, book readings and interviews. It also has a classical music station, and supports an orchestra in each state. The Australian airwaves have been deregulated for decades and across Australia there are more than 100 commercial stations on the AM band, more than 50 commercial FM stations, 200 community radio stations run by universities and ethnic groups and Aborigine-run radio stations which service the outback regions. Radio stations are often advertised on car bumper stickers, on television and in the newspapers, so it is easy to find something to your taste and tune in. Australians own nearly 30 million radio receivers and most households own four or more radios. The alternative music station Australia-wide is Triple J and it can be found on your FM radio dial. This station promotes alternative rock, as well as unearthing home grown talent. Many of Australia's biggest bands were discovered on this station. Also, every Australia Day they broadcast Australia's 'Hottest 100' – the countdown of all of the best tunes from the previous year. This will normally be blaring from radios during the many BBQs given on this hot public holiday. It also has a youth-driven, serious side with social issues being discussed and many topics covered.

ABC's main radio stations

- **Radio National:** Current affairs channel which hosts shows such as: *The Health Report*, *The Philosopher's Zone* and *The Science Show*
- **NewsRadio:** National radio network providing continuous news and information 24 hours a day. It can be heard in all Australia's capital cities plus Newcastle, the Gold Coast, and Gosford as well as on the Internet. Frequencies: www.abc.net.au/newsradio
- **Classic FM:** Playing world-renowned classic music to every state of Australia. Frequencies: www.abc.net.au/classic/freq
- **Triple J:** Youth-driven station. Plays unearthed local bands, live concerts and features programs on issues concerning the younger generation. To find the frequency, listen online or to watch a pod/vod cast go to: www.triplej.net.au/guide/
- **DIG:** Digital non-stop music and specialist jazz and country channels. Frequencies: www.abc.net.au/dig

■ SPORT

Sport is popularly considered to be the Australian national pastime and is central to the social life of many Australians. Most Australian children are encouraged to play at least one sport from a very early age. 'Little Athletics', an athletic training programme for children from the age of five upwards, is held on Saturday mornings around the country and is very popular. Regional and national competitions are attended by club scouts on the lookout for new talent. Similarly, cricket and football (Australian Rules) are enormously popular at every age and skill level, and most Australian boys play at some time or another for their local club (fathers often coach voluntarily). Cricket is becoming increasingly popular with girls, but usually not until secondary school age or even later.

Sporting centres all over the country also offer volleyball, netball and five-a-side soccer, and single-sex or mixed teams often have their own leagues. Many young working Australians will play in one such team at least one night per week as a way of keeping fit and meeting their friends. Children lucky enough to live close to a beach are also often enrolled in the 'Little Nippers', which is training at a junior level to become a surf lifesaver.

Popular sports

Australian Rules football

Australian football is the most popular winter game and is a predominantly male sport. Aussie Rules football is a national institution and the Australian Football League (AFL) Grand Final is comparable to the FA Cup Final in the UK in the level of interest it excites around the country. Every state has its own team or teams that play in the national league, with the West Coast Eagles, the Sydney Swans, Carlton, the Geelong Cats and the Essendon Bombers among the big names. Aussie Rules is a fast and athletic game, with much handling of the ball and some impressive jumping and mid-air collisions. The game is played by two teams of 18 players who try to score goals against each other. The goal posts consist of four tall, evenly spaced poles, the two outer ones slightly shorter than the inner ones, and there is a goal at each end of the oval. The oval-shaped football field is about three times the size of a soccer pitch.

If a player touches the ball over the line between the two middle posts, he has scored a goal, the team gains six points, and the goal umpire (always dressed in a white coat) will gesture and energetically wave two white flags. If the player touches the ball over the line between middle and an outer pole, he will have only scored a single point, and the goal umpire will gesture with one of his index fingers, waving just one of the flags. The game consists of four quarters, each quarter lasting 45 minutes.

Running with the ball is allowed, as long as it is bounced every three seconds; failure to do this means being 'caught with the ball'. Bouncing the ball while on the run is in fact not easy as the ball is oval-shaped, like a rugby ball. Although some of the players at the interstate level have started to wear head protection and gloves (to give them a better grip on the ball), Aussie Rules players pride themselves on their toughness and fitness. The game is gruelling and extremely hard on the players. It is long and very physical, but can also be intense and exciting. The best way to see a game is to go to an important interstate match and catch the enthusiasm of the crowd.

Rugby and football

In the eastern states, rugby (both league and union) is also known as football, and Queenslanders in particular take the game very seriously. Western Australia, Victoria the Northern Territory and Tasmania do not share the enthusiasm of the other states for rugby, but the nation as a whole is proud of its top-level international rugby team, the Wallabies. Football of the kind played in the UK is always known as soccer and has a small but enthusiastic following, particularly among European ethnic communities who often field their own teams in state soccer competitions.

A-League Soccer

Founded in 2004, A-league is the premier Australasian domestic association football (soccer) competition. The league is contested by eight teams: seven covering Australia's major cities and regional centres and one from New Zealand (Wellington Phoenix replaced the New Zealand Knights for the 2007–08 season). The team that finishes on top of the league table at the end of the 21–round regular season is awarded the Premiership, with the winner of the subsequent four-team finals series awarded the Championship. In the 2007–08 season, these were awarded to Central Coast Mariners and Newcastle Jets respectively. Over 35,000 people crammed into the Sydney football stadium in February 2008 to watch the Jets defeat the Mariners 1–0.

The A-League salary cap has spawned much controversy in the close season with champions Melbourne Victory unable to re-sign star midfielder Fred (Helbert Frederico Carreiro da Silva) due to an offer from Major League soccer club, DC United, that is reportedly worth three times the amount the Victory can afford to pay him. As well as this, Sydney FC have been unsuccessful in signing ex-Liverpool FC striker, Robbie Fowler because the club could not offer as much money as other English clubs.

Hockey

Hockey is very popular with men, women and children, and Western Australia prides itself on its exceptional facilities at Curtin University, and on its track record of providing most of the players in the national team. The Australian Institute of Sport trains its specially selected hockey stars of the future at these facilities. The Australian men's and women's hockey teams are respected and feared worldwide and they both compete at the very top of the international circuit.

Basketball and tennis

These are widely played throughout the country and Australia has produced many Wimbledon champions. Basketball is played at regional and interstate levels and the national league is extremely well supported and avidly watched on television. Australian players have gone on to positions in America's NBL teams, and there is considerable interchange between the two countries. Obtaining a ticket for an interstate match can prove to be very difficult as they are snapped up as soon as they become available. Baseball is an even newer sport to Australia, but there is a national league, which is becoming increasingly popular.

Netball and softball

Netball and softball enjoy almost universal participation among young girls. Around 90% of Australian schoolgirls play in non-school netball teams during winter, and there are also summer competitive leagues, playing on weekday evenings, which are very popular.

Sport and schools

The Australian school curriculum incorporates sport into the normal school day and each school, whether private or state, usually participates in both an interschool swimming carnival and an interschool athletics carnival every year. In addition, there are interschool cricket, netball, football and softball leagues with games scheduled during school time or immediately after school. Sport classes at school are known as PE (physical education). Many private schools, however, hold their interschool sporting matches on Saturdays. In fact, Saturday mornings and afternoons are unofficially dedicated to sport around the country, and parents should resign themselves to the inevitability that for at least five years they will have to get out of bed early on a Saturday morning to deliver their offspring to the relevant sporting venue.

Modified rules for children

An important difference in Australian sport for children is the widespread use of 'modified rules' in almost every game. Under modified rules sports, even quite young children are able to compete in complete safety, while learning the basic skills of the sport. Primary schools will undertake careful coaching in every sport played and there is a strong emphasis on skill development. Modified rules sports are known by names which differentiate them from their big brother sports: junior hockey is called 'minkey', a game based on baseball and softball for kids is called 'tee ball' (and is very popular), junior Aussie rules is 'touch football' and junior tennis, 'short tennis'.

Water sports

Water sports are the cornerstone of Australian social and sporting life. Water-skiing, windsurfing, surfing, boating and diving are all common leisure activities, as well as highly competitive sports. Many Australians own their own pleasure boat, whether a yacht, power boat or launch. Swimming is an essential part of every school's sporting curriculum at both primary and secondary levels, and in summer students will swim in either the school or local pool at least two or three times a week, if not every day. Pupils are divided into classes according to their age and swimming ability and are rigorously coached by qualified instructors. Students are expected to attain swimming qualifications to a high level and from the

FACT

■ Squad sizes in A league Soccer were increased from 20 players to 23 players for the 2007–08 season.

Kite surfing on a blustery day

age of 13 are coached towards attainment of life-saving qualifications. Most students will leave high school with the Royal Life Saving Society's Bronze Medallion and Instructors Certificate.

Every public swimming pool is home to a competitive swimming club, and many young Australians join these at an early age, often eventually swimming at a state or even national level. Almost every Australian child is a safe swimmer by the age of six and school classes are focused on the development of refined technique and stamina. If you are moving to Australia with children, it is advisable to have swimming coaching before you leave, so that they are not left high and dry at school. Once in Australia, do not allow your children to swim widths in public swimming pools: this is considered highly antisocial and derisory, and even three-year-olds will be expected to tackle the length or keep to the baby pool. The Australian swimming, diving and water polo teams are among the world's best, and proved the point during the 2000 Olympic Games in Sydney.

Other outdoor pursuits

White water rapids, surfing, bungee jumping, skydiving, caving, hiking, swimming or snorkelling with dolphins, whales or sharks – if you have ever wanted to try any of these activities, then Australia is the place. Here are a list of other options and a rough guide to how much they will cost:

- Canoeing (A$40)
- Caving (A$40)
- Cricket (usually free to play)
- Dolphin swim (A$80)
- Football (usually free or A$20–30 to watch)
- Go karting (A$40)
- Golf (depending on club – A$20)
- Harbour Bridge climb (A$180)
- Harbour Bridge pylon lookout (A$10)
- Horse riding (A$40)
- Jet boat ride (A$50)
- Kayaking (A$30)

- Kite surfing (A$50)
- Mountain biking (A$20 to hire)
- Outdoor Tai Chi (A$10)
- Rugby (A$30 to watch)
- Scenic flight (A$250)
- Scuba diving (A$150)
- Skydiving (A$150)
- Snorkelling (free if you have your own snorkel)
- Surf lessons (A$150 – 3 days' course)
- Wet n' Wild amusement park (A$50)
- Whale watching (A$50)
- Whitewater rafting (A$60)

Sydney Harbour bridge climb: www.bridgeclimb.com
Harbour bridge-Pylon look out : www.pylonlookout.com.au
Wet N Wild on the Gold Coast: http://wetnwild.myfun.com.au
DreamWorld on the Gold Coast:www.dreamworld.com.au

FACT

Did you know that before finding fame, fortune and marrying his co-star, Crocodile Dundee actor and comedian Paul Hogan was once a rigger on the Sydney Harbour Bridge?

Australian activities by state: www.virtualtourist.com/travel/Australia

■ ENTERTAINMENT

Entertainment in Australia revolves around many outdoor pursuits, from playing or watching sport, getting soaked at a water theme park, to surfing, barbequing, sunbathing, climbing or walking. There are however a plethora of indoor activities that are perfect for the chilly winter months. Cinema complexes are found in every area, as are theatres, entertainment complexes for concerts and Opera houses in most states, not to mention the many pubs, clubs and casinos on offer. Australia also has world-renowned restaurants with a melting pot of cuisine influences. Below is a brief guide of entertainment choices for your stay down under.

Restaurant and pub guides

Best restaurants in Australia: www.yourrestaurants.com.au
Best pubs in Sydney: www.sydneypubguide.net
Brisbane's best pubs, clubs and restaurants:
www.ourbrisbane.com/dining/pubsandclubs

Public barbeques mean that you can have a meal and chill out in a park all at once

Best pubs, clubs and bars in Perth: www.streetsofperth.com.au/guides
Pubs, bars and clubs in Melbourne: www.melbournepubs.com
Things to do in Darwin:
http://darwin.citysearch.com.au
Tasmania's top watering holes:
www.pubjury.com/county/pub/guide/Tasmania
Adelaide's top pubs: www.pubscene.com.au

Bars and clubs

Australia, as you would imagine, is brimming with trendy pubs, bars and clubs. In every city and country town, you are also bound to find a couple of big ol' traditional pubs. Here are some ideas, for Melbourne and Sydney, to point you in the right direction so you can quench that thirst.

Top Sydney bars

The Daddy of all Sydney bars is Justin Hemmes' Ivy. This visually enticing palace at 320 George Street comprises the grand sum of 18 bars (just like a game of golf, but with drinks), nine restaurants, a decadent ballroom and a 25-metre swimming pool. It's almost as if Dubai has moved to the centre of Sydney. This place is definitely worth a look, even if you cannot afford the cost of a drink. Second on the list of hot bars to frequent is also owned by Mr Hemmes and is located just down the road at number 252 – Establishment. This is tiny in comparison, with only 3 bars-including the members only 'Hemmesphere' bar.

Ivy and Establishment: www.merivale.com/

Hugo's Lounge in Kings Cross (33 Bayswater Road) is now a firm favourite with local Sydney bar dwellers wanting to hang with the celebrity clientele. Other local fashionable haunts include the atmospheric Favela (1 Kellett Way) or the Gazebo Wine Garden (2 Elizabeth Bay Road).

Hugos Lounge: www.hugos.com.au
Favela: www.favela.com.au
Gazebo Wine Garden: www.gazebowinegarden.com.au

For those wanting to soak up the twinkling harbour view, while downing their glass of vino, head to either the Bennelong bar (under the sails of the Opera house) or the Opera Bar (Lower Level Concourse, Sydney Opera House). If you would like a bird's eye view from above the harbour, then take the lift to the 36th floor of the Shangri-La Hotel in Circular Quay and settle down for drinks and nibbles in the **Blu Horizon bar** (176 Cumberland Street, The Rocks).

Bennelong: www.guillaumeatbennelong.com.au
Opera Bar: www.operabar.com.au
Shangri-La www.shangri-la.com

Sydney clubs

Sydney's Oxford Street in Paddington is the place to head to, if you want to dance the night away surrounded by sweaty ravers. You have the choice between popular gay bars such as **Midnight Shift** (85 Oxford Street) and **The Colombian** (117 Oxford Street) or old school dance venues such as the **Goodbar Sydney** (11a Oxford Street), the **Grand Pacific Blue Room** (1 Oxford Street) and **Ruby Rabbit** (231 Oxford Street). Most places charge cover charges on weekend nights, which is usually around A$20–A$30.

Midnight Shift: www.themidnightshift.com
Good Bar: www.clubzone.com/c/Sydney/Nightclub/Goodbar
Grand Pacific Blue Room: www.gpblueroom.com
Ruby Rabbit: www.rubyrabbit.com.au

Top Melbourne bars

Cookie, (Level 1, 252 Swanston Street; 03 9663 7660) serves up a dizzying array of beers, many on tap. **Town Hall Hotel**, (33 Errol Street, North Melbourne; 03 9328 1983) is a relaxed and casual bar, once frequented by hardworking manual labourers. It is now packed with mellow young things, dressed down, relaxed and not giving a damn. **St Jerome's** (7 Caledonian Lane) was once a humble Swiss café down a grimy bin-strewn alleyway. It's now the little bar that grew and grew. The front section still has the squeezy wooden tables that once graced the café, but it balloons out into a disused loading bay at the back.

Cookie: www.cookie.net.au
Town Hall Hotel: www.melbournepubs.com/v/748/

Section 8 (27 Tattersalls Lane; 0408 971 044) is housed in a shipping container with wooden pallets for seating, meaning everyone is exposed to the open air, though there is cover from rain. **Madame Brussels**, (Level 3, 59 Bourke Street; 03 9662 2775) is named after an infamous brothel owner from the CBD's shady past. The old-fashioned charm spills over into the drinks list, with jugs of exotically flavoured punch; and the view from the laid-back rooftop area is impressive. **The Order** (Level 2, 401 Swanston Street; 03 9663 6707) is another place joining the rooftop bar fraternity. The roof level is a small open terrace, hemmed around by the decorative work on the building's upper walls. At night, this is a great place to take in the stars and sip a beer.

Section 8: www.section8.com.au
Madame Brussels: www.madamebrussels.com
The Order: www.theorder.com.au

Melbourne Supper Club, (161 Spring Street ; 03 9654 6300) is an oldie, but a goodie still worth mentioning. It's all very grown-up and sophisticated: everyone is seated, the knowledgeable waiters are welcoming and there are quality bar snacks to accompany the contents of the compendious wine list. **Borsch Vodka & Tears**, (173 Chapel Street, Prahran ; 03 9530 2694) is a Polish bar and restaurant with dozens of varieties of vodka on its menu. Sample a cherry vodka, a honey vodka, a bison grass vodka or the spectacular Goldwasser, speckled with gold flakes. **Paris Cat**, (6 Goldie Place; 03 9642 4711) is a cellar jazz club and its old exposed brickwork works with the sleek furniture and bar to create bags of ambience. There's music most nights, with regular jazz gigs and spoken word sessions.

Melbourne Supper Club: www.melbournepubs.com
Borsch Vodka and Tears: www.borschvodkaandtears.com
Paris Cat: www.pariscat.com.au

Loop, (23 Meyers Place; 03 9654 0500) is the place to watch a movie while you're sipping a cocktail. Fitted out with audiovisual equipment, this contemporary space is often used to premiere ambitious short films or to stage a challenging experimental music night. At **Kent Street**, (201 Smith Street, Fitzroy, 03 9419 6346), the split-level bar is scattered with sofa seating and the green and brown tones match the moody lighting. Via a screen above the door, you can watch a live relay of events unfolding outside on Smith Street, while you sip a lazy beer and earn hipness points.

Loop: www.looponline.com.au
Extracted from: www.theage.com.au/news/bar-reviews
Melbourne clubs guide: go to www.melbournenightclubs.com.au

Cinema

The two biggest cinema chains in Australia are Hoyts and Greater Union. There are also independent and art house cinemas in each state. These cinemas show all international and local films. The average ticket price is between A$12 and A$15, but there are discounts for senior citizens and students. Also keep your eye out for cheap Tuesdays, when tickets are often slashed to half price. If you are based in Sydney, try a different cinema experience by going to one of Govinda's dinner and film nights. For A$15 you can fill up on the 'all you can eat' vegetarian buffet, as well as chilling out on cushions and beanbags, while watching a double billing of the latest films.

 Greater Union: www.greaterunion.com.au
Hoyts: http://hoyts. ninemsn.com.au
Govindas: www.govindas.com.au

■ ARTS AND CULTURE

Although Australians are famous for their love of sport, they are also enthusiastic supporters of the arts. Their expenditure on arts products ranks among the highest in developed countries, and research shows that they read more newspapers per head than any other nation. Australia's cultural scene is a product of its unique blend of ancient traditions and new influences. Australia is home to some of the world's oldest continuous cultural traditions and has a rich mix of migrant cultures that have left their mark on current culture. Modern Australians are responsible for

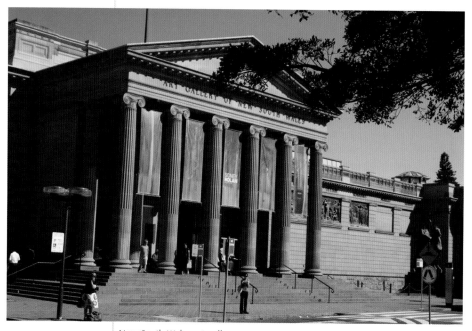

New South Wales art gallery

many cultural exports, such as music, art, film, theatre, touring dance and performance arts. It's not all *Neighbours* and Dame Edna Everage! Think of Nick Cave, INXS, The Australian Ballet, The Australian Philharmonic Orchestra, The Wiggles, Cate Blanchett, Geoffrey Rush, Naomi Watts, Kylie, Nicole Kidman, and artists such as Brett Whiteley. Thomas Keneally and Peter Carey have both won the Booker Prize for Literature in Britain. The Australian Youth Orchestra is widely regarded as one of the best in the world and is the training ground for the country's finest musicians.

The Australian Government also plays a large role in the growing culture and arts industry. Its advisory body, The Australia Council, annually provides more than 1,700 grants throughout Australia to arts organisations that are directly involved in dance, literature, community cultural development, new media, theatre, music, visual arts and Aboriginal and Torres Strait Islander arts. Government support has been an important factor in developing the arts and funding totals about A$3.8bn per annum. Funding for the development of Australia's cultural heritage comes from all three levels (federal, state/territory and local) of government. The Arts are also heavily supported by corporate and business sponsorship.

Australia has a vibrant cultural and artistic life and all forms of the visual and performing arts have strong followings. More than 88% of adult Australians attended a cultural event or performance in 2007. Film was the most popular event, with 70% attendance for the year; music concerts had the second highest attendance rate, with 26% of Australians aged 15 years or more attending at least one in the 12 month period; while 25% opted for an art gallery or museum. Other popular cultural pursuits include live theatre, dance performance, classical music concerts, visiting aquariums, libraries, botanical gardens and zoos. This industry is so popular that the total size of Australia's arts and related industries sector is estimated at A$32bn.

Film industry

The Australian film industry has been thriving for the last 30 years and is one of Australia's major cultural exports. The Australian Film Commission assists in the growth of this industry by aiding project development through script, pre-production assistance grant giving and international promotion. The locations in Australia double for numerous places worldwide, including major cities such as LA and New York, where costs and filming restrictions are prohibitive. Film makers from all across the globe are drawn to Australia by its lucrative tax incentives (which can afford up to 40% of a films budget) and its highly skilled, but affordable work force, whose skills have been honed servicing Hollywood blockbusters. The Government is keen to support a vigorous and diverse cultural environment and this is reflected in Australian films, which find a big audience both at home and abroad. Recent hits have included Baz Luhrmann's *Moulin Rouge, Muriel's*

Wedding, The Castle, Shine and *Chopper* and Australian actors are a big feature of Hollywood these days. The Hollywood blockbusters *X-Men, The Matrix* trilogy, *Star Wars*, Episodes Two and three, *Independence Day, Indiana Jones and the Last Crusade, Peter Pan, Jurassic Park, Happy Feet, Mad Max, Dark City, Pitch Black* and *Superman* were all shot in various locations down under.

While the industry is modest in international terms, it nevertheless employs about 50,000 people and more than 2,000 businesses are involved in film, television and video production. In 2005–06, 32 feature films started production in Australia – 25 Australian films, three co-productions and four foreign productions.

All the big international releases find their way to Australian cinemas, generally about six months before they hit the screens in Britain. Film going is a popular pastime, and tickets cost about A$5. In some cities, certain weeknights are 'concession nights', with all tickets costing under A$6, and this has greatly boosted mid-week sales. In the summer months, the Festival of Perth hosts the Lotteries Film Season, which shows art-house movies at the two outdoor venues of the Somerville Auditorium in Crawley and the Joondalup Pines Picture Garden at Edith Cowan University. It is one of the great pleasures of life in Perth to take a picnic to the Somerville at dusk and sit in a deck chair under the pine trees by the banks of the Swan River, sharing a bottle of wine and watching a movie. Similarly, Sydney hosts the annual (January/February) Outdoor Open Air Cinema. Patrons bring along picnics and blankets and watch a screen that pops up in the Harbour (and has the impressive Harbour Bridge and Opera house behind it, which can often be distracting). Similar outdoor events occur in both Melbourne and Brisbane.

> Australian Film Commission: www.afc.gov.au

FACT

■ Australia has film co-production treaties with the United Kingdom, Canada, Italy, Ireland, Israel and Germany, and memorandums of understanding with France and New Zealand. Treaties with Singapore and China have been signed, and are expected to become operative in the first half of 2008. A treaty with South Africa is also under negotiation.

Australian cultural achievements are now well known internationally, through the awards gained by its many arts exports. The movie *Strictly Ballroom* won the Prix de la Jeunesse at Cannes in 1992, and *The Piano,* the Palme d'Or in 1993. Australian actors such as Russell Crowe (originally from New Zealand), Nicole Kidman, Mel Gibson, Naomi Watts, Cate Blanchett and Geoffrey Rush are now big players in Hollywood.

Orchestra and chamber music

The Australian Broadcasting Commission (ABC) supports orchestras in each capital city, and the Sydney and Melbourne orchestras are flagship ensembles, which frequently tour internationally. Musica Viva, established in 1945 to promote chamber music in Australia, now co-ordinates one of the largest ensemble music concert networks in the world. It also organises overseas tours for Australian chamber music groups and commissions works by Australian composers. Youth Music Australia, formed in 1948, has helped the careers of thousands of young musicians and the Australian Chamber Orchestra is at the cutting edge of early music performance.

 The Australian Philharmonic Orchestra: www.auspops.com.au/about1.html
The Australian Chamber Orchestra: www.aco.com.au
Musica Viva: www.musicaviva.com.au
The Australian Youth Orchestra: www.ayo.com.au
Youth Music Australia: www.culture.com.au/exhibition/yma

Ballet and opera

There are two major organisations involved in ballet and opera on a national basis, the Australian Ballet and the Australian Opera, and most states also have state opera and ballet companies of a high standard. *The New York* Times described the Australian Ballet as 'world class' during one of its recent world tours. As well as touring theatre and dance productions, the iconic Sydney Opera house is also home to Opera Australia, The Sydney Theatre Company and the Sydney Symphony.

 Australian Ballet: www.australianballet.com.au
Australian Opera: www.opera-australia.org.au
Sydney Opera House: www.sydneyoperahouse.com

The Sydney Opera House tour

Working with new, rich audio-visual components, where images are projected onto the fabric of the building guides will take you on an emotional journey, engrossing you in a story to rival any opera plot with its dramatic twists and turns.

 Duration: Approx. 1 hour Adults: A$35/Concession: A$24; Family: A$74

Art galleries

There are excellent art galleries in every state, and a strong commitment to bringing international touring exhibitions to Australia. You will find both modern and historical pieces in galleries by artists such as Picasso, Brett Whiteley, Turner, Monet, Degas and the Australian surrealists Nolan, Boyd and Tucker.

 Art galleries Australia-wide: www.australianartgalleries.com

The emergence of symbolic surrealists such as Sidney Nolan (1917–1992), Arthur Boyd (1920–1999) and Albert Tucker (1914–1999) introduced

The Sydney Opera House

- Over 1,500 performances, from opera to circus, rock and cabaret, are staged each year to audiences totalling around 1.5 million.
- The Concert Hall, with 2,679 seats, is the home of the Sydney Symphony and used by a large number of other concert presenters. It contains the Sydney Opera House Grand Organ, the largest mechanical tracker action organ in the world with over 10,000 pipes.
- The Opera Theatre, a proscenium theatre with 1,547 seats, is the Sydney home of Opera Australia and The Australian Ballet.
- The Drama Theatre, a proscenium theatre with 544 seats, is used by the Sydney Theatre Company and other dance and theatrical presenters
- The Playhouse, is end-stage theatre with 398 seats.
- The Studio, a flexible space, has a maximum capacity of 400 people, depending on configuration.

a new dimension into Australian art, with Nolan focusing on Australian icons, especially the legendary bushranger Ned Kelly. Other notable artists of the mid to late 20th century include Russell Drysdale, John Olsen, Margaret Olley, Fred Williams, Howard Arkley, Margaret Preston, Jeffrey Smart, Clifton Pugh, William Dobell and Brett Whiteley.

Aboriginal arts

Aboriginal art, indigenous dance and music have begun to be introduced to national and international audiences. Companies like Bangarra and the Tjapukai Dance Theatre now take their performances around Australia and the world. Aboriginal art, once confined to the ethnographic sections of local museums, now takes its place in contemporary art galleries internationally. Aboriginal writers, such as Sally Morgan and Jack Davis, the late Kevin Gilbert and Oodgeroo Nunuccal, are well known throughout Australia. Sally Morgan's *My Place* is a moving account of the discovery of her Aboriginal heritage, and provides a keen insight into some regrettable episodes in Australia's history.

The Australian Museum

Established back in 1827, the Australian Museum in Sydney is Australia's very first museum. It holds unique, extensive collections of natural science and cultural artefacts. It also has an international reputation in the fields of natural history and indigenous research, community programmes and exhibitions. There are often temporary exhibitions from around the world and a series of permanent exhibits

 Australian Museum: www.amonline.net.au

Australian writing

Australian writing can be traced back to the early indigenous stories of 'Dream time'. These were never written but simply retold to future generations, becoming woven into the fabric of their rich history. The next storytellers to enter Australian history were the convicts and first settlers from the late 18th century.

The short stories and bush ballads of Henry Lawson and Andrew 'Banjo' Paterson's poems, including the classics *The Man from Snowy River* and *Waltzing Matilda,* were to be the most memorable from that period. The early 20th century produced classics such as *My Brilliant Career* by Miles Franklin (1901). Australia has one Nobel Prize for Literature to its credit, with novelist Patrick White receiving the award in 1973.

Peter Carey tops the current list of most memorable Australian authors, with titles such as *Oscar and Lucinda* (winning the Man Booker prize in 1988, with having a film made shortly afterwards) and *The True History of the Kelly Gang* (2001). Other notable Aussie writers have been Thomas Keneally (winner of the 1982 Man Booker prize for *Schindler's Ark*) Elizabeth Jolly, Geraldine Brooks (who won the 2006 Fiction Pulitzer Prize for her novel *March*) David Malouf and DBC Pierre (who won the 2003 Man Booker prize for *Vernon God Little*).

◼ JOINING COURSES

There are hundreds of courses on offer at colleges and TAFE Institutions (Technical and Further Education) throughout Australia. Many teenage school leavers opt to study at a TAFE rather than a University as it offers a wider selection of courses at a vastly reduced rate. This is because they are owned, operated and financed by the various state and territory governments. If you have always wanted to learn how to cook, teach, speak in public, program computers, learn public relations, speak Spanish, start up your own business, get your childcare certificate, learn first aid, sculpt, be an interiorior designer, be a photographer, nutritionist or a social worker then there is a course for you. There are also a multitude of other courses on offer, so read on.

Some of the colleges award degrees (such as tertiary institutions and medical and art schools) at the end of the course, but this is infrequent. The programs offered by these colleges can be used as employment-based training and qualifications or to enter one of the universities and in that way achieve a degree-level qualification.

Overall attending a TAFE course is beneficial, both in broadening your skills and for giving you newfound opportunities to meet locals. There are usually no age restrictions for TAFE courses, so don't be put off by that factor.

How to apply for a TAFE course

 Search for courses (over 11,000 Tafe and independent college courses listed): www.courses.com.au/tafe.php

Print off the application forms or use the relevant online forms for the individual college and start collecting the necessary documents needed for admission (each college will require individual documentation). You will perhaps need your GCSE or A Level certificate, your passport/driving licence or birth certificate, a credit card for payment of fees and a covering letter. Popular TAFE courses are listed in Appendix 7.

For a detailed list of TAFE options: www.courses.com.au/TAFE.php www.australian-universities.com/colleges

■ PUBLIC LIBRARIES

Every state has excellent library services both at the local and state level, and the National Library of Australia provides research facilities for scholars from all around the country (there are over 5,400 libraries throughout Australia). It is also home to the national archives.

 Australia's libraries: www.nla.gov.au/libraries

Many schools operate a mobile book van that literally drives up to the school gates and offers a library service to the children. Most libraries will have childrens' book reading hours and as well book clubs.

FACT

■ There are an estimated 54.9 million objects and artworks located in Australia's museums, and national and state libraries hold 11.3 million items.

To sign up for a library card

Australia operates its libraries in much the same way as the UK and America. When signing up for an account, you will need to provide a passport or picture identification (such as driving licence) and one piece of ID with your current postal address on it. So it is worth connecting your electricity and phone lines as soon as you can, so you have these documents (it will come in handy at the video store too). Normal borrowing time is 2–4 weeks, depending on the newness of the title.

MARRIAGE

If you are hoping to tie the knot, there are a few guidelines you have to consider. First you will be required to submit a 'Notice of the intended marriage' with your nominated celebrant/local church. The form must be submitted at least one month before the marriage is to take place, and no earlier than six months before the marriage. This form must be signed and witnessed either by an Australian Consular Official or Diplomatic Officer.

Other items you must take with you when submitting the notice include personal identification, such as a passport, visa and birth certificate. Be sure to check with your celebrant beforehand to ensure you have the correct legal identification. Outdoor weddings are legal in Australia (unlike the UK) as long as you have a qualified celebrant performing the ceremony. There are some beautiful locations throughout the nation, which are perfect for both ceremony and picture opportunities. If you are hoping to be married in a public park or, say, the Botanical Gardens, you must first get permission from the local council.

 Find a celebrant: http://mag. weddingcentral.com.au/weddings/legal/overseas.htm

About Australia

Australia is divided into six states – New South Wales (NSW), Victoria (VIC), Queensland (QLD), South Australia (SA), Western Australia (WA), and Tasmania (TAS) – and two territories, the Northern Territory (NT), and the Australian Capital Territory (ACT). The states and territories of Australia each have their own parliaments, capital city, flag and emblems depicting regional flora and fauna. Australian mapmakers, atlases and educationalists use cartographic projections that show Australia and the South-East Asian region at the centre of the world map, with Europe to the extreme left and the American continents to the right. The climate ranges from a hospitable 11°C in winter to a scorching 40°C (in some areas) at the peak of summer.

This chapter will give you a brief look into the different states, their characteristics and liveability (including real estate prices), so that you gain an insight into the state you would like to settle in. You will also get an idea of how Australia is governed and the idiosyncrasies, manners and customs of its people.

■ AUSTRALIAN PEOPLE

Australians are generally friendly and outgoing people. They find the British extremely reserved and often find it difficult to establish relationships with them because of this cultural barrier. Most Australians will quickly invite you into their home, often on introduction, and a barbecue is the most likely first point of association for both neighbours and colleagues. Nothing, however, will repel this friendly approach more than polite formality. First names rule in Australia, from top to bottom, and people are likely to be insulted by any other form of address. So, how can you break the ice, meet the locals and both accept and be accepted by them? This section tries to

> **Expat Joanna Davies enjoys the way Aussies socialise:**
>
> 'Social life revolves around barbeques and other gatherings, usually having a sporting theme as an excuse, like the AFL Grand Final, Melbourne Cup. We find Australians always bring food to a gathering and are happy to share. We find neighbours friendly and they will always pop over for a coffee or a chat. Social events revolve around food and drink, but meals seem lighter with more importance placed on the company and location than the food provided. Eating out seems more affordable (plenty of reasonably priced Asian restaurants) and social events can be organised spontaneously because the weather does not affect things too much.'

A dare-devil Australian gets close to a snake

give you a little insight into Australian social life and the kinds of people and attitudes you are most likely to meet.

Manners and customs

On the whole, Australians are a lot more casual than their British or European cousins. You will find that people, while friendly and courteous, will be far more direct in asking questions or in telling you what they think. You are much less likely to experience the occasionally chilling British reserve and are more likely to know exactly where you stand. When you meet an Australian for the first time at a social gathering you may find that you are asked a lot of questions that you may think 'forward' or even intrusive. This directness is the normal form of social discourse and a similar directness of response will be expected. It is generally considered to be a time-saver, enabling friendships to develop to a deeper and more interesting level more quickly.

Titles are rarely used and most people, regardless of their position, will expect to be addressed in first name terms. It would be quite normal, for example, for an undergraduate student to be comfortable calling the Vice-Chancellor of their university, say, 'Fay' or 'Derek'. It would also be extremely insulting for a person of senior position to address someone of

Pets are well-loved in Australia – a dog enjoys a ride to the shops

lower status as Mr or Mrs; far from being respectful, it would be considered patronising. Australian women will expect others to use the title Ms on occasions when a title is required, and eyebrows will be raised if a woman chooses to indicate her marital status by the use of Miss or Mrs.

One Australian custom that cuts across all social barriers is the use of 'mate' as a form of address. The concept of 'mateship' is a peculiarly Australian phenomenon and has been much studied anthropologically. Mateship generally refers to a specifically male bond and constitutes a somewhat macho, but nonetheless powerful, kind of friendship. Many

> **Canadian expat Scott Sumner finally feels at home in Australia, after finding it harder than he imagined to make friends:**
>
> 'It took me the better part of a year to really feel at home. Arriving at the age of 30, I discovered that most people, while friendly enough weren't actively looking for new friends as they were struggling to find the time to maintain their childhood friendships. I think that this would be the case in any country and is a reflection of the challenge of growing up and having different commitments. The catalyst for me in adjusting was making that one first friend who I really connected with and who then allowed me to share his massive network of friends.'

> **Expat Joanna Davies is full of praise of the Australian way of life:**
>
> 'We don't miss the highly competitive atmosphere we felt while in the UK. We find Australians more friendly and helpful than people in the UK. We were initially quite mistrustful of people's intentions when they spoke to us or tried to offer help – thinking they were out to con us, but we soon got used to the more friendly nature of people and have let our defences down. We are pleasantly surprised that generally teenagers and children are not as abusive or disrespectful to adults and we mostly feel safer in Australia than the UK. We have probably become much more laid-back ourselves. We have tried to avoid having only expat friends, although have unavoidably made a couple of English friends, as there are so many of them here, and you do share certain cultural backgrounds which make it easy to relate to each other and share support.'

Australian men consider their mates to be as important, or even more important, than their female partner and this bond often lasts to the grave. To be described as someone's lifelong mate is the highest of compliments. Conversely, however, Australians also often use the term 'mate' ironically, or as an aggressive indicator in potentially explosive situations. The tone of voice will clearly indicate the level of use. Australian men, regardless of ethnic origin, will almost invariably use this form of expression.

Australians have a great respect for people who get out there and try something new or difficult. They love to support the underdog, and newcomers who really 'give it a go' will readily win the admiration and friendship of their new acquaintances and colleagues (See *Settling in,* page 169.)

There are a number of associations of migrant communities in Australia, and all major cities will have branches of the Chung-Wah Chinese Association, and Greek, Italian, Yugoslav, and Irish Clubs. The United Kingdom Settlers' Association (03 9787 3112) is specifically intended to provide assistance and a point of contact for new migrants from Britain and publishes a journal, *Endeavour* every second month. Other clubs may be found in the Yellow Pages or your telephone directory, or by contacting the Department of Multicultural Affairs in your state. About 53,688 USA-born people live in Australia, mostly in NSW, followed by Victoria. The Australian American Association (see *Retirement,* page 369), based in Sydney and Melbourne, is a good place to start for support and information.

 Australian Yellow Pages: www.yellowpages.com.au

■ HISTORY

Although archaeological and historical evidence suggests that Australia was first settled over 50,000 years ago by Aborigines and later mapped by Dutch and Portuguese galleons in the 16th century, Australia's founding myths centre on the 'discovery' of the east coast by Captain James Cook in 1770. It was Cook who claimed the 'Great South Land' for the English Crown. Eighteen years later, in response to a crisis in English jails and a shortage of natural resources following the American Declaration of Independence, the First Fleet arrived in Port Jackson (now known as Sydney Harbour) with 11 ships, 736 convicts and a contingent of guards. Most convicts came from the cities of London, Manchester, Liverpool, Dublin and Glasgow and were transported for what now seem petty offences, such as stealing bread. A total of 160,000 convicts were brought to Australia over the next 70 years, and many of those who survived their sentences, chose to stay on in the country as farmers.

Up until the 1960s, schools taught children British history, leaving Australia as a country with no identity. It wasn't until the White Australia policy was abolished (in 1973) that schools started to teach about the diversities of the land they were occupying and the vibrant history of the indigenous people. White Australia policy is a term used to describe a collection of historical legislation and policies that intentionally restricted non-white immigration to Australia from 1901 to 1973.

The inauguration of White Australia as government policy is generally taken to be the passage of the Immigration Restriction Act in 1901, very soon after Australian federation. The policy was dismantled in stages by successive governments after the conclusion of the Second World War, with the encouragement of first non-British and later non-white immigration. From 1973 on, the White Australia policy was for all practical purposes defunct, and in 1975 the Australian government passed the Racial Discrimination Act, which made racially based selection criteria illegal.

Free settlement

The first free settlers, lured by the promise of cheap land and convict labour, began to arrive in 1815, while explorers gradually opened up new country, discovering rich grazing land to the west. Wool soon became one of Australia's most important industries and remains so to the present. The discovery of gold in the 1850s brought a fresh influx of immigrants from Europe, China and America, Rich gold seams were found at Ballarat, north of Melbourne and in central Western Australia, at Kalgoorlie. Large copper deposits were also found in the York Peninsula in South Australia. Settlements were also established in Hobart, Tasmania in 1803; on the Brisbane River, Queensland, in 1824; on the Swan River, in Western

Australia in 1829; on Port Phillip Bay, Victoria in 1835; and on Gulf St Vincent, South Australia in 1836. The capital cities of each state have grown from these sites. In 1900 the colonies, which were previously independent entities, united to encourage economic expansion, regulate the postal system and build a military defence force. The constitution was presented to the House of Commons in London in 1900 and was signed by Queen Victoria. Australia became the Commonwealth of Australia on 1 January 1901, and this date is known as Federation Day. Australia Day is celebrated on 26 January every year and commemorates the arrival of the First Fleet at Port Jackson.

Gold Rush: In a boom to Australia's economy, over 370,000 immigrants arrived in 1852, many seeking their fortunes in the Gold Rush.

Victoria contributed more than one third of the world's gold output in the 1850s and in just two years the State's population had grown from 77,000 to 540,000. The number of new arrivals to Australia was greater than the number of convicts who had landed here in the previous 70 years. The total population trebled from 430,000 in 1851 to 1.7 million in 1871.

Aboriginal man in traditional dress

■ GEOGRAPHY

Australia is one of the world's biggest islands, which is referred to by some as a continent. It has a landmass of 2,966,136 square miles (7,682,300 sq km), and is the sixth largest country in the world after Russia, Canada, China, the USA and Brazil. It is 31 times larger than the United Kingdom. The coastline, which stretches over 22,826 miles (36,735 km), encompasses a wide variety of coastal seascapes from the wild surf and dramatic cliffs of the Australian Bight, to the tranquil bays of the south-west. Australia is bounded by the Pacific Ocean to the east, the Indian Ocean to the west, the Arafura Sea to the north and the Southern Ocean to the south. The Great Barrier Reef, the largest natural reef in the world, runs almost parallel to the Great Dividing Range from the northernmost Tip of Queensland at

FACT

■ In 1851, Edward Hargraves discovered a grain of gold in a waterhole near Bathurst, he then named the place 'Ophir'. He received a reward of £10,000 and a life pension.

Ayres rock

Cape York down to Fraser Island, approximately 124 miles (200 km) north of Brisbane. Australia's marine conservation reserves cover more than 146,718 square miles (380,000 sq km).

Australia is characterised by the flatness of its topography and much of central Australia is a giant plateau; its highest mountain, Mount Kosciuzsko (7,309 feet/2,228m), is only half as high as the tallest peak on any other continent. The coastal strip is fertile, but it is insignificant in size compared to the vast inland deserts at the dry heart of the continent. This inland region, known as the Outback, is broken by salt lakes, starkly beautiful mountain ranges, such as the MacDonnell Ranges near Alice Springs and the Kimberly Ranges in Western Australia, and by mysterious rock formations such as Uluru (Ayers Rock) and Mount Olga (Kata Tjuta). Deserts such as the Great Sandy Desert, the Gibson Desert and the Great Victoria Desert are barren, unpopulated wastes of red dust, low scrub and spinifex (hardy tufts of spiny grass) and are extremely hot by day and freezing by night. The harshness of this land is sometimes reflected in the names given to geographical features, such as Lake Disappointment in Western Australia.

The Murray River and the Darling River are the main internal waterways of Australia and form the Murray–Darling River Basin. This drainage basin comprises the major part of the interior lowlands of Australia, and covers more than one million square kilometres (around 14% of the country). The headwaters of the Darling, Australia's longest river, are found in the Great Dividing Range between Queensland and NSW and finally reach the coast south-west of Adelaide some 2,094 miles (3,370km) later. Australia's three largest lakes, Eyre, Torrens and Gairdner, are located in the interior lowlands of South Australia and are fed by the rare run-off of heavy rains in the desert. Lake Eyre was filled only three times during the 20th century, and Lake Torrens only once.

Around 202,316 square miles (524,000 sq km) of public land in Australia has been designated as nature conservation reserves, and a further 424,710 square miles (1.1 million sq km) is preserved as aboriginal and Torres Strait Islander land.

Other territories

Australia is responsible for administering seven external territories: Norfolk Island, Cocos (Keeling) Island, Christmas Island, Ashmore and Cartier Island Territories, the Territory of Heard Island, Coral Sea Islands Territory, the sub-Antarctic McDonald Islands, and the Australian Antarctic Territories.

Neighbouring countries

Australia's nearest neighbour is Papua New Guinea, which lies less than 124 miles (200km) across the Torres Strait to the north of Cape York. To the north-west of Australia lies the Indonesian archipelago and further away to the north-east are the Solomon Islands, the French Island of New Caledonia, Fiji, Western Samoa and Tonga. Australia's nearest neighbour in a cultural sense is New Zealand, lying approximately 1,056 miles (1,700km) east of Sydney. Beyond Tasmania to the south, there is nothing but ocean until Antarctica, and to the west beyond Perth nothing before the islands of the Seychelles, Mauritius and Madagascar, near the African coast.

Population

The population of Australia is around 21.9 million. Most of this population is concentrated in cities situated in coastal areas, and although population density figures are as low as two people per sq km, this figure averages population over the vast inland areas of Australia and does not reflect Australia's urban environment. Population growth is in excess of 1.5% per annum, and the projected population for the year 2021 lies in the region of 24 million.

The ageing of Australia's population leads to the number of deaths exceeding births. It is possible that in the 2030s immigration may be the only source of growth in population. Around 92% of Australia's population are of Caucasian descent, a further 7% are Asian, and a mere 1.5% are of Aboriginal extraction. Approximately 76% of Australians are Christians (mainly Roman Catholic and Anglican). Australia's official language is English and 100% of Australians are functionally literate.

FACT

■ Western Australia is Australia's fastest growing state at 2.4% per annum.

Migration through the years

Australia prides itself on its multicultural composition. Its multicultural policies enshrine the right to individual cultural identity and to social justice regardless of race, ethnicity, culture, religion, language, birthplace or gender. All Australians, whatever their background, are expected to have an overriding commitment to Australia (and are for the most part overtly patriotic) and its interests and to accept the basic structures and principles of Australian society. Australia's multicultural policies have gone through three main phases over the decades. Until the 1960s, a policy of assimilation was in place, which drew its rationale from the long-discredited and disbanded White Australia policy. This policy effectively excluded non-European immigration but was weakened by attitudinal changes after the Second World War and is now regarded with shame by younger generations of Australians. From the mid-1960s through to 1972, the Government adopted a policy of integration, recognising that large numbers of migrants, especially those whose first language was not English, required direct assistance and intervention to help them become integrated into Australian society. Finally, multiculturalism became established as government policy in 1973 and today minority groups are assisted in promoting the survival of their language and heritage in mainstream institutions.

In 1978 a comprehensive review of immigration in Australia led to the adoption of new policies and programmes as a framework for Australia's population development. Three-year rolling programmes were implemented to replace annual immigration targets, as well as developing a more consistent and structured approach to migrant selection, emphasising the need for skilled people who would represent a positive gain to the nation. Today, nearly one in four of Australia's population were born overseas and numbers for 2006–07 were around the 180,000 mark, making it 72% more than in 1996-97. Of these, 17.7% were from the United Kingdom (23,300) and 14.4% from New Zealand (19,000). Other large migrating countries during this period were China (excludes SARs and Taiwan Province) 8.0% (10,600), India 8.6% (11,300), Sudan 2.9% (3800), South Africa 3.0% (4.000), Philippines 3.7% (4,900) and Singapore 2.0% (2,700).

There are around 1.5 million British-born permanent residents and citizens in Australia, more than in any other country except the UK.

◤ CLIMATE

Australia's size means that it encompasses several climatic zones. The more southerly regions have a temperate, Mediterranean climate with hot, dry summers and mild, wet winters while areas nearer the equator are sub-

tropical. Northern Queensland and parts of the Northern Territory experience heavy rainfall between January and March ('known as the wet').

The seasons in the southern hemisphere are inverted: the summer months are from December to February, autumn is from March to May, winter from June to August and spring from September to November.

Sun protection

Australians these days are highly aware of the dangers of their climate. The hole in the ozone layer, which is concentrated over the southern hemisphere, means that more and more ultra-violet rays are penetrating the atmosphere, creating an increased risk of skin cancer. The greatest damage is done in childhood, and today everyone is prepared to cover up to an extent undreamed of by British holidaymakers. Factor 15+ sunscreen should be worn at all times and many people choose to wear the impenetrable zinc cream on their faces; often seen smeared on the noses of the Australian cricket team. Most adults and all children wear hats

> 'The biggest difference is the weather – you quickly learn to walk on the side of the street with the shade!'
> **Simon Bloom**

> Expat Joanna Davies loves the unique climate of Melbourne: 'I like the cooler, drier climate. It is less humid than other areas of Australia and has a more European/Mediterranean feel. It does not have the long weeks of endless rain, or grey damp depressing skies of the UK. Generally the weather enables you to be outside most of the time and is more conducive to outdoor pursuits'.

every time they step outside and clothing often comes with a protection rating, depending on sleeve length, colour and fabric. Sunglasses are not a fashion accessory but an essential item and you should choose a pair with high quality lenses, such as Ray-Bans. All sunglasses are sold with a removable sticker on the lens indicating the level of ultraviolet rays against which they offer protection; you should only buy those that screen 100% of these dangerous rays. Sunglasses are available for all ages, from babies upwards; baby glasses come with colourful elasticised straps to keep them in place. All of the above points apply in winter as well as summer.

Appendix 8 shows average temperatures, rainfall and sunshine hours.

Skin cancer

- Over 380,000 Australians are treated for skin cancer each year – that's over 1,000 people every day
- Over 1,600 Australians die from skin cancer each year
- Skin cancer costs the health system around A$300m annually, the highest cost of all cancers
- Australia has the highest rate of skin cancer in the world. Skin cancers account for around 80% of all new cancers diagnosed each year in Australia
- Each year Australians are four times more likely to develop a common skin cancer than any other form of cancer

Suncare

On the beach, throw away those ideas of going topless and frying your body to achieve a great tan. Today, although tans are still relatively fashionable, sunbathing is out and fake tan and covering up are in. Although women still wear itty-bitty bikinis, they try and cover up with trendy kaftans and 15–25+ sunscreen. Both men and women cover up with t-shirts and hats. There is even an ad campaign (which has been airing for decades) which urges all to 'Slip, Slop, and Slap – Slip on a shirt, slop on sunscreen and slap on a hat'. Children all, without exception, wear swimsuits reminiscent of the Victorian era neck-to-knee bathing costume. These sun suits are made of UV-resistant Lycra and come in fluorescent colours. They have wrist or elbow length sleeves, cover the whole body and extend to the knees or even the ankles, zipping up at the front like a diver's wetsuit. They are quick drying, designed for speed in the water and are generally thought 'cool' by children. Should you let your children on the beach in a European-style swimming costume, the under-the-breath tut-tutting all around you will probably drown out the sound of the waves. Australian-style children's swimsuits are available in all surf shops and department stores as well as, and more cheaply, from Cancer Foundation Shops in most cities.

Skin cancer: www.cancercouncil.com.au
How to cover up: www.sunsmart.com.au

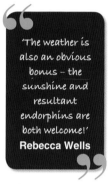

'The weather is also an obvious bonus – the sunshine and resultant endorphins are both welcome!'
Rebecca Wells

'Getting used to the heat on some days is a challenge – no long walks at lunchtime unless you can take a shower afterwards!'
Matthew Morrison

■ POLITICS AND GOVERNMENT

System of government

Australia is governed by three levels of elected government – local, state, and federal – and has been called the most over-governed country in the world. Local government operates through city and shire councils who have responsibility for local amenities, town planning, parks and pet and vermin control. State governments fund and administer roads, vehicle licensing, the police force, education and healthcare (among many other departments) while the Government of Australia (the Federal or Commonwealth Government) takes care of international trade, foreign affairs and the national treasury. State governments are located in the capital city of each state and the national parliament is in Canberra, the administrative capital of Australia. Although there are both state and federal taxes, income earners fill out only one tax return per year, remitted to the Australian Taxation Office, which then distributes revenue to the various states to fund their public services.

State and federal governments are run according to the British Westminster system, with two key differences. Firstly, unlike Britain, Australia has a written constitution, inspired by the constitution of the United States and secondly, Australia's upper house, the Senate (equivalent in function to the British House of Lords) is a democratically elected body. The lower house is known as the House of Representatives, and its parliamentarians as Members of the House of Representatives (MHR). The legislative power of the Commonwealth of Australia is vested in the Parliament of the Commonwealth. Queen Elizabeth II is Australia's Head of State (under the Australian Royal Styles and Titles Act of 1973 her title is 'Queen of Australia and Her Other Realms and Territories, Head of the Commonwealth') and her representative in Australia is the Governor-General, who has the powers to prorogue Parliament and to dissolve the House of Representatives and to assent in the Queen's name to any proposed law passed by both the Houses of the Parliament.

The Governor-General is Commander-in-Chief of the Australian Defence Forces. In practice, the Governor-General's role is largely ceremonial and there has been only one occasion in recent memory where he has interfered in the democratic government of the nation. This incident, widely considered by Australians to have been an insupportable intrusion of monarchical power in Australian affairs, occurred in 1975 when the then Governor-General, Sir John Kerr, dismissed the democratically elected Prime Minister Gough Whitlam, after backroom manoeuvring by opposition parties. Australia's real political power is held by the Prime Minister, currently Kevin Rudd, who was elected on 24 Nov, 2007 after a 6 week campaign and votes from over 13 million voters, who opted for change.

Many thought the previous Prime Minister, John Howard, had overstayed his welcome after 11 years and were looking for a fresh start with new Labor policies. All 150 seats in the House of Representatives and 40 seats in the 76-member Senate were contested in the election. Rudd wasted no time in fulfilling his election promise of apologising to the Australian indigenous people; on 13 February 2008, Rudd apologised to the 'stolen generation' for wrongdoings in their past.

The previous PM, John Howard, had been Prime Minister since 1996. He was re-elected in 1998, 2001, and in 2004 won a fourth term, making him the second longest serving leader in Australia's history. Kevin Rudd's victory means that the Labor party coalition now controls the Senate and the House of Representatives. The House of Representatives formulates and debates proposed legislation, which is then passed on to the Senate for further reading and eventual ratification. A cabinet of ministers with responsibilities for various portfolios, such as trade and foreign affairs, is appointed by the Prime Minister on election, and is subject to frequent reshuffles during the lifetime of a parliament. The Australian Labor Party website shows how the new PM is trying to align himself with the younger generation and its technology.

 Australian Labor Party: www.alp.org.au

State governments

State governments are constituted under the same two-house system as the federal parliament, except in Queensland, which abolished its upper house in 1992. The lower house of the state parliaments of New South Wales, Victoria and Western Australia is known as the Legislative Assembly and in South Australia and Tasmania as the House of Assembly. The governments of Queensland, the Northern Territory and the Australian Capital Territory are known as the Legislative Assembly. In each state a

The 'Stolen Generation'

Kevin Rudd's iconic and emotional apology to the stolen generation marked a turning point in government policy and was seen as both a huge gesture in reconciliation and a massive event in Australian culture

On 13 February 2008, Prime Minister Kevin Rudd put a motion to the Parliament of Australia.

"I move:

That today we honour the Indigenous peoples of this land, the oldest continuing cultures in human history.

We reflect on their past mistreatment. We reflect in particular on the mistreatment of those who were Stolen Generations – this blemished chapter in our nation's history.

The time has now come for the nation to turn a new page in Australia's history by righting the wrongs of the past and so moving forward with confidence to the future.

We apologise for the laws and policies of successive Parliaments and governments that have inflicted profound grief, suffering and loss on these our fellow Australians.

We apologise especially for the removal of Aboriginal and Torres Strait Islander children from their families, their communities and their country.

For the pain, suffering and hurt of these Stolen Generations, their descendants and for their families left behind, we say sorry.

To the mothers and the fathers, the brothers and the sisters, for the breaking up of families and communities, we say sorry.

And for the indignity and degradation thus inflicted on a proud people and a proud culture, we say sorry.

We the Parliament of Australia respectfully request that this apology be received in the spirit in which it is offered as part of the healing of the nation.

For the future we take heart; resolving that this new page in the history of our great continent can now be written.

We today take this first step by acknowledging the past and laying claim to a future that embraces all Australians.

A future where this Parliament resolves that the injustices of the past must never, never happen again.

A future where we harness the determination of all Australians, Indigenous and non-Indigenous, to close the gap that lies between us in life expectancy, educational achievement and economic opportunity.

A future where we embrace the possibility of new solutions to enduring problems where old approaches have failed.

A future based on mutual respect, mutual resolve and mutual responsibility.

A future where all Australians, whatever their origins, are truly equal partners, with equal opportunities and with an equal stake in shaping the next chapter in the history of this great country, Australia."

Governor acts as the representative of the Queen, exercising prerogative powers conferred by Letters Patent issued under the Great Seal of the United Kingdom, as well as various statutory functions defined by the state constitution and by the Commonwealth Australia Act 1986. A Governor of a State assents in the Queen's name to bills passed by the Parliament of the State, but acts on the advice of state cabinet ministers.

Voting

Australia has universal adult suffrage and electoral registration and voting in both state and federal elections is compulsory for all eligible persons. To qualify to vote, you must be either an Australian citizen (or a British subject who was on the Commonwealth Roll on 25 January 1984), over 18 years of age and resident in Australia. People who fail to vote in an election may be charged and fined; currently A$70 for a first offence.

Political parties

There are five mainstream political parties in Australia: the Australian Labor Party (ALP), the Liberal Party (LP), the National Party of Australia (NPA), the Australian Democrats (AD), and the Australian Greens. The ALP is traditionally a left-wing party but has become increasingly centrist so that it now embraces such previously right-wing policies as privatisation. It is currently the party of federal government and The Liberal Party, which is conservative in orientation and held power until 2007, is in a coalition with the National Party. The National Party is also a conservative organisation whose power base lies in rural areas, and although it is never likely to hold power in its own right, they inevitably enter into a coalition with the Liberal Party when that party is in government. In many cases, the Liberal Party holds power only by the consent and cooperation of the NPA. The Greens are active in environmental issues, particularly in states such as Tasmania where development threatens natural wildernesses. They, together with the Australian Democrats, are usually successful in gaining seats in the Senate rather than in the House of Representatives.

FACT

■ The Stolen Generation is a term used to describe those children of Australian Aboriginal and Torres Strait Islander descent who were removed from their families by the Australian and State government agencies and church missions, under various acts of their respective parliaments. This occurred in the period between approximately 1869 and 1969. Many were removed for their safety; others were removed under a government initiative to acclimatise them with European settlers. It is thought that many were abused and most were never reunited with their families.

How to vote

There are ballot offices in every main town on voting day. They are largely based in the auditoriums of local schools. You are given your voting form and asked to tick your preference (in the privacy of your own booth) and then place the form into the nominated box.

An ugly development in Australian politics is the foundation and expansion of the One Nation Party, which espouses overtly racist policies. Sadly, the platform of this party appeals to redneck communities in highly conservative outback areas, particularly in Queensland. It is, however, reviled by most Australians, and its leader, Pauline Hanson, is generally considered an embarrassment to the country. The antics of the One Nation Party have caused several diplomatic incidents between Australia and its South-East Asian neighbours and the Government is at pains to stifle its sphere of influence as far as democratically possible. At the time of writing One Nation has a Senator, as well as local government councillors. In January 2002, Pauline Hanson resigned from the National Executive as National President of One Nation. In the 2006 South Australian state election, six One Nation candidates stood for the lower house. Their highest levels of the primary vote was 4.1% in the district of Hammond and 2.7% in Goyder, with the other four hovering around 1%. They attracted 0.8% (7,559 votes) of the upper house vote. One Nation consequently won no seats in that election.

Republicanism

Support for a republican Australia has been growing steadily since the 1970s, taking centre stage in national debate in the 1990s. In 1993, the Prime Minister of the day, Paul Keating, established a Republican Advisory Committee, which founded its enquiries on the premise of 'when and how' rather than 'if', enraging pro-monarchy factions. Although traditionally the conservative Liberal Party has opposed the formation of a republic (in the 1960s, Liberal PM Sir Robert Menzies was an arch-monarchist), the Liberal Government, under John Howard, has been forced to bow to the public clamour for independence and a referendum was held in 1999. In February 1998, a Constitutional Convention, comprising democratically nominated delegates from all areas of Australian society, was held in Canberra to consider firstly, whether or not Australia should become a republic and secondly, which republican model of government should be adopted. The Convention found in favour of the formation of a republic under the 'Bipartisan Appointment of President' model, and subject to a successful referendum outcome in 1999, it had been likely that the new republic would come into effect on 1 January 2001. However, although public support for a republic was high, on 6 November 1999 the majority of Australians – around 55% – voted to keep the Constitutional Monarchy. The only state to return a vote of 'yes' to a Republic was Victoria, and that by the narrowest of margins – 49.6% for a republic and 49.4% against.

The word 'referendum' is Latin and means something referred (to the people for a decision). A referendum is a vote by all voters on a question. In Australia it's normally on a proposal to change the Constitution or to gauge the opinion of electors on a certain issue – e.g. daylight saving. Electors are simply required to vote either 'yes' or 'no' in response to one or more questions.

A change to the Commonwealth Constitution can only be made if, in the referendum, the majority of electors and the electors in a majority of the states, (that is four out of six states) vote yes. Referendums have failed four times when there have been national majorities in favour of the amendments but there has not been a majority in favour in at least four of the six states.

Originally only electors in the states voted in referendums, but the Commonwealth Constitution was amended in 1977 to give electors in the two territories an opportunity to be included in the count for the national majority. However the territories are not counted for the requirement that a majority of the states must also be in favour

Since 1991, the Labor party has supported constitutional change to become a republic and has incorporated republicanism into its platform. Labor spokesperson Nicola Roxon said that reform will:

'...always fail if we seek to inflict a certain option on the public without their involvement. This time round, the people must shape the debate.'

In other words, the idea of Australia becoming a republic still grows strong; it was the past model that failed to win overall support.

If, and when, Australia does become a republic (and it is very likely that this will occur at some point in the future), it may be initiated by Australia, or by Britain itself. A new flag without the Union Jack inset will have to be invented. It is likely that it will be designed, probably by public competition, and will be placed before the voters in a referendum before being formally

FACT

The word 'referendum' is Latin and means something referred (to the people for a decision). A referendum is a vote by all voters on a question. In Australia it's normally on a proposal to change the Constitution or to gauge the opinion of electors on a certain issue – e.g. daylight saving. Electors are simply required to vote either 'yes' or 'no' in response to one or more questions.

adopted. The Australian national anthem, *Advance Australia Fair*, which replaced *God Save the Queen* in 1984, will be retained.

Local government

Below the level of state government, the administration of local areas is undertaken by an elected town or shire council. This body is responsible for the provision and maintenance of public facilities and amenities, such as leisure centres, libraries and rubbish collections. Payments for all housing rates, and even dog licensing, are made to the local government. Planning permission for new buildings, demolitions and extensions are also the responsibility of the local government and vocal public meetings are frequently held to hear public discussion over topical local issues such as town planning and new developments. The local government level is the only one at which voting is not compulsory and, in general, most Australians are somewhat apathetic and avoid close involvement in local government decisions. Addresses and telephone numbers of local governments are available under the 'Local Government' section at the front of state telephone directories and in the Yellow Pages.

 Australian Yellow Pages: www.yellowpages.com.au

> '...always fail if we seek to inflict a certain option on the public without their involvement. This time round, the people must shape the debate.'

■ RELIGION

Australians are free to choose their own religion, as governed by section 116 in the 1900 Australian constitution:

> 'The Commonwealth of Australia shall not make any law establishing any religion, or for imposing any religious observance, or for prohibiting the free exercise of any religion, and no religious test shall be required as a qualification for any office or public trust under the Commonwealth.'

As such, there is no state religion in Australia. An astounding one-sixth of the population have no religious beliefs (according to the latest census in 2006) and over two-thirds of the population have a Christian-based religion. The remaining one-sixth of the population has diverse religious beliefs, which are a direct result of the huge multicultural element of Australia's population.

The indigenous people believed in their own religion or belief system, made up of their Dreamtime stories, passed down by generations. In 1788, European settlement brought Christianity to the shores of Australia;

STATES OF AUSTRALIA

NORTH →

INDIAN OCEAN

SOUTHERN OCEAN

SOUTH PACIFIC OCEAN

INDONESIA

INDIAN OCEAN

SOUTHERN OCEAN

AUSTRALIA

PAPUA NEW GUINEA

SOUTH PACIFIC OCEAN

NEW ZEALAND

WESTERN AUSTRALIA

Exmouth
Geraldton
Bussleton
Albany
PERTH
Kalgoorlie
Esperance
Karratha
Broome
The Kimberley

NORTHERN TERRITORY

DARWIN
Kakadu NP
Katherine
Alice Springs
Uluru (Ayers Rock)

SOUTH AUSTRALIA

Flinders Ranges
ADELAIDE
Barossa Valley

QUEENSLAND

Cairns
Townsville
Airlie Beach
Rockhampton
Bundaberg
Noosa Heads
Toowoomba
BRISBANE

NEW SOUTH WALES

Port Macquarie
Newcastle
SYDNEY
CANBERRA
ACT

VICTORIA

Great Ocean Road
Snowy Mountains
MELBOURNE

TASMANIA

HOBART
Freycinet Peninsula

Sydney Opera House, New South Wales

South Australian vineyards

Ayers Rock, Northern Territory

Melbourne, Victoria

denominations represented were predominantly Roman Catholic found among Irish convicts and Anglican among other convicts and their gaolers.

One of the more popular religions in modern Australia is the Church of England, which is now known as the Anglican Church. Other main religions include the Methodist, Catholic, Presbyterian, Congregationalist and Baptist churches. Recent waves of immigration from the Middle East and South-East Asia have seen Buddhist and Muslim numbers expand considerably, and increased the ethnic diversity of existing Christian denominations. Every state has its fair share of religious communities and congregations.

 Find your local church: www.yellowpages.com.au

◼ REGIONAL GUIDE

Western Australia (WA)

Capital: Perth

Area: 1,515,300 square miles (2,525,500 sq km) = over 10 times the size of the UK

Total area of Australia: 32.87%

Coastline: 7,813 miles (12,500 km)

Climate: Average Perth daily maximum temperature in January (Summer) 81°F (27°C); in July (Winter) 59°F (15°C). Note that there is significant variation in temperatures throughout the state from the temperate south to the tropical north

Western Australia's huge size (the whole of Western Europe can easily fit into Western Australia and still leave room for more) encompasses the whole range of climatic and geographical zones. From the endless white sands and crystal waters of the tropical north to the arid zones of the Nullarbor Plain, through to the vineyards of the south-west, WA is the Australian landscape encapsulated. Its features include the spectacular

> **Life coach Rebecca Wells on her first impressions of the west coast of Australia:**
>
> 'My first impressions of the west coast – I just loved it. It's home to the most glorious national parks and host to some beautiful, booming red gorges. The beaches around that coast are idyllic – gorgeous fine sand near Turquoise Bay and some spectacular snorkelling spots!'.

Ningaloo Reef, a marine reserve less well-known than the Great Barrier Reef but equally impressive, majestic Karri forests, ancient and massive gorges and geological formations such as Wave Rock and the Pinnacles (an ancient fossilised forest now standing in a desert landscape). The Stirling and Porongorup Ranges very occasionally see snow in winter.

Economy

Western Australia's healthy economy (due to the commodities boom), its growing population, developing industries and technology, outdoor lifestyle, relatively affordable real estate and prime facilities contribute to a general feeling of well-being, which occasionally borders on smugness, and most locals consider themselves lucky to live there. Since the 1960s, the Western Australian economy has grown faster than that of any other State, with an average real Gross State Product growth of 4.9%. The state's economy is export-based and its overseas trade surplus is more than double that of the rest of Australia. Its major export markets are Japan and the South-East Asian nations as well as the USA and the EU. It has the second lowest levels of unemployment in the country. Western Australia is second to New South Wales as the most popular destination for business migrants.

Exports/imports

The state is rich in a wide variety of natural resources and is a leading producer of iron ore, gold, industrial diamonds, alumina, mineral sands, wool, wheat, salt and forest products. While wheat and wool account for around two-thirds of the state's income from primary industry, Western Australia is also developing more unusual primary industries; farming cashmere and angora goats, emu and deer. Western Australia's fishing industry produces rock lobster, prawns, shrimp and scampi, which are mainly exported to the USA and Japan. Mineral and petroleum production adds a further A$8bn per annum to the State's economy and comprises 84% of the value of the State's overseas exports and about 50% of Australia's total mineral and energy exports. The minerals and petroleum industry in WA contribute about 30% of the Gross State Product.

People

More than a quarter of Western Australia's population was born overseas, and it consequently enjoys a broad and cosmopolitan lifestyle. It also has a young population, second only to the Northern Territory, with an average age of 30.4 years. Western Australian medical and health services are considered among the best in the world. At a doctor–patient ratio of 1:288, the state now ranks with Norway, Sweden, Finland, Denmark, France and the Netherlands, and is considerably ahead of the USA, UK and Japan. The average life expectancy in Western Australia is high, and currently stands at 76 years for men and 82 for women.

Education

Western Australian education is of a very high standard, both in the public and private sector. With five universities and over a thousand schools and colleges throughout the state, Western Australia has world-class education facilities and is a world-leader in research, such as wave technology.

Real estate

Real estate costs were once among the lowest in the country, but with high levels of migration (the highest of any state in 2007, due to the commodities boom) and rising inflation, this is no longer true. The Government have recently had to step in and implement a cut of 5% on stamp duty for homes. Regardless of increased prices, Western Australians enjoy a high rate of home ownership with more than two-thirds of all residences being privately owned.

Capital: Perth

Perth is the most geographically isolated capital city in the world and has a population of 1.5 million people (WA has a total population of 2.1 million). The city is stunning, situated along the banks of the Swan River, and has a relaxed and friendly atmosphere and easy-going lifestyle. The most popular residential areas are built along the river and coastal strip, with suburban sprawl extending inland to the edge of the escarpment of the coastal plateau. Perth summers are very hot, and although the average temperature is only 80°F (27°C), the mercury frequently hovers around 104°F (40°C) for days at a time. The heat is very dry and as it is not sticky or cloying can easily be dealt with by staying in the shade. In the afternoons, the sea breeze comes in off the Indian Ocean and by sunset the weather is usually extremely pleasant. This breeze is known affectionately as 'The Fremantle Doctor', for its remedying effect on the wilting population. Perth is, in fact, Australia's windiest city and the third windiest city in the world. It enjoys more sunshine and clear days than any other Australian capital and while it also has one of the wettest winters, rains are usually short and sharp, interspersed with cool, sunny periods.

The centre of Perth is dominated by King's Park, which consists of approximately 1,000 acres (404,686 ha) of natural bushland, wildflowers and landscaped gardens. This park is a focus for family life and its various

Expat Jane Smith considers herself lucky to have bought, before Perth's real estate boom hit:

'We bought a house in 2003, with a price that was just over the medium price. We are so glad that we did though, as in 2006 Perth property went up 46%, it's tough out here now.'

cycle tracks, nature walks, adventure playgrounds and water features are popular with all sections of the community. King's Park is the home of the state botanical gardens, which features the full array of native flora, and hosts the Wildflower Festival in September.

Culture

Perth has an active cultural scene, with a permanent symphony orchestra, ballet company and opera company performing year-round at the city's two main arts venues: the Perth Concert Hall and His Majesty's Theatre. The enormous Entertainment Centre hosts large-scale popular events and commercial productions such as the Moscow Circus and ice shows. The Festival of Perth is held every year and is centred on the venues of the University of Western Australia. Major national and international performing artists in the fields of music, dance and theatre are brought in for the four week event, so that every year, the world's best can be seen on the local stages. In addition, the Festival Fringe offers cutting-edge comedy and experimental theatre and music, and the concurrent film festival screens art movies from around the world. Musica Viva operates a national and international chamber music touring scheme, the largest of its kind in the world.

Transport

Perth has an efficient public transport system made up of ferries, electric trains and buses, all run by Transperth. In Perth, travel on the Central Area Transport (CAT) system is free throughout the central business district (CBD). City planners are actively seeking to improve public transport to alleviate congestion in the city centre. Long distance commuting is rare in Perth, and most people live with in about 20 minutes of their place of work.

Outdoor pursuits

The beaches and the Swan River provide a perfect water-playground for Perth's population; the swimming, water-skiing, windsurfing, surfing and sailing are the cornerstone of Perth leisure activities. There are more boats per capita in Perth than in any other Australian city. The other major sports played in Perth include cricket (the Western Australian Cricket Association, affectionately known as the WACA, often hosts One-Day International and Test matches), various codes of football (Aussie rules, soccer, rugby),

English Expat Jane Smith comments on the practicalities of Perth's infrastructure:

'The infrastructure in Perth is fantastic, transport is efficient, on time, clean and caters for the disabled and people with prams etc. People complain about the health service, but after one surgery, two children and several trips to A & E as a public patient, I cannot fault the treatment we have received.'

horseracing, tennis, hockey, lawn bowls and golf. Basketball and baseball are also increasingly popular.

First-home buyers should consider buying an older-style apartment in an inner city area as an entry point in the housing market.

'There are currently a large number of Perth suburbs where you can still buy an older style apartment for under A\$300,000.
(*Source: http://wa. professionals.com.au*)

Useful resources

Online WA: Portal website for the Government of Western Australia: www.wa.gov.au

Real Estate Institute of Western Australia: 08 9380 8222; admin@reiwa.com.au; www.reiwa.com.au. REIWA produces an illustrated weekly property guide, *The Homebuyer*, available free every Friday from REIWA and local REIWA Agents

Department of Education and Training of Western Australia: 08 9264 4111; www.eddept.wa.edu.au

Department of Industry and Resources: 08 9222 8333; www.doir.wa.gov.au. The DOIR produces a quarterly economic briefing on Western Australian economy. Business help at www.doir.wa.gov.au/BusinessAssistance

Northern Territory (NT)

Capital: Darwin

Area: 807,720 square miles (1,346,200 sq km) = 5.5 times the size of the UK

Total area of Australia: 17.52%

Coastline: 3,720 miles (6,200km)

Climate: Average daily maximum temperature in January 87°F (31°C); in July 87°F (31°C). In Alice Springs temperatures vary more widely, as the town lies in the semi-arid central region rather than the tropics. The average daily maximum summer and winter temperatures for Alice Springs are 95°F (35.2°C) and 68°F (20.5°C)

TIP

■ First-home buyers should consider buying an older-style apartment in an inner city area as an entry point in the housing market.

TIP

■ 'There are currently a large number of Perth suburbs where you can still buy an older style apartment for under A\$300,000.'

The Northern Territory (also known as 'The Top End') is situated in central northern Australia, to the east of Western Australia. It is bordered by South Australia in the south and Queensland to the east. The Northern Territory's history of development is closely linked with that of South Australia, as in 1863 the British Government handed over control of the Northern Territory to the Colony of South Australia. In a year, the first sale of land in the Territory was held in Adelaide. In 1869 an expedition led by the Surveyor-General George Goyder resulted in the establishment of a permanent settlement, now known as Darwin. South Australia's control was relinquished in 1901 after Federation, and control over the Northern Territory was held by the Commonwealth Government until 1 July 1978, when the Territory was granted self-government. The powers of government differ from those of other states in the title only. Its assembly consists of a single lower house, and its leader is known as the Chief Minister. For inter-governmental financial purposes the Northern Territory has been regarded as a state by the Commonwealth since July 1988.

The remoteness and harshness of the Northern Territory has made it unique in many ways, not the least of which is its relatively tiny population. Its 216,500 residents (September 2007) comprise 0.75% of Australia's population and it has a population density of only one person per nine sq km. The population of Darwin is around 108,000 and of Alice Springs, 27,000. The annual population growth rate in 2006 was 0.8%. This rate has slowed due to changing patterns of interstate migration, but the Northern Territory continues to have the youngest population in Australia, with an average age of 29 years, compared with the Australian average of 34.7 years. Almost 28% of the population are Aboriginal, although overall Aboriginal and Torres Straits account for only 1.5% of the Australian population. More than 50 different ethnic groups are represented in Darwin, and 24% of people speak a language other than English.

Economy

Although the Territory is hampered by its distance from major Australian economic and political centres, and by restricted transport and communication links, its economy has experienced a growth rate in Gross Domestic Product (GDP), which has generally exceeded that of Australia as a whole. Its rapid growth can be attributed mainly to developments in mining, to tourism and especially to oil. The abundance of natural resources such as alumina, manganese, gold, bauxite and uranium, as well as oil and gas, has enabled the Northern Territory to participate substantially in the international market and the value of exports for the Northern Territory per capita is almost double the national figure.

Roads

There are three main interstate highway links in the Northern Territory: the Stuart Highway from Darwin to the South Australian border, the Barkly

Highway from Tennant Creek to the Queensland border, and the Victoria Highway from Katherine to the Western Australian border. Although there are roadhouses along these highways, there are stretches of road that are not serviced for more than 174 miles (280km). It is always advisable to notify the Automobile Association of the Northern Territory before embarking on an unfamiliar road (especially in the wet season), or before undertaking long journeys over unsealed or unserviced roads. You should ensure that you take supplies of petrol, water and food, and if possible a CB radio. In the case of breakdown or emergency, stay with your vehicle at all times.

Cost of housing

The cost of housing varies widely in the Northern Territory. Rented accommodation in Darwin is among the most expensive of all Australian capital cities, and suitable properties may be scarce. Average price of a two-bedroom apartment is A$470,000.

Education

Education has been the responsibility of the Northern Territory government since 1979, and in recent years it has modified its schools' curriculum to reflect the multicultural nature of its classrooms, promoting intercultural understanding and literacy. There are also correspondence schools, known as 'Schools of the Air', which use two-way radio, video and computers, to bring the classroom to isolated students. The Northern Territory Secondary Correspondence School offers an excellent range of secondary courses up to university entrance level for those who do not have access to normal school facilities. Tertiary education in the Northern Territory is usually undertaken through Charles Darwin University or the University's Institute of Technical and Further Education, which specialises in trade and technical courses. In 1985, the postgraduate research institution, the Menzies School of Health Research, was established at the Royal Darwin Hospital and it is enjoying a reputation as a centre of scientific excellence in its field. One of its primary objectives is to assist in improving the health of people in tropical and central Australia. The School has an academic link with the Charles Darwin University and its students may qualify for the higher degrees of that university.

Health service

The Northern Territory Health Services are remarkable, considering the distance and difficult terrain that must be covered. There are modern, well-equipped hospitals in Darwin, Alice Springs, Katherine, Tennant Creek and Nhulunbuy. All hospitals provide general in and outpatient care as accident and emergency services. The Royal Darwin and Alice Springs Hospitals offer a wide range of specialist services and are both special teaching hospitals affiliated with the University of Sydney. A private hospital is also available in Darwin. Mobile services are provided in remote areas and the Northern Territory government subsidises missions and Aboriginal organisations in the provision of health services. While there are health centres in all major towns and settlements, in extremely remote regions the Royal Flying Doctor Service (RFDS) and the Aerial Medical Service operate in cases of serious injury or illness. The Patient Assisted Travel Scheme (PATS) provides financial assistance to people from isolated areas that have had to travel for specialist consultation and treatment. The Northern Territory government also provides mental healthcare, blood banks, services for the aged, caring for family, youths and children, services for the disabled and women's information services as well as women's refuges and shelters, alcohol and other drug treatment programmes, a Sexual Assault Reference Centre. There is also the Ruby Gaea Darwin Centre Against Rape which provides counselling, support services and emergency accommodation.

Geography and climate

The Northern Territory lies in the torrid zone of the Tropic of Capricorn and much of its area is semi-arid. Although its landscape contains Australia's great 'dead heart' of claypan desert, which covers an area 500 miles (805km) long and 200 miles (322km) wide, the tropical northern part

of the Territory is luxuriantly verdant. These two climatic regions result in a diversity of vegetation in the Territory, ranging from mangrove and freshwater swamps and billabongs (pool or backwater), rainforest, eucalyptus and mulga woodlands, to spinifex grasslands, gibber plains and sandy deserts. There are no major rivers in the Northern Territory's interior, and rivers and creeks flow only after rains in the wet season (October–April). The Todd River, on which Alice Springs is located, is usually dry. 'The wet' is a period of high humidity and torrential rain and thunderstorms occur in the transition from 'the dry' to the wet season. These rains often cause flooding and transport and communications in the Northern Territory can be difficult or even disrupted at times. All of the Territory's major rivers are on the coastal fringe. The Roper River, which flows into the Gulf of Carpentaria, is the Territory's largest. Among other smaller rivers are the Daly, Victoria, Adelaide, Mary, South and North Alligator rivers. The Northern Territory is prone to cyclones or

Exploring the Australian outback

hurricanes, the most famous of which, Cyclone Tracy, destroyed Darwin on 24 December 1974. The city has subsequently been rebuilt and is now a modern showcase of urban planning. Houses are constructed to withstand cyclone conditions, and government authorities maintain crisis plans against future disasters.

Culture

Although the Northern Territory is best known to non-Territorians as one of the world's great wildernesses, the capital, Darwin, is a modern city that provides the services and lifestyle expected of any Australian city. Like any other Australian state, the Northern Territory offers a huge range of outdoor activities, including a wide variety of sports, as well as diverse cultural events, including theatre and festivals. In general, the towns are small, sparsely populated but have a relaxed atmosphere and a strong sense of community.

Useful resources

The Territory: Portal website for the Northern Territory Government: www. nt.gov.au

Department of Business, Industry and Resource Development: 08 8982 1700; info. dbird@nt.gov.au; www.dbird.nt.gov.au

South Australia (SA)

Capital: Adelaide

Area: 380,070 square miles (984,377 sq km) = four times the size of the UK

Total area of Australia: 12.81%

Coastline: 2,300 miles (3,700km)

Climate: Average daily maximum temperature in January 84°F (29°C); in July 59°F (15°C)

South Australia is situated in the middle of the southern coast of Australia, along the Great Australian Bight. It is bordered by Western Australia to the west, the Northern Territory to the north and Victoria to the east. It has a Mediterranean climate, ideally suited to the production of wine and vineyards established by early European settlers are prolific throughout the Barossa Valley. South Australia produces more wines than any other state or territory in the country and has a population of 1.5 million, which is around 8.5% of the total population of Australia. Most of South Australia's population lives in Adelaide, the capital, which has a population of 1.1 million. Adelaide is situated on the River Torrens, between the waters of the gulf and a range of low hills on the coastal plateau. The city stretches 56 miles (90km) from its southernmost to northernmost suburbs. The rest of the state's population is scattered throughout the major regional centres of Whyalla, Mount Gambier, Port Augusta, Murray Bridge, Port Pirie and Port Lincoln.

Transport

Adelaide's transport system is a well-oiled machine that rarely experiences breakdown or congestion. This is largely due to the city's first planner, Colonel William Light, who planned Adelaide with such geometric symmetry that all major city roads are straight and wide. Adelaide enjoys a unique bus service called the O-Bahn, which is a right-of-way guided transport system on which commuters are shuttled to and from the city at speeds of up to 62 miles/h (100km/h).

Housing

Most of the housing follows the pattern of single-storey houses on spacious blocks, ensuring off-street parking and a private back garden. The standard of homes in South Australia is among the highest in the country, and rented accommodation is cheaper than most other states. Industrial property rental is on average 35% cheaper than in other Australian capitals. For four-bedroom houses for rent in Adelaide, expect to pay A$400–A$600 per week, or A$320,000 to buy a two-bedroom apartment.

 Adelaide real estate: www.realestate.com.au

Industry

South Australia is an important industrial and scientific centre and is home to a rapidly expanding electronics industry. The Advanced Engineering, Electronic Research and Electronic Surveillance laboratories at the Defence Science Technology Centre are world-leaders in laser research, and the academic centres of the Adelaide and Flinders Universities support this research, as well as enjoying a fine reputation in many other disciplines. The University of Adelaide is one of Australia's premier universities and consistently ranks high among the top universities in the Asia-Pacific region in winning research funds. Australia's first planned centre for high-tech development and manufacture, Technology Park Adelaide, is integrated with the campus of the University of South Australia. South Australia's industrial base is supported by vast mineral resources in the form of oil, gas and other hydrocarbons, which are tapped in the Cooper Basin area. Brown coal is mined at Leigh Creek and copper, uranium and gold are extracted at Roxby Downs. Australia's biggest opal fields are at Andamooka.

Culture and people

South Australia has a warm, friendly ambience and Adelaide is a rapidly developing city. The capital has the highest ratio of health professionals per capita in Australia and has 173 public and private hospitals. It has excellent sporting and entertainment facilities and a highly regarded education system. The city has a permanent symphony orchestra, ballet and opera company, and hosts the world-famous Adelaide Festival every summer. Adelaide offers a very attractive environment with some fine architectural features and is known as the 'City of Churches'. The cost of living and real estate is generally low in South Australia, making it an appealing place in which to live.

Useful resources

South Australia Central: Portal website for the Government of South Australia: www.sa.gov.au

Department of Trade and Economic Development: 08 8303 2400; www.southaustralia.biz

Department of Immigration and Multicultural and Indigenous Affairs: 131 881; www.immi.gov.au

Immigration South Australia: 08 8204 9250; www.immigration.sa.gov.au

Tasmania (TAS)

Capital: Hobart

Area: 26,375 square miles (68,331 sq km) = 0.22 times the size of the UK

Total area of Australia: 0.88%

Coastline: 1,920 miles (3,200km)

Climate: January 71°F (22°C); July 51°F (11°C)

Tasmania is Australia's smallest state. It is an island separated from the south-east corner of the mainland by the Bass Strait, a shallow body of water with an average width of 149 miles (240km). Tasmania's coastline is bounded by the Southern Ocean to the south and west, and the Tasman Sea to the east. Tasmania spans 184 miles (296km) from north to south and 196 miles (315km) from east to west. Despite the fact that it is Australia's smallest state it is, nonetheless, more than twice the size of Wales. Tasmania is the only Australian state that does not have a desert region and it is fertile throughout. It is the most mountainous state and one of the almost completely mountainous islands in the world. It has the largest rural population in relation to its size of all the Australian states, and is one of the world's most richly mineralised areas. Tasmania is the leading Australian state in terms of the production of minerals in point of value of output per capita, and almost all of Australia's tungsten is extracted from King Island, situated in the Bass Strait.

Industry and geography

Orchard and berry fruits are grown in the south of the state and due to its high production of apples and because of its shape, Tasmania is often referred to as the Apple Isle. Industries in the southern region include the Cadbury Schweppes cocoa and confectionery factory, the Electrolytic Zinc Company, the Australian Newsprint Mills, Stanley Works (manufacturers of hand tools such as the Stanley knife), Sheridan Textiles, International Catamarans and the Cascade Brewery, which was established in 1824 and is the oldest brewery still in operation in Australia.

Fishing is the major industry on the east coast of Tasmania and is based in the ports of St. Helens and Bicheno. Catches include crayfish and abalone. Tasmania has a rapidly developing fisheries industry and now farms salmon and oysters for the international market.

In the north-east of the state, the fertile soil provides ideal farming land. Beef and dairy cattle, wool sheep and prime lambs are all farmed in this region. Market gardening is also important, as it is in the north-west of the state, where vegetable and dairy farming predominate. Other types of farming in the north-west include pig, sheep and also poppy farming, to provide oil for pharmaceutical preparations. Manufacturing here is dominated by forest-based industries, whereas in the central northern region of the state industries include the knitting yarn producers Coats Patons, the automotive parts manufacturers ACL Bearing Company and the aluminium smelter and refinery Comalco. Central and northern Tasmania has developed a viticulture industry and is the home of the Ben Lomond Ski Fields.

The west of the state is a region of dense forests and mountain ranges, raging rivers and rugged hills, and has a treacherous coastline and wild, inaccessible beaches. Mining is the predominant industry in the west and metal ores such as copper, zinc, tin and iron are extracted here. Much of the south-west region is inaccessible and uninhabited, containing some of the most spectacular scenery in the world. The south-west wilderness area has been listed by the World Heritage Commission and consists of dense rain forests, scrub, wild rivers, rapids, ravines and harsh mountains, which can only be tackled by experienced bush-walkers.

Approximately 20% of Tasmania is World Heritage Area, and there are extensive cave systems, many of which are Ice Age aboriginal cave art sites.

The central lakes area is dominated by the hydroelectric schemes, which produce the state's electricity. Trout fishing is also popular. In the flatter midland area sheep farming, particularly for wool, and beef cattle grazing are also popular.

Many parts of Tasmania are reminiscent of the green but windswept landscapes of some parts of Scotland and over the decades a large number of British and other European immigrants have settled on the island. The resident population of Tasmania is currently 498,200 of which two-fifths were born outside Australia (mostly in England, Scotland and Germany) and approximately 23% of whom are under the age of 15. Tasmania's climate and farming conditions are most comparable to those of northern

European countries such as France and the UK, which also helps new British settlers feel more 'at home' than they might in the harsh dry regions of the Northern Territory or the tropical areas of Queensland.

Capital: Hobart

Hobart is Tasmania's capital city. It was founded in 1804 and is situated in the south-west of the state, 12 miles (20km) from the mouth of the Derwent River. It is Australia's second oldest city, with a population of around 190,000, and extends over both sides of the river. To the west of the city lies Mount Wellington (4,163 feet/1,269 m), which is usually snow-capped in winter. The city was founded as a penal colony and was reputed to be one of the harshest prison settlements. Transportation to Van Diemen's Land (as Tasmania was originally called) was as good as a death sentence and many convicts did not survive. Despite its ruthless beginnings, the city flourished in the mid-nineteenth century thanks to its shipbuilding, whaling and port facilities. Today, Hobart is more likely to make the shipping news during the famous Sydney–Hobart yacht race held every year commencing on Boxing Day.

Education and employment

In 1869 Tasmania became the first colony in the British Empire to make education compulsory and in 1898 school attendance was made obligatory between the ages of seven and 13, expanding to between six and 14 years in 1912. In 1946 Tasmania became the only Australian state to make attendance up to the age of 16 compulsory. It has its own university, the University of Tasmania, as well as numerous colleges of advanced education and conservatorium of music. Tasmania's main employment sectors are retailing and manufacturing, however, employment is depressed and the outlook for young people is considered poor. Unemployment continues to rise in Tasmania and it currently has the highest unemployment rate of all states.

Immigration

Tasmania is becoming increasingly popular as a migration destination. The high standard of education, modern health facilities and cheap housing (the average price of a three-bedroom rental is A$350 per week) are all strong attractions. However, the cost of living can be slightly higher than in other states due to freight costs. Although some love the small-community feel of the state, others feel that the sense of isolation that almost inevitably affects new settlers is exacerbated by Tasmania's separation from mainland Australia.

Flora and fauna

Tasmania's geographical isolation has meant that the state has developed a unique flora and fauna. Tasmania has 10 species of mammal not found elsewhere, including the Tasmanian Devil (a carnivorous, nocturnal marsupial), the 'Tasmanian Tiger' (generally believed to be extinct although occasional sightings are claimed) 14 indigenous species of birds and two species of indigenous reptiles. The duck-billed platypus is more common in Tasmania than elsewhere and the Tasmanian mountain shrimp, which is only known outside Tasmania as a fossil, has remained obstinately unaltered and very much alive.

In terms of natural environment, Tasmania is breathtaking and perhaps feels a little more familiar to the European settler than the harsh, sandy, sun baked land of mainland Australia.

Useful resources

Tasmania Online: Portal website for the Government of Tasmania: www.tas.gov.au

Department of Economic Development: 03 6233 5888; info@development.tas.gov.au; www.dsd.tas.gov.au

Victoria (VIC)

Capital: Melbourne

Area: 136,560 square miles (227,600 sq km) = 0.93 times the size of the UK

Total area of Australia: 2.96%

Coastline: 1,080 miles (1,800km)

Climate: January 77°F (25.1°C); July 57°F (14°C), but the weather in Victoria, particularly in Melbourne, is notoriously unpredictable. Victoria's exposure to frequent cold fronts and southerly winds results in changeable weather patterns, is popularly known as the 'Four Seasons in One Day' phenomenon.

Victoria is situated in the south-eastern corner of Australia, bordered by South Australia to the west and New South Wales to the north. Even though Victoria is the smallest of all Australian States, it still offers a wide geographical diversity ranging from the Victorian Alps, which lie on the shared border with New South Wales, fertile wine-growing regions in the Murray and Yarra River Valleys, rainforest in the Gippsland region in the south-east corner of Victoria on the Errinundra Plateau and desert beauty in the north-west inland Mallee region. Victoria has the world's third largest volcanic plain, situated in the Western District. The Great Dividing Range, which forms a spine down the inland 'back' of Victoria and New South Wales, is known as the 'High Country'.

The land on which Melbourne was built was purchased in 1835 from Aborigines of the local Dutigalla clan. The Aborigines had no concept of land as a commodity at that time, and in exchange for their ancestral home they received articles of clothing, 50 pounds of flour, handkerchiefs, knives, tomahawks, looking glasses and blankets.

Great Ocean Road, Victoria

Capital: Melbourne

In 1990 the Population Crisis Committee, based in Washington DC, rated Melbourne the world's most liveable city in terms of safety, health and air quality. Melbourne's location on the coastal plain between the Pacific Ocean and the beautiful Dandenong hills provides a superb living environment and its cultural and sporting facilities are unequalled elsewhere in Australia.

Melbourne flourished during the great gold rush of the 1850s and as a consequence it became the Australian centre of business and commerce. Today, 16 of Australia's top 50 innovative companies have their headquarters in Melbourne. In the 1880s Melbourne was known as 'The Paris of the Antipodes' and it was the capital of Australia from 1901 (Federation) until 1927, when the capital was moved to Canberra (to avoid in-fighting between Melbourne and Sydney).

Melbourne is one of Australia's leading exporters of computers, engines and pharmaceuticals and it is the location of eight major medical research institutes, including the Walter and Eliza Hall Institute, the home of modern immunology and one of the world's best known medical research centres. Australia's main telecommunications research and development facilities are based in Melbourne and Victoria accounts for more than 30% of Australia's information and telecommunications technology turnover. Melbourne is a popular destination in the Asian region for conventions, meetings and exhibitions.

Federation Square, Melbourne

Population

The 3.4 million population of Melbourne is a cosmopolitan one and, with nearly 200 different nationalities represented, it is one of the most multicultural cities in the world. It has the world's third largest Greek community, behind Athens and Thessalonia.

Culture

Melbourne is widely considered to be the cultural capital of Australia, and it enjoys the facilities of a world-standard Arts Centre. The Australian Ballet Company is based in the city. Melbourne is also the home of the Australian

> **Expat Joanne had this to say about her adopted home, Melbourne:**
>
> 'Melbourne is a fairly quiet and clean city with relatively good transport links. It sprawls a long way, but you can live near the beach or in the hills and still be able to commute to the city by public transport for work. There are lots of cycle paths and parks. Trees line most streets so many suburbs are quite pleasant places to live. There are lots of cheap and free events and you don't need to earn a lot of money to have a good lifestyle. Housing is getting more expensive but currently my husband and I are managing to survive on one salary, rather than both of us having to work full-time.'

film industry and of much of Australian television output (including Neighbours). The city is Australia's premier shopping location, with an unlimited selection of designer shops and other stores. Melbourne also hosts the Melbourne Cup, the nation's richest horse race, the Australian Rules Football Grand Final, and the Australian Open at the impressive Koorong Tennis Centre. Melbourne also successfully played host to the Commonwealth Games in 2006.

See the section on best places to live in Melbourne on pages 113–131.

Useful resources

Victoria Online: www.vic.gov.au
Business Victoria: 132 215 (local) or 03 9651 9387 (International); email enquiries@iird.vic.gov.au; www.business.vic.gov.au
Department of Innovation, Industry and Regional Development: 03 9651 9999; www.dsrd.vic.gov.au

History

The driving force behind the founding of Melbourne was John Pascoe Fawkner, the son of a convict. A self-educated bush lawyer who also established several newspapers, Fawkner sat on the Legislative Council of Victoria for 15 years, where he was an energetic campaigner for the rights of small settlers and convicts, and instrumental in ending the transportation of convicts from Great Britain to Australia. His energy was drawn from his own personal experience of the harsh penal code – he received 500 lashes when he was 22 for assisting seven convicts to escape and he bore the scars for the rest of his life.

The population of Victoria (the most densely populated state in Australia) is currently around 5.3 million, and consists of immigrants from the UK and EU as well as the Middle East and South-East Asia. There are approximately 12,000 Aborigines in Victoria. All of these different ethnic groups give the state a real cultural diversity and have a positive influence on Victorian culture. Melbourne has a population of around 3.9 million, and other major regional centres include Geelong, Bendigo, Ballarat, Horsham, Mildura, Warrnambool, Castlemaine and Shepparton.

Victoria's economy has suffered in the past from industrial unrest and from poor economic government. In an attempt to boost the State's economy, the Victorian Government sponsors successful overseas entrepreneurs and senior executives intending to live permanently in Victoria through the Australian Government's State/Territory Nominated Independent Scheme Migration Category. Victoria is the site of research and development in the areas of food, paper, chemicals and petroleum, transport equipment, electrical equipment and biotechnology.

The standard of tertiary education in Victoria is particularly high. There are eight universities in the State, three of which specialise in technology, as well as numerous technical and further education institutions. The

Commonwealth Scientific and Industrial Research Organisation is based in Victoria.

New South Wales (NSW)

Capital: Sydney.

Area: 309,572 square miles (802,000 sq km) = 3.25 times the size of the UK.

Total area of Australia: 10%.

Climate: The mean January temperatures along the coast are usually between 46°F (8°C) and 69°F (21°C), but 71°F (22°C) at Sydney. The plateaux are about 39°F (4°C) cooler and the temperatures in the plains increase in direct relation to the distance from the sea. Temperatures at the Queensland border are about 80°F (27°C) to 87°F (31°C). The maximum temperature in July is 62°F (17°C) and the minimum is 46°F (8°C).

New South Wales is probably the Australian state most visited by tourists and business people, and is the state that receives most international publicity. This is largely due to its spectacular capital city, Sydney, which played host to the hugely successful Olympic Games in 2000. There is, however, so much more to New South Wales than Sydney, and it is well worth venturing beyond the city limits to explore its diverse regions. For details of the best suburbs to live in outer Sydney, see page 98.

Geography

New South Wales is bordered to the north by Queensland, to the east by South Australia and to the south by Victoria. The Australian Capital Territory

lies wholly contained in the south-east corner of New South Wales. From Sydney, it is 719 miles (1,157km) west to Broken Hill, almost on the South Australian border, 564 miles (908km) north to Tweed Heads which borders Queensland, and 309 miles (498km) south to Eden, the last sizeable town before Victoria. In these extremes lie mountain ranges, beaches, fertile farmland, rainforests and arid desert.

The Blue Mountains, 62 miles (100km) west of Sydney, is a national park containing some of the most breathtaking scenery in the world. Standing at one of the numerous lookouts it is possible to survey hundreds of miles of unbroken, uninhabited bush and to view the immense unusual rock formations at Echo Point known as 'The Three Sisters'. The area was home to Aboriginal people at least 14,000 years ago and they have left their mark in the numerous rock carvings and cave paintings. The rugged 617,762-acre (250,000 ha) park is composed mainly of sandstone, which has been eroded over the ages by rivers and creeks, to form dramatic valleys and sheer escarpments. The hundreds of Eucalyptus trees which line the valley floor, are responsible for naming this area the Blue Mountains, as when it is humid the eucalyptus oil evaporates and gives the area a blue haze.

Wine regions

Approximately 93 miles (150km) north of Sydney lies the main wine-producing region of New South Wales, Hunter Valley. The Valley is divided into two distinct regions, the Lower and the Upper Hunter areas. Cessnock, 113 miles (183km) from Sydney, is the centre of the Lower Hunter region and was originally founded on the coalmining industry. The area produces some of the state's best wines and famous wineries include McWilliams, Mount Pleasant, Lindemans, Hungerford Hill, Tyrrells and Brokenwood. One hundred kilometres further to the north-west is the smaller and less well-known Lower Hunter, home of the renowned Rosemount Estate. Muswellbrook is the centre of this region and is known for its coal and agriculture. See more about the wine growing regions on pages 183–187.

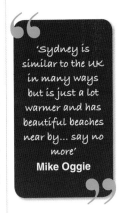

'Sydney is similar to the UK in many ways but is just a lot warmer and has beautiful beaches near by... say no more'

Mike Oggie

Snowy Mountains and ski season

To the south-east of the state lie the Snowy Mountains, less than a three-hour drive from Canberra in the ACT. Thredbo is a popular ski resort, which has hosted various World Cup Ski events, and it is possible to take a chair lift to the top of Crackenback and then hike up Australia's highest mountain, Mount Kosciuzsko which, at 7,328 feet (2,241 metres), is less than half the height of Mont Blanc in France. On the northern side of Mt. Kosciuzsko, in Perisher Valley, lie two of the most popular ski resorts, Perisher and Smiggins Holes. This is Australia's 'alpine country' that, surprisingly, contains more snow-covered area than Switzerland. Instead of pine trees and alpine scenes be prepared for ghostly eucalypts silhouetted against the snow. The Australian ski season runs from June to October and the snow is usually best between late July and mid-September. Mount Kosciuzsko is located at the heart of the Kosciusko National Park, which contains 1,554,290 acres (629,000 ha) of rugged moorland, glacial lakes, caves and the source of the Murray River, Australia's largest waterway. There are more than 200 species of birds here, and an abundance of wildlife including kangaroos, possums and wombats. The Snowy Mountains support seven hydroelectric stations, which supply a large proportion of the state's power grid.

Murray River and crops

The Murray River rises in the Great Dividing Range and flows for more than 1,553 miles (2,500km), forming the border between Victoria and New South Wales. From Wentworth, in the far west of New South Wales, the Murray continues through South Australia and veers south, flowing into Lake Alexandrina and to the ocean. The river is used extensively for irrigation and is crucial to the region's agricultural industries. One of the state's most important agricultural districts is the Riverina, which lies along the northern borderlands of the Murray River. Crops as diverse as rice, vegetables and citrus fruits are grown here, and cattle and merino sheep are also important. Albury is at the heart of this fertile region and its population is approximately 44,000. It is a National Growth Centre, the aim of which has been to encourage the decentralisation of industry from major state capitals. Wentworth is important as the heart of the region's irrigation scheme and both the citrus and avocado growing areas.

Broken Hill and mining

Broken Hill is one of the state's most easterly settlements, lying almost on the border with South Australia. It is isolated and remote, but nearly 28,000 people live here and it is famous for its silver mines and the Royal Flying Doctor Services. The mining industry has survived, and silver, lead and zinc are still mined in significant quantities. In the northern desert region of the state, along the border with Queensland, lies the town of Lightning Ridge, famous for its opal mines. Over 1,200 people from 30 different nations are based at Lightning Ridge, and manage to survive the extreme weather conditions and limited water supply (artesian bore water is the only kind available here) to mine the fields for the highly prized black opals. Visitors are allowed to tour various mines and to fossick (prospect) for the gems.

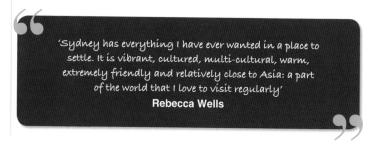

'Sydney has everything I have ever wanted in a place to settle. It is vibrant, cultured, multi-cultural, warm, extremely friendly and relatively close to Asia: a part of the world that I love to visit regularly'

Rebecca Wells

North Coast Beach Region/Byron Bay/Coffs Harbour

New South Wales' north coastal region is one of the state's favourite holiday destinations, and the region contains spectacular surf beaches, lakes, rivers, small coastal towns and beautiful inland scenery. Byron Bay, Australia's most easterly point, is considered to be the unspoilt gem of the New South Wales coast. Cape Byron is home to many people who prefer an alternative lifestyle away from the rat race of the busy cities and is a haven for surfers. Coffs Harbour, closer to Sydney, is a popular harbour and port town, with many top-class tourist resorts. There is plenty of good surf, and it is also a famous yachting centre and is also home to the iconic 'Big Banana'. Bananas are grown in this semi-tropical area and the nearby Dorrigo National Park contains rainforest, waterfalls and lush vegetation. Inland from Coffs is the Nymboida River, a popular spot for white-water rafting. Grafton is situated in this area, some 40 miles (65km) inland, and is at the centre of a region that specialises in both dairy and sugarcane industries.

Lord Howe Island and Norfolk Island

New South Wales also controls Lord Howe Island and originally owned Norfolk Island, although this is now a Territory of Australia. Lord Howe Island is a tiny island, 6 miles (11km) long and 1.7 miles (2.8km) at its widest point, some 435 miles (700km) north-east of Sydney. It has a population of around 400 and was listed as a World Heritage area in 1982 because of its soaring volcanic peaks, the world's most southerly coral reef, exceptional bird life and scenic beauty. Lord Howe Island was first sighted in 1788 and was named after the first Lord of the Admiralty. The numbers of visitors to the island is strictly controlled to protect it from becoming overrun by crowds, and the island's 23 miles (37km) coastline provides plenty of opportunity for fishing, coral reef viewing and relaxation. Norfolk Island is a much larger and more isolated island, 994 miles (1,600km) to the east of Sydney. It was first discovered by Captain Cook in 1774 and later became a penal settlement for the colony of New South Wales between 1788 and 1855. Norfolk Island was the home of the Pitcairn Islanders who included descendants of the Bounty mutineers. There are still many Pitcairn descendants on the island who speak 'Norfolk', a curious mixture of Tahitian and English. The island has a population of about 2,300, most of whom are involved in either tourism or agriculture.

Capital: Sydney

Sydney has a population of nearly 4.3 million people, around 63% of the state's total population of 6.9 million. The second largest city in New South Wales is Newcastle, on the northern coast 105 miles (170km) from Sydney, with a population of 360,000, and Wollongong, some 51 miles (82km) south of Sydney, is the third urban area. The city of Sydney is open and spacious, surrounded on three sides by national parks and on the fourth by 37 miles (60km) of beautiful and quite spectacular coastline. Sydney Harbour, on which the city is built, has 149 miles (240km) of foreshore, much of which remains as it was when the First Fleet made its initial investigative journey up the waterway in 1788. Sydney has been described as 'the best address on earth', and although Sydney has its share of the problems associated with big cities, such as pollution, ugly industrial areas, traffic congestion, homelessness, unemployment, drugs and crime, one still cannot help but feel that Sydney is perhaps even more beautiful now than it was over 100 years ago. The Sydney Harbour Bridge and the Opera House, which are the most dramatic features of the Harbour, were opened in 1932 and 1973 respectively.

The total financial cost of building the Harbour Bridge was £10,057,170.7s.9d (double the original quote). This was not paid off in full until 1988 and there is still a toll in place for crossing it. The bridge links East Sydney to the Northern suburbs. Over 800 homes were demolished in the preparation for construction. The toll is currently A$3.00.

History

Sydney is one of Australia's most historical cities, as it was into Botany Bay, just south of Sydney that Captain Cook sailed in the Endeavour in 1770. In May 1787, the First Fleet of 1,044 people, including 759 convicts (191 of whom were women) set sail from Portsmouth and arrived in Australia eight months later. Unimpressed with Botany Bay's windswept barrenness, the Fleet moved north in search of a more suitable site and six days later the ships arrived at what became Port Jackson, described by Captain Phillip as 'the finest harbour in the world'. Even though Port Jackson was superior to Botany Bay, the first years of the colony were harsh, as crops failed and the anticipated supply ships failed to arrive. However, the colony managed to survive and slowly, began to grow. Captain Phillip was replaced by Governor Macquarie, known as the 'Father of Australia' (his name graces many street signs and buildings), in 1810, and over the next 11 years streets were laid down and fine new buildings erected. Convict transportation to New South Wales continued until 1840, but free settlers began to arrive from 1819. From 1831 to 1850 more than 200,000 government-assisted migrants streamed into the colony to begin a new life as far away as possible from the urban nightmare of Victorian Britain. During the 1850s, a gold rush brought a new influx of settlers, which continued until the end of the 19th century, and by 1925 the area around Sydney had a population in excess of one million.

Attractions

Sydney today boasts Australia's most influential Central Business District (CBD) and most national and international businesses choose to have their

FACT

■ The total financial cost of building the Harbour Bridge was £10,057,170.7s.9d (double the original quote). This was not paid off in full until 1988 and there is still a toll in place for crossing it. The bridge links East Sydney to the Northern suburbs. Over 800 homes were demolished in the preparation for construction. The toll is currently A$3.00.

major Australian offices in Sydney. Darling Harbour houses the Sydney Aquarium, Chinese Gardens, Powerhouse Museum and the National Maritime Museum, and is linked to the CBD by monorail. The Rocks is Sydney's most historic area, and much of it has been restored to its former glory. Doyle's Restaurant at the foot of the Rocks is a haven for the seafood connoisseur, with fresh fish a house speciality. There are many beaches around the Sydney area, the most famous being Bondi and Manly However, the most beautiful, unspoilt and uncrowded beaches lie further north and south of the city. The northern coastal suburbs are particularly beautiful as the coastline is made up of rugged headlands interspersed with long sandy beaches. Most beaches have seawater swimming pools naturally carved out of the rocky headland, which provide safe, sheltered swimming areas. The beaches of Dee Why, Long Reef, Collaroy, Narrabeen, Newport, Avalon, Whale Beach and Palm Beach are among the most beautiful Sydney beaches. See our section on the best beaches on pages 396–398.

Culture

Sydney is a cultural centre and is home to the Australian Opera and the Sydney Symphony Orchestra, both based at the Opera House. Standing tickets for the opera can be bought for as little as A$35, and many agents sell last-minute tickets at half price. Sydney is also home to the Museum of Contemporary Art and the Sydney Observatory. The city's Gay and Lesbian Mardi Gras (in early February) is an international crowd-puller, as the country's gay, bisexual and transvestite population take to the streets in bizarre and outlandish costumes. The Queen Victoria Building houses many chic boutiques and plenty of bargain shops, but better bargains can be found at Paddy's Markets in Paddington.

In 1988 a re-enactment of the First Fleet entering Sydney Harbour was staged as part of the bicentennial celebrations and the view included a bank-to-bank flotilla of small pleasure boats, the old 'Coathanger' and Centrepoint Tower in the background, in front of which stood the Sydney Opera House, the sun gleaming off the millions of highly polished white tiles that make up its shell. Mark Twain described the harbour as 'the darling of Sydney and the wonder of the world.' There is no doubt that Sydney Harbour is stunning and the city is an exciting place in which to live. Some Australians do, however, tire of the bright lights and relatively fast pace and prefer to move to quieter, calmer and perhaps safer cities.

Real estate and employment

Sydney is one of the most expensive areas in Australia in which to live, but many of the outer suburbs and regional areas are less expensive. Rent in Sydney is very high by Australian standards, but is still markedly lower than current rental rates in London or New York for comparable properties. See our section on this in Setting up home. The state's unemployment rate is

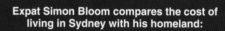

> **Expat Simon Bloom compares the cost of living in Sydney with his homeland:**
>
> 'I can only compare Sydney to London so it's a fair bit cheaper. People from Brisbane and Melbourne think Sydney costs are high, but again it's all down to what you're used to. I think Perth is now up there for living costs. Ultimately coming from England, it'll seem cheap.'

the lowest in Australia. Major employment sectors in the city are commerce (banking, insurance and finance), retail, manufacturing, hospitality and tourism. Agriculture and tourism are the biggest employment sectors in regional areas.

Education and health services are exceptionally good in New South Wales, which is home to many large and excellent tertiary educational institutions. New South Wales attracts more new settlers than any other state/territory.

Useful resources

New South Wales Government: www.nsw.gov.au.

Department of State and Regional Development: 02 9228 3111; www.business.nsw.gov.au

New South Wales Government Trade and Investment Office: The Australia Centre; 020 7887 5871; invest@nswq.co.uk

Australian Capital Territory (ACT)

Capital: Canberra

Area: 1,440 square miles (2,400 sq km) = 0.01 times the size of the UK

Total area of Australia: 0.0003%

Coastline: 0 (except 21 miles/35km in Jervis Bay Territory)

Climate: January 82°F (28°C); July 51°C (11°C)

Canberra was established in 1901 (at Federation) to provide a 'neutral' headquarters for the new seat of government. Sydney had threatened to refuse to join the Federation unless the capital was in New South Wales; Melbourne, for its part, considered it had the greater claim. As a compromise, the Australian Capital Territory was established mid-way between the two states in a move which was, as it was said, 'acceptable to everyone, but satisfactory to nobody'. The American architect, Walter Burley Griffin, won the international competition to design the new capital city, resulting in a completely planned city where even the sites of trees have been carefully selected. The effect can appear sterile, and this sterility is reinforced by the fact that 60% of Canberra's residents are civil servants. The weekend sees an evacuation of politicians back to their state of origin, giving Canberra the reputation for city without a soul. During the week, however, Capitol Hill, through which the artificial Lake Burley Griffin cuts, is the hub of the nation's political activity.

Canberra is a derivative of an Aboriginal word kambera, which means 'meeting place'. The city is home to the Australian National University, the Australian Institute of Sport, the Australian National Gallery and the Australian War Memorial and Museum. Canberra does not have a commercial centre and its big shopping centres are all located in suburban areas. Instead, the city has many parks and recreational areas, and traffic congestion is virtually unknown.

Canberra, with a population of 350,800, is an attractive city, although it is much derided by most Australians who find its planned and highly ordered environment less than easy to appreciate. Nonetheless, it has a friendly atmosphere, and is not inferior to other Australian cities, merely different.

One irregularity to Canberra's stiff image is the fact, that it is the only state of Australia to have a legalised porn industry. There are numerous warehouses, which stock upper shelf DVD titles and other unmentionables. Well, they have to amuse the politicians somehow!

Average price for a three-bedroom house in Canberra is A$400–A$500 per week.

Australian Capital Territory: www.act.gov.au.
Business ACT, Nara Centre: 1800 244 650;
www.business.gateway.act.gov.au.

Queensland (QLD)

Capital: Brisbane.

Area: 1,035,000 square miles (1,725,000 sq km) = seven times the size of the UK.

Total area of Australia: 22.48%.

Coastline: 4,440 miles (7,400km).

Climate: In Brisbane, the average daily maximum in January is 84°F (29°C) and in June is 69°F (21°C). In Cairns, the average daily maximums for the same months are 87°F (31°C) and 78°F (26°C).

Queensland is Australia's second largest state, but has the largest habitable area defined by rainfall. Queensland's habitable area is a staggering 599,999 square miles (1,554,000 sq km). By contrast, a mere 57% of Western Australia is considered habitable (555,984 square miles/1,440,000 sq km). Queensland is situated in the north-eastern corner of Australia and it is bounded by the Northern Territory to the west, South Australia to the south-west and New South Wales to the south. It stretches from the temperate and densely populated south-east to the tropical and sparsely populated Cape York Peninsula in the north.

Queensland epitomises the marketed image of Australia overseas. Queensland Tourism's catch tag says it all- 'Queensland beautiful one day, perfect the next'. With the Great Barrier Reef, the Whitsunday Islands, World Heritage areas such as the Daintree Rainforest and Fraser Island, and a beautiful climate, it is not surprising that Queensland is one of the most popular tourist destinations in Australia. Queensland is known as the 'Sunshine State' and Queenslanders are affectionately called 'banana-benders'. They are also considered to be the rednecks of Australia, and as such are renowned for their very conservative political outlook.

Like most of Australia, Queensland is rich in natural resources. Its four major products are sugar, meat, grains and wool, and the growing areas are spread throughout the state. Australia is the world's second largest exporter of raw cane sugar, and 95% of Australia's production comes from Queensland. The State also contains vast mineral deposits, including coal, bauxite, gold, copper, lead, zinc, silver and magnesite. Besides agricultural and mining industries, Queensland's biggest industries are manufacturing and tourism. Queensland's economic growth is significantly higher than the national average, and tourism accounts for 10% of Gross State Product.

Population

For more than 20 years, Queensland has experienced a consistently higher rate of population growth than the national average. Queensland's population growth can be attributed to overseas immigration, natural increase, and most importantly, to interstate migration. Queensland, it seems, is the place where most Australians want to live, and more Australians are moving to Queensland than to any other state or territory. In 2007 102,200 moved to Queensland from other Australian states and territories (that's almost 2000 people per week). Popular opinion has it that more and more Australians are moving to Queensland to retire. Census figures from the Australian Bureau of Statistics show that 31% of Queensland's population lies in the 25–44 year age range, however, it is predicted that by 2021 at least 43% of the population will be over 45.

In 2007, movement from Queensland to other states and territories was 75,200 (just over 1400 people per week). This resulted in a net gain for Queensland of 27,000 people from other states and territories. (Source: www.smartcompany.com.au)

Queensland's population is much more decentralised than that of any other state. The population of around 4.3 million is scattered over major regional centres such as the Gold Coast, Bundaberg, Toowoomba, Rockhampton, Longreach, Townsville, Cairns and Mount Isa, as well as Brisbane, which is home to 1.9 million people.

FACT

In 2007, movement from Queensland to other states and territories was 75,200 (just over 1400 people per week). This resulted in a net gain for Queensland of 27,000 people from other states and territories. (Source: www.smartcompany.com.au)

Government

The Queensland Government has for many years had a reputation for ultra-conservativism. For most of those years the state was under the leadership of the Premier, Sir Joh Bjelke-Peterson, and became notorious for its repressive and racist attitudes. Vestiges of this xenophobia remain, and Queensland is the seedbed of the racist One Nation Party, until recently led by Pauline Hanson. Antipathy is particularly directed towards the Japanese who have invested large sums in Queensland property, however, most Queenslanders recognise that Japanese investments play a significant part in promoting Queensland's healthy economy. The Queensland Government has suffered from allegations of corruption at the highest levels. When the Labour Party was elected in September 1992, its leader, the Hon. W K Goss, became the first Labour Premier in Queensland since 1957. The new government represented the desire of Queenslanders to end the corruption and hypocritical moralising of the old government, and stood for a fresh start.

Health and education

Queensland's health and education services are broadly comparable with the national standard. Brisbane is home to the University of Queensland and to Australia's first private university, Bond University, established by entrepreneur Alan Bond. The multimillionaire Western Australian, after whom it is named, served a three-year prison sentence for illegal business ventures and was released in March 2000; however, the university that bears his name is nonetheless regarded as a centre of excellence.

Real estate

Most Queensland residents own their own home, and the high standard of living combined with an extraordinary natural environment makes Queensland a popular choice for settlement. Rental prices vary (Brisbane is more expensive than the outer suburbs) from A 450–1000 per week for a three-bedroom house

Useful resources

Queensland Government: www.qld.gov.au
State Development and Innovation: 07 3225 1915; www.sd.qld.gov.au
Queensland Government Trade and Investment Office (Europe),
Queensland House: 020 7836 1333.

Appendices

◼ RECOMMENDED READING

- ◼ *The Oxford Companion to Australian History* by Graeme Davison, John Hirst and Stuart Macintyre. (Oxford University Press, 2001)
- ◼ This mammoth book is full of alphabetically organised articles that include: Australian people (such as Olympic athletes, opera singers, comedians, politicians) Aboriginal topics (history, Dreamtime, languages, art), important events (such as the Castle hill rising), cities, religious bodies and movements.
- ◼ *The History of Australia* by Frank G Clarke (Greenwood Press, 2002).
- ◼ Includes chapters on the timeline of historical events, the nuts and bolts of modern Australia, Aboriginal Australia, European arrivals and colonisation, the history of the sheep wool industry and the Gold Rush era.

 Read an excerpt: www.questia.com

The Use and Abuse of Australian History by Graeme Davison. (Allen & Unwin, 2000).

This collection of engaging and vigorous essays which examine what makes the 'history business' tick. Davison demonstrates that Australia's history can be relevant to the issues Australians confront everyday at the governmental level, at work and in communities.

100 Years: The Australian Story by Paul Kelly (Allen & Unwin, 2001).

Based on a TV series presented by one of Australia's most respected political and economic commentators, this is an exploration of 'who we are as a nation, where we have come from and where we are going'.

Down Under by Bill Bryson. (Black Swan, 2001).

Bill Bryson, who in the past has written amusing anecdotes about his beloved USA and his adopted country of Britain, decides to write an account of a land that is unfamiliar to him - Australia. This book is hugely entertaining, yet incredibly informative and some say the best example of his work. It includes an energetic and amusing account of the history of Oz, its people and unique wildlife. If you would prefer to read an amusing summary of Australian history, rather than a simple factual history guide, then this is the perfect choice!

30 days in Sydney: the Writer and the City by Peter Carey (Bloomsbury, 2008)

After living in New York for 10 years, successful Australian novelist, Peter Carey returned home to Sydney with the idea of capturing its character via the four elements of Earth, Fire, Air and Water. An amusing short read which transports the reader into the very life and soul of Sydney.

True History of the Kelly Gang by Peter Carey (Faber and Faber, 2004).

'Through Kelly's keen eyes, we see the rural landscapes of 19th-century Australia: the stunted white-trunked gum trees, the mustard-coloured puddles, the ramshackle homesteads with swaybacked roofs. But it is the moral aspect that is most apparent. In this "colony made specifically to have poor men bow down to their gaolers", injustice suffocating darkens the atmosphere. "They were Australians," Kelly observes, "they knew full well the terror of the unyielding law the historic memory of unfairness were in their blood." *True History of the Kelly Gang* is a handsome act of reparation to a figure that Carey sees as an outstanding victim of that great unfairness.' (Review by Peter Kemp, *The Sunday Times*)

The Songlines by Bruce Chatwin. (Viking, 2001).

A travel book which adds a sincere attempt to explain the plight of the Australian indigenous population. A beautiful read.

Thumbs Up Australia: Hitchhiking the Outback by Tom Parry. (Nicholas Brealey, 2006)

This book tells of a spiritual, historical and physical journey across the harsh Australian terrain. Parry manages to document both his own personal, spiritual quest as well as highlighting the best bits of the outback (with its colourful/slightly mad inhabitants).

The Dig Tree: The Extraordinary Story of the Ill-fated Burke and Wills 1860 Expedition by Sarah Murgatroyd. (Bloomsbury, 2003).

The title says it all, a factual yet entertaining story of Australia's iconic explorers.

A Traveller's History of Australia by John H Chambers. (Interlink, 2001)

An informative read on Australia's chequered history before and after European settlement.

Ten Pound Poms: Australia's Invisible Migrants by A James Hammerton and Alistair Thomson. (Manchester University Press, 2005).

More than a million Britons emigrated to Australia between the 1940s and 1970s. They were the famous 'Ten Pound Poms' and this is their story.

◣ USEFUL WEBSITES

Expat forum
www.expatforum.com/expats/australia-expat-forum-expats-living-australia/2628-please-read-helpful-websites-your-move-australia.html

Immigration
Immigration is managed by the Department of Immigration and Citizenship.

Application forms online and for more detailed information on individual visas: www.immi.gov.au

Details on business and independent visas: www.visabureau.com

Help and advice on obtaining Australian visas:
www.emigrationgroup.co.uk

Studying
Details on bridging courses and studying in Australia:
www.goingtouni.gov.au www.dest.gov.au/noosr

Temporary jobs
Australian job network: https://jobsearch.gov.au

Private health insurance
Government private health insurance database and information site:
www.privatehealth.gov.au
Private health funds: www.phiac.gov.au/healthfunds/reglist.htm

Time zones for Australia
http://wwp.au-australia.com/time-zones

Sending money internationally
Western Union: www.westernunion.com

Cheap flights
www.expedia.com
www.lastminute.com

■ METRIC CONVERSIONS

Australia fully adopted the metric system in the late 1970s and imperial measurements were dropped completely. Consumers were never given conversions on packaging, for example 1lb/454g, or alternative Fahrenheit and Celsius weather reports, so people learned new ways very quickly. If you ask for a pound of mince at the butcher you will not be understood. All street signs and road maps note distances in kilometres, as do speedometers. Weights are calculated in grams and kilograms, and temperatures are given in degrees Celsius.

Distances and measurements are invariably expressed as a decimal rather than as a fraction. If you have children at school, they will be expected to be conversant with the metric system and no instruction will be given in calculating imperial measurement. The modern Australian child is unlikely to have any idea how many inches there are in a foot, ounces in a pound or yards in a mile; in fact, this probably applies to anyone under 40.

■ EMBASSIES

Australian embassies, high commissions and consulates outside Australia
Wellington, New Zealand: Australian High Commission, 72–76 Hobson Street, Thorndon, Wellington +64 (0) 4 473 6411; www.newzealand.embassy.gov.au

London: Australian High Commission, Australia House, The Strand, London WC2B 4LA; 020 7379 4334; Recorded information line (24 hours) 09001 600 333; www.australia.org.uk. Open: 9:00am–5:00pm Monday to Friday (Office hours); 9:00am–11:00am Monday to Friday (Migration/ Visas); telephone service hours 2pm–4pm Monday to Friday.

Edinburgh: Australian Honorary Consul, 69 George Street, Edinburgh EH2 2JG; 0131 624 3333

Manchester: Australian Consulate, First Floor, Century House, 11 St Peter's Square, Manchester M2 3DN; 0161 237-9440; www.australia.org.uk. Passport interviews only. Open: 1:00pm–3:00pm Monday to Friday.

Dublin: Australian Embassy Ireland, 7th Floor, Fitzwilton House, Wilton Terrace, Dublin 2, Ireland; 01 664 5800; www.australianembassy.ie. Open: 8:30am–4:30pm Monday to Friday. There is no visa office at the Embassy. Visa services for those living in Ireland can be obtained from the Australian High Commission in London only.

France: Australian Embassy, 4 Rue Jean Rey, Paris 75015; (33 +1) 4059 3301; www.france.embassy.gov.au. Open: 9.00am–5.00pm Monday to Friday, except public holidays

USA: Australian Embassy, 1601 Massachusetts Avenue, NW, Washington DC 2006; 202 797 3000; www.austemb.org. General office hours: 8:30am–5:00pm Monday to Friday; Visa office hours: 9:00am–11:00am Monday to Friday.

Canada: Australian High Commission, Suite 710, 50 O'Connor Street, Ottawa, ON K1P 6L2; 613 236 0841; www.canada.embassy.gov.au. General office hours: 8:30 am–5:00 pm Mon–Thur and 8:30 am–4:30 pm Friday, except public holidays. Visa and immigration office hours: 10:00 am–12 noon Monday to Friday except public holidays.

South Africa: Australian High Commission, 292 Orient Street, Arcadia, Pretoria; +27 12 423 6000 (Admin and Consular); www.southafrica.embassy.gov.au. Open 8:00am–4.10 pm Monday to Friday, except public holidays.

Embassies in Australia

British High Commission: Commonwealth Avenue, Yarralumla ACT 2606 02 6270 6666; information.section@uk.emb.gov.au; www.uk.emb.gov.au

Canadian High Commission: Commonwealth Ave, Canberra ACT 2600; 02 6270 4000; enqserv@dfait-maeci.gc.ca; www.dfait-maeci.gc.ca/australia

New Zealand High Commission: Level 10, 55 Hunter Street, Sydney NSW 2000; 02 8256 2000; Passport office 02 9225 2300; nzcgsydney@bigpond.com

Embassy of Ireland: 20 Arkana Street, Yarralumla, Canberra ACT 2600; 06 273 3022

Embassy of France: 6 Perth Ave, Yarralumla ACT 2600; 02 6216 0100; embassy@france.net.au; www.france.net.au

Royal Danish Consulate General: Gold Fields House,1 Alfred St, Circular Quay, Sydney NSW 2000; 02 9247 2224; dkconsul@dkconsul-sydney.org.au; www.dkconsul-sydney.org.au

Embassy of Italy: 12 Grey Street, Deakin ACT 2600; 02 6273 3333; ambital2@dynamite.com.au; www.netinfo.com.au/italembassy

Embassy of Austria: 12 Talbot Street, Forrest ACT 2603; 61 2 6295 1533; austria@dynamite.com.au; www.austriaemb.org.au

South African High Commission: Cnr Rhodes Place and State Circle, Yarralumla ACT 2600; 02 6273 2424; info@rsa.emb.gov.au; www.rsa.emb.gov.au

US Embassy: Moonah Place, Yarralumla ACT 2600; 02 6214 5600; usfcs@australia.net.au; www.usis-australia.gov/embassy.html

■ AUSTRALIAN NATIONAL CLASSIFICATION OF OCCUPATIONS (ASCO)

Managers and Administrators	code
Child Care Coordinator	1295-11

Professionals	code
Accountant	2211-11
Anaesthetist	2312-11
Architect	2121-11
Chemical Engineer	2129-17
Civil Engineer	2124-11
Computing Professional*	2231-79
Dental Specialist	2381-13
Dentist	2381-11
Dermatologist	2312-13
Electrical Engineer	2125-11
Emergency Medicine Specialist	2312-15
External Auditor	2212-11
General Medical Practitioner	2311-11
Hospital Pharmacist	2382-11
Mechanical Engineer	2126-11
Medical Diagnostic Radiographer	2391-11
Mining Engineer (excluding Petroleum)	2127-11
Obstetrician and Gynaecologist	2312-17

Occupational Therapist	2383–11
Ophthalmologist	2312–19
Paediatrician	2312–21
Pathologist	2312–23
Petroleum Engineer	2127–13
Physiotherapist	2385–11
Podiatrist	2388–11
Psychiatrist	2312–27
Quantity Surveyor	2122–11
Radiologist	2312–29
Registered Mental Health Nurse	2325–11
Registered Midwife	2324–11
Registered Nurse	2323–11
Retail Pharmacist	2382–15
Specialist Medical Practitioners (not elsewhere classified)	2312–79
Specialist Physician	2312–25
Speech Pathologist	2386–11
Sonographer	2391–17
Surgeon	2312–31
Surveyor	2123–13
Associate Professionals	**code**
Chef (excluding Commis Chef)	3322–11 (part)
Aircraft Maintenance Engineer (Avionics)	4114–15
Aircraft Maintenance Engineer (Mechanical)	4114–11
Automotive Electrician	4212–11
Baker	4512–11
Boat Builder and Repairer	4981–13
Bricklayer	4414–11
Cabinetmaker	4922–11
Carpenter	4411–13
Carpenter and Joiner	4411–11
Cook	4513–11
Drainer	4431–15
Electrical Powerline Tradesperson	4313–11
Electrician (Special Class)	4311–13

Continued

Electronic Equipment Tradesperson	4315–11
Fibrous Plasterer	4412–11
Fitter	4112–11
Floor Finisher	4423–11
Furniture Finisher	4929–13
Furniture Upholsterer	4942–11
Gasfitter	4431–13
General Electrician	4311–11
General Plumber	4431–11
Hairdresser	4931–11
Joiner	4411–15
Lift Mechanic	4311–15
Locksmith	4115–15
Mechanical Services and Air-conditioning Plumber	4431–19
Metal Fabricator (Boilermaker)	4122–11
Metal Machinist (First Class)	4112–13
Motor Mechanic	4211–11
Optical Mechanic	4999–11
Painter and Decorator	4421–11
Panel Beater	4213-11
Pastry Cook	4512–13
Pressure Welder	4122–13
Refrigeration and Air-conditioning Mechanic	4312–11
Roof Plumber	4431–17
Roof Slater and Tiler	4413–11
Solid Plasterer	4415–11
Sheetmetal Worker (First Class)	4124–11
Stonemason	4416–13
Toolmaker	4113–11
Vehicle Body Maker	4215–11
Vehicle Painter	4214–11
Wall and Floor Tiler	4416–11
Welder (First Class)	4122–15

*specialising; in CISSP, C++/C#/C, Java, J2EE, Network Security/Firewall/ Internet security, Oracle, Peoplesoft, SAP, SIEBEL (esp. Siebel Analytic), Sybase SQL Server

TECHNICAL AND FURTHER EDUCATION (TAFE) COURSES

Arts and media	Code
Advanced Photography Skills and Techniques	23491
Digital Photography Introduction	26022
Digital Video Production Introduction	26019
Drawing Skills and Techniques	23484
Figurative Clay Sculptures – Summer School	26866
Interior Design	26148
Jewellery Fabrication	26403
Life Drawing Introduction	26049
Painting Skills and Techniques	23486
Photoshop – Introduction	23506
Printmaking Skills and Techniques	23492
Using Advanced Photoshop and Illustrator Basics	24363
Web Page Design	26188

Business and computing	Code
Advanced Legal Terminology	26365
Advanced Medical Terminology	26359
Assessment in VET	17078
Basic Legal Terminology	26366
Build Your Own Computer	26409
CCNA Sem 1 Cisco Networking Academia Program	24528
Computer Care	26415
Computer Crash Course – Women Starters Only	26416
Excel Skills	26354
Linux – an Introduction	24527
Network Cabling	26418
Property (Real Estate Agent's Licence) – Statement of Attainment	17335

Health and community services	Code
Child Protection – TAFE PLUS Statement	21255
Enrolled Nurse Conversion (Medication Administration) – Certificate Level IV (NRT)	716
Marine First Aid (Stcw95)	22154
Medication Administration for Enrolled Nurses – Statement of Attainment	3271
Spray Tanning/Airbrushing for Beauty Services	26828

Industry and natural resources	Code
Airbrushing Skills 1	22181
Asbestos Removal (Friable Asbestos)	8036
Authorised Contractors Scheme Core Modules	21250
Building on Your Foundations – CPD (Program for Licensed Contractors)	6499
Chainsaw Operations (Level 1) – Statement of Attainment	17230
Demolition Supervision (Restricted) – Course	6454
Owner-Builder Information – Course	9052
Project Management – Diploma (NRT)	8557
Restricted Electrical Work – Disconnect/ Reconnect – Statement of Attainment	433
RTA Examiner – Light Vehicle – Course	9022
Surfboard Making Skills	21549

Tourism and hospitality	Code
Bar Skills, Cocktail Mixology & Espresso Art	24705
Canteen Operations – School – Statement of Attainment	9551
Food Safety Workshop	22293
Gaming Skills – Statement of Attainment	9523
Hotel Licenses – Statement of Attainment	6649
Introduction to Barista	24760
Responsible Conduct of Gambling – Statement of Attainment	4515

Weather chart

Average temperature (°C), rainfall (mm), sunshine in hours per day

	Jan	Feb	Mar	Apr	May	Jun	Jul	Aug	Sep	Oct	Nov	Dec
Adelaide												
Max	29	29	26	22	19	16	15	16	19	22	25	27
Min	17	17	15	12	10	8	7	8	9	11	14	15
Rainfall	21	11	25	38	58	79	82	69	62	43	29	29
Rainy days	4	4	6	8	12	15	17	17	14	10	8	7
Sunshine	10	10	9	7	5	4	5	6	7	8	9	9
Brisbane												
Max	29	29	28	26	23	21	21	22	24	26	27	29
Min	21	21	20	17	14	11	9	10	12	16	18	20
Rainfall	160	173	140	89	98	70	62	41	33	93	96	126
Rainy days	13	14	14	11	10	7	7	6	7	10	10	11
Sunshine	8	8	8	7	6	7	8	8	9	9	9	9

	Jan	Feb	Mar	Apr	May	Jun	Jul	Aug	Sep	Oct	Nov	Dec
Canberra												
Max	28	27	24	20	15	12	11	13	16	29	22	26
Min	13	13	11	7	3	1	0	1	3	6	9	11
Rainfall	62	55	53	50	49	39	42	46	51	66	64	53
Rainy days	8	7	7	8	8	9	10	11	10	11	10	8
Sunshine	9	9	8	7	6	5	6	7	7	9	9	9
Darwin												
Max	32	31	32	33	32	31	30	31	32	33	33	33
Min	25	25	24	24	20	19	21	23	25	25	25	25
Rainfall	431	344	316	98	22	1	1	6	16	72	141	234
Rainy days	21	20	19	9	2	1	0	1	2	6	12	16
Sunshine	6	6	7	9	10	10	10	10	10	9	8	7
Hobart												
Max	22	22	21	18	15	13	12	13	15	17	19	20
Min	12	12	11	9	6	4	4	5	6	7	9	11
Rainfall	42	36	37	46	37	29	47	49	41	49	45	58
Rainy days	9	8	10	11	12	11	14	14	14	14	14	12
Sunshine	8	8	7	6	5	4	5	5	6	7	7	8

	Jan	Feb	Mar	Apr	May	Jun	Jul	Aug	Sep	Oct	Nov	Dec
Melbourne												
Max	26	26	24	20	17	14	13	15	17	19	22	24
Min	14	14	13	11	9	7	6	7	8	9	11	13
Rainfall	49	47	52	58	57	50	48	51	59	68	60	60
Rainy days	8	7	9	12	14	14	15	16	15	14	12	11
Sunshine	9	8	7	6	4	4	4	5	6	7	7	8
Perth												
Max	32	32	29	25	21	19	18	18	20	22	25	29
Min	17	17	16	13	10	9	8	8	9	10	13	15
Rainfall	7	16	15	42	106	174	163	118	70	47	27	12
Rainy days	2	3	4	8	13	17	18	16	13	10	7	4
Sunshine	12	11	9	8	7	6	6	7	8	9	10	12
Sydney												
Max	26	26	25	22	19	17	16	18	20	22	24	25
Min	19	19	17	15	11	9	8	9	11	13	16	17
Rainfall	7	16	15	42	106	174	163	118	70	47	27	12
Rainy days	2	3	4	8	13	17	18	16	13	10	7	4
Sunshine	12	11	9	8	7	6	6	7	8	9	10	12

■ INDEX

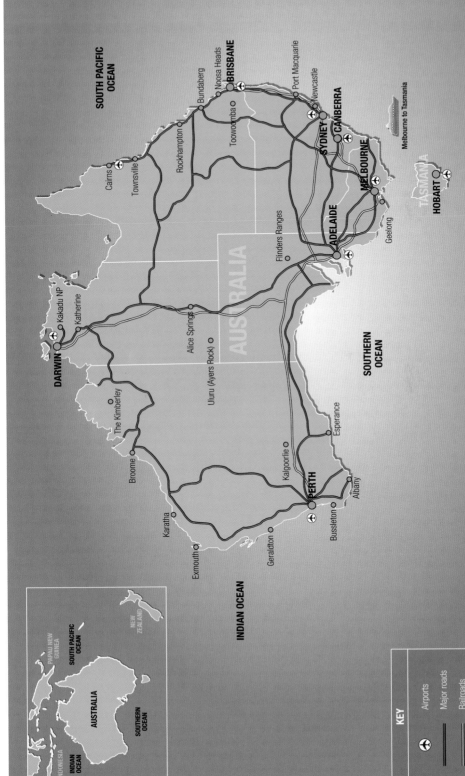

TRANSPORT**OF**AUSTRALIA

NORTH

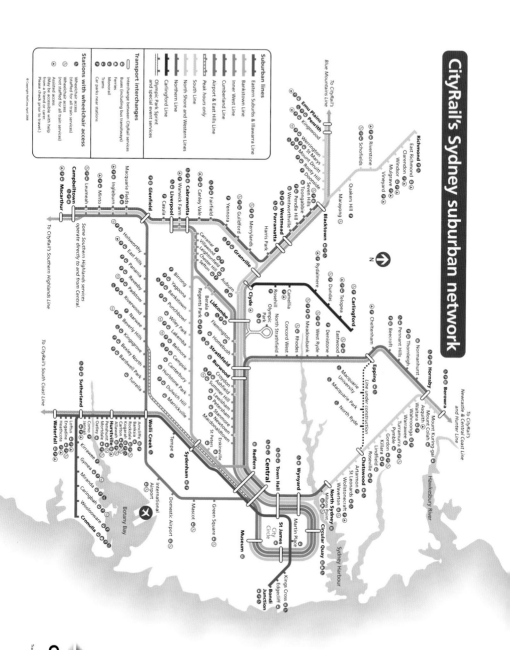

CityRail's Sydney suburban network

Reproduced with kind permission from Railcorp

Melbourne Train Network

connex | metlink

NORTH

MAP NOT TO SCALE
Effective October 2007

Information

Ticketing Zones

City Saver
Zone 1
Zone 2

▲ Connecting Bus
▬ Connecting Tram
● Premium Station
○ Host Station
P Parking

Premium Station:
Customer service centre staffed from first train to last, seven days a week.
Host Station:
Customer service staff at station during morning peak.
*Line to Showgrounds and Flemington Racecourse, only open for special events.

For train, tram and bus information,
call **131 638** / (TTY) **9619 2727** or
visit **metlink.melbourne.com.au**

PORT PHILLIP

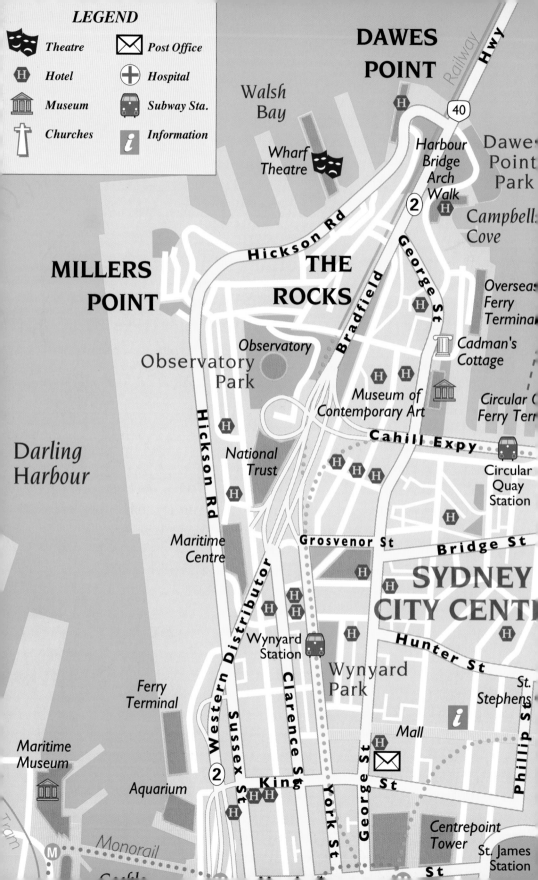

LEGEND

🎭 Theatre   ✉ Post Office

🏨 Hotel   ➕ Hospital

🏛 Museum   🚐 Subway Sta.

✝ Churches   ℹ Information

DAWES POINT

Walsh Bay

Wharf Theatre

MILLERS POINT

Hickson Rd

THE ROCKS

Harbour Bridge Arch Walk

40

2

Dawes Point Park

Campbell's Cove

Observatory

Observatory Park

Bradfield

George St

Overseas Ferry Terminal

Cadman's Cottage

Darling Harbour

Hickson Rd

National Trust

Museum of Contemporary Art

Cahill Expy

Circular Ferry Terr

Circular Quay Station

Maritime Centre

Grosvenor St

Bridge St

SYDNEY CITY CENTRE

Maritime Museum

Western Distributor

Sussex St

Wynyard Station

Clarence St

Wynyard Park

Hunter St

St. Stephens

Phillip St

Ferry Terminal

Mall

ℹ

Aquarium

2

King St

York St

George St

Mall

✉

Centrepoint Tower

St. James Station

Monorail

M

Tram

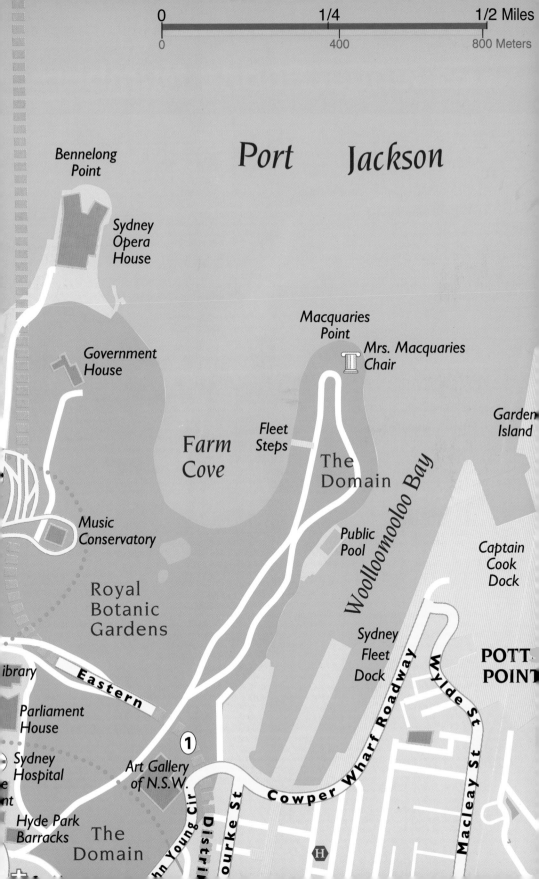

Port Jackson

Bennelong
Point

Sydney
Opera
House

Government
House

Macquaries
Point

Mrs. Macquaries
Chair

Garden
Island

Farm
Cove

Fleet
Steps

The
Domain

Woolloomooloo Bay

Captain
Cook
Dock

Music
Conservatory

Public
Pool

Royal
Botanic
Gardens

Sydney
Fleet
Dock

POTT
POINT

ibrary

Eastern

Parliament
House

Sydney
Hospital

1

Cowper Wharf Roadway

Wylde St

Macleay St

Hyde Park
Barracks

Art Gallery
of N.S.W.

The
Domain

John Young Cir

Distri

ourke St

H

0   1/4   1/2 Miles
0   400   800 Meters

Essential Phone Numbers

Emergency services

Fire service, police, ambulence	**000**
Emergency contact	**1800 641 792**

Health
Nurse on call	
Victoria	1300 60 60 24
Medicare	13 20 11

Utilities State Emergency
Service (SES)	**132 500**
Power cut	
Gas leak ACT	13 19 09
Phone fault	
Stolen bankcard	

Phone Information
Directory enquiries	013 or 0175
Operator	1234
International access	
Code	0011 +61

Travel
Melbourne Airport	+61 3 9297 1600
Sydney Airport	+61 2 9667 9111
Brisbane Airport	+61 7 3406 3000
Adelaide Airport	+61 8 8308 9211
Perth Airport	+61 8 9478 8888

Transport line for each area
(find on gov website)
Melbourne	131638
Sydney	131500
Queensland	131230
South Australian Transit	
Authority	8 210 1000
Perth	136213

Other information
Road traffic information	
Victoria	+61 3 9854 2160
Queensland	13 23 80
New South Wales	131 700

Weather report	1196
Fire information	

Embassies
Canada	
New South Wales	(02) 9364 3000
Victoria	(03) 9653 9674
Western Australia	(08) 9322 7930
India	
New South Wales	(02) 9223 9500
Queensland	(07) 3371 5198
Victoria	(03) 9384 0141
Western Australia	(08) 9486 9011
Ireland	
New South Wales	(02) 9264 9635
Western Australia	(08) 9385 8247
Victoria	(03) 9397 8940
New Zealand	
New South Wales	(02) 8256 2000
Victoria	(03) 9642 1586
South Africa	
Queensland	(07) 3258 6666
Southern Australia	(08) 8139 7330
Victoria	(03) 8825 4114
Western Australia	(08) 9321 0355
United Kingdom	
New South Wales	(02) 9247 7521
Queensland	(07) 3223 3200
Southern Australia	(08) 8232 9817
United States	
New South Wales	(02) 9373 9200
Victoria	(03) 1902 941641
Western Australia	(08) 9202 1224